THE STATESMAN'S YEAR-BOOK
HISTORICAL COMPANION

THE
STATESMAN'S
YEAR-BOOK
HISTORICAL
COMPANION

EDITED BY

JOHN PAXTON

**MACMILLAN
REFERENCE
BOOKS**

First published 1988 by
THE MACMILLAN PRESS LTD
London and Basingstoke

Associated companies in Auckland, Delhi, Dublin,
Gaborone, Hamburg, Harare, Hong Kong, Johannesburg,
Kuala Lumpur, Lagos, Manzini, Melbourne, Mexico
City, Nairobi, New York, Singapore, Tokyo.

British Library Cataloguing in Publication Data

Paxton, John
   The statesman's year-book historical
   companion.—(Macmillan reference books)
   1. History, Modern—19th century
   2. History, Modern—20th century
   I. Title
   909.8   D358

   ISBN 0–333–43659–8

Printed in Great Britain by
Richard Clay Ltd, Bungay, Suffolk

CONTENTS

THE

STATESMAN'S YEAR-BOOK

A STATISTICAL, GENEALOGICAL, AND HISTORICAL
ACCOUNT OF THE STATES AND SOVEREIGNS
OF THE CIVILISED WORLD

FOR THE YEAR

1864

BY FREDERICK MARTIN

London and Cambridge

MACMILLAN AND CO.

1864

THE FIRST ONE HUNDRED AND TWENTY-FIVE YEARS OF THE STATESMAN'S YEAR-BOOK

The summer of 1988 sees the publication of the 125th edition of *The Statesman's Year-Book*. Since the first edition in 1864 there have been dramatic changes in the political systems and the frontiers of the countries of the world. Two world wars have hastened economic and social change. All these evolutionary and sometimes revolutionary events are recorded in the 125 annual volumes of *The Statesman's Year-Book*.

In this long period there have been only five editors; Frederick Martin 1864–1883, Sir John Scott-Keltie 1883–1926, Mortimer Epstein 1911/27–1946, Henry Steinberg 1946–1969, and the present editor who joined the publication in 1963 and became editor on the death of Henry Steinberg. Throughout this period, five generations of the Macmillan family, Alexander (who commissioned the first edition), Sir Frederick, Harold (the first Earl of Stockton), Maurice and again Alexander (the second Earl of Stockton) have shown considerable interest and have given encouragement to the successive editors of *The Statesman's Year-Book*. Richard Clay of Bungay have been the printers throughout most of the years and John Bartholomew of Edinburgh have undertaken the cartography.

The originator and first editor of *The Statesman's Year-Book* was Frederick Martin who was amanuensis to the historian, Thomas Carlyle. It seems that Carlyle and W. E. Gladstone, then Chancellor of the Exchequer, introduced Martin to Alexander Macmillan and an agreement for 'A Statistical, Genealogical and Historical Account of the States and Sovereigns of the Civilised World' was signed in Dec. 1862. The first edition appeared on 20 Jan. 1864 running to 684 pages and selling at 8s. 4d.

The first edition was divided into 2 parts, one dealing with 15 European states – the 33 members of the German confederation receiving separate consideration – and the other dealing with 'Principal States not in Europe', the USA, the Confederate States, Mexico, the Argentine Republic, Chile, Brazil, Canada, China, Japan, India, New Zealand and the 5 separate colonies in Australia. Numerous pages at the beginning and end of the volume were given over to advertisements for other Macmillan publications and for *The Statesman's Year-Book's* continental model and rival, the

Almanach de Gotha 'Annuaire Genealogique, Diplomatique et Statistique', then more than 100 years old, and now unfortunately extinct.

When Frederick Martin retired from the editorship in 1883, *The Statesman's Year-Book* was well-established and had built the foundations of its international reputation for accuracy, impartiality and usefulness.

Whatever changes *The Statesman's Year-Book* has undergone at the hands of his successors, the basic features established by Martin have been preserved, although, of course, there have been countless minor changes and improvements. Martin's main bequests to all subsequent editors have been his dissociation from any party-political and denominational considerations, his firm resistance to pressure groups of any description and his co-operation with governmental and other official agencies while always preserving the editor's final right of decision. The 'official' documents which provided much of the information for the early editions gave way about 1870 to the issuers of these documents – government departments, embassies, learned societies, statistical offices – on whose help the accuracy and reliability of *The Statesman's Year-Book* has rested ever since.

The editors however have always shown a healthy scepticism about official statistics provided by governments whose motives they consider to be suspect. In the very first issue Frederick Martin rejected the official estimate of expenses at the Tsarist court as ridiculously low in view of the 'boundless pomp and splendour displayed on all occasions'. Attempts, too, have been made to influence *The Statesman's Year-Book* in the interest of particular political or economic groups.

Frederick Martin, while possessing the ideal qualifications for the establishment of a great reference book, showed increasing instability towards the end of his editorship, and for a time *The Statesman's Year-Book's* continued existence was threatened when he mislaid the revised proofs of the 1883 edition in a railway carriage. Macmillans called on John Scott-Keltie, who saved the situation and brought the 1883 edition out on time. In 1884 Scott-Keltie succeeded Martin as editor, a position he held actively until about 1917, and in name until 1927. This remarkable man had considerable gifts as a writer, an organizer and a scholar, and was a liberal-imperialist and an ardent promoter of Anglo-American co-operation. He was a regular contributor to *The Times*, inspector of geographical education to the Royal Geographical Society, the creator and editor of the *Geographical Journal*, as well as an accepted expert on the geographical aspects of imperial expansion, especially in Africa. He was awarded many medals by learned societies, was decorated by foreign governments and was knighted in 1918. It is hardly surprising, then, that under his editorship *The Statesman's Year-Book* was expanded to include every country 'that can be regarded as a state, however rudimentary', and to take account of political developments all over the globe.

Maps were introduced in 1892 illustrating, as Scott-Keltie put it, 'subjects of great moment'. An important milestone in the history of *The Statesman's Year-Book* came in 1906, when the USA was given a section of its own. The increasing interest of Macmillan in the American market, especially after the foundation of the Macmillan Company of New York in 1896, fortified by marriage bonds, had in 1898 made Frederick Macmillan suggest a special American edition. Scott-Keltie received this news with enthusiasm: 'several US correspondents', he said, 'have written to me suggesting that larger space might be given to so great a country'. Beginning in 1906 each of the then 46 states of the Union was allotted a special chapter, and the co-operation of the state governors and the state secretaries was warmly acknowledged. The phrase used in the preface, that the reorganization of the USA section was done 'in compliance with influential suggestions from America', discreetly veils a friendly hint Scott-Keltie had received from the then occupant of the White House, Theodore Roosevelt.

The third editor, appointed in 1927, was Mortimer Epstein, who had been joint-editor with Sir John Scott-Keltie since 1911. Born in Lithuania in 1880, Epstein had come to England and settled in Manchester. He joined *The Statesman's Year-Book*, but was also editor of the *Annual Register*, and ran both annual publications with undiminishing vigour until the day of his death. Whereas Frederick Martin had been able to undertake the compilation of early editions with only casual assistance, the greatly increased scope of *The Statesman's Year-Book*, and the flood of information pouring into the office of the editor now made the task far beyond the ability of one man. Scott-Keltie had begun to employ regular assistants, and Mortimer Epstein now reorganized them into a regular team.

The Second World War inevitably caused a disruption in the organization of *The Statesman's Year-Book*, and on the death of Mortimer Epstein in 1946, the fourth edi'or, Henry Steinberg, was faced with the task of making entirely new arrangements with the host of new countries, old countries under new régimes, and newly created international agencies. Henry Steinberg was an exile from Nazi Germany and his books included *Five Hundred Years of Printing* and a *History of the Thirty Years' War*. His astonishing gift of acquiring the friendship as well as the professional services of people he never met helped considerably in re-establishing the vast network of correspondents following the war.

The present editor joined Henry Steinberg in 1963, the year that *The Statesman's Year-Book* was celebrating its centenary. He became assistant editor in 1964 and editor in 1969, and the main editorial changes in the last 25 years have been to rearrange the layout to give even quicker accessibility to facts. Previously the publication was divided into four parts: International Organizations, the Commonwealth, the United States of America, and Other Countries. Changing over from hot metal printing to computer setting gave the opportunity to move to alphabetical order for the independent countries of the world and with this *The Statesman's Year-Book* lost its imperialistic feel and became truly international. Also the opportunity was taken to rearrange the sections within each country into a more logical sequence and to add new sections such as tourism and climate where felt necessary.

The aim has always been to produce a one-volume encyclopaedia of the nations of the world and with judicious planting and weeding this is achieved in just over 1,700 pages. It is obviously impossible to give many details of individual towns and regions and this is why in 1975 *The Statesman's Year-Book World Gazetteer* was published as a companion to the main volume. The *Gazetteer* is now in its third edition.

Continuity has been the great strength, continuity of publishers, editors, printers and cartographers. However, thousands of people have helped to make *The Statesman's Year-Book* what it is today and a mention of long-serving assistants is not out of order in what is, in fact, a publishing celebration.

From 1900 until 1916 Fred T. Jane of *Jane's Fighting Ships* was the expert adviser on the navies of the world, and for the last 40 years, R. V. B. Blackman, MBE, a former editor of *Jane's Fighting Ships*, has undertaken this task. Between the two world wars the late Sir Basil Liddell Hart gave advice on the armies, and the advisers on the Arab world were St John Philby and Edward Atiyah. The index has been compiled by Dora Fetherstonhaugh for over 25 years and many of the eastern European countries are 'looked after' by Brian Hunter who has worked for *The Statesman's Year-Book* for 28 years and who last year compiled the name index to add to the 50 pages or so of general index. Sheila Fairfield, the editor's chief assistant, has put up with the editor for 20 years.

Without these wonderful people and the many, many others who write in with constructive and informed criticism *The Statesman's Year-Book* would not have reached its 125th birthday and now be found in most reference libraries of the world.   J.P.

PREFACE

This *Companion* is a celebration. It celebrates the publication of 125 annual editions of *The Statesman's Year-Book*. SYB, as it is affectionately known, is found in most reference libraries of the world and during this century and a quarter dramatic changes in the constitutions, the boundaries and the economies of the nations of the world have taken place. These changes have been faithfully recorded year by year in *The Statesman's Year-Book*. Obviously in a one-volume reference book it is not possible to retain all this data year by year, and so the publishers responded to the need for a separate publication, *The Statesman's Year-Book Historical Companion*, which would dig into earlier editions of *The Statesman's Year-Book* and record the salient constitutional and political events over these momentous years. Particular attention has been given to the turbulent political histories of countries becoming independent in this century. Most entries give the name of a reliable general history for further reading and many of the name changes are recorded in the index for quick reference.

I'm extremely grateful to my many correspondents throughout the world for providing valuable data and also to the following for drafting and giving advice on entries: Sheila Fairfield, Jesús Pérez Cavero, Jonathan Derrick, Brian Hunter, Rif Winfield, Basil Wright. At Macmillan, Penelope Allport and Nigel Quinney gave tremendous support as did my secretary Penny White.

J.P.

Bruton, Somerset
June 1988

AFGHÁNISTÁN

Ahmad Sháh Durráni consolidated Afghánistán as a kingdom, ruling with an advisory council of tribal chiefs from 1747 until his death in 1773. His capital was Kandahar, replaced in his lifetime by Ahmad Shahi. His frontiers extended into modern Kashmir and Pakistan, although by 1770 he had suffered reversals at the hands of the Sikhs in the Punjab.

After 1773 the unity of Afghánistán was threatened by internal quarrels. In 1816–24 there was civil war, ending in victory for the Barakzay clan whose leader Dost Mohammed became Amir in 1826. His capital was Kábul.

By then the Punjab and Kashmir had been lost, the British had become dominant in India and the Russian empire was ambitious to expand southwards. The British, believing that Dost Mohammed was unwilling or unable to resist Russia, invaded Afghánistán in 1839 in an attempt to replace him with their own protégé, Shah Shoja. An apparent British victory in 1840 was followed by actual defeat when the Afghans murdered Shah Shoja and British forces were forced to retreat from Kábul with heavy losses.

Dost Mohammed was restored in 1843 and made friendship treaties with Britain in 1855 and 1857; he died in 1863 and was succeeded by his third son Shír 'Ali Khan. There was then civil war between two branches of the family and once more the Russians and the British tried to exploit internal instability. There was a second war with Britain 1878–79. In 1879 Shír 'Ali Khan fled leaving his son Ya'qúb Khan on the throne. In 1880 the British recognized the rival, 'Abdor Rahmán Khan, in return for his undertaking to accept British control of his foreign policy. He defeated internal uprisings. In 1893 he accepted the Durand Line as his frontier with Russia.

Habíbolláh Khan (1901–19) continued the relationship with Britain in return for a subsidy. During the First World War he succeeded in remaining neutral. However, there was popular support in Afghánistán for the Ottoman Turks, and Habíbolláh's refusal to ally himself with them against Britain led to his assassination in 1919. His son and successor Amánolláh declared total independence from Britain at his coronation. Fighting broke out, but Britain then recognized the independence of Afghánistán at the Treaty of Rawalpindi, 1919.

Amánolláh was a reforming Khan who antagonized the conservatives of traditional society. Tribal revolt and banditry reached a climax in 1928 and the Khan abdicated in 1929 to be replaced first by Habíbolláh (soon murdered) and then by Mohammed Nadir (1929–33). The latter signed a friendship treaty with Russia. He was murdered in 1933 and succeeded by Mohammed Záhir who (like Nadir towards the end of his reign) took the title of Shah. Záhir Shah ruled with the advice, and under the influence, of his family for 40 years. In 1964 he was able to overcome opposition and put through a constitution establishing parliamentary democracy (effective 1965). In 1973 there was a military *coup* led by his cousin and brother-in-law Mohammed Daoud who abolished the 1964 constitution and declared a republic. Záhir Shah abdicated on 24 Aug. 1973.

The republic inherited pressure for tribal autonomy and economic crises mainly brought about by drought and famine. In April 1978 President Daoud was overthrown and killed in a further *coup* which installed a pro-Soviet government led by the People's Democratic Party. The new president was Noor Mohammad Taraki who signed a new treaty of friendship with the Soviet Union. In Sept. 1979 Taraki was overthrown, whereupon the Soviet Union invaded Afghánistán in Dec., deposed his successor and placed Babrak Karmal at the head of government.

In Dec. 1986 Sayid Mohammed Najibullah became president amid continuing civil war between government and rebel Moslem forces. Whereas in the 1960s both the USSR and the USA had financed government projects, in 1987 the USSR provided considerable military support and development aid to the pro-Soviet administration while the USA extended more limited support to the rebels. In the mid-1980s the UN began negotiations on the withdrawal of Soviet troops and the establishment of a government of national unity. Soviet troops began withdrawing from Afghánistán in early 1988.

Further Reading
Sykes, P. M., *A History of Afghanistan*. 2 vols. New York, 1975

ALBANIA

Of Illyrian origin, the Albanian clans were compelled to recognize the suzerainty of the expanding Ottoman empire in 1385. Split since 1054 between Rome (Catholics) and Constantinople (Orthodox), many Albanians converted to Islam and were able to rise high in the Ottoman administration. One such was Gjergj Kastrioti (1405–68), surnamed Skanderbeg, who defected from his Turkish commandership in 1443, reconverted to Christianity and maintained, with help from Naples, Venice and the Papal States, a successful guerrilla resistance to the Turks. After his death, Turkish rule was emancipated though sporadic uprising continued. Many Albanians fled to Sicily and Calabria to form communities still existing today. The Northern Highlands, however, were never brought under total control. In 1431 the Turks introduced their fiefdom system, whereby land was held in return for military or civil service. With the thwarting of Ottoman expansionism in the mid-16th century, these fiefdoms became hereditary estates, and a class of large landowners developed. With the decline of central power, some lords acquired a wide measure of local autonomy.

Turkish attempts at modernizing reform in the 19th century were ineffective, and the prospect of Turkish collapse produced apprehension amongst Albanian nationalists about the aspirations to Albanian territory both of the Balkan successor states and some great powers (notably Italy and Austria-Hungary). After the Russo-Turkish war of 1877–78, an Albanian League was set up at Prizren to resist the cession of Albanian territory ordered by the Treaty of San Stefano and the Congress of Berlin. Demands grew for autonomy from the Turkish government, and although the League was suppressed by force in 1881, revolts continued. Expectations of reform from the Young Turk government of 1909 were disappointed. After the defeat of Turkey in the Balkan war of 1912, Albanian nationalists under the leadership of Ismail Kemal, a liberal opposition deputy in the Turkish parliament, proclaimed Albania's independence at Vlorë on 28 Nov. 1912 and set up a provisional government with Kemal at its head.

The powers' ambassadors' conference (London 1912–13) recognized Albania's independence and delimited its boundaries; Kosovo was assigned to Serbia. The conference chose the German, Prince William of Wied, as ruler, aided by a government of landowners and an international control commission. Wied's reign was ineffective and bedevilled by subversion, and after 6 months he left on 3 Sept. 1914 at the powers' request. During the First World War Albania became a battlefield for warring occupation forces. By the secret Treaty of London (26 April 1915) Britain, France and Russia offered Italy large tracts of Albania as an inducement to enter the war; and on 3 June 1917 the Italian commander in Albania declared Albania's independence under Italian protection. Such clandestine arrangements, however, were in conflict with the US President Woodrow Wilson's 'Fourteen Points' enunciated at the Versailles peace conference, which emphasized self-determination and open treaties. In Jan. 1920 50 Albanian regional delegates met at Lushnjë to protest to the peace conference against partitioning. They set up a regency council of 4 (representing the religious denominations) and formed a government under Sulejman Delvina. Irregular forces ejected the Italians who, however, retained the island of Sazan. Albania was admitted to the League of Nations on 20 Dec. 1920. In Nov. 1921 the conference of ambassadors confirmed her 1913 frontiers with minor alterations.

A parliament was elected in April 1921 in which 2 factions emerged led respectively by Ahmet Zogu, representing conservative landowners, and the Orthodox Bishop Fan Noli, representing the intelligentsia and urbanized middle class. Zogu became prime minister in 1922 and secured 40 out of 95 seats in the elections of Dec. 1923, but his government's harshness and corruption provoked a military *coup* on 10 June 1924. Zogu fled to Yugoslavia and Fan Noli set up a government which was idealistic but ineffective and made the fatal step of recognizing the Soviet Union. In Dec. 1924, with Yugoslav help Zogu drove Noli into exile and set up a personal authoritarian régime. On 1 Sept. 1928 he proclaimed himself King Zog I.

Italian influence grew from the mid-1920s. In 1925 the Bank of Albania was set up with 51% Italian capital. A friendship pact was signed with Italy in 1926 and a defence treaty in 1927. Despite Zog's tardy efforts to reverse this trend, Albania became economically dependent on Italy. In April 1939 Mussolini invaded Albania outright and set up a puppet state, uniting the Italian and Albanian crowns. Zog went into exile.

During the Second World War Albania suffered first Italian and then German occupation. Resistance was carried on by royalist, nationalist republican and communist movements, often at odds with each other. The latter enjoyed the support of Tito's partisans, who were instrumental in forming the Albanian Communist Party on 8 Nov. 1941. Communists dominated both the ostensibly nonpartisan National Liberation Movement (set up in Sept. 1942) and the Anti-Fascist National Liberation Committee (formed on 24 May 1944). The latter became the Provisional Democratic Government on 22 Oct. 1944 after the German withdrawal, with Enver Hoxha, a French-educated school teacher and member of the Communist Party Central Committee, at its head. The provisional government took immediate steps to gain full control of the administration and economy. Large estates were broken up and the land distributed, though full collectivization was not brought in until 1955–59. Britain, the USA and the USSR recognized the provisional government on condition that free elections were held, but at the elections of 2 Dec. 1945 only communists and their sympathizers were allowed to stand. The new national assembly met in Jan. 1946, proclaimed a people's republic and promulgated a Soviet-type constitution.

In 1946 Yugoslav plans to incorporate Albania were set in motion with a customs union and Treaty of Mutual Aid. Hoxha emerged as an opponent, and managed to delay the tactics of the pro-Yugoslav faction until the Stalin–Tito rift of 1948 gave him a chance to espouse the Moscow line. The Moscow-trained Mehmet Shehu supplanted the pro-Yugoslav Koçi Xoxe as minister of the interior. Close ties were forged with the USSR, but following Khrushchev's reconciliation with Tito in 1956 China replaced the Soviet Union as Albania's powerful patron from 1961 until the end of the Maoist phase in 1977. The régime was in 1987 pursuing 'revolutionary self-sufficiency'. In Dec. 1981 Mehmet Shehu, then prime minister, allegedly committed suicide. Hoxha died on 11 April 1985.

Further Reading

Logoreci, A., *The Albanians: Europe's Forgotten Survivors*. London, 1977

ALGERIA

The French took Algiers in 1830 and, despite formidable resistance, by 1857 the whole country was in French control. The French settlers who subsequently arrived developed political and economic power at the expense of the indigenous Moslem population. In Nov. 1954 the *Front de Libération Nationale* (FLN), representing the Moslem majority, sought national independence by open warfare against the French administration and armed forces. There was extensive loss of life and property during the fighting which continued unabated until in March 1962 a cease-fire was agreed between the French government and the nationalists. The conflict marked the only successful challenge to colonialism by a Middle Eastern country. Against the wishes of the French in Algeria, Gen. de Gaulle declared Algeria independent on 3 July 1962.

The Political Bureau of the FLN took over the functions of government, a National Constituent Assembly was elected and the Republic was declared on 25 Sept. 1962. The founder of the FLN, Ahmed Ben Bella, became prime minister, becoming president the following year. On 15 June 1965 the government was overthrown by a junta of army officers, who established a Revolutionary Council under Col. Houari Boumédienne. After 10 years of rule, Boumédienne proposed that elections should be held for a president and a National Assembly. The proposed new constitution was accepted in a referendum in Nov. 1976 and Boumédienne was elected president (unopposed), securing more than 99% of the votes cast. A National Assembly was elected in Feb. 1977, only FLN members being allowed as candidates.

On the death of the president in Dec. 1978 the Revolutionary Council again took over the government. Col. Bendjedid Chadli was proposed president, and a referendum accepted him. When he stood for re-election in 1984, as the sole candidate, he was chosen for a further 5 years. The president appoints the prime minister, and this office is now obligatory under the constitution; the president, however, also wields executive power.

Economic and broad cultural problems have plagued the country since independence. The Algerian brand of socialism has yet to win the battles against crippling unemployment and for greater Arabization of education.

Further Reading

Horne, A., *A Savage War of Peace: Algeria 1954–1962*. London, 1977

ANDORRA

Andorra was said to be declared a free state by Charlemagne but by the *Paréage* of 1278 it was placed under the joint suzerainty of the Bishop of Urgel and the Comte de Foix. The rights vested in the House of Foix later passed to the French crown. Sovereignty is now exercised jointly by the President of the French Republic and the Bishop of Urgel. The co-princes, as they are designated, are represented in Andorra by the *Viguier français* and the *Viguier Episcopal*. The Andorran valleys pay every second year a due of 960 francs to France and 460 pesetas to the Bishop.

The Andorrans' elective body is the General Council of the Valleys, composed of 28 members, which submits motions and proposals to the Permanent Delegations of the co-princes. The franchise had been granted only to third-generation Andorran males until 1970, when it was extended to second-generation inhabitants and to women. In 1977 first-generation Andorrans over 28 years were included, and very recently the voting age has been lowered to 18 years.

Andorra has no clear international status and has, in the 20th century, experienced many difficulties in gaining control of its essential services.

ANGOLA

The earliest people in Angola, as in most of sub-Saharan Africa, were hunter-gatherers. They were displaced by Bantu-speaking farmers who by the 14th century were organized in several powerful states such as the kingdoms of Kongo and Mbundu. The rulers of Mbundo were called *ngola*, from which the Portuguese derived the name Angola. The Portuguese first made contact with Kongo in 1491, and for some time thereafter its kings were Catholic and their capital was renamed São Salvador.

Only brief Dutch occupation in the 1640s interrupted four centuries of Portuguese rule along the coast, from which hundreds of thousands of slaves were shipped and where, by the 19th century, a small Portuguese-speaking African and *mestiço* (half-European) elite had emerged. Inland, African states remained independent until the 19th century.

The Portuguese founded Luanda in 1875, and from the 1870s gradually occupied the interior of Angola, often called Portuguese West Africa. The occupation was slow in the face of strong African resistance (such as the Bailundo rising of 1902), and Portuguese rule was only fully established about 1920. That rule involved many impositions, such as conscription for forced labour. Only a very few Africans who fully absorbed Portuguese culture, *assimilados*, had some rights. Portugal built the Benguela railway linking the Belgian Congo (now Zaïre) copper mines to Lobito, and developed coffee cultivation in Angola. From the 1950s thousands of Portuguese settlers moved to Angola which was declared an Overseas Province of Portugal in 1951.

While legal African nationalist activity was banned, underground activity grew and led in 1961 to the creation of the *Movimento Popular de Libertação de Angola* (MPLA) and the *União das Populacões de Angola* (UPA). In 1961 both staged uprisings, the MPLA in Luanda and the UPA in the Kongo country near the north-east border. Portugal fiercely suppressed these and for 14 years successfully contained African guerrillas and Angola boomed economically. The nationalist parties and their leaders, Holden Roberto of the UPA and then of its successor the FNLA, and Dr Agostinho Neto of the MPLA, were rivals, and in 1966 another rival group started, the *União Nacional para a Independéncia Total de Angola* (UNITA).

As Portugal moved towards withdrawal following the 1974 revolution, the three nationalist movements briefly joined in a transitional government in Luanda in 1975, but were in fact at war and open fighting led to each movement occupying a part of the country, the MPLA holding the capital. Portugal handed over power without passing it to any Angolan government, and independence came on 11 Nov. 1975 amid civil war. The MPLA in three months drove the FNLA out of its strongholds in the north and north-east, and UNITA out of most of its area in the south. Headed by Neto as President, the MPLA was recognized as the Angolan government by most of the world, but not by the USA which had backed its opponents. The Republic of South Africa began military attacks, justified by Pretoria on the grounds of Angola's backing for the Namibia independence movement, SWAPO. The government called on Cuban troops for aid and they were still present in 1988.

The left-wing MPLA, although affected by factional rivalries which culminated in a *coup* attempt in 1977, installed a one-party régime with a socialist programme over much of Angola. Neto died in 1979 and was succeeded by José Eduardo dos Santos. While the FNLA never recovered from its defeat, from 1981 UNITA did, and with the Republic of South Africa has increasingly challenged the MPLA government. South Africa launched many major invasions, and kept troops in Kunene province until April 1985. Even then constant South African raids continued. UNITA, under Jonas Savimbi, controlled large areas in the south by 1982, and the following year spread its guerrilla activity throughout the country; by 1984 it claimed to be striking all over Angola. It became evident that South African military aid, protection and commando intervention underpinned UNITA'S performance.

In 1984 the government created a Defence and Security Council as its senior decision-making organ, and Military Councils with sweeping powers in war zones. It faces a critical situation, with huge numbers of people displaced and normal life disrupted over vast areas. In 1985, the US Congress voted more aid to UNITA, and South Africa launched another major raid in May 1986 and again in February 1988. The Angolan government managed to repel the attack, and it continues to refuse suggestions of talks with UNITA.

Further Reading

Bender, G. J., *Angola under the Portuguese: Myth and Reality*. London, 1979
Marcum, J., *The Angolan Revolution*. 2 vols. MIT Press, 1969 and 1978

ANGUILLA

Anguilla was probably given its name by the Spaniards or the French because of its eel-like shape. It was inhabited by Arawaks for several centuries before the arrival of Europeans. Anguilla was colonized in 1650 by English settlers from neighbouring St Kitts. In 1688 the island was attacked by a party of Irishmen who then settled. Anguilla was subsequently administered as part of the Leeward Islands, and from 1825 became even more closely associated with St Kitts. In 1875 a petition sent to London requesting separate status and direct rule from Britain met with a negative response. Again in 1958 the islanders formally petitioned the Governor requesting a dissolution of the political and administrative association with St Kitts but this too failed. From 1958 to 1962 Anguilla was part of the Federation of the West Indies.

Opposition to rule from St Kitts erupted on 30 May 1967 when St Kitts policemen were evicted from the island and Anguilla refused to recognize the authority of the State Government any longer. During 1968–69 the British Government maintained a 'Senior British Official' to advise the local Anguilla Council and devise some solution to the problem. In March 1969, following the ejection from the island of a high-ranking British civil servant, British security forces occupied Anguilla. A Commissioner was installed, and in 1969 Anguilla became *de facto* a separate dependency of Britain; a situation rendered *de jure* on 19 Dec. 1980 under the Anguilla Act 1980 when Anguilla formally separated from the state of St Kitts, Anguilla-Nevis. A new constitution came into effect in 1982 providing for a large measure of internal autonomy under the Crown.

Further Reading

Petty, C. L., *Anguilla: Where there's a Will, there's a Way*. Anguilla, 1984

ANTIGUA AND BARBUDA

Antigua and Barbuda make up the island nation of the lesser Antilles in the Eastern Caribbean. Most of the population is made up of decendents of African slaves who had been brought there during colonial times to work on sugar plantations – today most of the population is engaged in agricultural pursuits and tourism.

The country was discovered when Christopher Columbus made his second voyage to the West Indies in 1493. The Spaniards attempted to settle on the island in 1520 as did the French in 1629. Antigua was eventually colonized in the year 1632 and in 1667, under the Treaty of Breda, it became a British Colony. Barbuda was colonized in 1628 and granted to the Cordrington Family in 1680. By the late 19th century, however, it reverted to the British Crown.

Although planned as a slave-breeding colony, it never became one; the slaves became self-reliant sailors, hunters, fishermen and skilled workers, coming to regard the land as communually owned.

Antigua was the only British island to possess a good harbour, and English Harbour was the dockyard for the British West Indies throughout the period of the Napoleonic wars. The naval dockyard was commissioned in 1725 and closed in 1854.

On 27 Feb. 1967 Antigua assumed a status of association with the UK, and the island exercised full internal self-government and was accorded executive authority over a wide field of internal affairs. Antigua and Barbuda became fully independent on 1 Nov. 1981.

Further Reading

Dyde, B., *Antigua and Barbuda: The Heart of the Caribbean.* London, 1986

ARGENTINA

In 1515 Juan Díaz de Solis discovered the Río de la Plata. In 1534 Pedro de Mondoza was sent by the King of Spain to take charge of the 'Gobernación y Capitania de las tierras del Rio de la Plata', and in Feb. 1536 he founded the city of the 'Puerto de Santa María del Buen Aire'. In 1810 the population rose against Spanish rule, and in 1816 Argentina proclaimed its independence. Civil wars and anarchy followed until, in 1853, stable government was established.

In this century there have been a succession of military *coups*. The first took place in 1930, the second in 1943 when Gen. Juan Domingo Peron won control. His regime was autocratic but popularist and nationalistic and propogated some social reforms. His wife Eva (Evita), played a major role, giving the regime an almost cult-like following. She died in 1952. He was overthrown in 1955 and a civilian administration followed until 1966 when the next military *coup* led to seven years of government by the military. However, a political party had established itself around the Perons, and when elections were held in 1973 the Peronists were the victors; Gen. Peron was elected president. When he died in 1974, his widow Isobel succeeded him as president. She was deposed in 1976 following another military *coup*, which established a three-man junta with Gen. Jorge Videla, C.-in-C. of the army, as president. The new government instituted a savagely repressive attitude towards any opposition.

Videla was succeeded as president first by Gen. Viola and then by Gen. Leopoldo Galtieri, the army C.-in-C. In April 1982 Galtieri, in an effort to distract attention from domestic failings, decided to invade the Falkland Islands (Islas Malvinas). The subsequent military defeat helped to precipitate the fall of Galtieri and the junta in July 1982. In elections held in Oct. 1983 the *Unión Cívica Radical* party triumphed and its leader, Raul Alfonsín, became president. His government has been preoccupied with trials of army leaders and the consequences of the debt crisis.

Further Reading

Rock, D., *Argentina 1516–1982: From Spanish Colonization to the Falklands War.* London, 1986

AUSTRALIA

Various dates are given for the discovery of Australia, including 1522 in which year it was sighted by Magellan's followers. Capt. Cook discovered the east coast in 1770 and initially the British planned to establish a colony there; instead, however, the government decided to set up a penal settlement. In 1801 Matthew Flinders, a British naval officer, completed the charting of Australia. He suggested that the name Australia replace New Holland, and this took place in 1817.

The appointment of Lachlan Macquarie as Governor in 1809 began a period of development in which Australia ceased primarily to be a penal settlement. The crossing of the Blue Mountains in 1813 was the first of many expeditions which led to discovery and use of vast areas of good grazing land.

On 1 Jan. 1901 the 6 separately constituted colonies of New South Wales, Victoria, Queensland, South Australia, Western Australia and Tasmania were federated under the name of the Commonwealth of Australia, the designation of 'colonies' being at the same time changed into that of 'states' – except in the case of Northern Territory which was transferred from South Australia to the Commonwealth as a 'territory' on 1 Jan. 1911.

In 1911 the Commonwealth acquired from the State of New South Wales the Canberra site for the Australian capital. Building operations were begun in 1923 and a Federal Parliament was opened at Canberra in 1927. A further area at Jervis Bay was acquired in 1915.

Territories under the administration of Australia in Jan. 1987, but not included in it, include Norfolk Island, the territory of Ashmore and Cartier Islands, and the Australian Antarctic Territory (acquired on 24 Aug. 1936), the latter comprising all the islands and territory, other than Adélie Land, situated south of 60° S. lat. and between 160° and 45° E. long. The Coral Sea Islands became an External Territory in 1969.

The British Government transferred sovereignty in the Heard Island and McDonald Islands to the Australian Government on 26 Dec. 1947. Cocos (Keeling) Islands on 23 Nov. 1955 and Christmas Island on 1 Oct. 1958 were also transferred to Australian jurisdiction.

AUSTRALIAN TERRITORIES

AUSTRALIAN CAPITAL TERRITORY

The area which is now the Australian Capital Territory was explored in 1820 by Charles Throsby, who named it Limestone Plains, and settlement commenced in 1824. Until its selection as the seat of government it was a quiet pastoral and agricultural community with a few large holdings and a sprinkling of smaller settlers.

In 1901 the Commonwealth constitution stipulated that a land tract of at least 260 sq. km in area and not less than 160 km from Sydney be set aside from New South Wales and reserved as a capital district. The Canberra, formerly called Yass-Canberra, site was adopted by the Seat of Government Act 1908. The present site, together with an area for a port at Jervis Bay, was surrendered by New South Wales and accepted by the Commonwealth in 1909, and by subsequential proclamation the Territory became vested in the Commonwealth from 1 Jan. 1911. In 1911 an international competition was held for the city plan. The plan chosen was that of W. Burley Griffin, of Chicago. Construction was delayed by the First World War, and it was not until 1927 that, with the transfer of parliament and certain departments, Canberra became in fact the seat of government.

NORTHERN TERRITORY

The Northern Territory, after forming part of New South Wales, was annexed on 6 July 1863 to South Australia and in 1901 entered the Commonwealth as a corporate part of South Australia. The Commonwealth Constitution Act of 1900 made provision for the surrender to the Commonwealth of any territory by any state, and under this provision an agreement was entered into on 7 Dec. 1907 for the transfer of the Northern Territory to the Commonwealth, and it formally passed under the control of the Commonwealth Government on 1 Jan. 1911.

On 1 Feb. 1927 the Northern Territory was divided for administrative purposes into two territories, but in 1931 it was again administered as a single territory under the control of an Administrator in Darwin.

The Legislative Council for the Northern Territory, constituted in 1947, was reconstituted in 1959. On 1 July 1978 self-government was granted to the Northern Territory.

AUSTRALIAN EXTERNAL TERRITORIES

AUSTRALIAN ANTARCTIC TERRITORY

An Imperial Order in Council of 7 Feb. 1933 placed under Australian authority 'all the islands and territories other than Adélie Land which are situated south of 60° S. lat. and lying between 160° E. long. and 45° E. long.' The Order came into force on 24 Aug. 1936. The boundaries of Adélie Land (the French enclave of Terre Adélie) were definitively fixed by a French decree of 1 April 1938 as the islands and territories south of 60° S. lat. lying between 136° and 142° E. long. In 1954 the laws of the Australian Capital Territory were declared to be in force, as far as applicable, in the Antarctic Territory.

A meteorological and research station named Mawson was set up in Feb. 1954 in MacRobertson Land; in Jan. 1957 another station, named Davis, was established in the Vestfold Hills some 400 miles east of Mawson. In Feb. 1959 the Australian Government accepted custody of Wilkes station, established by the USA.

COCOS (KEELING) ISLANDS

The islands were discovered in 1609 by Capt. William Keeling of the East India Company. The islands were uninhabited until 1826, when the first settlement was established on the main atoll by an Englishman, Alexander Hare, who left the islands about 1831. In 1827 a second settlement was formed on the main atoll by John Clunies-Ross, a Scottish seaman and adventurer, who landed with several boat-loads of Malay seamen. In 1857 the islands were declared a British possession; in 1878 responsibility for their supervision was transferred from the Colonial Office to the Government of Ceylon, and in 1882 to the Government of the Straits Settlement. By indenture in 1886 Queen Victoria granted the islands to the Clunies-Ross family in perpetuity, a grant that was honoured when the islands passed to Australia in 1955. In 1903 the islands were incorporated in the Settlement of Singapore and in 1942–46 temporarily placed under the Governor of Ceylon. In 1946 a Resident Administrator, responsible to the Governor of Singapore, was appointed.

On 23 Nov. 1955 the Cocos Islands were placed under the authority of the Commonwealth of Australia under the Cocos Islands Act 1955.

In 1978 the Clunies-Ross family agreed to sell their entire interests in the island except for a family residence.

CHRISTMAS ISLAND

The island was first sighted by Capt. William Mynors, of the British East India Company, on Christmas Day in 1643.

The island was formally annexed by Great Britain on 6 June 1888, was placed under the administration of the Governor of the Straits Settlements in 1889, and was incorporated with the Settlement of Singapore in 1900. Sovereignty was transferred to the Commonwealth of Australia on 1 Oct. 1958. Christmas Island was occupied by Japanese forces from March 1942 until 1945 and was a base for British hydrogen bomb tests in 1957–58.

NORFOLK ISLAND

The island was first discovered by Capt. Cook in 1774, and was made a penal settlement shortly afterwards.

Formerly part of the colony of New South Wales and then of Van Diemen's Land, Norfolk Island has been a distinct settlement since 1856, when the majority of the descendants of the mutineers of H.M.S. *Bounty* resettled there from Pitcairn Island, under the jurisdiction of the state of New South Wales. By the passage of the Norfolk Island Act 1913, the island was finally accepted as a Territory of the Commonwealth Government.

A modern whaling station went into operation in 1956 but work was suspended in 1962 owing to a shortage of whales.

HEARD AND MCDONALD ISLANDS

These islands, about 2,500 miles south-west of Fremantle, were transferred from UK to Australian control as from 26 Dec. 1947. The laws of the Australian Capital Territory were declared to be in force in the Territory by the Heard and McDonald Islands Act, 1953. Heard Island was occupied continuously from 1947 to 1954 by the Australian National Antarctic Research Expeditions. The McDonald Islands have not been occupied.

TERRITORY OF ASHMORE AND CARTIER ISLANDS

Britain took possession of the Ashmores in 1878 and Cartier Island in 1909.

By an Imperial Order in Council of 23 July 1931, Ashmore Islands (known as Middle, East and West Islands) and Cartier Island were placed under the authority of the Commonwealth.

On 16 Aug. 1983 a national nature reserve was declared over Ashmore Reef which is now known as Ashmore Reef National Nature Reserve.

The islands are uninhabited, but Indonesian fishing boats, which have traditionally plied the area, fish within the Territory and land to collect water in accordance with an agreement between the governments of Australia and Indonesia.

Periodic visits are made to the islands by ships of the Royal Australian Navy, and aircraft of the Royal Australian Air Force make aerial surveys of the islands and neighbouring waters.

TERRITORY OF CORAL SEA ISLANDS

The British naval vessels H.M.S. *Cato* in 1803, H.M.S. *Frederick* in 1812 and H.M.S. *Herald* from 1854 to 1860, discovered these islands and reefs scattered over a sea area of about 1m. sq. km. All the islands except Willis Island (where there has been a manned Australian Bureau of Meteorology station since 1921) are uninhabited, but they are occasionally visited by scientists, fishermen, and prospectors for oil and minerals.

Since 1967 extensive surveying has been undertaken by the Australian Department of National Development.

The Coral Sea Islands became a Territory of the Commonwealth of Australia under the Coral Sea Islands Act 1969.

AUSTRALIAN STATES

NEW SOUTH WALES

Originally, the name New South Wales was applied to the entire east coast of Australia when Capt. James Cook claimed the land for the British Crown on 23 Aug. 1770. The separate colonies of Tasmania, South Australia, Victoria and Queensland were proclaimed in the 19th century, and in 1911 and 1915 the Australian Capital Territory around Canberra and Jervis Bay was ceded to the Commonwealth. New South Wales was thus gradually reduced to its present area. The first settlement was made at Port Jackson in 1788 as a penal settlement; a partially elective council was established in 1843, and responsible government in 1856.

Gold discoveries from 1851 had brought a large influx of immigrants and responsible government was at first unstable, 7 ministries holding office in the 5 years after 1856. The times were somewhat lawless, and bitter conflict arose from loose land laws enacted in 1861. Lack of transport hampered agricultural expansion.

New South Wales federated with the other Australian states to form the Commonwealth of Australia in 1901.

QUEENSLAND

Queensland was first visited by Capt. Cook in 1770. From 1788 it was a part of New South Wales and was formed into a separate colony, with the name of Queensland, by letters patent of 8 June 1859, and responsible government was conferred.

Although by 1868 gold had been discovered, wool was the colony's principal product. The first railway line was opened in 1865.

Queensland federated with the other Australian states to form the Commonwealth of Australia in 1901.

Further Reading

Johnston, W. R., and Zerner, M., *Guide to the History of Queensland.* Brisbane, 1985

SOUTH AUSTRALIA

South Australia was surveyed by Tasman in 1644 and charted by Flinders in 1802. It was formed into a British province by letters patent of Feb. 1836, and a partially elective legislative council was established in 1851.

From 6 July 1863 the Northern Territory was placed under the jurisdiction of South Australia until the establishment of the Commonwealth of Australia in 1901.

Further Reading

Gibbs, R. M., *A History of South Australia: From Colonial Days to the Present.* Adelaide, 1984

TASMANIA

Abel Janzoon Tasman discovered Van Diemen's Land on 24 Nov. 1642. The island became a British settlement, mostly of convicts, in 1803 as a dependency of New South Wales; in 1825 its connexion with New South Wales was terminated and it was proclaimed a separate colony. In 1851 a partially elective legislative council was established, and in 1856 responsible government came into operation and the name of Van Diemen's Land was changed to Tasmania. On 1 Jan. 1901 Tasmania was federated with the other Australian states into the Commonwealth of Australia.

Further Reading

Townsley, W. A., *The Government of Tasmania*. Brisbane, 1976

VICTORIA

The first permanent settlement in the area was formed at Portland Bay in 1834. Regular government was first established in 1839. Victoria, formerly a portion of New South Wales, was, in 1851, at much the same time as gold was discovered, proclaimed a separate colony, with a partially elective legislative council. A new constitution giving responsible government to the colony was proclaimed on 23 Nov. 1855. This event had far-reaching effects, as the population increased from 76,162 in 1850 to 589,160 in 1864. By this time the main impetus behind the search for gold had waned and the new arrivals availed themselves of the opening of the pastoral and agricultural lands to smaller holders and the gradual development of manufacturing industries.

Victoria federated with the other Australian states to form the Commonwealth of Australia in 1901.

Further Reading

Priestley, S., *The Victorians: Making Their Mark*. Melbourne, 1984

WESTERN AUSTRALIA

In 1791, the British navigator George Vancouver, in the *Discovery*, took formal possession of the country around King George Sound. In 1826 the Government of New South Wales sent 20 convicts and a detachment of soldiers to King George Sound and formed a settlement then called Fredericks Town. The following year Capt. James

Stirling surveyed the coast from King George Sound to the Swan River, and in May 1829 Capt. Charles Fremantle took possession of the territory. In June 1829 Capt. Stirling founded the Swan River Settlement, now the Commonwealth State of Western Australia, and the towns of Perth and Fremantle, and was appointed Lieut.-Governor.

Large grants of land were made to the early settlers, and agricultural and pastoral occupations were pursued by a small population with varying success until, in 1850, with the colony in a languishing condition, the inhabitants' petition that it might be made a penal settlement was acceded to. Between 1850 and 1868 (in which year transportation ceased), 9,668 convicts were sent out.

In 1870 partially representative government was instituted, and in 1890 the administration was vested in the Governor, a legislative council and a legislative assembly. The legislative council was, in the first instance, nominated by the Governor, but in 1893 it became elective.

Western Australia federated with the other Australian states to form the Commonwealth of Australia in 1901.

Further Reading

Crowley, F. K., *Australia's Western Third: A History of Western Australia from the First Settlements to Modern Times*. Rev. ed. Melbourne, 1970

AUSTRIA

From 1282 the possession of the Hapsburgs, Austria served there-after as the centre of their expanding power and empire; an empire (under which Austria and Bohemia came in 1526) which lasted until 1918. At their greatest extent under Charles V (1519–55) the Hapsburg dominions included part of Hungary (wholly conquered from the Turks in 1688), Belgium, Italian territories, Spain and its vast empire. Spain was soon separated, and the Hapsburgs struggled to gain international recognition for the integrity of their dynastic holdings. The Pragmatic Sanction of 1713 was only partially successful in this, but the Empire survived, with only the loss of Silesia, the War of the Austrian Succession (1740–48) and the Seven Years War (1756–63). Polish territory was annexed in 1772 and 1795. The Empire, represented by Prince Metternich at the Congress of Vienna, in 1815, recovered the influence in Germany and Italy it had lost during the French Revolutionary and Napoleonic Wars. It remained the major power in Central Europe till defeated in 1866 by Prussia and her German allies, a position confirmed by the unification of Germany in 1870–71 under Prussian leadership. Hungarian nationalism, the main obstacle to the integration of the Empire, was in 1867 appeased by the *Ausgleich* or Compromise: the state became known as the Dual Monarchy of Austria-Hungary.

As national feeling spread to the other peoples in the Empire, politics turned increasingly on national rivalries and aspirations. Tension was particularly high among the Serbs of Bosnia (annexed 1908) who could also look to the independent state of Serbia. It was at Sarajevo in Bosnia on 28 June 1914 that the heir to the throne, Archduke Franz Ferdinand, was assassinated by Serbian nationalists, an event that triggered the First World War. The Empire, allied with Germany, suffered severely in the war with 1·2m. dead out of a population of 52m. In defeat in 1918 the Empire disintegrated into its national units.

The Treaty of St Germain (1919) left substantial populations of German speakers in Italy and Czechoslovakia. The federal constitution of 5 Oct. 1920 introduced proportional representation; Christian Socialists dominated the governments (except for 1929–30) until 1938. But the Socialists were strong, and the general strike of July 1927 and the rising of Feb. 1934 induced Chancellor Dolfuss to end parliamentary democracy and introduce the Fatherland Front backed by the paramilitary Heimwehr. The Nazis who assassinated Dolfuss on 25 July 1934 helped to bring about the *Anschluss* or Union with Germany which was achieved by a German invasion on 12 March 1938. Until 1945 Austria was Ostmark, a province of the Third Reich.

Although the 1943 Moscow Conference of Allied Foreign Ministers regarded Austria as the first victim of German aggression, Austria was occupied by Britain, France, USA and USSR (and paid reparations to the last over a ten-year period). Independence came with the Austrian State Treaty of 15 May 1955, when the four powers withdrew and Austria entered the UN and inaugurated a policy of neutrality.

The first elections had been held on 25 Nov. 1945 with an almost complete Communist failure. The People's Party and the Socialists formed coalitions which lasted until 1966 and then continued under Chancellor B. Kreisky (1969–83). 'Social partnership' in the economy also brought stability. Austria is a member of EFTA. On 4 May 1986 the former UN Secretary-General, Kurt Waldheim, was elected president. His war record as an officer in the German Army brought tense international controversy as the 50th anniversary of the *Anschluss* approached.

Further Reading

Sotriffer, K., *Greater Austria: 100 Years of Intellectual and Social Life from 1800 to the Present Time.* Vienna, 1982

BAHAMAS

The Commonwealth of the Bahamas is an island state in the Atlantic Ocean, comprising some 700 islands. They were originally inhabited by a group of Arawak Indians known as Lucayan. Coming from the South American continent, some of the Arawak had been driven north into the Caribbean by the Carib. A peaceful race, the Arawak were more involved with fishing than with agriculture. The Bahamas were then discovered in 1492 by Columbus who named them Lucayos. The Spaniards made no attempt to settle but operated slave raids on the Arawak. By the time the English arrived, in the 17th century, the Bahamas were uninhabited. In 1671 'The Lords Proprietors of Carolina', armed with a Royal Grant, established a Governor and an elective House of Assembly. The Proprietors surrendered their rights to the Crown in 1717. In 1776 American rebels captured the islands, and in 1781 the Spaniards also occupied the islands until the Peace of Versailles in 1783 returned the islands to Britain.

During the American Civil War, gun-running provided lucrative employment as did smuggling during the period of prohibition in the USA.

In 1964 a new constitution was established with internal self-government, cabinet responsibility and universal adult suffrage. On 10 July 1973 independence was granted to the Commonwealth of the Bahamas.

Further Reading

Albury, P., *The Story of the Bahamas*. London, 1975

BAHRAIN

Bahrain was controlled by the Portuguese from 1521 until 1602. The Khalifa family gained control in 1783 and has ruled since that date, rejecting claims of suzerainty from Persia (Iran) and the Ottoman Empire. British assistance was sought to retain independence and in 1861 Bahrain and Britain signed a treaty of peace and friendship, and from 1861 until 1971 Bahrain was in all but name a British protectorate. Treaties signed in 1882 and in 1892 gave Britain responsibility for defence and foreign policy.

In 1970 a Council of State was established, so that the ruling family was no longer the sole executive power.

On 15 Aug. 1971 a new treaty of friendship was signed with Britain. This replaced all earlier treaties, and at the same time Bahrain declared its independence. Shaikh Isa bin Salman Al-Khalifa became the Amir, and the Council of State became the cabinet. A constitution was ratified in June 1973 providing for a National Assembly of 30 members, popularly elected for a 4-year term, together with all members of the cabinet (appointed by the Amir). Elections took place in Dec. 1973. However, the relationship between the National Assembly and the Khalifa family was not successful, and in 1975 the National Assembly was dissolved and the Amir has since ruled solely through the cabinet. The main island was, in 1987, joined to the Saudi mainland by a causeway, the social and economic effects of which await to be seen.

Further Reading
Rumaihi, M. G., *Bahrain: Social and Political Change since the First World War*. New York and London, 1976

BANGLADESH

The eastern territory of the Bengali people was ruled by the Nawab of Bengal, governor for the Moghul Empire, who declared himself independent of the emperor in 1740. His defeat by the British East India Company in 1757 and the company's assumption of control of the area marked the beginning of the British Empire in India. By 1764 his lands had been conquered by the British East India Company who kept Bengal as a unit, adding Assam to it in 1838.

The first formal partition of Bengal was made by the Government of India in 1905. East Bengal, which was predominantly Moslem and also rural and poor, was united with Assam to form a new province. The partition was extremely unpopular with Bengali Hindus who claimed that their Bengali nationality was more important than their religious diversity. In 1912 East and West Bengal were reunited – a move unpopular with Moslems.

Independent India was partitioned according to religion in 1947. West Bengal became part of India while East Bengal elected to join Pakistan as East Pakistan. The province, however, was separated from West Pakistan physically and ethnically, it was still poor and it continued to be neglected. Differences became unmanageable when East Pakistan's Awami League, campaigning for greater autonomy, won the majority of seats in the federal parliament in Dec. 1970. There was civil war from March to Dec. 1971, and with the help of Indian troops the Pakistani forces were defeated and the East broke away as an independent state; it became the Republic of Bangladesh and the Awami League leader, Sheikh Mujibur Rahman, became its first president. The constitution of 1972 provided parliamentary democracy, but in Jan. 1975 the president banned political parties and began to rule with an advisory parliament. In Aug. 1975 he was murdered and martial law was introduced. His successor as head of state, Maj.-Gen. Ziaur Rahman, was murdered by a group of army officers in May 1981. In March 1982 there was a further army *coup* after a short period of ineffective civilian government. Lieut.-Gen. Ershad was installed at the head of a military government and assumed the presidency in Dec. 1983. Parliamentary elections were held again in April 1986, but the Awami League boycotted the new parliament.

Further Reading

O'Donnell, C. P., *Bangladesh: Biography of a Muslim Nation*. Boulder, 1986

BARBADOS

Barbados was settled by the British during the 1620s and in 1627 a Governor was appointed and a legislative council established. In 1639 a House of Assembly was created. The sovereignty of Barbados never changed hands as the constitution gradually developed. The British developed Barbados as a sugar plantation economy, initially on the basis of slavery until its abolition in the 1840s.

In the 19th century an executive council or committee with ministerial powers was established. In 1951 universal adult suffrage was introduced, followed in 1954 by a complete ministerial system with cabinet government. Full internal self-government was attained in Oct. 1961.

From 1958–62 Barbados was a member of the short-lived Federation of the West Indies. On 30 Nov. 1966 Barbados became an independent sovereign state within the Commonwealth.

Further Reading

Hoyos, F. A., *Barbados: A History from the Amerindians to Independence.* London, 1978

BELGIUM

The Netherlands became part of the duchy of Burgundy in the late 14th century and through dynastic marriage came under the control of the Spanish Hapsburgs in 1504. When the northern provinces rebelled against Spanish rule in the 1570s, the southern provinces pledged their allegiance to Catholicism and the Spanish crown. The War of the Spanish Succession (1701–14) ended with the cession of Belgium to the Austrian Hapsburgs. Briefly annexed to France during the Napoleonic war, Belgium and Holland were reunited by the Treaty of Paris (1815) to form one state. The Belgians rose in revolt against this arrangement, and the 'Kingdom of Belgium' was formed as an independent state in 1830. A National Congress elected Prince Leopold of Saxe-Coburg as 'King of the Belgians', and he ascended the throne as Leopold I on 21 July 1831. By the Treaty of London, 15 Nov. 1831, the neutrality of Belgium was guaranteed by Austria, Russia, Great Britain and Prussia. It was not until after the signing of the Treaty of London, 19 April 1839, which established peace between Leopold I and the King of the Netherlands, that all the states of Europe recognized the Kingdom of Belgium.

In 1914 Belgian neutrality was violated by the Germans whose troops invaded. As a consequence Britain declared war on Germany.

In the Second World War Belgium was again invaded by Germany in 1940. On this occasion the king, Leopold III, immediately surrendered, although an exiled Belgian Government operated from Britain during the war. In 1950 Leopold III abdicated in favour of his son, Baudouin.

In the post-war years linguistic problems have caused persistent quarrelling between the Flemish (Dutch)-speaking north of the country and the French-speaking Walloons of the south. This animosity has been accentuated by increasing industrialization and consequent population movements.

BELIZE

A low-lying country on the Central American mainland, Belize was the home of the Mayan civilization, which flourished there from about 300 BC to 900 AD . In 1502, Columbus sailed into and named the Bay of Honduras, although he did not actually visit the area later known as British Honduras. European settlement was established in 1638 by shipwrecked British sailors. These were later joined by British soldiers and sailors disbanded after the capture of Jamaica from Spain in 1655. Spain claimed sovereignty over the entire New World except for certain Portuguese possessions, and so there were numerous attacks from nearby Spanish settlements during the next century. Victory was won by the settlers in the Battle of St George's Caye in 1798. In 1862 British Honduras was formally declared a British colony.

From an early date the settlers had governed themselves under a system of democracy by public meeting. A constitution was granted in 1765 and, with some modification, continued until 1840 when an executive council was created.

In 1853 the public meeting was replaced by a legislative assembly, with the British Superintendent, an office created in 1786 at the settlers' request, as chairman. British settlers began to penetrate the interior as coastal timber became exhausted. The Indians resisted this penetration and the 19th century was punctuated by clashes between the two. When the settlement became a colony in 1862, the Superintendent was replaced by a Lieut.-Governor under the Governor of Jamaica. The frontier with Guatemala was agreed by Convention in 1859 but was declared invalid by Guatemala in 1940.

The Crown Colony system of government was introduced in 1871, and the legislative assembly by its own vote was replaced by a nominated legislative council with an official majority, presided over by the Lieut.-Governor.

The administrative connection with Jamaica was severed in 1884 when the title of Lieut.-Governor was changed to that of Governor.

Universal adult suffrage was introduced in 1964, and thereafter the majority of the legislature were elected rather than appointed; the ministerial system was adopted in 1971. In June 1974 British Honduras became Belize.

Independence was achieved on 21 Sept. 1981 and a new constitution introduced.

Further Reading

Dobson, D., *A History of Belize*. Belize, 1973

BENIN

The People's Republic of Benin is the former Republic of Dahomey. Dahomey was called after the historic kingdom of Dahomey or Abomey, conquered by the French in 1892–94. The new name given to the country on 30 Nov. 1975 came from the Bight of Benin and the former 'French Bight of Benin Settlements', themselves called after the ancient kingdom of Benin in modern Nigeria. The kingdom of Dahomey was a powerful, well-organized state from the 17th century, trading extensively in slaves through the port of Whydah with the Portuguese, British and French. On the coast an educated African élite grew up in the 19th century.

After the defeat of Dahomey, whose monarchy was abolished, the French occupied territory inland up to the River Niger, and created the colony of Dahomey as part of French West Africa. Subsequently, there were several African revolts, a number occurring during the First World War. The African élite protested frequently at French rule and, as African nationalism blossomed after the Second World War, Dahomey saw lively political activity and the formation of several parties.

Dahomey became independent on 1 Aug. 1960 with a coalition of three parties in power and Hubert Maga as president. Opposition to his rule led to a military *coup* by Gen. Christophe Soglo in Oct. 1963. Soglo handed over power to another political leader, Sourou-Migan Apithy, but returned to power in late 1965. Two years later he was deposed and replaced by another military régime, led by Col. Alphonse Alley. Alley handed over in 1968 to a civilian president, Emile-Derlin Zinsou. In Dec. 1969 a three-man military junta took control; elections were held in early 1970, after which a Presidential Council was installed in power, consisting of Maga, Apithy and Justin Ahomadegbe. Maga chaired the Council until May 1972 when he handed over to Ahomadegbe.

In Oct. 1972, Gen. Mathieu Kerekou seized power and installed a new left-wing régime committed to socialist policies. A constitution was adopted in 1977, based on a single Marxist-Leninist party, the *Parti de la Révolution Populaire du Bénin* (PRPB). Despite persistent economic problems, factional fighting within its ranks and frequent plots and attempts at its overthrow, the régime has retained power.

Further Reading
Herskovitz, M. J., *Dahomey, An Ancient West African Kingdom*. London, 1967

BERMUDA

Bermuda is composed of a group of 300 coral islands in the North Atlantic Ocean. The Spaniards visited the islands in 1515, but, according to a 17th-century French cartographer, they were first discovered in 1503 by Juan Bermudez, after whom they were named. They were uninhabited until a party of colonists under Sir George Somers was shipwrecked there in 1609. In 1612 Bermuda was included in the Third Charter of the Virginia Company and 60 English settlers were sent to colonize the islands. Indian and African slaves were transported to Bermuda, beginning in 1616, and soon outnumbered the white settlers. A company was formed for the Plantation of the Somers Islands, as they were originally called, but in 1684 the company's charter was annulled and the Crown took over the government.

During the American Civil War, Bermuda was a resting point for blockade runners. Rum was smuggled into the USA from the islands during the prohibition period (1919–33). The US government acquired a 99 year lease for naval and air bases in 1941, and the British naval garrisons diminished.

Although a House of Assembly was created, only those with property were enfranchised. Gradually the electorate was extended and in 1962 those over 25 years of age were given the vote, with property owners allowed two votes. The latter privilege was abolished in 1966 when the voting age was reduced to 21 years. Internal self-government was established on 8 June 1968. The new constitution gave considerable powers to the elected head of the majority political party. Political tensions increased in 1973 with the assassination of the Governor. A period of further civil unrest with riots in 1977 led to official efforts to end racial discrimination and begin independence talks, which were later suspended. A movement to reopen independence discussions resurfaced in the early 1980s.

Further Reading

Zuill, W. S., *The Story of Bermuda and Her People*. London, 1973

BHUTÁN

A sovereign kingdom in the Himalayas, Bhután was governed by a spiritual ruler and a temporal ruler – the Dharma and Deb Raja – from the 17th century. The capital was Funakha. The interior was organized into districts for defence. Districts were controlled by governors and each district's central fort *(dzhong)* by a fort commander. These officials formed the electoral council appointing the Deb Raja.

The British East India Company made a treaty with Bhután in 1774, but relations were uneasy and there were violent incidents. The British annexed a number of borderland areas in an attempt to contain Bhutánese raiders.

During the 19th century civil wars were fought between district governors for the office of the Deb Raja. The election became a formality, and the governors of Tongsa and Paro were the most frequently chosen, because the strongest. The appointment of new governors was likewise settled by force.

By 1860 the British in India were disturbed by the instability of Bhután. An attempt to interfere in 1863 resulted in a short frontier war, ending with a treaty in 1865. The British annexed part of Dewangiri and agreed to pay the rulers of Bhután an annual subsidy.

In 1907 the office of Dharma Raja came to an end. The governor of Tongsa, Ugyen Wangchuk, was then chosen Maharajah of Bhután, the throne becoming hereditary in his family (the title is now King of Bhután). He concluded a further treaty with the British in 1910 allowing internal autonomy but British control of foreign policy. The treaty was renewed with the Government of India in 1949; the subsidy was further increased and the annexed area of Dewangiri returned to Bhután.

The Chinese occupation of Tibet in 1949 caused a flow of Tibetan refugees into Bhután, where their assimilation has proved extremely difficult.

Since 1953 there has been a partly-elected national assembly exercising some influence on the decisions of the king and his ministers. Thimphu became the capital in 1962.

Further Reading
Mehra, G. N., *Bhutan: Land of the Peaceful Dragon*. Rev. ed. New Delhi, 1985

BOLIVIA

Bolivia was part of the Inca Empire until conquered by the Spanish in the 16th century. In 1776 it became part of the viceroyalty of Buenos Aires. Independence was won and the Republic of Bolivia was proclaimed on 6 Aug. 1825. The first constitution was adopted on 19 Nov. 1826. Since then there has been considerable political unrest and constant, often violent, changes of government.

Expansion in the production of tin in the early 20th century brought greater political stability for a time.

Until 1884, when she was defeated by Chile, Bolivia had a strip bordering on the Pacific which contains extensive nitrate beds and at that time the port of Cobija (which no longer exists). She lost this area to Chile; but in Sept. 1953 Chile declared Arica a free port and, although it is no longer a free port for Bolivian imports, Bolivia still retains certain privileges. Further territory was lost to Paraguay in 1935 at the end of the Chaco War.

During the first 154 years of its independence, Bolivia had 189 governments, many of them installed by coups. Largely civilian governments from 1880 gave way to mainly military ones after 1936. In 1952 a major revolution was led by the MNR (National Revolutionary Movement), but its social reforms were soon undone. In the 1960s the Argentinian revolutionary, and former minister of the Cuban Government, Ernesto 'Che' Guevara, was killed while fighting with a left-wing guerrilla group. In 1971 Bolivian instability reached a peak with the brief establishment of a revolutionary Popular Assembly during the regime of Gen. Torres. Later repression under Gen. Hugo Banzer took a heavy toll of the left-wing parties. An attempt to hold elections in July 1978 led to Gen. Juan Pereda Asbún (supported by the army) carrying out a military *coup*. In Nov. he was in turn overthrown by Gen. David Padilla Arancibia, the army commander. Elections in July 1979 proved indecisive, and an interim government was formed until it was overthrown in Nov. by yet another army *coup*, which won power for a mere two weeks.

The failure of any candidate to win a clear majority at the presidential elections has added to the country's serious economic problems. The power of the army has helped to keep governments unstable. The 1980 elections were as inconclusive as those of the previous year and a *coup* followed, led by the army C.-in-C., Gen.

Luis Garcia Meza. However, in 1981 he was forced to resign in favour of Gen. Celso Torrelio Villa. When the new president tried introducing civilians to the Cabinet and adopting a liberal attitude to trade unions, he was superseded by Gen. Guido Vildoso Calderón. In Oct. 1982 Dr Siles Zuazo (who had won a small majority in the two previous elections) became president. However, his Cabinet resigned twice during 1983. In 1985 Dr Victor Paz Esstensoro was elected president, and he has dealt firmly with disturbances and declared strikes illegal.

Further Reading

Dunkerley, J., *Rebellion in the Veins: Political Struggle in Bolivia 1952–1982*. London, 1984

BOTSWANA

The Tswana or Batswana people are the principal inhabitants of the country formerly known as Bechuanaland and now called Botswana. The 8 main communities of the Batswana are the Bakgatla, Bakwena, Bangwaketse, Bamalete, Bamangwato, Barolong, Batawana and Batlokwa.

Dominant in the area from the 17th century, the Batswana were disturbed in the early 19th century by invasions of Nguni peoples fleeing from Shaka in the mass migration called the *Mfecane*, and by Boers moving east in the Great Trek. They clashed with the Boers, but obtained the support of British missionaries (including David Livingstone). King Khama III, a Christian who became ruler of the Bamangwato in 1872, appealed with other chiefs to Britain because of the Boer danger. In 1885 Britain declared the country under Queen Victoria's protection and it was formally declared a protectorate in 1895. Britain ruled through her High Commissioner in South Africa and a Resident Commissioner whose office was at Mafeking. When the post of South African High Commissioner was abolished in 1964, the British representative was restyled Commissioner and placed directly under the Colonial Secretary in London. The seat of government was moved to Gaborone in 1965. Frequent suggestions for the addition of Bechuanaland and the other two High Commission Territories to South Africa were rejected, the Africans being strongly against the idea. Economically, however, the country was very closely tied to that of South Africa and has remained so.

The British left much day-to-day administration in the hands of the Tswana chiefs. They set up an African Advisory Council in 1920 and a European Advisory Council for the (never very numerous) white residents in 1921; a Joint Advisory Council was created in 1950.

Seretse Khama, ruler of the Bamangwato since 1923 when he was four, was deposed in 1950 because of South African opposition to his marriage to a white woman. He returned in 1956 and joined the African Advisory Council in 1957. In Dec. 1960 Bechuanaland received its first constitution. Elections followed in 1961 for African members of the Legislative Council, of whom Seretse was one. In 1962 he formed the Bechuanaland Democratic Party, now the Botswana Democratic Party (BDP). Further constitutional change brought full self-government in 1965 and full independence on 30 Sept. 1966. Sir Seretse Khama became president.

Botswana, unusually for Africa, has continued to tolerate opposition parties. Nonetheless, the BDP easily won elections in 1969, 1974 and 1979. President Khama died on 13 July 1980 and was succeeded by Dr Quett Masire, without any change of policy. For years Botswana had great difficulties with the neighbouring settler régime in Rhodesia, until that country became Zimbabwe in 1980. Such difficulties have continued with South Africa, Botswana supporting African resistance to the Pretoria régime but at the same time being economically dependent on it. Many border clashes and other incidents between Botswana and South Africa culminated in a South African raid on alleged African National Congress offices in Gaborone in June 1985, May 1986 and again in March 1988.

Further Reading

Coclough, C., and McCarthy, S., *The Political Economy of Botswana*. OUP, 1980

BRAZIL

Brazil, South America's largest country, was colonized by the Portuguese following the arrival of Admiral Pedro Alvares Cabral on 22 April 1500. In 1815 the colony was declared 'a kingdom'. When, in 1822, the Portuguese king, João VI, returned home after using Rio de Janeiro as his capital during the French occupation of Portugal, his eldest surviving son, Dom Pedro, was chosen 'Perpetual Defender' of Brazil by a National Congress. He proclaimed the independence of the country on 7 Sept. 1822, and was chosen 'Constitutional Emperor and Perpetual Defender' on 12 Oct. 1822, with the title Emperor Pedro I. He abdicated in 1831 and was succeeded in 1840 by his son, Pedro II. Pedro ruled for nearly 50 years. His policies were liberal and included the gradual abolition of slavery.

Under the dictatorship of President Vargas from 1930 to 1945, some areas (such as San Paulo) saw considerable economic development. Vargas was succeeded by Presidents Kubitschek and Quadros.

In 1961 the left-wing João Goulart was elected president. For a period he had to share some of his executive powers with a prime minister and then was overthrown by a reactionary *coup* in 1964. The Army Chief-of-Staff, Gen. Humberto Castelo Branco, became president until Marshal Artur da Costa e Silva was elected to take office in 1967. The new constitution named the country República Federativa do Brasil. In 1969 da Costa e Silva was compelled to resign and a junta of the 3 heads of the armed services assumed power. An amendment to the constitution on 17 Oct. 1967 provided for the indirect election of the president through an electoral college. It also gave him increased powers as he was authorized to issue decree-laws on matters connected with the economy and national security. Gen. Emilio Garrastazu Medici assumed the office of president on 30 Oct. 1969, and was succeeded by Gen. Ernesto Geisel on 15 March 1974. The latter began to allow very limited democratic developments, a policy that his successor in 1979, Gen. João Baptista de Oliveira Figueiredo, promised to continue. In 1979 provision was made for the development of political parties and as a result the government party, *Partido Democratico Social* (PDS), could not establish a satisfactory majority in the lower house of Congress, the Chamber of Deputies. Considerable demand followed for direct presidential elections, and 1984 saw huge rallies in the main cities. When the more liberal members of PDS moved towards the democratic demands of the opposition parties, a civilian, Tancredo de Almeido Neves, was elected president in 1985 by the electoral college. As he died in the same year, the vice-president, Jose Sarney, who was sympathetic to Neves' ideals, assumed office. President Sarney's government has been dominated by the problem of Brazil's external debt.

In 1988 a new constitution was being drafted and discussions taking place on the timing of direct presidential elections.

Further Reading

Dickenson, J. P., *Brazil.* Harlow, 1982

BRITISH ANTARCTIC TERRITORY

The South Shetland Islands were discovered in 1819, the Antarctic Peninsula in 1820 (although it was 1832 before Britain formally possessed the area), and the South Orkney Islands in 1821. The whole area was part of the Falkland Islands Dependencies until 1962. Under the Antarctic Treaty of 1961, 12 countries agreed to co-operate scientifically in the Antarctic and to keep it free of any military or nuclear exercises. An Order in Council separated those areas of the Falkland Islands Dependencies which lay within the treaty area from those which did not, and they were then designated the British Antarctic Territory.

BRITISH INDIAN OCEAN TERRITORY

The British Indian Ocean Territory, a British dependency since 1965, comprises the Chagos Islands. The islands have been British territory for nearly 170 years, having been ceded with Mauritius and Seychelles to Britain by France in 1814. Thereafter, for reasons of administrative convenience, they were administered from Mauritius, until 1965 when they were detached to form, with 3 island groups formerly administered by Seychelles, the new dependency. The last 3 groups – Aldabra, Desroches and Farquhar – became part of Seychelles when it became an independent republic within the Commonwealth in 1976.

In 1966 it was agreed to make the Territory available for the defence purposes of the USA and Britain. The Crown purchased the islands in 1967 and 3,000 inhabitants were moved to Mauritius. The islands remain Crown property, administered from London by a Commissioner. Mauritius continues to call for the return of Diego Garcia, an atoll in the territory, and along with the Seychelles argues that the Indian Ocean should become a 'zone of peace' free of US and Soviet bases.

BRUNEI DARUSSALAM

Situated on the northern coast of Borneo, Brunei was trading with China during the 6th century, and through allegiance to the Javanese Majapahit Kingdom in the 13th-15th centuries, it came under Hindu influence. In the early 15th century, with the decline of the Majapahit Kingdom and widespread conversion to Islam, Brunei became an independent Sultanate.

When Magellan anchored his ships off Brunei in 1521, Bolkiah (the fifth Sultan) controlled most of Borneo, its neighbouring islands and the Suhi Archipelago. By the end of the 16th century, however, the power of Brunei was on the wane because of the activities of the Portuguese and Dutch in the region.

Brunei became a British protectorate in 1888 and in 1906 accepted a British Resident who exercised control over all matters except the Islamic faith and Malay custom. The discovery of major oil fields in the western end of the State in the 1920s brought economic stability to Brunei and created a new style of life for the population. Brunei was occupied by the Japanese in 1941 and liberated by the Australians in 1945.

Self-government was introduced in 1959 but Britain retained responsibility for foreign affairs. In 1962 an attempt was made by a section of the community to overthrow the Sultan, Sir Omar Ali Saifuddin. In 1965 constitutional changes were made which led to direct elections for a new Legislative Council. In 1967 Sultan Sir Omar Ali Saifuddin abdicated in favour of his eldest son, Sultan Sir Muda Hassanal Bolkiah, who was crowned in 1968.

The sultan negotiated a new treaty with the British in 1979 and full independence and sovereignty was gained on 1 Jan. 1984.

Further Reading

Brunei: The Land and its People. State Secretariat, Brunei, 1978

BULGARIA

The Bulgarians take their name from an invading Asiatic horde (Bulgars) and their language from the Slav population with whom they merged after 680. From 681 to 1018 and 1185 to 1389 the Bulgarians carved out empires against a background of conflict with Byzantium and Serbia, and established a civilization of which the Orthodox missionaries Cyril and Methodius, credited with the invention of the Slavonic alphabet, are noteworthy exemplars.

After the Serb-Bulgarian defeat at Kosovo in 1389 Bulgaria finally succumbed to Ottoman encroachment. The Bulgar landowners were replaced by military and civil officials who held land in return for state service. The Orthodox church was permitted to practise. The Ottoman empire's decline, however, engendered corruption and exactions, uprisings and reprisals. National liberation consciousness owed much to the patriotic *History* (1762) of the monk Paisi, and was reinforced by the cultural-educational movements which brought intelligentsia and peasantry together in the 19th century. Bulgarian control of the church was secured from the Greeks in 1870. In 1872 a Bulgarian Revolutionary Central Committee was formed which organized a rebellion in 1876. The brutal repression of this provoked great power intervention; Russia successfully invaded Turkey in 1877 and imposed upon her the Treaty of San Stefano (March 1878) which established a 'big Bulgaria' extending into Macedonia and Thrace. Conceiving this a threat to the balance of power, Britain and Austria-Hungary pressurized Russia into revising these boundaries by the Treaty of Berlin (July 1878): Macedonia and Thrace reverted to Turkey, Eastern Rumelia became semi-autonomous and Bulgaria proper a principality under Turkish suzerainty.

Under the Treaty a constituent assembly at Tŭrnovo voted a liberal constitution which provided for a single-chamber parliament elected by male suffrage. The throne was offered to the German prince Alexander of Battenberg. In 1885 Eastern Rumelia was united to Bulgaria by a *coup d'état*. Alexander accepted the unification against the wishes of Russia, who forced his abdication in 1886. He was replaced by Ferdinand of Saxe-Coburg-Gotha, who did not gain Russian recognition until 1896. Prime Minister Stefan Stambolov achieved a period of prosperity, but Ferdinand engineered his resignation in 1894 and henceforth ruled personally through manipulation of the political parties.

After Austria annexed Bosnia in 1908, Bulgaria declared itself independent. To block Austrian expansion into the Balkans Russia encouraged Greece, Serbia, Montenegro and Bulgaria to form a Balkan League in 1912. The League successfully attacked Turkey (first Balkan War, 1912), but in the dispute which followed over the territorial spoils (principally in Macedonia) Bulgaria failed to secure her claims against her former allies by force (second Balkan War, 1913). Territorial aspirations led Bulgaria to join the First World War on the German side in Oct. 1915, but the peace settlement (Neuilly, 1919) left her with little gained.

Economic decline caused by the war produced social unrest. Ferdinand was forced to abdicate in favour of his son, Boris III, in Oct. 1918, and the radical Agrarian Party took office, headed by Alexander Stamboliiski. The latter's reformism, friendship with Yugoslavia (a contender for Macedonia) and high-handed behaviour generated various currents of opposition, and he was assassinated after a *coup* in June 1923. The Communist Party held its hand during this, but launched an abortive rising in Sept. 1923, and bombed Sofia cathedral in April 1925, killing 120 people. This led to a reign of government terror against all radicals. Bedevilled by Macedonian terrorism and the effects of the world economic depression, parliamentary government was ended by a military *coup* in May 1934. In 1935 Boris established a royal dictatorship under which political parties were banned. Boris died in 1943 and was succeeded by a regency.

Increasingly drawn into the German economic orbit, and in pursuit of the San Stefano territories, Bulgaria joined the Nazis against Britain in March 1941, but retained diplomatic relations with the Soviet Union. On 8 Sept. 1944 the Soviet Union declared war and sent its troops across the frontiers. Wartime opposition to the government had centred round the Communist-dominated Fatherland Front, which formed a government on 9 Sept. A referendum on 8 Sept. 1946 abolished the monarchy, and a people's republic was proclaimed. In 1947 the Soviet-type 'Dimitrov' constitution replaced the Tŭrnovo constitution of 1879. Georgi Dimitrov, a veteran Communist leader who had secured acquittal from a Nazi court after charges of complicity in the arson of the Reichstag, was prime minister until his death in 1949. The 'Titoist' purges of late Stalinism were presided over by Vulko Chervenkov, who was eclipsed in the 1950s by the present leader, Todor Zhivkov.

Further Reading

Crampton, R. J., *A Short History of Modern Bulgaria*. CUP, 1987

BURKINA FASO

Formerly known as Upper Volta, the country's name was changed in 1984 to Burkina Faso, meaning 'the land of honest men'. The area it covers was settled by farming communities until their invasion by the Mossi people in the 11th century, who set up several powerful kingdoms – Ouagadougou, Yatenga and Tenkogodo. These successfully resisted Islamic crusades and attacks by neighbouring empires for seven centuries until conquered by the French between 1895 and 1903.

France made Upper Volta a separate colony in 1919, only to abolish it as such in 1932, dividing its territory among Ivory Coast (now Côte d'Ivoire), French Sudan (now Mali) and Niger. In 1947 the territory of Upper Volta was reconstituted. For much of the colonial era the people of Upper Volta suffered from military and labour conscription, forced labourers being often sent to Ivory Coast. After the abolition of forced labour in 1946 Voltaic men continued to emigrate to the Ivory Coast and Ghana, this time voluntarily.

Upper Volta has had a troubled political history since independence, and has remained, however, a desperately poor country often hit by drought, particularly in 1972–74 and again in 1982–84.

After independence, President Maurice Yameogo and his *Union Démocratique Voltaique* (UDV) ruled until 3 Jan. 1966, when the army took power under Gen. Sangoule Lamizana. His régime surrendered some power to civilians in 1971, under a new constitution allowing for an elected assembly and with a government consisting of two-thirds civilians and one-third military officers. But after three years Lamizana, who had remained president, and his military colleagues took back all power into their hands in 1974. Their régime created a new governmental political party in 1975. A new constitution was drawn up and approved by referendum in 1977, and elections were held to a new national assembly in 1978. Joseph Conombo, as prime minister, formed a coalition government. Gen. Lamizana was elected president.

In 1980 a *coup d'état* overthrew this new régime and Col. Saye Zerbo, at the head of a *Comité Militaire de Redressement pour le Progrès National* (CMRPN), held power for two years. Then, on 7 Nov. 1982, the CMRPN was overthrown in another *coup* and replaced by the *Conseil du Salut de Peuple* (CSP), headed by Jean-

Baptiste Ouedraogo. Younger, more radical officers now came to the fore, but there was serious tension within the CSP, leading to the arrest of the leading radical, Capt. Thomas Sankara, on 17 May 1983 and then, on 4 Aug. 1983, to a new *coup d'état* which put him in power.

Sankara and his radical military colleagues formed a *Conseil National de la Révolution* (CNR) and installed a left-wing régime, with Revolutionary Defence Committees *(Comités de Défense de la Révolution*, CDR) operating at local level. The régime aimed at ending exploitation, and sought to curb food traders. Although it established close relations with the similar régime in Ghana, and with Libya, it also maintained fairly normal relations with France and remains in the franc zone.

A border dispute between Burkina Faso and Mali led to fighting in 1974 and again in Dec. 1985. A year later, on 22 Dec. 1986, the International Court of Justice ruled on the dispute, dividing the contested area into roughly equal shares for each; both countries accepted the judgment. Sankara was overthrown and killed in a *coup* on 15 Oct. 1987, the fifth since 1960, led by his friend Captain Blaise Compaore.

Further Reading

MacFarlane, D. M., *Historical Dictionary of Upper Volta*. Metuchen, 1978

BURMA

In 1785 the Alaugpaya dynasty of Burma conquered Arakan in the south-west. Arakanese refugees fled into India in large numbers and turned Chittagong into a base for guerrilla raids on Burma, thus provoking reprisal raids into India by Burmese forces.

This was followed by Burma's invasions of the kingdom of Assam. The British East India Company then took action in defence of its Indian interests and in 1826 finally drove the Burmese out of India and annexed territory in south Burma. The kingdom of Upper Burma, ruled from Mandalay in the north, remained independent. A second war with Britain in 1852 ended with the British annexation of the Irrawaddy Delta.

In 1862 and 1867 trade treaties were concluded with Upper Burma. However, in 1885 the British invaded, deposed the king and occupied Upper Burma. In 1886 all Burma became a province of the Indian empire. The Chin tribes of the Burmese-Indian borderlands were subdued in 1889–90. The Indian system of administration was not suitable for the country and exacerbated resentment at imperial economic policies and Britain's refusal to support Buddhism as the state religion. There were violent uprisings in the 1930s and in 1937 Burma was separated from India and some degree of self-government was introduced.

Following the Japanese invasion and occupation of 1942–45, Britain and Burma began to negotiate the establishment of independence, which was achieved in 1948 with the creation of the Union of Burma, an independent republic outside the Commonwealth. The president was Sao Shwe Thaike.

In 1958 there was an army *coup*, and another in 1962 led by Gen. Ne Win who installed a Revolutionary Council and dissolved parliament. The Council lasted until March 1974 when the country became a one-party socialist republic, a new constitution having been approved by referendum in Dec. 1973. The name was changed to Socialist Republic of the Union of Burma. U Ne Win became president, serving until 1982 when he was succeeded by U San Yu.

In 1988 there was still unrest among the ethnic minorities. Most of the country remains closed to foreign visitors.

Further Reading

Steinberg, D. I., *Burma*. Boulder, 1982
Taylor, R. H., *The State of Burma*. 1988

BURUNDI

Tradition recounts the establishment of a Tutsi kingdom under successive Mwamis as early as the 16th century. German military occupation in 1890 incorporated the territory into German East Africa. From 1919 Burundi formed part of Ruanda-Urundi administered by the Belgians, first as a League of Nations mandate and then as a UN trust territory. Internal self-government was granted on 1 Jan. 1962, followed by independence on 1 July 1962.

On 8 July 1966 Prince Charles Ndizeye deposed his father Mwami Mwambutsa IV, suspended the constitution and made Capt. Michel Micombero prime minister. On 1 Sept. Prince Charles was enthroned as Mwami Ntare V. On 28 Nov., while the Mwami was attending a Heads of State Conference in Kinshasa (Congo), Micombero declared Burundi a republic with himself as president.

On 31 March 1972 Prince Charles returned to Burundi from Uganda and was placed under house arrest. On 29 April 1972 President Micombero dissolved the Council of Ministers and took full power; that night heavy fighting broke out between the ruling Tutsi and Hutu rebels from both Burundi and neighbouring countries apparently intent on destroying the Tutsi hegemony. Prince Charles was killed during the fighting which was estimated to have claimed 120,000 lives. On 14 July 1972 President Micombero reinstated a government with a prime minister. On 1 Nov. 1976 President Micombero was deposed by the army. A Supreme Revolutionary Council was established which appointed Col. Jean-Baptiste Bagaza president.

In Sept. 1987 President Bagaza was himself deposed in a *coup* and succeeded by Major Pierre Buyoya.

Further Reading
Weinstein, W., *Historical Dictionary of Burundi*. Metuchen, 1976

CAMBODIA

The recorded history of Cambodia starts at the beginning of the Christian era with the Kingdom of Fou-Nan, whose territories at one time included parts of Thailand, Malaya, Cochin-China and Laos. The kingdom was absorbed at the end of the 6th century by the Khmers. Attacked on either side by the Vietnamese and the Thai from the 15th century onwards, Cambodia was saved from annihilation by the establishment of a French protectorate in 1863. Thailand eventually recognized the protectorate and renounced all claims to suzerainty in exchange for Cambodia's north-western provinces of Battambang and Siem Reap, which were, however, returned under a Franco-Thai convention of 1907, confirmed in the Franco-Thai treaty of 1937. In 1904 the province of Stung Treng, formerly administered as part of Laos, was attached to Cambodia.

A nationalist movement began in the 1930s, and anti-French feeling strengthened in 1940–41 when the French submitted to Japanese demands for bases in Cambodia and allowed Thailand to annex Cambodian territory. On 9 March 1945 the Japanese suppressed the French administration and King Norodom Sihanouk proclaimed Cambodia's independence. British troops occupied Phnom Penh in Oct. 1945, and the re-establishment of French authority was followed by a Franco-Cambodian *modus vivendi* of 7 Jan. 1946, which promised a constitution embodying a constitutional monarchy. Elections for a National Consultative Assembly were held on 1 Sept. 1946 and a Franco-Thai agreement of 17 Nov. 1946 ensured the return to Cambodia of the provinces annexed by Thailand in 1941.

In 1949 Cambodia was granted independence as an Associate State of the French Union. The transfer of the French military powers to the Cambodian government on 9 Nov. 1953 is considered in Cambodia as the attainment of sovereign independence. In Jan. 1955 Cambodia became financially and economically independent, both of France and the other two former Associate States of French Indo-China, Vietnam and Laos.

Anti-French guerrilla bands had operated in the jungle from 1945, the most important being a nationalist group known as the Khmer Issarak led by Son Ngoc Thanh. By 1953 Communist bands drawn from the Vietnamese minority and controlled by the Vietminh were active, and in 1954 regular Vietminh forces invaded Cambodia.

Fighting came to an end with the conclusion on 21 July 1954, at the Geneva Conference, of the agreement on Cambodia. This ensured the withdrawal of French and Vietminh troops, and most of the Khmer Issarak bands then surrendered. The International Control Commission responsible for the implementation of the Geneva Agreements was withdrawn in Dec. 1969 at the request of Prince Sihanouk.

Following a period of increasing economic difficulties and growing indirect involvement in the Vietnamese war, Prince Sihanouk was deposed in March 1970 and on 9 Oct. 1970 the Kingdom of Cambodia became the Khmer Republic. From 1970 hostilities extended throughout most of the country involving North and South Vietnamese and US forces as well as republican and anti-republican Khmer troops. During 1973 direct US and North Vietnamese participation in the fighting came to an end, leaving a civil war situation which continued during 1974 with large-scale fighting between the Khmer Republic supported by US arms and economic aid and the United National Cambodian Front including 'Khmer Rouge' communists supported by North Vietnam and China.

After unsuccessful attempts to capture Phnom Penh in 1973 and 1974, the Khmer Rouge ended the five-year war in April 1975, when the remnants of the republican forces surrendered the city.

From April 1975 the Khmer Rouge instituted a harsh and highly regimented régime. They cut the country off from normal contact with the world and expelled all foreigners. All cities and towns were forcibly evacuated and the population were set to work in the fields.

The régime had difficulties with the Vietnamese from 1975 and this escalated into full-scale fighting in 1977–78. On 7 Jan. 1979, Phnom Penh was captured by the Vietnamese, and the prime minister, Pol Pot, fled. In Dec. 1985 the Khmer Rouge still had 30,000 guerrillas fighting the Vietnamese in Cambodia (Kampuchea).

In June 1982 the Khmer Rouge (who claim to have abandoned their Communist ideology and to have disbanded their Communist party) entered into a coalition with Son Sann's Kampuchean People's National Liberation Front and Prince Sihanouk's group. This government is recognized by the UN.

Further Reading

Barron, J., and Paul, A., *Murder of a Gentle Land*. New York, 1977

CAMEROON

The name Cameroon is derived from the Portuguese *camarões* (prawns), applied by the Portuguese navigators who from 1472 came for the crayfish in the Wouri river estuary. Called Kamerun in German and Cameroun in French, that estuary was later called the Cameroons River by British navigators. The Duala people living there were important traders, selling slaves and later palm oil to Europeans. They signed on 12 July 1884 a treaty establishing German rule over Kamerun. Originally covering the Dualas' territory on the Wouri, this German colony later expanded to cover a large area inland, to which the name Kamerun was also applied.

The area occupied was home to a large number of African peoples; Betis, Bassas, Bamilekes, Bamouns, Tikars, Fulanis and many others. Some, like the Betis and Bassas, had only small traditional states; others had larger ones, notably in the 19th century, the kingdom of Bamoun and the Moslem Fulani state of Adamawa, whose territory was largely incorporated in German Kamerun although its capital, Yola, was included in Nigeria. Resistance to German colonization was strong, and it was about 20 years before German rule was established over the whole territory. In 1911 France ceded large adjoining areas of its neighbouring colonies (Chad, Ubangi-Shari, Middle-Congo and Gabon) to the Germans, who called this new territory Neu-Kamerun.

The Duala people, advanced in education and important as traders, planters and junior government officials, became increasingly critical of German rule, especially when many were evicted from their homes in Douala city in 1914 and one Duala paramount chief, Rudolf Duala Manga Bell, was executed.

In the First World War Allied forces rapidly occupied Douala and then fought the Germans over a wide area, until the last Germans left early in 1916. The occupied territory was provisionally partitioned between France and Britain in 1916, a division confirmed in 1919 when each obtained a League of Nations mandate over its section. British Cameroons consisted of 2 areas, British Southern Cameroons and British Northern Cameroons, adjoining Nigeria. France's mandated territory of Cameroun occupied most of the former German colony. Its capital was at first at Douala, and then, from 1921, at Yaoundé. The French, like the Germans before them, using forced labour. The Dualas continued to take the lead in anti-colonial protest, and in 1929 their paramount chiefs signed a petition calling for self-government.

In the Second World War French Cameroun was occupied at an early stage (when Leclerc landed at Douala on 27 Aug. 1940) by the Free French. From 1944 reforms in the French colonial empire allowed African trade unions and parties, and nationalism spread rapidly. In 1946 the French and British territories became Trust Territories of the UN. Africans in British Cameroons joined in the nationalist politics of Nigeria, and for some years British Southern Cameroons was represented in the parliament and government of Nigeria's Eastern Region. In French Cameroun the *Union des Populations du Cameroun* (UPC), founded in 1948, became the major nationalist party, calling for independence and 'reunification' with British Cameroons and appealing for UN support.

In the 1950s other parties emerged, encouraged by the French, to rival the radical UPC, notably the *Bloc des Democrates Camerounais* led by André Mbida. In 1955, after rioting, the UPC was banned. In Dec. 1956, when elections were held prior to self-government, the UPC began guerrilla war, but other parties took part in the elections and Mbida became prime minister in 1957. In Feb. 1958 Ahmadou Ahidjo, leader of the northern-based *Union Camerounaise* (UC), became prime minister, while the UPC remained illegal and fought against the French and the new Cameroonian government. On 1 Jan. 1960 French Cameroun became independent; elections were held, and Ahidjo became president. The UPC guerrillas were largely defeated by 1963.

On 11 Feb. 1961 British Southern Cameroons voted in a referendum to join ex-French Cameroun, while British Northern Cameroons chose to join Nigeria. On 1 Oct. 1961 the Republic of Cameroon and British Southern Cameroons were united to form the Federal Republic of Cameroon.

On 2 June 1972 the limited powers of the West and East Cameroon governments were ended when the country became the United Republic of Cameroon.

Ahidjo resigned on 6 Nov. 1982 and was succeeded as president by Paul Biya, previously prime minister. After a crisis between Biya and his predecessor in 1983, and a *coup* attempt on 6 April 1984, Biya was confirmed fully in power. He was elected without opposition early in 1984 when the country's name was changed to the Republic of Cameroon. In March 1985 the ruling party was renamed the *Rassemblement Démocratique du Peuple Camerounais*.

Further Reading

Rubin, N., *Cameroon*. New York, 1972

CANADA

The territories which now constitute Canada came under British power at various times by settlement, conquest or cession. For the most part such efforts were directed at gaining advantage over the indigenous Indian and Eskimo communities as well as displacing French colonial rule; conflict also broke out, however, with the fledgling United States in the Anglo-American war of 1812–14. Since then, Canadian-American relations have been described in terms of the world's longest undefended border. Nova Scotia was occupied in 1628 by settlement at Port Royal, was ceded back to France in 1632, and was finally ceded by France in 1713, by the Treaty of Utrecht; the Hudson's Bay Company's charter, conferring rights over all the territory draining into Hudson Bay, was granted in 1670; Canada, with all its dependencies, including New Brunswick and Prince Edward Island, was formally ceded to Great Britain by France in 1763; Vancouver Island was acknowledged to be British by the Oregon Boundary Treaty of 1846; and British Columbia was established as a separate colony in 1858. As originally constituted, Canada was composed of the provinces of Upper and Lower Canada (now Ontario and Quebec), Nova Scotia and New Brunswick. They were united under the provisions of an Act of the Imperial Parliament known as 'The British North America Act, 1867.' The Act provided that the constitution of Canada should be 'similar in principle to that of the United Kingdom'; that the executive authority should be vested in the Sovereign, and carried on in his name by a Governor-General and Privy Council; and that the legislative power should be exercised by a Parliament of two Houses, called the 'Senate' membership of which is by appointment and the 'House of Commons' whose members are elected.

In 1931 the House of Commons approved the enactment of the Statute of Westminster emancipating the Provinces as well as the Dominion from the operation of the Colonial Laws Validity Act, and thus removing what legal limitations existed as regards Canada's legislative autonomy.

Provision was made in the British North America Act for the admission of British Columbia, Prince Edward Island, the Northwest Territories and Newfoundland into the Union. In 1869 Rupert's Land, or the Northwest Territories, was purchased from the Hudson's Bay Company; the province of Manitoba was erected from this territory and admitted into the confederation on 15 July 1870. On 20 July 1871 the province of British Columbia was admitted, and Prince Edward Island on 1 July 1873. The provinces of Alberta and Saskatchewan were formed from the provisional districts of Alberta, Athabaska, Assiniboia and Saskatchewan, and admitted on 1 Sept. 1905. Newfoundland formally joined Canada as its 10th province on 31 March 1949.

In Feb. 1931 Norway formally recognized the Canadian title to the Sverdrup group of Arctic islands. Canada thus holds sovereignty in the whole Arctic sector north of the Canadian mainland.

In Nov. 1981 the Canadian government agreed on the provisions of an amended constitution, to the end that it should replace the British North America Act and that its future amendment should be the prerogative of Canada. These proposals were adopted by the Parliament of Canada and were enacted by the UK Parliament as the Canada Act of 1982.

The enactment of the Canada Act was the final act of the UK Parliament in Canadian constitutional development. The Act gave to Canada the power to amend the constitution according to procedures determined by the Constitutional Act 1982, which was proclaimed in force by the Queen on 17 April 1982. The Constitution Act 1982 added to the Canadian constitution a charter of Rights and Freedoms, and provisions which recognize the nation's multicultural heritage, affirm the existing rights of native peoples, confirm the principle of equalization of benefits among the provinces, and strengthen provincial ownership of natural resources.

Further Reading
Creighton, Donald G., *Canada's First Century*. Toronto, 1970.—*Towards the Discovery of Canada*. Toronto, 1974

CANADIAN PROVINCES

ALBERTA

The southern half of Alberta was administered from 1670 by the Hudson's Bay Company, as part of Rupert's Land. As the northwest was opened to fur-trappers, trading posts were established. In 1869 the area was transferred to the new dominion of Canada and was combined with the crown land of the Northwest Territories in 1870 to form the North-West Territories. Alberta achieved provincial status in 1905.

Further Reading
MacGregor, J. G., *A History of Alberta*. 2nd ed. Edmonton, 1981

BRITISH COLUMBIA

British Columbia, formerly known as New Caledonia, originally formed part of the Hudson's Bay Company's concession. In 1849 Vancouver Island was given crown colony status and in 1853 the Queen Charlotte Islands became a dependency. The discovery of gold on the Fraser river and the following influx of population resulted in the creation in 1858 of the mainland crown colony of British Columbia, to which the Strikine Territory (established 1862) was later added. In 1866 the two colonies were united.

Further Reading
Ormsby, M., *British Columbia: A History*. Vancouver, 1958

MANITOBA

Manitoba was known as the Red River Settlement before it entered the dominion in 1870. During the 18th century its only inhabitants were fur-trappers, but a more settled colonization began in the 19th century. The area was administered by the Hudson's Bay Company until 1869 when it was purchased by the new dominion. In 1870 it was given provincial status. It was enlarged in 1881 and again in 1912 by the addition of part of the North-West Territories.

Further Reading
Morton, W. L., *Manitoba: A History*. Univ. of Toronto Press, 1967

NEW BRUNSWICK

Visited by Jacques Cartier in 1534, New Brunswick was first explored by Samuel de Champlain in 1604. With Nova Scotia, it originally formed one French colony called Acadia. It was ceded by the French in the Treaty of Utrecht in 1713 and became a permanent British possession in 1759. It was first settled by British colonists in 1764 and was separated from Nova Scotia and became a province in June 1784 as a result of the great influx of United Empire Loyalists. Responsible government came into being in 1848, and consisted of an Executive Council, a Legislative Council (later abolished) and a House of Assembly.

Further Reading
Thompson, C., *New Brunswick Inside Out*. Ottawa, 1977

NEWFOUNDLAND AND LABRADOR

Archaeological finds at L'Anse-au-Meadow in northern Newfoundland show that the Vikings had established a colony there at about 1000 AD.

Newfoundland was rediscovered by John Cabot on 24 June 1497, and was soon frequented by the English, Portuguese, Spanish and French for its fisheries. In 1537 the island was proclaimed to be British territory, but it was not until 1564 that the first serious attempt at permanent settlement was made. It failed, as had several previous efforts, because of the antagonism of the various fishing concerns towards such settlements and continual conflicts between Britain and France over sovereignty. British sovereignty was recognized in 1713 by the Treaty of Utrecht and after the appointment of the first governor in 1729 permanent settlements came into being. Disputes over fishing rights with the French, who also had a station on the island, were not finally settled till 1904.

The colony became self-governing in 1855, decided to stay out of the Canadian confederation in 1867 and continued to govern itself until 1934, when a commission of government appointed by the British Crown assumed responsibility for governing the colony and Labrador. This body controlled the country until union with Canada in 1949.

Further Reading
Perlin, A. B., *The Story of Newfoundland, 1497–1959*. St John's, 1959

NOVA SCOTIA

Nova Scotia was visited by John and Sebastian Cabot in 1497–98. In 1605 a number of French colonists settled at Port Royal. The old name of the colony, Acadia, was changed in 1621 to Nova Scotia by Sir William Alexander who received a grant of what are now the Maritime Provinces from James I. The French were granted possession of the colony by the Treaty of St-Germain-en-Laye (1632). In 1654 Oliver Cromwell sent a force to occupy the settlement. Charles II, by the Treaty of Breda (1667), restored Nova Scotia to the French. It was finally ceded to the British by the Treaty of Utrecht in 1713.

In the Treaty of Paris (1763) France resigned all claim, and in 1820 Cape Breton Island united with Nova Scotia. Representative government was granted as early as 1758 and a fully responsible legislative assembly was established in 1848. In 1867 the province entered the dominion of Canada.

Further Reading

Hamilton, W. B., *The Nova Scotia Traveller*. Toronto, 1981

ONTARIO

The French explorer Samuel de Champlain began to explore the Ottawa River in 1613. From 1627 the area was governed by the French, first under a joint stock company and then as a royal province, until ceded to Great Britain in 1763.

Before the American War of Independence the country was sparsely populated by Indian tribes, but in 1783 thousands of British Empire Loyalists crossed into Canada. The Ontario region was called Upper Canada until 1867, when it received provincial status.

Further Reading

Schull, J., *Ontario since 1867*. Toronto, 1978

PRINCE EDWARD ISLAND

Jacques Cartier visited the island in 1534 and named it Isle St-Jean, but it is alleged that Cabot had sighted it first in 1497.

In 1603 Samuel de Champlain took possession of it for France. It was first settled by the French, but was taken from them in 1758. By the Treaty of Paris (1763) it became a British possession annexed to Nova Scotia. In 1769 the island was constituted a separate colony and received its present name in 1798. Responsible government was set up in 1851. Prince Edward Island entered the Confederation on 1 July 1873.

Further Reading

Hocking, A., *Prince Edward Island*. Toronto, 1978

QUEBEC

Quebec was known as New France from 1535 to 1763; as the province of Quebec from 1763 to 1790; as Lower Canada from 1791 to 1846; as Canada East from 1846 to 1867; and when, by the union of the four original provinces, the Confederation of the Dominion of Canada was formed, it again became known as the province of Quebec.

The Quebec Act, passed by the British Parliament in 1774, guaranteed to the people of the newly conquered French territory in North America security in their religion and language, their customs and tenures, under their own civil laws.

The territory of Ungava was added to the province under the Quebec Boundaries Extension Act 1912.

Further Reading
Jacobs, J., *The Question of Separatism: Quebec and the Struggle for Sovereignty*. London, 1981

SASKATCHEWAN

In 1670 Charles II granted to Prince Rupert and his friends a charter covering exclusive trading rights in 'all the land drained by streams finding their outlet in the Hudson Bay'. This included what is now Saskatchewan. The trading company was first known as The Governor and Company of Adventurers of England; later as the Hudson's Bay Company.

In 1774 the first trading post built by the Hudson's Bay Company in the interior was established on the Saskatchewan River. Soon this company and its great rival, the Northwestern Company, had established numerous posts around which settlements sprang up. More generally, however, settlement began only after 1870, when the Hudson's Bay Company Territory was acquired by Canada.

In 1869 the North-West Territories was formed, and this included Saskatchewan. A year later the Dominion Lands Act provided free homesteads for settlers and attracted many people. In 1882 the District of Saskatchewan was formed. By 1885 the North-West Mounted Police had been inaugurated, with headquarters in Regina, a bitter rebellion had been crushed and its leader, Louis Riel, executed, and the Canadian Pacific Railway's transcontinental line had been completed, bringing a stream of immigrants to southern Saskatchewan. The Hudson's Bay Company surrendered its claim to territory in return for cash and land around the existing trading posts. Legislative government was introduced. Saskatchewan became a province on 1 Sept. 1905.

Further Reading
Archer, J. H., *Saskatchewan: A History*. Saskatoon, 1980

CANADIAN TERRITORIES

NORTHWEST TERRITORIES

In 1863 all British North America lying north-west of the St Lawrence basin was called Northwest Territory. The population consisted of nomadic Eskimo and Indian hunters; isolated trading posts were operated by the Hudson's Bay Company. The British North America Act 1867, provided that 'Rupert's Land and the North-West Territory' might be admitted to Canada. Manitoba, Saskatchewan, Alberta and Yukon were subsequently formed out of this vast territory.

Further Reading

Zaslow, M. *The Opening of the Canadian North 1870–1914.* Toronto, 1971

YUKON TERRITORY

The territory owes its fame to the discovery of gold in the Klondike at the end of the 19th century. The Yukon Territory was constituted a separate political region in 1898.

Further Reading

William, A. A., *The Discovery and Exploration of the Yukon.* Sydney, 1986

CAPE VERDE

The Cape Verde Islands were uninhabited, except perhaps by some Lebou fishermen from Senegal, when first visited by Portuguese in 1456. During centuries of Portuguese rule the islands were gradually peopled with Portuguese, slaves from Africa, and people of mixed African-European descent who became the majority. While retaining some African culture, the Cape Verdians came to speak Portuguese or the Portuguese-derived Crioulo (Creole) language, and became Catholics. Because of constant drought in the islands, the people have for long emigrated in large numbers, so that today over half the Cape Verdians live outside Cape Verde, especially in Senegal, Portugal and the USA.

Cape Verde included Portuguese Guinea until 1879, when that mainland territory was separated. Ruled as a colony and then, from 1951 to 1974, as an Overseas Territory of Portugal, Cape Verde had a governor, a government council, and latterly a partly elected legislative council. While many Cape Verdians were taken to São Tomé as labourers on cocoa plantations, because of their Portuguese culture and some degree of education Cape Verdians were in some ways privileged among Portuguese-ruled Africans; they held subordinate government positions in other colonies, such as Portuguese Guinea.

In 1956 6 nationalists from Cape Verde and Portuguese Guinea formed the *Partido Africano da Independência da Guiné e do Cabo Verde* (PAIGC). In the 1960s the PAIGC led by Amilcar Cabral waged a successful guerrilla war. While armed resistance was not possible in the Cape Verde Islands, the PAIGC won control there also after the Portuguese revolution of 1974. On 5 July 1975 Cape Verde became independent, ruled by the PAIGC which was already the ruling party in ex-Portuguese Guinea-Bissau. Aristides Pereira became president of the new republic.

On 14 Nov. 1980 Luis Cabral, brother of the PAIGC's founder and president of Guinea-Bissau since 1974, was overthrown in a *coup d'état* caused partly by resentment at Cape Verdians' privileged position in Guinea-Bissau. Ensuing tension led to the end of the ties between the two countries' ruling parties. Although the PAIGC retained its name in Guinea-Bissau, in Jan. 1981 it was renamed the *Partido Africano da Independênecia do Cabo Verde* (PAICV), in Cape Verde.

Further Reading
Carriera, A., *The People of the Cape Verde Islands*. London, 1982

CAYMAN ISLANDS

The Cayman Islands were discovered by Columbus on 10 May 1503. Called Las Tortugas by the Spaniards, the group of islands were ceded, along with Jamaica, to Britain in 1670. The Grand Cayman was settled in 1734, but the other islands, which were considered as separate from Grand Cayman, only in 1833. In 1887 all the islands were administered as one. Turtle fishing was the main economic activity until the end of the 18th century, by which time the turtles had been all but exterminated.

On 4 July 1959 the islands became a separate Crown Colony administered by the same Governor as Jamaica. When Jamaica became independent in 1962 the Cayman Islands were given their own Administrator, a title changed to Governor in 1972.

The 1972 constitution provided for a legislative assembly.

CENTRAL AFRICAN REPUBLIC

The present area of the Central African Republic may be where African people first developed into the continent's Bantu-speaking inhabitants, although many tribes such as the Banda and Mbaka came to the area only in the 19th century. The most important precolonial states in the area were those of the Azande. France occupied the country from the 1890s and created there the colony of Ubangi-Shari, a part of French Equatorial Africa, called French Congo until 1910.

For many years under French rule part of Ubangi-Shari was shared out among concessionary companies which employed brutal methods to force the collection of wild rubber. Force was also used later to impel Africans to grow cotton. There were many African revolts, including a number during the First World War and the great uprising of the Bayas, provoked by conscription of labourers for the building of the Congo–Ocean Railway, from 1928–31.

When African nationalist politics developed in the French colonies a Catholic priest, Father Barthélemy Boganda, formed the *Mouvement pour l'évolution sociale de l'Afrique noire* (MESAN). When in late 1958 the colony attained self-government under his leadership he changed its name to the Central African Republic. A few months later he was killed in an air crash. His relative David Dacko took the country into independence on 13 Aug. 1960.

On 31 Dec. 1965 President Dacko was overthrown by another relative, Col. Jean-Bédel Bokassa, in a military *coup*. For 13 years Bokassa ruled the country as one of Africa's most notorious tyrants. In 1976 he proclaimed himself Emperor and changed the name of the country to the Central African Empire. Besides his extravagance and his waste of the few resources of one of Africa's most deprived countries, Bokassa personally committed many acts of brutality and sadism. France organized his removal by 'Operation Barracuda' on 20 Sept. 1979. Abroad at the time of his deposition, Bokassa went initially to Côte d'Ivoire and then to France. Dacko, although he had worked closely with Bokassa for years, became head of state again.

Dacko had strong opposition, his victory in presidential elections on 15 March 1981 was contested, and on 1 Sept. 1981 the army seized power under General André Kolingba and a Military Committee for National Recovery (CMRN). The country remained near bankruptcy, with France subsidizing half the budget. The military régime announced in May 1986 the creation of a new governmental party, the *Rassemblement démocratique centrafricain*.

In late 1986 Bokassa suddenly returned and was put on trial for murder and other crimes; he was sentenced to death but the sentence was commuted to life imprisonment. A single political party, Centrafrican Democratic Assembly (RDC), was launched in Nov. 1986 by Kolingba. Elections in 1987 confirmed the party in power in the National Assembly.

Further Reading

Kalck, H. P., *Historical Dictionary of the Central African Republic*. Metuchen, 1980

CHAD

The present area of Chad had many important traditional states including Kanem, which began expanding in the 11th century in the region of Lake Chad where previously the Sao civilization had stood; it was succeeded by the Bornu Empire, powerful in the 16th and 17th centuries. Further east were the Moslem kingdoms of Baguirmi and Wadai (or Ouaddai) which flourished for long on the trans-Sahara caravan trade.

In the late 19th century Rabih ibn Fadlallah conquered Baguirmi and Bornu and soon afterwards France began occupation; three French armies met and defeated and killed Rabih at Kousseri in 1900. France occupied the vast area of Chad only gradually, occupying Wadai in 1909. The Derde, ruler of the Toubou people of the Tibesti mountains, surrendered in 1920, but the Borkou-Ennedi-Tibesti (BET) region in the north remained for long under French military rule. Chad formed part of French Equatorial Africa (earlier called French Congo). In the Second World War Chad rallied to the Free French and became an important operational base.

Chad achieved independence on 11 Aug. 1960. After forming part of a coalition initially, the *Parti progessiste tchadien* (PPT) became the sole party, headed by President François Tombalbaye. Under his rule the Sara, his people, and other southerners predominated in administration and politics. Maladministration by them led to an uprising in the north and east starting in 1966. As it spread, Tombalbaye's government received help from French troops in 1968 and again in 1969. But the rebellion under the Chad National Liberation Front (FROLINAT) went on. In 1972 Tombalbaye signed an agreement with Col. Qadhafi, the Libyan ruler, which led to Libyan occupation of the Aouzou Strip, a desert area of Chad bordering Libya. In 1973 President Tombalbaye, changing his first name to Ngarta, launched an 'authenticity' campaign for revival of African culture, at the same time forming a new ruling party, the National Movement for Cultural and Social Renewal (MNCRS). Excesses in the 'authenticity' drive and other acts discredited Tombalbaye's régime; he was overthrown and killed on 13 April 1975, and the army took power under Gen. Felix Malloum. FROLINAT fought on, however, and it launched a major successful offensive southwards from its northern stronghold in 1977. French forces delayed their triumph, but in 1979 Malloum fell, and other

African states, especially Nigeria, intervened to secure agreement on a new government including all the various factions then in existence.

As a result a Transitional Government of National Unity (GUNT) was formed in 1979 under Goukouni Weddeye. But the Defence Minister, Hissène Habré and his forces turned against it and marched across Chad and captured Ndjamena on 7 June 1982.

Goukouni Weddeye and others reconstituted the GUNT and, with Libyan help, ran it from Bardai in northern Chad, claiming it was the lawful government. Although in the south Habré's rule was challenged by guerrillas, called *codos*, Habré controlled most of Chad and won international recognition. He was installed as president in Oct. 1982 and on 27 June 1984 created a new governmental party, the *Union nationale pour l'indépendence et la révolution*.

GUNT forces advanced far to the south in 1983 until a French force saved Habré's government. That French force left in 1984 after a Franco-Libyan agreement, but Libyan forces continued to help the GUNT. In 1985–86, however, the *codos* in the south surrendered to the Habré government, while the GUNT split gradually apart until in the latter part of 1986 Goukouni Weddeye lost the leadership and his followers in the Tibesti declared support for Habré.

Government forces then attacked in the north, with French help. In the first months of 1987 the Libyans and their Chadian allies steadily retreated. In April, Weddeye appealed for Habré to be recognized as head of state and his position was stabilized.

Further Reading
Thompson, W., and Adloff, R., *Conflict in Chad*. London and Berkeley, 1981

CHILE

Magellan sighted what is now Chile in 1520. Subsequently Spaniards colonized the land in the 1530s and 1540s, defeating the Incas in the north and subjugating the Araucanian Indians in the south. Santiago, the capital, was founded in 1541, and Chile, as a colony, was attached to the viceroyalty of Peru.

In 1810 the Republic of Chile threw off allegiance to the Spanish crown, establishing a national government on 18 Sept. 1810. However, there were seven years of fighting before Chile was recognized as an independent republic in 1818. A constitution was adopted in 1883, and the country enjoyed stable government. Peru and Bolivia, which had been in dispute with Chile over their boundaries, were defeated in the War of the Pacific 1879–1884. In 1925 the constitution was amended so as to strengthen the executive at the expense of the legislature.

1964 saw the election of the first Christian Democratic president, Eduardo Frei Montalava; but in 1970 Dr Salvador Allende Gossens was elected president as the Marxist leader of five left-wing parties which formed a coalition, the Popular Unity, which attempted to speed up social reform. This government was overthrown in 1973 by a *coup* of the three armed services and the *carabineros* (para-military police). These forces formed a government headed by a four-man junta. Gen. Augusto Pinochet Ugarte, C.-in-C. of the Army, took over the presidency. President Allende died in the course of the *coup*. Tens of thousands of Popular Unity supporters were massacred and all political activities banned. The new government assumed wide-ranging powers, but the 'state of siege' ended in March 1978. A new constitution came into force on 11 March 1981 and provided for a return to democracy after a minimum period of eight years. Anti-government protests increased over the years while relations with the Roman Catholic church deteriorated. However, by 1988 Gen. Pinochet still showed no sign of willingness to abandon his military dictatorial rule.

Further Reading
Smith, B. H., *Church and Politics in Chile: Challenges to Modern Catholicism*. Princeton Univ. Press, 1983

CHINA

The Han dynasty (216 BC–220 AD) was founded by an official who retained the Ch'in bureaucracy and made Confucianism a state philosophy. The system of civil service recruitment by public competitive examination was instituted in this period, and Buddhism was introduced from India. The Han dynasty collapsed amid intrigues and was followed by centuries of division and disorder. Unity was restored under the T'angs (618–906), but was lost again until the Sung period (960–1279). Mongol invaders succeeded in imposing a foreign dynasty (Yuan) but were quickly assimilated to the higher cultural and technological level of the Chinese. A peasant rising drove the last Mongol from the throne in 1368 and ushered in the Ming dynasty.

Although unity and tradition were restored, the Ming empire was not as efficient as the T'ang nor as enlightened as the Sung. A new imperial capital was built at Beijing only 40 miles from the Wall and thus vulnerable to attack; preoccupation with the defence of this frontier contributed to a neglect of the defence of the sea, whence came the ultimately most dangerous invaders: the Portuguese in 1516, the Dutch in 1622, and the English in 1637. A second wave of nomad invaders, the Manchus, breached the Wall to capture Beijing in 1644 and found the Ch'ing dynasty, which lasted until 1912. The Manchus, who used Dutch ships to subdue Taiwan in 1683, were not sea-going, and confined foreign trade to Canton after 1757. The court would not enter into diplomatic relations with Europe, and would receive foreigners only if they paid homage. Catholic missionaries were tolerated and even employed in state service, but outside ideas made little impression on the ossified and complacent traditionalism of the court and mandarins. Though gradually assimilated, the Ch'ing did not forget they were a foreign dynasty in an occupied country: a quota of posts was reserved for Manchus, and a system of garrison governorships was set up which degenerated into sinecures doing nothing to modernize the armed forces.

A British expeditionary force sent to overturn a Chinese ban on imports of opium forced the empire to cede Hong Kong and grant Britain economic and diplomatic privileges. Other western nations followed suit. Foreigners established concessions in 'treaty ports' administered by their own officials. In 1851 a neo-Protestant *T'ai P'ing* rebellion broke out, which was put down with western help in

1864. The British and French had seized Beijing in 1860 and burnt the imperial palace. In 1895 China was defeated by a modernized Japan and forced to cede Korea and Taiwan. The emperor became converted to the necessity for reforms, but these were blocked by court intrigue. An anti-foreigner *Boxer* rebellion was suppressed by western forces in 1900.

Sun Yat-sen founded the Kuomintang (Nationalist Party) in 1905. When troops at Hangchow mutinied in Oct. 1911 and proclaimed a republic, the emperor's mediator Yuan went over to them and made himself president; the infant emperor abdicated. Yuan attempted to make himself emperor but was overthrown in 1916 after acceding to Japan's demands which would have made China a virtual protectorate. The Beijing government lost all real authority and the country disintegrated into the hands of squabbling warlords. At Versailles the Allies failed to restore territory seized by Japan. Sun Yat-sen, who had formed a separatist government in Canton, turned to the Soviet régime. The Communist Party (founded 1921) co-operated with the Kuomintang, led after 1926 by Chiang Kai-shek, in attacking both warlords and foreign concessions, but in 1937 Chiang turned on the Communists and suppressed them. Communism was then carried on by Mao Tse-tung's rural 'Soviet', at first in Kiangsi, and then, after the Long March, in Yenan. Chiang came to terms with the warlords and foreign concessionaries, but his aims to create a modern state were thwarted by Japanese invasions in 1931 and 1937, and by his campaign against the Communists. In 1936 he was forced (after being kidnapped) to declare a joint front with them against Japan, but hostilities continued.

After the Second World War full-scale civil war broke out. Chiang was defeated and took refuge on Taiwan where the Republic of China was set up. Mao proclaimed a People's Republic on 1 Oct. 1949. The Maoist period was marked by innovatory excesses: the agricultural communes (now abolished); the conscription of intellectuals to till the fields; the disastrous 'Great Leap Forward' with its backyard blast furnaces; the Thought (and cult) of Mao; the Cultural Revolution. After Mao's death in 1976 moderates within the Communist Party triumphed and the radical Gang of Four led by Mao's wife Chang Ch'ing were first publicly denounced and then arrested. China has since emerged as a major international power with a liberalized economy under Deng Xiaoping.

Denounced in the Cultural Revolution, Deng was formally rehabilitated in 1973 and became one of Mao's vice-premiers for a time in the 1970s. The keynote of his administration has been political and economic pragmatism. He has sought 'readjustment, restructuring, consolidation and improvement'. In 1979 China and the US established full diplomatic relations. From that time contacts with the west have grown considerably. Relations with the USSR, though better than under Chairman Mao, remain cool.

Further Reading
Dietrich, C., *People's China: A Brief History*. OUP, 1986
Morton, W. S., *China: Its History and Culture*. 1980

TAIWAN
'Republic of China'

The Republic of China (Nationalist China) consists of the island of Taiwan, 15 islands in the Taiwan group and a further 64 islands in the Pescadores Archipelago. Taiwan, christened Formosa (beautiful) by the Portuguese, was ceded to Japan by China by the Treaty of Shimonoseki in 1895. After the Second World War the island was surrendered to Gen. Chiang Kai-shek in Sept. 1945, who made it the headquarters for his crumbling Nationalist Government.

Since 1949 the Nationalist Government in Taiwan has continued to claim jurisdiction over the Chinese mainland. Chiang Kai-shek used the ideology of eventual Kuomintang victory as an excuse for authoritarian, military backed rule and the maintenance of a large standing army on the island. On Chiang Kai-shek's death in 1978 he was succeeded by his son, Chiang Ching-Kuo.

Until 1970 the US fully supported Taiwan's claims to represent all of China. Only then did the government of the People's Republic of China manage to replace that of Chiang Kai-shek at the UN. In Jan. 1979, the US established formal diplomatic relations with the People's Republic of China, breaking off all formal ties with Taiwan.

Taiwanese fears that US recognition of China spelt the end of the island's independence have not so far been realized. The US Congress in the Taiwan Relations Act subsequently authorized continuing economic and social ties with Taiwan. Taiwan itself has continued to reject all attempts at reunification talks broached by mainland China, but both sides appear to be moderating their previously rigid ideological positions in favour of greater economic and social contacts.

Further Reading
Kuo, S. W., *The Taiwan Economy in Transition*. Boulder, 1963

COLOMBIA

Columbus sighted what became Colombia in 1499. The conquest of the territory began in 1509; and 30 years later the Spaniards were well established. In 1564 the Spanish Crown appointed a President of New Granada, which included the territories of Colombia, Panama and Venezuela. In 1718 a viceroyalty of New Granada was created. This viceroyalty gained its independence from Spain in 1819, and together with the present territories of Panama, Venezuela and Ecuador was officially constituted on 17 Dec. 1819 as the state of 'Greater Colombia'. This new state lasted only until 1830 when it split up into Venezuela, Ecuador and the republic of New Granada. The constitution of 22 May 1858 changed New Granada into a confederation of eight states, under the name of *Confederación Granadina*. Under the constitution of 8 May 1863 the country was renamed *Estados Unidos de Colombia*, which were nine in number. The revolution of 1885 led the National Council of Bogotá, composed of two delegates from each state, to promulgate the constitution of 5 Aug. 1886, forming the Republic of Colombia. The constitution abolished the sovereignty of the states, converting them into departments with governors appointed by the President of the Republic. The department of Panama, however, became an independent country in 1903.

The two political parties, Conservatives and Liberals, since the 19th century regularly alternated in power. Both have faced unrest, rioting and civil war. Liberal governments were in power 1860–84, Conservatives 1884–1930, Liberals 1930–46, and Conservatives 1946–53. In 1953 Gen. Gustavo Rojas Pinilla established a dictatorship, but he was deposed in 1957.

The Conservatives and Liberals fought a civil war from 1948 to 1957 *(La Violencia)* during which some 300,000 people were killed. In a plebiscite in 1957 the two political parties agreed to support a single presidential candidate and to divide government posts equally. This arrangement was modified in 1974 and the growing strength of a third party, ANAPO (the *Alianza Nacional Popular*), led to it being abandoned in 1978. The Liberal, Virgilio Barco Vargas, was elected president in 1986 and although the transfer of power from the Conservatives was successful, increasing violence has continued through right-wing guerrilla attacks often allied with the drug trafficking empires.

COMOROS

The three islands forming the present state, and originally with inhabitants of mixed African, Malagasy and Arabic descent, became French protectorates at the end of the 19th century, and were proclaimed colonies on 25 July 1912. With neighbouring Mayotte they were administratively attached to Madagascar from 1914 until 1947, when the four islands became a French Overseas Territory, achieving internal self-government in Dec. 1961.

In referenda held on each island on 22 Dec. 1974, the three western islands voted overwhelmingly for independence, while Mayotte voted to remain French. The Comoran Chamber of Deputies unilaterally declared the islands' independence on 6 July 1975, but Mayotte remained a French dependency.

The first government of Ahmed Abdallah was overthrown on 3 Aug. 1975 by a *coup* led by Ali Soilih (who assumed the Presidency on 2 Jan. 1976), but Ahmed Abdallah regained the Presidency after a second *coup* ousted Ali Soilih in May 1978. Abdallah's use of mercenaries in returning him to power led to the Comoros' expulsion from the Organization of African Unity (OAU). After foiling a *coup* attempt in 1983, Abdallah was reconfirmed as president in an election where he was the sole candidate. Elections in Feb. 1987 saw his party, the *Union Comorienne pour le progrès* (Udzima), retaining full control of the legislature.

Further Reading
Newitt, N., *The Comoro Islands*. London, 1985

CONGO

The People's Republic of the Congo, formerly called Congo-Brazzaville to distinguish it from the ex-Belgian Congo (now Zaïre), and before that French Congo or Moyen-Congo, is named after the Kongo people, whose historic kingdom, founded probably in the 14th century and at its height in the 16th century, included territory now covered by the Congo, Zaïre and Angola. Another important African state in the area was the kingdom of Loango, where Europeans traded for centuries before penetrating inland in the late 19th century.

French occupation began in 1880 with a treaty between the Makoko, ruler in the Stanley Pool area, and the explorer, Pierre Savorgnan de Brazza. France gradually occupied areas further upstream along the Congo and further inland, and in 1903 created the colony of Moyen (Middle) Congo. Moyen Congo was part of the larger territory first called French Congo and then, from 1910, French Equatorial Africa, and shared with this larger territory the capital, Brazzaville. African resistance lasted until 1917. Early French rule was particularly harsh in the Congo as much of the area was assigned to Concessionary Companies allowed to use any and all methods to enforce wild rubber collection. France built the Congo–Ocean Railway, linking Brazzaville and Pointe Noire, from 1921 to 1934, with massive use of forced labour.

The Congo attained self-government in 1958 and independence in 1960. At independence on 15 Aug. 1960 the country was ruled by an unfrocked Catholic priest, Father Fulbert Youlou, but in 1963 President Youlou was overthrown after a popular rising now recalled as the 'three glorious days' *(trois glorieuses)*. Power was taken by a left-wing régime headed by President Alphonse Massemba-Débat and the *Mouvement National de la Révolution* (MNR). Massemba-Débat was forced to resign in 1968 and Major Marien Ngouabi and the *Conseil National de la Révolution* (CNR) installed a considerably more left-wing régime. In 1969–70 a new ruling party, the *Parti Congolais du Travail* (PCT), was formed, and the country's name was changed to that of a 'People's Republic'.

Although beset by factions, intrigues and quarrels, which led to some fighting in 1972–73, the régime has stayed in power, and adopted a socialist economic programme whose implementation, however, has been difficult. On 18 March 1977 President Ngouabi was assassinated; a week later ex-President Massemba-Débat was executed for organizing the assassination, but the truth about the affair is unclear. Col. Joachim Yhombi-Opango took over power, but he resigned on 2 Feb. 1979 and was succeeded by Major (now Col.) Denis Sassou Nguesso. These changes meant no major policy changes, but the economic crisis, worsening in the 1980s with the fall in price of Congo's oil exports, has forced modification of the socialist programme. Close relations with communist countries, such as the USSR which concluded a Treaty of Friendship and Co-operation (without military clauses) in 1981, exist alongside continued good relations with France and increasingly pro-western foreign policy. In 1984, Sassou Nguesso was re-elected as president.

Further Reading

Thompson, V. and Adloff, R., *Historical Dictionary of the People's Republic of the Congo.* 2nd ed. Metuchen, 1984

COSTA RICA

Discovered by Columbus in 1502 on his last voyage, Costa Rica (Rich Coast) was part of the Spanish viceroyalty of New Spain from 1540 and was thought to be rich in gold. The region was administered as part of the captaincy general of Guatemala. Costa Rica became independent of Spain in 1821. From 1822 to 1823 it was part of Mexico and then part of the Central American Federation until 1838 when it left this confederation and achieved full independence. The first constitution was promulgated on 7 Dec. 1871.

Coffee was introduced in 1808 and became a mainstay of the economy, helping to create a peasant land-owning class. Bananas, another important crop, were introduced in 1878.

In 1917 Federico Tinoco overthrew the elected president but the USA intervened and Tinoco was deposed in 1919.

In 1948 a charge of fraud over the victory of Ulate in a close presidential election caused the congressional invalidation of the election. This was followed by a 6-week civil war, at the conclusion of which José Figueres Ferrer won power at the head of a revolutionary junta.

A new constitution was promulgated with, amongst other changes, the abolition of the army. Ferrer, the founder and leader of the *Partido de Liberacion Nacional* (PLN), became the elected president from 1953 to 1958, and again in 1970–74. More conservative governments held office between Ferrer's 2 presidencies, and again after Ferrer's PLN successor's single 4-year term. In 1982 the PLN candidate, Luis Alberto Monge, was elected president. These regular changes of parties in office, and of individual presidents, by elections show the stability of democracy in Costa Rica. In 1986 Oscar Arias Sánchez was elected to succeed Monge. He has promised to prevent Nicaraguan anti-Sandinista *(contra)* forces using Costa Rica as a base. In 1987 he received the Nobel Peace Prize as recognition of his Central American peace plan, agreed to by the other Central American states.

Further Reading

Ameringer, C. D., *Democracy in Costa Rica*. New York, 1982

CÔTE D'IVOIRE

The territory covered by the Côte d'Ivoire had well-organized kingdoms in the 18th and 19th centuries until colonial occupation in the mid-19th century.

Although the coast was originally explored by the Portuguese, France obtained rights in 1842, actively and continuously occupying the territory after 1882. On 10 Jan. 1889 the Ivory Coast was declared a French protectorate, and it became a colony on 10 March 1893. In 1904 it became a territory of French West Africa. More than 20,000 Africans fought in the First World War, but there was widespread revolt in 1916 against a hut tax. From 1933 until 1948 most of the territory of Upper Volta was added to the Ivory Coast. On 1 Jan. 1948 this area was returned to the reconstituted Upper Volta (now Burkina Faso). By this time, a nationalist movement centred around African planters' opposition to European settler domination was being organized by Felix Houphouët-Boigny. In 1946, the movement succeeded in persuading the French to abolish forced labour and to introduce a territorial assembly offering Africans some representation. The Ivory Coast became an autonomous republic within the French community on 4 Dec. 1958. Full independence was achieved on 7 Aug. 1960, and a constitution established in Oct. Felix Houphouët-Boigny was elected as the first president, and was re-elected in 1985 for his sixth successive five-year term.

The *Parti Démocratique de la Côte d'Ivoire* (PDCI), founded in 1946, is the sole legal party.

From 1 Jan. 1986 the Côte d'Ivoire, the French version, became the only name of the country.

Further Reading
Zartman, I. W., and Delgado, C., *The Political Economy of Ivory Coast*. New York, 1984

CUBA

Cuba was discovered by Columbus in 1492 and, except for the brief British occupancy in 1762–63, remained a Spanish possession until 10 Dec. 1898. Sovereignty was then relinquished under the terms of the Treaty of Paris at the end of the Spanish-American War. Cuba became an independent republic in 1901, although the US continued to influence Cuban internal affairs and foreign policy until 1934. Since 1903 the USA has maintained a military and naval base at Guantanamo in Oriente province.

In 1933 Fulgencio Batista Zladivar led a successful military revolution. He ruled the country until 1944, as elected president from 1940, and again, after seizing power in a *coup*, from 1952 until 1959. A revolutionary movement against the corrupt Batista dictatorship, led by Dr Fidel Castro from 26 July 1953, was eventually successful and Batista fled the country on 1 Jan. 1959.

Under Castro, Cuba's relationship with the US became increasingly strained while relations with the USSR became closer. In Jan. 1961 the USA severed diplomatic relations after US business interests in Cuba had been expropriated without compensation for refusing to co-operate with the government's economic plans. On 17 April an invasion force of émigrés and adventurers, encouraged by the USA, landed in Cuba but was defeated at the Bay of Pigs. At the end of 1961 Castro declared Cuba to be a Communist state.

The US Navy imposed a blockade of Cuba from 22 Oct. until 22 Nov. 1962 in order to force the USSR to withdraw Soviet missile bases detected on the islands. Cuba continued to receive financial aid and technical advice from the USSR. The USA has maintained an economic embargo against the island and relations between Cuba and the USA have remained embittered in the 1980s.

The first socialist constitution came into force on 24 Feb. 1976. Under the constitution there are elected municipal assemblies, elected delegates to the National Assembly of People's Power, which, in turn, chooses the Council of State of which Castro is president.

Further Reading

Dominguez, J. I., *Cuba: Order and Revolution*. Harvard Univ. Press, 1978
Thomas, H., *The Cuban Revolution: 25 Years Later*. Epping, 1984

CYPRUS

About the middle of the second millennium BC Greek colonies were established in Cyprus, and later it formed part of the Persian, Roman and Byzantine empires. In 1193 the island became a Frankish kingdom, in 1489 a Venetian dependency, and in 1571 was conquered by the Turks. The Turks retained possession of it until its cession to Britain for administrative purposes under a convention concluded with the Sultan of Constantinople in 1878. In 1914 the island was annexed by Great Britain, and on 1 May 1925 it was given the status of a Crown Colony.

In the 1930s the Greek Cypriots began to agitate for ENOSIS (Union with Greece), and continued their struggle after the war. In 1955 they started a guerrilla movement (EOKA) against the British for ENOSIS, with Archbishop Makarios, the head of the Greek Orthodox Church in Cyprus, as the leader and Gen. Grivas in charge of military operations. As the British suspected Makarios of advocating violence, he was banished from the island. However, in 1959 the Greek and Turkish Cypriots agreed on a constitution for an independent Cyprus, and Makarios returned to be elected president. On 16 June 1960 Cyprus became an independent state.

In Dec. 1963 the Turkish Cypriots withdrew from the government, and there was fighting between them and the Greek Cypriots, so that in 1964 the UN sent a peace-keeping force to stop physical disputes. At this stage the Turkish Cypriots began to organize their own administration. In 1968 Makarios was elected President.

In 1971 Gen. Grivas returned to the island and began to encourage ENOSIS and EOKA. He died in Jan. 1974, but on 15 July a military *coup* drove out Makarios and appointed as president, Nicos Sampson, an EOKA supporter. The *coup* was short-lived as Sampson resigned on 23 July and Makarios was recalled as President.

Turkish forces invaded Cyprus on 20 July 1974 and secured a northern 40% of the island for the Turkish Cypriots. Many Greek Cypriots fled south, and the so-called Attila Line divided the 2 groups. The crisis was raised in the UN, and the General Assembly unanimously adopted resolutions calling for the withdrawal of all foreign troops from Cyprus and the return of the refugees to their homes, but without result.

On 13 Feb. 1975, at a special meeting of the executive council and legislative assembly of the Autonomous Turkish Cypriot Administration, a Turkish Cypriot Federated State was proclaimed. Rauf Denktash was appointed president and he declared that the state would not seek international recognition. The proclamation was denounced by President Makarios and the Greek prime minister, but was welcomed by the Turkish prime minister.

Discussion in the Security Council led to a resumption of talks in April 1975 and to 6 further rounds of talks thereafter.

On 3 Aug. 1977 President Makarios died and was succeeded by President Spyros Kyprianou, who was re-elected for 5-year terms in 1978 and 1983.

On 15 Nov. 1983, while UN talks continued to prove fruitless, the Turkish Cypriots announced a unilateral Declaration of Independence. Only Turkey among the nations has recognized the 'Turkish Republic of Northern Cyprus'. The UN Secretary-General has made various attempts to resolve the situation including the submission on 29 March 1986 of a revised draft framework agreement. In 1988 he continues to keep in contact with the 2 sides within the framework of the good-offices mission entrusted to him by the Security Council.

Further Reading

Plyviou, P. G., *Cyprus: The Tragedy and the Challenge*. London, 1975.–*Cyprus in Search of a Constitution*. Nicosia, 1976.–*Cyprus: Conflict and Negotiation, 1960–1980*. London, 1980

CZECHOSLOVAKIA

Bohemia and Moravia. Although the name Bohemia is Celtic, Slav settlers were well established in the area by the 6th century. The Czechs were one tribe who rose to dominance there in the 8th century. Charlemagne imposed a tribute, but after his death the Greater Moravian state arose whose ruler sent to Byzantium for the Slav Orthodox missionaries Cyril and Methodius in 863. Moravia was engulfed by Magyars around 905, though part was recovered by one of the Přemysl ruling family (895–1306). By the 11th century Roman Catholicism had prevailed.

The early Přemysl dukes ruled over 'castle-holders' who were not to evolve into hereditary feudal lords until the 13th century. Dynastic squabbles, exacerbated by German interference, weakened the power of the dukes, but in 1212 Otakar I (1197–1230) received a hereditary kingship from the Holy Roman Emperor (of whom the Přemysls had been electors since 1198) by the Golden Bull of Sicily. A period of prosperity developed, aided by the immigration of German miners and merchants who were encouraged with special privileges. Bohemia expanded under the last Přemysl kings: Wenceslas I (1230–53) seized Austria in 1251, though it passed to the Habsburgs when Otakar II was killed at the battle of Marchfeld in 1278; Wenceslas II was elected king of Poland in 1300. During the minority of his reign the custom began of summoning the 'estates' of nobles, clergy and burgesses to assist in government. Wenceslas was assassinated in 1306 and was succeeded in 1310 by John of Luxemburg. His son, Charles (1346–78), became Holy Roman Emperor as Charles IV in 1355. Bohemia attained a high degree of prosperity and civilization at this time.

The clerical reform movement with which the name of Jan Hus is associated began as a protest against the corruption and venality of the church and was inspired by the teachings of John Wycliffe, but it had undertones of anti-German Czech nationalism and found support amongst the urban middle classes and lesser rural gentry as well as the urban poor and peasantry. Hus was burned at the stake in 1415, but the Hussite movement continued and repelled efforts ('crusades') to enthrone the Hungarian king Sigismund until 1436. There was some post-war recovery under the enlightened Hussite king, George of Poděbrad (1457–71). After his death the Jagiellonian dynasty succeeded, from 1490 ruling Hungary jointly, until the death of Louis against the Turks at Mohács in 1526. During this period the provincial diet of 3 estates (nobility, gentry, burgesses) acted to enhance the power of the nobility and diminish that of the burgesses. Peasants were bound to landowners' estates in 1497.

In 1527 the diet elected the Hapsburg Ferdinand as king. The Hapsburgs gradually encroached upon Czech rights and religious freedom. In 1618 Protestants threw 2 Czech Catholic governors out of a window in Prague Castle. This incident sparked off the Thirty Years War. The estates deposed Emperor Ferdinand II in favour of the Calvinist Frederick V, but the latter's forces were defeated at the battle of the White Mountain on 8 Nov. 1620, and a period of Hapsburg hegemony ensued: the Czech nobility were replaced by German-speaking adventurers; the burgesses lost their rights; burdens were piled on to the peasantry and Catholicism was enforced. Risings were savagely repressed. Some relief came with the ideas of the Enlightenment: amongst other reforms Emperor Joseph II granted the peasantry freedom of movement in 1781, a precondition for the burgeoning industrial revolution of the next century. At first Czech nationalism could find an outlet only in cultural activities. Uprisings in the revolutionary episode of 1848 were ineffective. The increasingly political aspirations of Czech nationalists were not for the resuscitation of old Bohemia but for the formation of a new Czechoslovakia, an idea fostered by Thomas Masaryk. Manhood suffrage was granted in 1906, but the chamber of deputies was constantly bypassed by the emperor. The First World War brought a complete estrangement between the Czechs and the Germans, the latter supporting the war effort. Masaryk and other leaders went into exile and in 1916 a Czechoslovak National Council was set up under his chairmanship. In 1918 he was in the USA and secured the support of Woodrow Wilson for Czech and Slovak unity. On 18 Oct. 1918 the National Council transformed itself into a provisional government, and was recognized by the Allies.

Slovakia. The 6th-century Slav settlers were incorporated into Moravia in the 9th century, and passed to Hungary after the latter's conquest of Moravia in the 10th century. Hussites overran the country in the 15th century, but Catholicism was restored with the Habsburgs in 1526. After the Austro-Hungarian Compromise of 1867 Slovakia was subjected to intense Magyarization. Slovaks elected to join Czechoslovakia at the end of the First World War.

During the Second World War a puppet state of Slovakia was set up under German auspices.

Czechoslovakia. Austria accepted President Woodrow Wilson's terms on 27 Oct. 1918, and the next day a republic was proclaimed with Masaryk as president and Edvard Beneš as foreign minister. On 29 Oct. the Slovak leaders declared Slovakia was part of the Czechoslovak nation. In drawing up the frontiers of the new state it was impossible to apply strictly the principles of Wilsonian self-determination because of the ethnic mix; other criteria employed were the partial restoration of the historic provinces and the need to establish an economically viable and defensible state. Amongst the minorities were 3·25m. Sudeten Germans. The constitution of 1920 provided for a 2-chamber parliament elected by adult suffrage. The electoral system worked so that all governments were coalitions. Slovakia was granted an assembly in 1927, but the state was basically centralist, and the Slovaks maintained their own parties. Czechoslovakia developed into a prosperous democracy, but was hard hit by the economic depression of the 1930s. Nationalist agitation amongst the Sudeten Germans was fomented by Hitler. Czechoslovakia relied for her defence against the threat of German aggression on her treaty with France of 1925, but France sided with Britain in the Munich agreement of 29 Sept. 1938 which stipulated that all districts with a German population of more than 50% should be ceded to Germany. Beneš resigned the presidency and left for the west. On 14 March 1939 Slovakia declared itself independent under German hegemony and the next day the German army occupied the rest of the country and proclaimed the 'Protectorate of Bohemia-Moravia'. Czechoslovaks who managed to escape joined Beneš to form a government in exile; Britain repudiated the Munich agreement in Aug. 1942. In Dec. 1943 Beneš signed a 20-year treaty of alliance with the USSR. In March 1945 he went to Moscow to talk to communists who had spent the war there about the nature of the post-war government, which was established in April at Košice in the wake of the Soviet army. Prague was retaken in May. The Sudeten Germans were expelled to Germany during 1946.

At the elections of May 1946 the Communist party won a victory with 38·7% of the vote. Klement Gottwald became prime minister. Collaboration between the Communist and other parties became increasingly difficult. In Feb. 1948 the cabinet ordered the Communist minister of the interior to stop packing the police force with Communists. When he refused, most of the non-Communist ministers resigned, but Gottwald did not, and took over the ministries vacated by resigning ministers. Beneš reluctantly appointed a new government which left the Communists in control, but refused to sign the Soviet-style constitution of 9 May and resigned. A single list of Communist-dominated National Front candidates was presented at the elections of 30 May: Gottwald became president.

Progressive ossification of the economy under the Stalinist Antonín Novotný led to the consideration of new economic principles moving from command planning to a mixed economy in the mid-1960s. This went alongside critical rumblings from the intelligentsia and the dissatisfaction of Slovaks with the 1960 constitution which had further limited Slovak autonomy. At the beginning of 1968 the Slovak Alexander Dubček replaced Novotný. The liberalizing tendencies were crushed, however, by the military intervention of the Soviet Union and other Warsaw pact countries in Aug. 1968. Gustáv Husák replaced Dubček as party leader in 1969 and the country relapsed into rigidity and mediocrity, though one lasting gain has been the establishment of Slovak equality within a federal structure.

Further Reading

Wallace, W. V., *Czechoslovakia*. London, 1977

DENMARK

Denmark was first organized as a unified state in the 10th century, with a Christian monarchy. King Canute was also King of England and King of Norway in the 11th century, but the union of the 3 countries was soon dissolved. In 1363 a royal marriage united Denmark and Norway and these two countries joined with Sweden in 1397. Sweden separated herself in 1523 and thereafter was in conflict with Denmark until the Peace of Copenhagen in 1660. Denmark acquired approximately its present boundaries in 1815 at the end of the Napoleonic Wars. Having supported Napoleon, it was forced to cede Norway to Sweden by the Treaty of Kiel (1814); it lost its north German territory to Prussia 1864–66 and only in 1920 was North Schleswig returned to Denmark.

After 1815 there was much pressure for a more liberal form of government in preference to the traditional absolute monarchy and on 5 June 1849 the royal assent was given to a new constitution. A parliament, the *Rigsdag*, was created, divided into an upper house, the *Landsting*, and a lower house, the *Folketing*. The franchise was granted to men over 30 years old.

During the First World War (1914–18) Denmark remained neutral, and in 1939, at the commencement of the Second World War it again declared its neutrality. On this occasion, however, it was soon overwhelmed by the German forces which invaded on 9 April 1940. Throughout the war there was a considerable Danish resistance movement to which the Germans responded by taking over power and inaugurating a reign of terror.

Immediately after the Second World War Denmark recognized the independence of Iceland. Home rule was granted to the Faroes in 1948 and to Greenland in 1979.

The constitution was amended in 1953 and this allowed for a female succession to the throne, abolished the *Landsting* (the upper house) and extended the franchise to all men and women over 18 years of age. Denmark joined NATO in 1949, took the lead in the formation of the consultative Nordic Council in 1953 and joined the EEC after a referendum held in 1972.

Since the Second World War Denmark has been ruled by coalition governments, usually headed by prime ministers drawn from the Social Democratic Party. Since 1982, however, the prime minister has been Poul Schlüter, a member of the Conservative Party.

Further Reading
Lauring, P., *A History of Denmark*. 5th ed. Copenhagen, 1981

DANISH DEPENDENCIES

FAROE ISLANDS

A Norwegian province from 1380 to 1709, the islands secured the restoration of their parliament in 1852 and since 1948 they have been a self-governing region of the Kingdom of Denmark. From 1 Jan. 1972 the Faroe Islands were no longer members of EFTA.

GREENLAND

A Danish possession since 1380, Greenland became on 5 June 1953 an integral part of the Danish kingdom. Following a referendum in Jan. 1979, home rule was introduced from 1 May 1979, and full internal self-government was attained in Jan. 1981 after a transitional period. Greenland left the European Communities in 1984.

DJIBOUTI

Djibouti in the 19th century was inhabited by pastoral nomadic African muslims notably the Afars and Issas, as well as by Arabs originating from Yemen. France established a protectorate over the Sultanates of Tadjoura and Obock in 1881 and in 1884 annexed the whole of the Gulf of Tadjoura region as the colony of French Somaliland. The port of Djibouti was founded in 1888 and became the colony's capital in 1892. A railway link to the Ethiopian capital of Addis Ababa, completed in 1917, became the colony's principal economic strength when Djibouti became a free port in 1947.

At a referendum held on 19 March 1967, 60% of the electorate voted for continued association with France, and a new statute for the territory, renamed the French Territory of the Afars and Issas after the two principal ethnic groups, came into being on 5 July 1967. Following an agreement signed on 8 June 1976 between France and the territorial government, a second referendum on 8 May 1977 approved independence, which was achieved on 27 June as the Republic of Djibouti. In Oct. 1981 it was declared a one-party state and elections held the following year. The past decade has seen a flow of refugees fleeing the conflicts in Eritrea and the Ogaden in neighbouring Ethiopia. President Hassan Gouled Aptidon was head of state in 1986, and maintained a policy of close links with France.

Further Reading

Thompson, V., and Adloff, R., *Djibouti and the Horn of Africa.* Stanford Univ. Press, 1967

COMMONWEALTH OF DOMINICA

The earliest known inhabitants of this island in the Caribbean were two Amerindian tribes: the Arawaks who migrated from South America and the Caribs, who later drove them out. At the time of Columbus' arrival, Dominica was inhabited by the fierce, warlike Caribs who were at war with the inhabitants of neighbouring islands. Dominica was discovered by Columbus on Sunday (hence the island's name), 3 Nov. 1493. Neither the Spanish nor the Earl of Carlisle, who was granted the island in 1627 by Charles I, established settlements, and instead it was French settlers who began to create plantations on the island. The island's strategic position, however, later caused it to become the centre of a threefold conflict between the Carib Indians, the British and the French. Control of the island was contested between the British and French until it was ultimately awarded to the British in 1783.

However, in 1778 the island was captured and held until 1783 by the French from Martinique. Twice during the French Revolutionary and Napoleonic wars the island was attacked, but on each occasion the invaders withdrew.

Dominica became part of a federation on four occasions: in 1833 with the Leeward Islands, in 1871 in an extended Leeward Islands Colony, in 1940 as part of the Windward Islands group and in 1958–62 as a member of the Federation of the West Indies.

In March 1967 Dominica became an Associated State of the UK, allowed internal self-government, and became an independent republic as the Commonwealth of Dominica on 3 Nov. 1978.

Further Reading
Atwood, T., *History of the Island of Dominica*. London, 1971

DOMINICAN REPUBLIC

On 5 Dec. 1492 Columbus discovered the island of Santo Domingo, which he called La Isla Espanola and which for a time was also known as Hispaniola. The city of Santo Domingo, founded by his brother, Bartholomew, in 1496, is the oldest city in the Americas. The western third of the island – now the Republic of Haiti – was later occupied and colonized by the French, to whom the Spanish colony of Santo Domingo was also ceded in 1795. In 1808 the Dominican population, under the command of Gen. Juan Sánchez Ramirez, routed an important French military force commanded by Gen. Ferrand at the battle of Palo Hincado. This battle was the beginning of the end for French rule in Santo Domingo and culminated in the successful siege of the capital. Eventually, with the aid of a British naval squadron, the French were forced to capitulate and the colony returned again to Spanish rule, from which it declared its independence in 1821. It was invaded and held by the Haitians from 1822 to 1844, when they were expelled, and the Dominican Republic was founded and a constitution adopted. In 1850 Great Britain was the first country to recognize the Dominican Republic.

Thereafter the rule was dictatorship interspersed with brief democratic interludes. Between 1916 and 1924 the country was under US military occupation. From 1930 until his assassination in 1961, Rafael Trujillo was one of Latin America's legendary dictators. The rise of radicalism following the election of Juan Bosch to the presidency in 1963 led in 1965, to a further US invasion. The conservative pro-American Joaquín Balaguer was president from 1966 to 1978 when an opposition candidate, Antonio Guzuén, was elected. Resistence to repression of popular movements led to the election of the moderate leftist Salvador Jorge Blanco in 1982. In 1986 Balaguer returned to power at the head of the Socialist Christian Reform Party.

Further Reading

Wiarda, H. J., and Kryzanek, M. J., *The Dominican Republic: A Caribbean Crucible.* Boulder, 1982

ECUADOR

The Incas of Peru conquered this territory in the 15th century but on 16 Nov. 1532 the Spaniards under Francisco Pizarro, after their victory at Cajamarca, founded a colony in Ecuador, then called Quito. This colony was in turn part of the viceroyalty of Peru and then of New Granada. Spanish rule was first challenged by the rising of 10 Aug. 1809. In 1821 a revolt under Marshal Sucre led to the defeat of the Spaniards at Pichincha in 1821, and thus the winning of independence from Spain. In 1822 Bolivar persuaded the new republic to join the federation of Gran Colombia. However, in 1830 Ecuador left this federation and on 13 March 1830 became the Republic of Ecuador instead of the Presidency of Quito. For 100 years thereafter considerable difficulty was found in creating a stable régime as presidents and dictators followed one another. Since 1948 first President Galo Plazo Lasso (1948–52) and then President José Maria Velasco Ibarra (1934–35, 1944–47, 1952–56, 1960–61, 1968–72) gave more continuity to the presidential régimes, although the last named was deposed by military *coups* from four of his five presidencies.

From 1963 to 1966 and from 1976 to 1979 military juntas ruled the country. The last of these juntas produced a new constitution which was accepted by a national referendum in Jan. 1978 and came into force on 10 Aug. 1979. A new Congress was elected, and Jaime Roldós Aguilera was elected president. Since then presidencies have been more stable, although President Roldós Aguilera (1979–81) died in an air crash. There have been occasional constitutional disagreements between the government and Congress. A state of emergency was declared in March 1986 when Gen. Frank Vargas Pazos led an anti-government revolt at Quito air base but this ended quickly. Further civil unrest eventually prompted a move for elections. Stage one of the presidential elections took place on 31 Jan. 1988, and the final election is planned for May 1988.

Further Reading

Martz, J. D., *Ecuador: Conflicting Political Culture and the Quest for Progress*. Boston, 1972

EGYPT

Egypt was part of the Ottoman Empire from 1517 until 1922 when it achieved independence, albeit qualified, from Britain which had exercised direct control over Egyptian affairs since occupying the country in 1882. Muhammad Ali (1805–40) succeeded in establishing a hereditary dynasty of Khedives, yet with the opening of the Suez Canal in 1869 and Britain's purchase of the Khedives shares, Egypt's strategic importance paved the way for foreign intervention and domination. In 1914 the country became a British protectorate and the Khedive was deposed. On 28 Feb. 1922 Egypt was declared an independent constitutional monarchy.

In the Second World War (1939–45) Egypt supported the Allies. Following a revolution in July 1952 led by Gen. Neguib, King Farouk abdicated in favour of his son, but in 1953 the monarchy was abolished. Neguib became president but encountered opposition from the military when he attempted to move towards a parliamentary republic. Col. Gamal Abdel Nasser seized power and Neguib resigned. Nasser became head of state on 14 June 1954 (president from 1956), and remained in office until he died on 28 Sept. 1970. In 1956 Egypt nationalized the Suez Canal, a move which led Britain, France and Israel to mount military attacks against Egypt until forced by the UN and the USA to withdraw.

In 1958 Egypt and Syria united to form the United Arab Republic (UAR), but Syria withdrew in 1961. For ten years Egypt retained the name UAR, but a new constitution, approved by a referendum on 11 Sept. 1971 renamed the country the Arab Republic of Egypt.

The 1960s and 1970s saw constant conflict with Israel until President Muhammad Anwar Sadat, who succeeded Nasser, made a dramatic peace treaty with Israel in March 1979. He was assassinated on 6 Oct. 1981, and was succeeded by the vice-president, Lieut.-Gen. Muhammad Hosni Mubarak.

Further Reading

Hopwood, D., *Egypt: Politics and Society 1945–1981*. London, 1982

EL SALVADOR

Conquered by Spain in 1526, El Salvador remained under Spanish rule until freeing itself in 1821. Thereafter, El Salvador was a member of the Central American Federation comprising the states of El Salvador, Guatemala, Honduras, Nicaragua and Costa Rica until this federation was dissolved in 1839. In 1841 El Salvador declared itself an independent republic.

The country's history has been marked by much political violence and a number of enforced changes of rulers. The repressive dictatorship of President Maximiliano Hernandez Martinez lasted from 1931 to 1944 when he was deposed, as were his successors in 1948 and 1960. The military junta that followed gave way to more secure presidential succession, although there were charges of corruption at the election. Left-wing guerrilla groups became increasingly large and strong and were engaged in constant fighting with government troops in the late 1970s. Many reports circulated of the violation of human rights, and in 1980 the Roman Catholic Archbishop of San Salvador, Oscar Romero y Galdames, an acknowledged advocate of human rights by government and army, was assassinated. As the guerrillas grew stronger and gained control over a part of the country, the USA sent economic aid and advisers to El Salvador and assisted in the training of Salvadorean troops. A new constitution was enacted in Dec. 1983 under which Agostin Duarte was elected president in May 1984, but it did nothing to pacify the situation. The Presidential election was boycotted as a fraud by the main left-wing organization, the Favabundo Marti National Liberation Front (FMLM). Since then fighting between government troops and left-wing guerrillas, as well as the activities of death squads apparently organized by the army, guerrilla disruptions of elections, kidnappings, the violation of human rights and many civilian deaths were still continuing in 1988.

Further Reading

Baloyra, E. A., *Salvador in Transition*. Univ. of North Carolina Press, 1982
Montgomery, T. S., *Revolution in El Salvador: Origins and Evolution*. Boulder, 1982

EQUATORIAL GUINEA

Equatorial Guinea consists of the island of Bioko, for centuries called Fernando Po; other, smaller islands, notably Pagalu, formerly Annobon; and the mainland territory of Rio Muni. The main ethnic group in Rio Muni is the Fang (or Pahouin), members of which also live in neighbouring Gabon; the Bubis, the original inhabitants of Fernando Po, still constitute the majority on Bioko. Fernando Po was called after the Portuguese navigator Fernão do Po who in 1471–72 became the first European visitor to the island; it was then ruled for 3 centuries by Portugal, but was in 1778 ceded to Spain, along with Annobon and a mainland area out of which Spain eventually retained a small area, Rio Muni, whose boundaries were recognized by other European countries in 1856.

For some decades after taking possession of Fernando Po Spain did not effectively occupy it and allowed Britain to establish an important consulate and naval base at Clarence (later Santa Isabel) which dominated the island and were important for suppression of slave trading over a wide area in the 19th century. Spain asserted its rule from the 1840s. Fernando Po and Rio Muni were together called the Spanish Possessions in the Gulf of Guinea, or simply Spanish Guinea. African resistance to Spanish occupation of the interior of Rio Muni continued for a long time. In Rio Muni timber became the major export; on Fernando Po the Spanish developed cocoa cultivation on European-owned plantations, for which African labour was imported from the early 20th century. This labour traffic led to an international scandal in 1930 when Liberians were found to be sold to virtual slavery. Later many Nigerians were employed, often in poor conditions, and a large Nigerian community came to live on the island.

For much of Spanish rule Africans were kept in a subordinate position under the system called *patronato de indígenas* (patronage over natives). On 30 July 1959 it was announced that Spanish Guinea was to be a part of Spain and its people Spanish citizens. It became 2 provinces, represented in the *Cortes* in Madrid.

African nationalist movements began in the 1950s and 1960s. Internal self-government was granted in 1963, with a joint legislative assembly for the 2 provinces. Bonifacio Ondo Edu, leader of the *Movimiento de Unión Nacional de Guinea Ecuatorial* (MUNGE), became head of government. Other parties included the *Idea Popu-*

lar de Guinea Ecuatorial (IPGE), of which Francisco Macias Nguema became the leader. In 1968 Spain briefly suspended the constitution after rivalry among the parties, but then, under pressure to grant independence, agreed to this on condition of its approval by a referendum, which was given on 11 Aug. 1968. The 2 parts of Equatorial Guinea were united in a state which became independent on 12 Oct. 1968 with Macias Nguema as president.

President Macias established the rule of a single party, the *Partido Unico Nacional de los Trabajadores* (PUNT), in 1970. His government was from early on a dictatorship. A third of the population was killed or else left the country.

On 3 Aug. 1979 President Macias was overthrown in a *coup d'état* led by a relative of his, Col. Teodoro Obiang Nguema. The military régime ended the extreme excesses of the rule of Macias, who was executed.

A constitution approved by a referendum on 3 Aug. 1982 restored some political institutions, but left the military régime in power, to stay until economic and social reconstruction is completed. Elections in Aug. 1983 returned candidates nominated by Nguema. He went on to establish the Democratic Party of Equatorial Guinea (DPEG). Efforts have been made to restore the shattered economy with aid notably from Spain and France, with which close ties are maintained.

ETHIOPIA

The ancient empire of Ethiopia has its legendary origin in the meeting of King Solomon and the Queen of Sheba. Historically, the empire developed at Aksum in the north, in the centuries before and after the birth of Christ, as a result of Semitic immigration from South Arabia. The immigrants imposed their language and culture on the indigenous Hamitic people. Ethiopia's subsequent history is one of sporadic expansion southwards and eastwards, checked from the 16th to early 19th centuries by devastating wars with Moslems and Gallas. Modern Ethiopia dates from the reign of the Emperor Theodore (1855–68).

Menelik II (1889–1913) defeated the Italians in 1896 and thereby safeguarded the empire's independence in the scramble for Africa. By successful campaigns in neighbouring kingdoms within Ethiopia (Jimma, Kaffa, Harar, etc.) he united the country under his rule and created the empire as it is today.

In 1923 the heir to the throne, Ras Tafari (crowned Emperor Haile Selassie five years later), succeeded in getting Ethiopia admitted as an independent country to the League of Nations. However, the League was ineffective in preventing a second Italian invasion in 1936. The Ethiopians fought a war of resistance but they were severely repressed in harsh reprisals carried out by the Italian army. They failed to dislodge the occupiers and the emperor fled the country, only returning when the Allied forces defeated the Italians in 1941. Ethiopia was initially treated as a conquered Italian colony, and only after a concerted campaign was the country's independence recognized again.

In accordance with a resolution of the General Assembly of the UN, dated 2 Dec. 1950, the former Italian colony of Eritrea, from 1941 under British military administration, was handed over to Ethiopia on 15 Sept. 1952. Eritrea thereby became an autonomous unit within the federation of Ethiopia and Eritrea.

This federation became a unitary state on 14 Nov. 1962 when Eritrea was fully integrated with Ethiopia although a secessionist movement has also been active, fighting a major guerrilla war for independence under the Eritrean Peoples' Liberation Front (EPLF) in the 1980s. A smaller war has been waged for similar reasons in neighbouring Tigray, led by the Tigray Peoples' Liberation Front (TPLF).

A provisional military government assumed power on 12 Sept. 1974 and came to be known as the Dirgue. It deposed the emperor, abolished the monarchy and acted against feudalism in the rural areas. Under the leadership of Lieut. Col. Mengistu Haile Miriam, it also took strong action against critics, and as part of its agricultural collectivization programme sent many students to do service in the rural areas. A political party, the Workers Party of Ethiopia (WPE), was set up by the Dirgue in 1984. The party drew up a constitution for a Peoples' Democratic Republic of Ethiopia, which was approved by a referendum in 1987. Elections took place in June, and all central committee members were returned to office, including Mengistu.

In mid-1977 Somalia invaded Ethiopia and took control of the Ogaden region. After an offensive mounted with strong Soviet and Cuban support the area was recaptured and in March 1978 Somalia withdrew all troops from the area. Control was re-established by Ethiopia later in 1978 and nationalist guerrillas were pushed back. Sporadic fighting continued in the Ogaden and along the border. Talks about the normalization of relations between Ethiopia and Somalia commenced in 1986.

Since 1973, the country has been ravaged by drought and famine, since compounded by war. In the 1980s, the government embarked on a massive programme to resettle people from the barren northern areas to the more fertile south.

Further Reading

Schwab, P., *Ethiopia: Politics, Economics and Society.* Boulder, 1985

FALKLAND ISLANDS

France established a settlement in 1764 and Britain a second settlement in 1765. In 1770 Spain bought out the French and drove out the British. In 1806 Spanish rule was overthrown in Argentina, and the Argentine claimed to succeed Spain in the French and British settlements in 1820. The British objected and reclaimed their settlement in 1832 as a Crown Colony.

On 2 April 1982 Argentine forces invaded the Falkland Islands and the Governor was expelled. At a meeting of the UN Security Council held on 3 April, the voting was 10 to 1 in favour of the resolution calling for Argentina to withdraw. British troops regained possession on 14–15 June after the Argentine surrendered.

Despite some international pressure to negotiate with Argentina over future sovereignty, Britain insists that the Falkland islanders should exercise self-determination and now maintains a sizeable garrison on the islands.

Further Reading

Hoffmann, F. L. and O. M., *Sovereignty in Dispute*. London, 1984

FIJI

The Fiji Islands were discovered by Tasman in 1643 and visited by Capt. Cook in 1774, but first recorded in detail by Capt. Bligh after the mutiny of the *Bounty* (1789). In the 19th century the search for sandalwood, in which enormous profits were made, brought many ships. Deserters and shipwrecked men stayed on; firearms salvaged from wrecks were used in native wars, new diseases swept the islands, and rum and muskets became regular articles of trade. Tribal wars became bloody and general until Fiji was ceded to Britain on 10 Oct. 1874, after a previous offer of cession had been refused. Fiji gained independent status on 10 Oct. 1970.

Fiji remained an independent state within the Commonwealth with a Governor-General appointed by the Queen until 1987. In the general election of 12 April 1987 a left-wing coalition headed by Dr Timoci Bavadra defeated the ruling Alliance Party of Ratu Sir Kanisese Mara. The new government had the support of the Indian population who outnumber the indigenous Fijians at a rate of 50% to 44%. It was, however, overthrown in a military *coup* on 14 May led by Lieut.-Col. Sitiveni Rabuka.

After a period of uncertainty in which civil government was largely restored, Brigadier Rabuka led a second *coup* on 25 Sept. On 7 Oct. Fiji declared itself a Republic, the Queen accepted the Governor-General's resignation and, on 15 Oct., Fiji's Commonwealth membership lapsed. On 5 Dec. Ratu Penaia agreed to accept the presidency and asked the former prime minister Ratu Mara to form a government. The majority of Mara's ministers are members of his old Alliance Party, four, including Rabuka (Minister of Home Affairs) are military officers and two are Fijian Indians, neither of them a member of Dr Bavadra's Coalition.

Further Reading

Scarr, D., *Fiji, A Short History*. Sydney, 1984

FINLAND

From the Middle Ages Finland was a part of the realm of Sweden. In the 18th century parts of south-eastern Finland were conquered by Russia, and the rest of the country was ceded to Russia by the peace treaty of Hamina in 1809. Finland became an autonomous grand-duchy which retained its previous laws and institutions under its grand duke, the Emperor of Russia. The Diet, elected since 1906 on universal suffrage, produced in 1916 a social democrat majority, the first in Europe. After the Russian revolution Finland declared itself independent on 6 Dec. 1917. The Civil War began in Jan. 1918 between the 'whites' and 'reds', the latter being supported by Russian Bolshevik troops. The defeat of the red guards in May 1918 consequently meant freeing the country from Russian troops. A peace treaty with Soviet Russia was signed in 1920 at Dorpat.

On 30 Nov. 1939 Soviet troops invaded Finland, after Finland had rejected territorial concessions demanded by the USSR. These, however, had to be made in the peace treaty of 12 March 1940, amounting to 32,806 sq. km and including the Carelian Isthmus, Viipuri and the shores of Lake Ladoga.

When the German attack on the USSR was launched in June 1941 Finland again became involved in the war against the USSR. On 19 Sept. 1944 an armistice was signed in Moscow. Finland agreed to cede to the USSR the Petsamo area in addition to the cessions made in 1940 (total 42,934 sq. km) and to lease to the USSR for 50 years the Porkkala headland to be used as a military base. Further, Finland undertook to pay 300m. gold dollars in reparations within six years (later extended to eight years). The peace treaty was signed in Paris on 10 Feb. 1947. The payment of reparations was completed on 19 Sept. 1952. The military base of Porkkala was returned to Finland on 26 Jan. 1956. To escape incorporation in the USSR, the post war premier and later president S. Passikivi pursued a policy of neutralism highly favourable to the Russians. This policy, known as Finlandization, has been continued under Presidents V. Kekkonen (1956–81) and M. Koivisto (1981–).

Further Reading
Jutikkala, E. and Pirinen, K., *A History of Finland*. 3rd ed. New York, 1979

94

FRANCE

Gaul, the area that is now France, was conquered by Julius Caesar in the 1st century BC and became a part of the Roman Empire. In the 3rd and 4th centuries it was overrun by Germanic tribes, and in the 10th century Norsemen invaded. There was a long period of conflict with England, typified by the Hundred Years' War (1337–1453); and this was followed by rivalry with Spain in the latter part of the 15th and in the 16th century. The Reformation caused a long religious civil war between 1562 and 1598, at the end of which the Huguenot leader, Henry of Navarre, was converted to Catholicism and reigned as the first Bourbon king, Henry IV. The two powerful ministers of the 17th century, Cardinal Richelieu and Mazarin, successively ensured that France, and not Spain, established itself as the dominant country in Europe. Militarily this was achieved by the treaties of Westphalia (which ended the Thirty Years' War in 1648) and of the Pyrenees (1659). There followed the brilliant reign of Louis XIV, the 'Sun King' (1643–1715).

The second half of the 18th century saw France defeated by England in the Seven Years' War (1756–63). The French Revolution began in 1789 when the 'Third Estate' assumed power as a National Assembly and overthrew the government. Riots and the storming of the Bastille were followed by the proclamation of a republic (1792) and the execution of the king, Louis XVI (1793). A Reign of Terror followed during which thousands were guillotined. After these excesses the Directory ruled from 1795 until 1799 when it was overthrown by Napoleon Bonaparte who became First Consul and then Emperor (1804) of the first French Empire. Napoleon went on to gain control of most of Europe until he was finally defeated at the Battle of Waterloo in 1815. The monarchy was restored, with the Bourbon family reigning (officially from 1814). A revolution in 1830 brought Louis Philippe, son of the Duke of Orleans, to the throne as a constitutional monarch. This 'July Monarchy' was overthrown in 1848 and superseded by the Second Republic, with Louis Napoleon (nephew of Napoleon I) elected president. In 1852 he took the title Emperor Napoleon III, and hence began the Second Empire. However, the early military failures of France in the Franco-Prussian War (1870–71) led to Napoleon being deposed and the proclamation of the Third Republic in 1870. This survived both the First World War, which was fought chiefly on French soil, and also 44 successive governments from the end of the war in 1918 until 1940. In 1940 German troops invaded France and the French government capitulated, and a pro-German government was established at Vichy. Gen. Charles de Gaulle headed a Free French government in London, while in France the Resistance continued to harass the German Army of Occupation and give secret aid to the Allies.

When France was liberated in 1944 a provisional government under de Gaulle ruled the country until the Fourth Republic was established in 1946, and de Gaulle retired. The country now faced problems in Algeria and in Indo-China; the government changed 25 times by 1958. In that year de Gaulle was recalled to be briefly prime minister and then president as the Fifth Republic began in 1958. He granted independence to Algeria (1962) and was successful in establishing a firm and stable government until rioting and strikes by students and workers led to his resignation in 1969. He was succeeded by Georges Pompidou, who died in 1974 and was in turn succeeded by Giscard d'Estaing. Both presidents tended to continue Gaullist policies, but in 1981 François Mitterand, a left-wing candidate was elected to the presidency. He invited four Communists to join his Council of Ministers, and pursued a policy of nationalization of some industries, improved conditions for the workers, and social benefits. He also began a process of developing stronger department governments at the expense of the central government. Since 1986 'cohabitation' between the Socialist president Mitterand and the Gaullist premier Chirac has worked reasonably smoothly.

Further Reading

Caron, F., *An Economic History of Modern France*. London, 1979
Ardagh, J., *France in the 1980s*. Harmondsworth, 1982

FRENCH OVERSEAS DEPARTMENTS

GUADELOUPE

Guadeloupe was discovered by Columbus, but the Carib inhabitants resisted Spanish colonization. A French colony was established on 28 June 1635. On 19 March 1946 Guadeloupe became an Overseas Department and in 1974 it additionally became an administrative region.

GUIANA

A French settlement was established in 1604 and Guiana finally became a French possession in 1817. Convict settlements, including the notorious Devil's Island, existed between 1852 and 1945. On 19 March 1946 the status of Guiana was changed to that of an Overseas Department, and in 1974 it also became an administrative region.

MARTINIQUE

Discovered by Columbus in 1493, the island was known as Madinina, from which its present name was corrupted. A French colony was established in 1635. On 19 March 1946 its status was altered to that of an Overseas Department, and in 1974 it also became an administrative region.

RÉUNION

Formerly Île Bourbon, Réunion became a French possession in 1638. On 19 March 1946 its status was altered to that of an Overseas Department, and in 1974 it also became an administrative region.

FRENCH TERRITORIAL COLLECTIVES

MAYOTTE

Mayotte was a French colony from 1843 until 1914 when it was attached, with the other Comoro Islands, to the governor-general of Madagascar until the Comoro group became an Overseas Territory in 1947. When the other islands voted to become independent as the Comoro state in 1974, Mayotte voted to remain a French dependency. In Dec. 1976 Mayotte became a *collectivité territoriale*.

ST PIERRE ET MIQUELON

This tiny remaining fragment of the once extensive French possessions in North America, the archipelago, was settled from France in the 17th century. It became a French territory from 1816, an Overseas Department in July 1976 and a *collectivité territoriale* in June 1985.

FRENCH OVERSEAS TERRITORIES

SOUTHERN AND ANTARCTIC TERRITORIES

The territory of the Terres Australes et Antarctiques Françaises was created on 6 Aug. 1955, with the administration's seat in Paris. In Nov. 1982 a Consultative Committee on the Environment was created for the territory.

NEW CALEDONIA

New Caledonia was annexed by France in 1853 and, together with most former French dependencies, became an Overseas Territory in 1958. Plans for the future of New Caledonia were announced in 1985 and in a referendum on independence held on 13 Sept. 1987 the inhabitants voted overwhelmingly in favour of retaining territorial ties with France. However, although this decision was popular with the Caldoches of European extraction, the indigenous Kalaks prefer independence.

FRENCH POLYNESIA

French protectorates since 1843, these islands were annexed to France in 1880 (the Society and Tuamotu Archipelagoes), 1882 (the Gambier and Marquesas Islands) and 1900 (the Austral Islands), in order to form 'French Settlements in Oceania'. In Nov. 1958 these settlements opted for the status of an Overseas Territory.

WALLIS AND FUTUNA

Wallis and Futuna have been French dependencies since 1842. On 22 Dec. 1959 the inhabitants of these islands voted in favour of exchanging their status to that of an Overseas Territory, which took effect from 29 July 1961.

GABON

Between the 16th and 18th centuries, the Fang and other peoples in the region of present-day Gabon were part of a federation of chiefdoms. Some collaborated in the slave-trade, while others suffered from it. The country's capital, Libreville, grew from a settlement of slaves who were rescued from captivity by the French in 1849. Colonized by France around this period, the territory was annexed to French Congo in 1888. There was resistance by the indigenous people between 1905 and 1911 to the depredations of colonial rule, but the country became a separate colony in 1910 as one of the four territories of French Equatorial Africa. In 1946, it became an overseas territory of France. Gabon became an autonomous republic within the French Community on 28 Nov. 1958 and achieved independence on 17 Aug. 1960. On 12 Feb. 1961 Leon M'ba, former mayor of Libreville and leader of *Bloc Démocratique Gabonais*, was elected president, and opposed federal grouping in Africa. This view was challenged by Jean Hilaire Aubame who led the opposition party which overthrew M'ba in a *coup* on 18 Feb. 1963. French intervention resulted in M'ba being restored to office. M'ba died on 30 Nov. 1967 and was succeeded on 2 Dec. by his vice-president, Albert Bernard (now Omar) Bongo. Bongo remained in power and was reconfirmed as president for a further seven years in elections in Nov. 1986. France retains a military base in the country, and Gabon's foreign policy remains moderate.

Further Reading

Remy, M., *Gabon Today*. Paris, 1977

THE GAMBIA

By the 15th century, the Wolof and Mandinka tribes were established in the territory that is now The Gambia. Portuguese navigators visited the area, but made no settlement. A strip of land that is surrounded on three sides by Senegal, its existence as a distinct country originates in historical rivalry and compromise between Britain and France for territory in West Africa.

During the 17th century various companies of merchants obtained trading charters and established a settlement on the river which, from 1807, was controlled from Sierra Leone; in 1843 it was made an independent Crown Colony; in 1866 it formed part of the West African Settlements, but in Dec. 1888 it again became a separate Crown Colony. The boundaries were delimited only after 1890. The Gambia achieved full internal self-government on 4 Oct. 1963, and became an independent member of the Commonwealth on 18 Feb. 1965 and a republic within the Commonwealth on 24 April 1970. The Gambia and Senegal formed the Confederation of Senegambia on 1 Feb. 1982.

The confederation continues, but with slow progress on economic integration. An attempted *coup* in 1981 was put down with Senegalese soldiers. Sir Dawda Jawara, president since 1970, was re-elected in March 1987.

Further Reading

Rice, B., *Enter Gambia: The Birth of an Improbable Nation*. London, 1968

GERMANY

At the outbreak of the Napoleonic wars Germany consisted of many small states, independent but loosely bound by a common allegiance to the Holy Roman Emperor, a title which was hereditary in the Austrian royal house of Hapsburg. In 1806 the Holy Roman Empire was destroyed by Napoleon, who then combined 16 German states as the Confederation of the Rhine.

Following Napoleon's defeat in 1815, a larger Confederation was formed with 38 members (39 after 1817). Austria remained the dominant power with a permanent right to the presidency of the Confederation. Prussia held the vice-presidency. The other important states were: Bavaria, Saxony, Hanover, Württemberg, Baden, Hesse-Kassel, Hesse-Darmstadt, Holstein and Lauenberg, Brunswick, Nassau, Mecklenburg-Schwerin and Mecklenburg-Strelitz.

In 1848–50 an attempt was made to draw up a constitution and elect a Confederation parliament. A new central authority replaced the Federal Diet from 12 July 1848 until 1 May 1850, when Austria proclaimed it defunct. Prussia did not agree to this until 29 Nov. 1850. A constitution was published in Dec. 1848 but few states accepted it; a revised version was accepted in May 1849, but not by Austria or Bavaria. The parliament which sat from 20 March to 29 April 1850 was neither recognized by Austria nor powerful enough to control the other dominant state, Prussia. The Federal Diet therefore resumed power and held it until 1866.

In 1866 Prussia defeated Austria in war and formed the North German Confederation in 1867, under her own control. She had annexed Hanover, Hesse-Kassel and Nassau in 1866 together with the smaller states of Homburg and Frankfurt.

In 1870 Prussia went to war with France, rallied the German states in support and, following German victory, went on to the creation of the German Empire in 1871. The Empire included all German states except Austria and had, therefore, deep North–South, Protestant–Catholic divisions. It was dominated by Prussia, and the Prussian king became emperor. Resentment developed in the previously powerful southern states. Conscious of arriving late on the world scene, Germany, nevertheless acquired colonies in West and South-West Africa in 1884 and at the end of the decade Zanzibar and Tanganyika in the East. The imperial government led Germany into the First World War in 1914 and when defeated,

101

national unity collapsed. The emperor abdicated on 28 Nov. 1918.

After an anarchic period a republican government, with a constitution drawn up at Weimar in 1919, attempted under Chancellor Ebert to restore the economy and political stability. But the scale of reparation demanded by the Treaty of Versailles, the onset of world depression and the loss of resources and territory through warfare were too great.

In 1933 the National Socialist leader Adolf Hitler was appointed Chancellor. The National Socialist ('Nazi') party appealed to national pride and offered a return to self-respect after humiliation. Hitler became president of the Third Reich in 1934. His policies involved the wide expansion of German power and a theory of Aryan racial supremacy which meant in practice that non-Aryans were persecuted, murdered, and their assets confiscated. Hitler's expansionism led to his annexation of Austria and of German-speaking Czechoslovakia in 1938. In March 1939 he declared all of Czechoslovakia a German protectorate, and in Sept. invaded Poland, attempting to restore the authority exercised there by Prussia before 1918. This latter act precipitated the Second World War.

The war ended in German defeat in 1945. The Allied forces occupied Germany; the UK, the USA and France holding the west and the USSR the east. By the Berlin Declaration of 5 June 1945 these governments assumed authority; each was given a zone of occupation, and the zone commanders-in-chief together made up the Allied Control Council in Berlin. The area of Greater Berlin was also divided into 4 sectors.

At the Potsdam Conference of 1945 northern East Prussia was transferred to the USSR. It was also agreed that, pending a final peace settlement, Poland should administer the areas east of the rivers Oder and Neisse, with the frontier fixed on the Oder and Western Neisse down to the Czechoslovak frontier.

By 1948 it had become clear that there would be no agreement between the occupying powers as to the future of Germany. Accordingly, the western allies united their zones into one unit in March 1948. In protest, the USSR withdrew from the Allied Control Council, blockaded Berlin until May 1949, and consolidated control of eastern Germany.

Further Reading

Conradt, D. B., *The German Polity*. 2nd ed. London, 1982
Craig, G., *The Germans*. Harmondsworth, 1982

GERMAN DEMOCRATIC REPUBLIC

The eastern zone of occupied Germany was administered after May 1945 by the USSR, through a military government. The only exception was the city of Berlin which had four zones, only one of them under Soviet authority. In 1948–49 the USSR attempted to blockade Berlin in order to bring American, British and French authority there to an end. The attempt was not successful, but the USSR established the German Democratic Republic in the Eastern zone and Soviet power in the Republic was consolidated.

A People's Council had been appointed in 1948 and in 1949 it became a provisional People's Chamber, which acted as a constituent assembly. The constitution which it drew up came into force in Oct. 1949, providing for a communist state of five Länder with a centrally-planned economy. In 1952 the government made a physical division between its own territory and that of the Federal Republic, in the form of a three-mile cordon fenced and guarded along the frontier. This left Berlin as the natural point of contact; it was closed as a migration route by the construction of a concrete boundary wall in 1961.

In 1953 there were popular revolts against food shortages and the pressure to collectivize. In 1954 the government eased economic problems, the USSR ceased to collect reparation payments, and sovereignty was granted. The GDR signed the Warsaw Pact in 1955. Socialist policies were stepped up in 1958, leading to an increased flight to the West of skilled workers; between 1945 and 1961, some three million left. The economy improved markedly after 1961; it remains centrally planned but there have been concessions to the play of market forces, notably in the New Economic System introduced in 1963 and revised in 1966. East German forces joined in the invasion of Czechoslovakia in 1968.

Relations with the Federal Republic improved after 1972 and E. Honeker, who succeeded W. Ulbricht in 1971, visited Bonn in 1987.

Further Reading
Childs, D., *East Germany*. London, 1969

FEDERAL REPUBLIC OF GERMANY

A constituent assembly met in Bonn in Sept. 1948 and drafted a Basic Law, which came into force in May 1949. In Sept. 1949 the occupation forces limited their own powers and the Federal Republic of Germany came into existence. The occupation forces retained some powers, however, and the Republic did not become a sovereign state until 1955 when the Occupation Statute was revoked.

The Republic consisted of the states of Schleswig-Holstein, Hamburg, Lower Saxony, Bremen, North Rhine-Westphalia, Hessen, Rhineland-Palatinate, Baden-Württemberg, Bavaria and Saarland, together with West Berlin.

The first chancellor, Konrad Adenauer (1949–63), was committed to the ultimate reunification of Germany and would not acknowledge the German Democratic Republic as a state. The two German states did not sign an agreement of mutual recognition and intent to co-operate until 1972, under Chancellor Willi Brandt.

The most marked feature of the post-war period was rapid population growth and the restoration of industry. Immigration from the German Democratic Republic, about 3m. since 1945, stopped when the Berlin Wall was built in 1961; however there was a strong movement of German-speaking people back into Germany from German settlements in countries now part of the Soviet bloc. Industrial growth also attracted labour from Turkey, Spain and the Balkans.

The Paris Treaty, which came into force in 1955, ensured the Republic's contribution to NATO, and NATO forces have since been stationed along the Rhine in large numbers, with consequent dispute about the deployment of nuclear missiles on German soil.

Even before sovereignty, the Republic had begun negotiations for a measure of European unity, and joined in creating the European Coal and Steel Community in 1951 and the European Economic Community in 1957. In Jan. 1957 the Saarland was returned to full German control. In 1973 the Federal Republic entered the UN. The occupied status of West Berlin continues to be strictly observed; West Berliners are not liable for military service in the Bundeswehr. After a decade (1972–82) of Social Democratic rule, Dr Adenauer's old party, the CDU, supported by its Bavarian affiliate the CSU under Dr F. J. Strauss, returned in 1982 under the chancellorship of H. Kohl.

Further Reading
Balfour, M., *West Germany, a Contemporary History*. London, 1982
Carr, W. A., *A History of Germany, 1815–1985*. London, 1986
Dahrendorf, R., *Society and Democracy in Germany*. London, 1968

THE LÄNDER

BADEN-WÜRTTEMBERG

The *Land* is a combination of former states. Baden (the western part of the present *Land*) became a united margravate in 1771, after being divided as Baden-Baden and Baden-Durlach since 1535; Baden-Baden was predominantly Catholic and Baden-Durlach, Protestant.

The margrave became an ally of Napoleon, ceding land west of the Rhine and receiving northern and southern territory as compensation. In 1805 Baden became a grand duchy and in 1806 a member state of the Confederation of the Rhine, extending from the Main to Lake Constance. In 1815 it was a founder-state of the German Confederation. A constitution was granted by the grand duke in 1818, but later rulers were less liberal and there was revolution in 1848, put down with Prussian help. The Grand Duchy was abolished and replaced by a *Land* in 1919.

In 1949 Baden was combined with Württemberg to form three states; the three were brought together as 1 in 1952.

Württemberg, having been a duchy since 1495, became a kingdom in 1805 and joined the Confederations as did Baden. A constitution was granted in 1819 and the state remained liberal. In 1866 the king allied himself with Austria against Prussia, but in 1870 joined Prussia in war against France. The liberal monarchy came to an end with the abdication of William II in 1918, and Württemberg became a state of the German Republic. In 1945 the state was divided between different Allied occupation authorities but the divisions ended in 1952.

BAVARIA

Bavaria was a political unit ruled by the Wittelsbach family from 1180. The duchy remained Catholic after the Reformation, which made it a natural ally of Austria and the Hapsburg Emperors.

The present boundaries were reached during the Napoleonic wars, and Bavaria became a kingdom in 1805. Despite the granting of a constitution and parliament, radical feeling forced the abdication of King Ludwig I in 1848. Maximilian II was followed by Ludwig II who allied himself with Austria against Prussia in 1866, but was reconciled with Prussia and entered the German Empire in 1871.

In 1918 the King Ludwig III abdicated. The first years of republican government were filled with unrest, attempts at the overthrow of the state by both communist and right-wing groups culminating in an unsuccessful *coup* by Adolf Hitler in 1923.

The state of Bavaria included the Palatinate from 1214 until 1945, when it was taken from Bavaria and added to the Rhineland. The present *Land* of Bavaria was formed in 1948.

Munich, which is the third largest city in the Federal Republic (not counting Berlin), became capital of Bavaria in the reign of Albert IV (1467–1508) and remains capital of the *Land*. Bavaria is the second largest *Land* in terms of population and, therefore, in the size of its representation in the federal parliament.

BERLIN

The western sectors of the city of Berlin form an enclave in the German Democratic Republic, as a detached part of the Federal Republic of Germany.

Greater Berlin was administered by the 4 occupying powers from the Berlin Declaration of 5 June 1945 until 1 July 1948, when the Soviet occupation was withdrawn and replaced by a municipal government; the latter continued to function when the German Democratic Republic was founded in 1949. West Berlin received a constitution in Sept. 1950 as a *Land* of the Federal Republic. The Democratic Republic constructed the Berlin Wall and closed all routes between the eastern and western cities in 1961.

Berlin Palace was built for the Electors of Brandenburg (1698–1706); the Electors were kings of Prussia from 1701 and Berlin became their Prussian capital. In 1871 it became capital of all Germany, and there was rapid industrialization and growth.

In 1945 the city was the seat of the Allied Control Council. With their failure to preserve a united Germany, Berlin (East) became the capital of the Democratic Republic but Berlin (West) could not remain capital of the Federal Republic from which it was physically detached.

Further Reading
Hillenbrand, M. J., *The Future of Berlin*. Monclair, 1981

BREMEN

The state is dominated by the Free City of Bremen and its port, Bremerhaven.

In 1815, when it joined the German Confederation, Bremen was an autonomous city and Hanse port with important Baltic trade. In 1827 the expansion of trade inspired the founding of Bremerhaven, on land ceded by Hanover at the confluence of the Geest and Weser rivers. Further expansion followed the founding of the Norddeutscher Lloyd Shipping Company in 1857.

Merchant shipping, associated trade, and fishing were dominant until 1940; there has been diversification in post-war years. In 1939 Bremerhaven was absorbed by the Hanoverian town of Wesermunde. The combined port was returned to the jurisdiction of Bremen in 1947.

The 1947 constitution provided for government of the *Land* by a city council which appointed an executive Senate, led by a Bürgermeister.

HAMBURG

The *Land* is co-extensive with the metropolitan area of the port and city of Hamburg.

Hamburg was a free Hanse town owing nominal allegiance to the Holy Roman Emperor until 1806. In 1815 it became part of the German Confederation, sharing a seat in the Federal Diet with Lübeck, Bremen and Frankfurt. During the Empire it retained its autonomy. By 1938 it had become the third largest port in the world, and its territory was extended by the cession of land (3 urban and 27 rural districts) from Prussia. On 3 May 1945 the city was captured by Allied forces. It became a *Land* of the Federal Republic with its 1938 boundaries. A constitution (in force 1 July 1952) provided for a House of Burgesses as the sovereign power, with an executive Senate.

HESSE (also called HESSEN)

The *Land* consists of the former states of Hesse-Darmstadt and Hesse-Kassel, and Nassau.

Hesse-Darmstadt was ruled by the Landgrave Louis X from 1790. He became grand duke in 1806 with absolute power, having dismissed the parliament in 1803. However, he granted a constitution and bicameral parliament in 1820.

Hesse-Darmstadt lost land to Prussia in the Seven Weeks' War of 1866, but retained its independence, both then and as a state of the German Empire after 1871. In 1918 the grand duke abdicated, and the territory became a state of the German Republic. In 1945 Allied forces occupied it; areas west of the Rhine were incorporated into the new *Land* of Rhineland-Palatinate, areas east of the Rhine became part of the *Land* of Greater Hesse.

Hesse-Kassel was ruled by the Landgrave William IX from 1785 until he became Elector in 1805. In 1807 the Electorate was absorbed into the Kingdom of Westphalia (a Napoleonic creation), becoming independent again in 1815 as a state of the German Confederation. In 1831 a constitution and parliament were granted, but the Electors remained strongly conservative.

In 1866 the Diet approved alliance with Prussia against Austria; the Elector nevertheless supported Austria. He was defeated by the Prussians and exiled, and Hesse-Kassel was annexed to Prussia. In 1867 it was combined with Frankfurt and some areas taken from Nassau and Hesse-Darmstadt to form a Prussian province (Hesse-Nassau).

Nassau had been divided into northern and southern states since the 13th century. In 1801 Nassau west of the Rhine passed to France; Napoleon also took the northern state in 1806. The remnant of the southern states allied in 1803, and three years later they became a duchy. In 1866 the duke supported Austria against Prussia, and the duchy was annexed by Prussia as a result.

In 1944 the Prussian province of Hesse-Nassau was split in two: Nassau, and Electoral Hesse, also called Kurhessen. The following year these were combined with Hesse-Darmstadt as the *Land* of Greater Hesse, which became known as Hesse. Its constitution was approved by referendum in Dec. 1946.

LOWER SAXONY

The *Land* consists of the former state of Hanover, with Oldenburg, Schaumburg-Lippe and Brunswick. It does not include the cities of Bremen *(q.v.)* or Bremerhaven.

Oldenburg, Danish from 1667, passed to the bishopric of Lübeck in 1773; the Holy Roman Emperor made it a duchy in 1777. As a small state of the Confederation after 1815, it supported Prussia, becoming a member of the Prussian Zollverein (1853) and North German Confederation (1867). The grand duke abdicated in 1918 and was replaced by an elected government.

Schaumburg-Lippe was a very small sovereign principality. As such it became a member of the Confederation of the Rhine in 1807 and of the German Confederation in 1815. Surrounded by Prussian territory, it also joined the Prussian-led North German Confederation in 1866. Part of the Empire until 1918, it then became a state of the new republic.

Brunswick, a small duchy, was taken into the Kingdom of Westphalia by Napoleon in 1806 but restored to independence in 1814. In 1830 the duke, Charles II, was forced into exile and replaced in 1831 by his more liberal brother, William. The succession passed to a Hanoverian claimant in 1913, but the duchy ended in 1918 with the Empire.

As a state of the republican Germany, Brunswick was greatly reduced under the Third Reich. Its boundaries were restored by the British occupation forces in 1945.

Hanover was an autonomous Electorate of the Holy Roman Empire, whose rulers were also kings of Great Britain from 1714 until 1837. After 1762 they ruled almost entirely from England. After Napoleonic invasions Hanover was restored in 1815. A constitution of 1819 made no radical change, and had to be followed by more liberal versions in 1833 and 1848.

Prussia annexed Hanover, despite its proclaimed neutrality, in 1866; it remained a Prussian province until 1946.

On 1 Nov. 1946 all four states were combined by the British military administration to form the *Land* of Lower Saxony.

NORTH RHINE-WESTPHALIA

Historical Westphalia consisted of many small political units, most of them absorbed by Prussia and Hanover before 1800. In 1807 Napoleon created a Kingdom of Westphalia for his brother Joseph. This included Hesse-Kassel, but was formed mainly from the Prussian and Hanoverian lands between the rivers Elbe and Weser.

In 1815 the kingdom ended with Napoleon's defeat. Most of the area was given to Prussia, with the small principalities of Lippe and Waldeck surviving as independent states. Both joined the North German Confederation in 1867. Lippe remained autonomous after the end of the Empire in 1918; Waldeck was absorbed into Prussia in 1929.

In 1946 the occupying forces combined Lippe with most of the

Prussian province of Westphalia to form the *Land* of North Rhine-Westphalia. On 1 March 1947 the allied Control Council formally abolished Prussia.

RHINELAND PALATINATE

The *Land* was formed from the Rhenish Palatinate and the Rhine valley areas of Prussia, Hesse-Darmstadt, Hesse-Kassel and Bavaria.

The Palatinate was ruled, from 1214, by the Bavarian house of Wittelsbach; its capital was Heidelberg. In 1797 its land west of the Rhine was taken into France, and Napoleon divided the eastern land between Baden and Hesse. In 1815 the land taken by France was restored to Germany and allotted to Bavaria. The area and its neighbours formed the strategically-important Bavarian Circle of the Rhine.

The rule of the Wittelsbachs ended in 1918 but the Palatinate remained part of Bavaria until the American occupying forces detached it in 1946.

The new *Land*, incorporating the Palatinate and other territory, received its constitution in April 1947 and confirmed it by referendum in May 1947.

SAARLAND

Long disputed between Germany and France, the area was occupied by France in 1792. Most was allotted to Prussia at the close of the Napoleonic wars in 1815.

In 1870 Prussia defeated France and when, in 1871, the German Empire was founded under Prussian leadership, it was able to incorporate Lorraine. This part of France was the Saar territory's western neighbour, so the Saar was no longer a vulnerable boundary state; it began to develop industrially, exploiting Lorraine coal and iron.

In 1919 the League of Nations took control of the Saar until a plebiscite of 1935 favoured return to Germany. In 1945 there was a French occupation, and in 1947 the Saar was made an international area, but in economic union with France. In 1954 France and Germany agreed that the Saar should be a separate and autonomous state, under an independent commissioner. This was rejected by referendum, and France agreed to return Saarland to Germany; it became a *Land* of the Federal Republic in June 1959.

SCHLESWIG-HOLSTEIN

The *Land* is formed from two states formerly contested between Germany and Denmark.

Schleswig was a Danish dependency ruled since 1474 by the King of Denmark as Duke of Schleswig. He also ruled Holstein, its southern neighbour, as Duke of Holstein, but he did so recognizing that it was a fief of the Holy Roman Empire. As such, Holstein joined the German Confederation which replaced the Empire in 1815.

Disputes between Denmark and the powerful German states were accompanied by rising national feeling in the duchies, where the population was part-Danish and part-German. There was war in 1848–50 and in 1864, when Denmark surrendered its claims to Prussia and Austria. Following her defeat of Austria in 1866 Prussia annexed both duchies.

North Schleswig (predominantly Danish) was awarded to Denmark in 1920. Prussian Holstein and south Schleswig became the present *Land* in 1946. The first parliament was elected in 1947.

GHANA

By the 17th century, several strong chiefdoms and warrior states, notably the powerful Ashanti state, ruled in the area. The Ashanti state was initially strengthened through its collaboration with the slave trade, but by 1874 it had been conquered by Britain and made a colony. The hinterland became a protectorate in 1901. A period of indirect British rule began, but was challenged after the Second World War by Kwame Nkrumah and his Convention People's Party (CPP) formed in 1949. The state of Ghana came into existence on 6 March 1957 when the former Colony of the Gold Coast and the Trusteeship Territory of Togoland attained Dominion status. In Dec. 1956 the UN General Assembly approved the termination of British administration in Togoland and the eventual union of Togoland with the Gold Coast.

The country was declared a Republic within the Commonwealth on 1 July 1960 with Nkrumah as the first president. On 24 Feb. 1966 this régime was overthrown in a military *coup* and ruled by the National Liberation Council until 1 Oct. 1969 when the military handed over power to a civilian régime under a new constitution. Dr K. A. Busia was the prime minister of the Second Republic. On 13 Jan. 1972 the armed forces and police took over power again from the civilian régime in a *coup*.

In Oct. 1975 the National Redemption Council was subordinated to a Supreme Military Council (SMC). In 1979 the SMC was toppled in a *coup* led by Flight-Lieut. J. Rawlings. The new government permitted elections already scheduled and these resulted in a victory for Dr Hilla Limann and his People's National Party. However, on 31 Dec. 1981 another *coup* led by Flight-Lieut. Rawlings dismissed the government and parliament, suspended the constitution and established a Provisional National Defence Council (PNDC) to exercise all government powers. People's Defence Committees were set up as a form of local government.

Although in 1984 Rawlings indicated that a future representative government would be organized differently, by 1988 government still operated through the committees. There have been several attempted *coups* against Rawlings, and economic problems bedevil his government.

Further Reading

Fage, J., *Ghana: A Historical Interpretation*. Wisconsin Univ. Press, 1959

GIBRALTAR

The Rock of Gibraltar was settled by Moors in 711 who named it after their chief (Tariq ibn-Ziyad) Jebel Tariq, 'the Mountain of Tarik'. In 1462 it was taken from the Moors by the Spaniards. It was captured by Admiral Sir George Rooke on 24 July 1704 and ceded to Great Britain by the Treaty of Utrecht (1713). The cession was confirmed by the treaties of Paris (1763) and Versailles (1783). Since the 18th century Gibraltar has been a British naval base. The British military garrison and naval dockyard, established during the Second World War, has continued to be an important part of Gibraltar's economy, and naval operations of NATO often use the port facilities.

On 10 Sept. 1967, in pursuance of a UN resolution on the decolonization of Gibraltar, a referendum was held in Gibraltar in order to ascertain whether the people of Gibraltar wished to retain their link with Britain or to pass under Spanish sovereignty. Out of a total electorate of 12,762, 12,138 voted to retain the British connexion, while 44 voted for Spain.

On 15 Dec. 1982 the border between Gibraltar and Spain was reopened for Spaniards and Gibraltarian pedestrians who are residents of Gibraltar. The border had been closed by Spain in June 1969. Following an agreement signed in Brussels in Nov. 1984 the border was fully opened on 5 Feb. 1985.

Further Reading
Dennis, P., *Gibraltar*. Newton Abbot, 1977

GREECE

Greece gained independence from the Ottoman Empire between 1821–29, and by the Protocol of London of 3 Feb. 1830 was declared a kingdom under the protection of Great Britain, France and Russia. Many Greeks were left outside the new state and the cause of the union of all Greeks was championed by Otto I, a Bavarian who was enthroned on 18 Jan. 1833. After his overthrow on 23 Oct. 1862, a Danish prince was elected George I, King of the Hellenes, in 1863. The 1844 constitution was replaced by one based on popular sovereignty in 1864. Under the premier Venezelos a programme of domestic renewal was launched after 1910, including important land reforms in 1917. In 1864 Great Britain had ceded the Ionian Islands; in 1881 Thessaly and part of Epirus had been taken. Under Venezelos, Greece's area increased by 70%, the population growing from 2·8m. to 4·8m. after the Treaty of Bucharest (1913) which recognized Greek sovereignty over Crete.

King Constantine who succeeded on his father's assassination on 18 March 1913 opted for neutrality in the First World War, while Venezelos favoured the Entente powers. This split or National Schism led to British and French intervention which deposed Constantine on 11 June 1917. When his son Alexander died on 25 Oct. 1920, he returned on 19 Dec. and reigned until 27 Sept. 1922. He was forced to abdicate by a *coup* after defeat by Turkey and the loss of Smyrna. The Treaty of Lausanne (1923) recognized this as Turkish with Eastern Thrace and the islands Imvros and Tenedos, all of which had been ceded to Greece by the 1920 Treaty of Sevres.

An exchange of Christian and Moslem populations followed. Over 1m. immigrants caused social problems, despite an effective peasant settlement in the countryside. The newcomers contributed strongly to the fall of the monarchy in a plebiscite on 13 April 1924. George II was restored after a new plebiscite on 25 Nov. 1935.

The authoritarian Metaxas, premier since 1937, was unable to preserve neutrality after the Italian ultimatum of 28 Oct. 1940. The successful resistance of the Greek army forced the Germans to aid Italy on 6 April 1941. Surrender followed on 20 April and Athens was occupied on 27 April. The harsh occupation lasted till 15 Oct. 1944.

The popular front EAM and its military wing ELAS, both dominated by the communists, took a leading part in resistance to the Germans. The king had moved in April 1941 to Crete, then to Cairo and London. On 30 Dec. 1944 he appointed Archbishop Damaskinos as regent before, backed by Britain and approved in a plebiscite, he returned on 28 Sept. 1946. On his death on 1 April 1947 he was succeeded by his brother Paul. A conflict with ELAS developed into a civil war in 1946–47, which made refugees of 10% of the population. Britain handed responsibility to the USA which pledged support against the communists who received only short-lived Yugoslav aid. Peace came after 1949.

The adoption, under US pressure, of a simple majority system rather than proportional representation, and the growing industrialization of the economy brought stability, especially after 1955 under the pro-western Karamanlis. The late 1950s saw the emergence of the Left, capitalizing on the movement for union with Cyprus and unease over NATO membership (1952). On 9 Aug. 1954 Greece, Turkey and Yugoslavia signed a 20-year treaty of friendship and mutual aid.

The election of 1963, based on proportional representation, undermined the position of the Right, and led to conflict with the new king Constantine, who succeeded his father Paul on 6 March 1964. A military *coup* on 21 April 1967, with fear of communism its stated reason, led to the departure the following year of the king after an unsuccessful counter-*coup*. The authoritarian rule of the 'Colonels' was headed by George Papadopoulos, prime minister, regent (1972) and president after the republic was declared on 29 July 1973. The régime was overthrown in a bloodless *coup* by Gen. Ghizikis on 25 Nov. 1973.

Inflation and the failure to defeat President Makarios of Cyprus or to prevent the Turkish invasion of the island led to the collapse of the military dictatorship on 23 July 1974. Karamanlis was recalled from exile to form a civilian government of national unity. On 17 Nov. 1974 he and his New Democracy Party won a large majority. The monarchy was abolished by a referendum on 8 Dec. 1974.

Hostility to the USA grew, especially as it was believed that America favoured Turkey, with whom conflicts persisted. Papandreou's socialist PASOK party won the election in 1981, the year in which Greece became the tenth member of the EEC. PASOK then moderated its hostility to the EEC and to NATO and found the economic recession made its economic reforms difficult. However, it won a second election in June 1985.

Further Reading

Clogg, R., *A Short History of Modern Greece*. CUP, 2nd ed., 1986
Woodhouse, C. M., *The Struggle for Greece, 1941–1949*. London, 1976.—*Karamanlis: The Restorer of Greek Democracy*. OUP, 1982

GRENADA

Grenada was discovered by Columbus in 1493. Colonized by the French, the island became a British possession by treaty in 1763. Under the West Indies Act of 1967 Grenada became an Associated State with internal self-government. It became an independent nation within the Commonwealth on 7 Feb. 1974.

On 13 March 1979 Sir Eric Gairy, the prime minister, was ousted in a *coup* led by Maurice Bishop, leader of the left-wing New Jewel Movement. The policy pursued by Bishop's government provoked concern in the USA that Grenada was becoming allied with the USSR and Cuba.

On 19 Oct. 1983 the army took control of the country following a power struggle between the prime minister and Bernard Coard, his deputy. Bishop was imprisoned, then freed by his supporters, and finally executed. A Revolutionary Military Council was established. At the request of a group of Caribbean countries, Grenada was invaded by US-led forces on 24–28 Oct. and the *coup* leaders were defeated.

At the General Election held in 1984 Herbert Blaize and the New National Party (a coalition of parties) were elected to power. In 1985 the last of the US-led forces evacuated the island.

Further Reading
Page, A., Sutton, P., and Thorndike, T., *Grenada and Invasion*. London, 1984

GUATEMALA

The remarkable Mayan civilization flourished in the area now known as Guatemala from 2500 BC until 1000 AD. Their decendants were subjugated by the conquistadores from 1523. From 1524 until 1821 Guatemala was part of a Spanish captaincy-general, comprising the whole of Central America. It became independent in 1821 and formed part of the Confederation of Central America from 1823 to 1839 when Rafael Carrera dissolved the Confederation.

Since then it has had a turbulent political history with periods of presidential dictatorship, democracy and military dictatorship. Boundary disputes with El Salvador, Honduras and Belize (formerly British Honduras) have caused some intermittent fighting.

The economic crisis of the 1930s brought the right-wing dictator Jorge Ubico to power. His overthrow by a revolution in 1944 opened a decade of rising left-wing activity which alarmed the USA. In 1954 the leftist régime of Jacob Arbenz Guzmán was overthrown by a CIA-supported *coup*. A series of right-wing governments failed to produce stability and since 1966 the toll in human life and the violation of human rights has been severe and caused thousands of refugees to flee to Mexico. Amnesty International estimate that over 50,000 people were killed in the 1970s.

On 23 March 1982, ignoring a presidential election of the same month, a junta consisting of Brig.-Gen. Efrain Ríos Montt and other army officers took part in a bloodless *coup*. Gen. Ríos Montt later became president. There was a demand for constitutional rule, especially because the president was using relatively junior army officers as his advisers. Consequently a further *coup* on 8 Aug. 1983 removed Montt from the presidency. Maj.-Gen. Oscar Humberto Mejia Victores became head of state. Elections to a National Constituent Assembly were held on 1 July 1984, and a new constitution was promulgated in May 1985. Amidst violence and assassinations, the presidential election was won by Marco Vinicio Cerezo Arévalo. On 14 Jan. 1986 Cerezo's civilian government was installed – the first for 16 years and only the second since 1954.

Further Reading

Plant, R., *Guatemala: Unnatural Disaster*. London, 1978

GUINEA

Present-day Guinea was historically a subordinate part of the broader Ghanain empire in the 10th and 11th centuries and the Malinke empire (Mali-based) until the 16th century. A powerful feudal state of Guinea's Fulani people in the early 18th century resisted intrusions by both the French and the Muslim states to the north east.

In 1888 Guinea became a French protectorate, and in 1893 a colony. It became a constituent territory of French West Africa in 1904. Forced labour and other colonial depredations ensued, although a form of representation was introduced in 1946. The independent Republic of Guinea was proclaimed on 2 Oct. 1958, after the territory of French Guinea had decided at the referendum of 28 Sept. to leave the French community rather than being self-governing within it. Ahmed Sékou Touré became the first president of the new republic. It became a single-party state. There were regular fears of possible *coups* and of interference from abroad. Ties with France were broken in 1965 and only restored in 1976. For a time Guinea was isolated, but in 1975 it joined its African neighbours in the Economic Community of West African States. Touré's strong measures to maintain his rule provoked riots in 1977. In 1977 and 1978, when a more liberal government policy was pursued, Touré spoke of his desire to co-operate with the West.

In 1980 Touré was elected for the fourth time for a seven-year term as president, but he died in 1984 and the armed forces staged a *coup* and dissolved the National Assembly and the *Parti démocratique de Guinée*. Col. Lansana Conté was appointed as head of a military committee. Many exiles returned to the country, political prisoners were released and former politicians were brought to trial. After an attempted *coup* in 1985, Conté tightened his control.

Further Reading

Rivière, C., *Guinea: The Mobilization of a People*. Cornell Univ. Press, 1977

GUINEA-BISSAU

The area began to be settled with the break up of the ancient Ghanaian and Mali empires. The Portuguese explorer Nuno Tristão visited the coast in 1446. Portugal remained the major influence in the area and in the 19th century established its rule on the coast; however, Portuguese rule was not extended into the interior until later, and met African resistance well into the 20th century. Portuguese Guinea came under Cape Verde until 1879 when it became a separate colony. Portuguese Guinea became an Overseas Territory in 1951.

Amilcar Cabral, one of the many Cape Verdians working in government service in Portuguese Guinea, in 1956 joined other nationalists to form the *Partido Africano da Independencia da Guiné e do Cabo Verde* (PAIGC). From 1963 this party waged a successful guerrilla war against Portuguese rule in Guinea, Guineans and Cape Verdians working together and by 1973 evicting the Portuguese from much of the interior where the PAIGC set up its own administration. On 20 Jan. 1973 Cabral was murdered, but elections to a national assembly had already been held in liberated areas and on 23–24 Sept. 1973 the assembly proclaimed the independence of Guinea-Bissau. A Council of State was chosen with Luis Cabral, brother of Amilcar, as chairman.

In 1974, after the Portuguese revolution, Portugal abandoned the struggle to keep Guinea-Bissau, and independence was formally recognized on 10 Sept. 1974. In 1975 Cape Verde also became independent under the rule of the PAIGC, but the secretary-general of the party, President Pereira of Cape Verde, did not in fact have authority over Guinea-Bissau and the two countries remained separate sovereign states.

On 14 Nov. 1980 Luis Cabral was overthrown in a *coup d'état* in part inspired by resentment in Guinea-Bissau over the privileges enjoyed by Cape Verdians, and Guineans obtained a more prominent rôle under the new government of Major João Bernardo Vieira, previously prime minister.

On 16 May 1984 a new constitution was approved which retained Marxist principles. But in Nov. 1986 the PAIGC Congress approved a return to private enterprises in an attempt to solve critical economic problems.

Further Reading
Rudebeck, L., *Guinea-Bissau: A Study of Political Mobilization*. Uppsala, 1974

GUYANA

The name Guyana derives from the name given to the land by its original American Indian inhabitants. The territory, including the counties of Demerara, Essequibo and Berbice, named from the three local rivers, was first partially settled by the Dutch West India Company between 1616 and 1621. The Dutch retained their hold on the area until 1796 when it was captured by the British. It was finally ceded to Britain in 1814 at the end of the Napoleonic War; in 1831 it became a colony with the name British Guiana.

To work the sugar plantations African slaves were transported here in the 18th century and East Indian and Chinese indentured labourers in the 19th century. From 1950 the anti-colonial struggle was spearheaded by the Peoples Progressive Party led by Cheddi Jagar and Faber Burnham. But after its victory with a left-wing programme in the elections of 1953, the British Government suspended the constitution. By the time internal autonomy was again granted in 1961 Burnham had split with Jagar to form the more moderate People's National Congress. After much internal conflict between the two parties Guyana became an independent member of the Commonwealth in 1966 with Burnham as the first prime minister.

On 3 Feb. 1970 Guyana became the world's first Co-operative Republic, with Arthur Chung as its first non-executive president. In Oct. 1980 the prime minister, Forbes Burnham, declared himself the executive-president. Two months later his party, the PNC (People's National Congress), won a large majority of votes at the election for the National Assembly; Forbes Burnham was then declared duly elected as president. When he died in Aug. 1985 his prime minister, Desmond Hoyte, succeeded as president. Like his predecessor, Hoyte was declared duly elected when the PNC gained a large majority at the general election for the National Assembly in Dec. 1985.

Further Reading
Spinner, T. J., *A Political and Social History of Guyana, 1945–83*. Epping, 1985

HAITI

Haiti occupies the western third of the large island of Hispaniola which was discovered by Christopher Columbus in 1492. The Spanish colony was ceded to France in 1697 and became her most prosperous colony. After the extirpation of the Indians by the Spaniards (by 1533) large numbers of African slaves were imported whose descendants now populate the country. Following the French Revolution the slaves obtained their liberation through the most famous of all slave rebellions. But subsequently Napoleon sent his brother-in-law, Gen. Leclerc, to restore French authority and reimpose slavery. Toussaint L'Ouverture, the leader of the slaves who had been appointed a French general and governor, was kidnapped and sent to France, where he died in gaol. However, the reckless courage of the Negro troops and the ravages of yellow fever forced the French to evacuate the island and surrender to the blockading British squadron.

The country declared its independence on 1 Jan. 1804, and its successful leader, Gen. Jean-Jacques Dessalines, proclaimed himself Emperor of the newly-named Haiti. After the assassination of Dessalines (1806) a separate régime was set up in the north under Henri Christophe, a Negro general who in 1811 had himself proclaimed King Henry. In the south and west a republic was constituted, with the mulatto Alexander Pétion as its first president. Pétion died in 1818 and was succeeded by Jean-Pierre Boyer, under whom the country became reunited after Henry had committed suicide in 1820. From 1822 to 1844 Haiti and the eastern part of the island (later the Dominican Republic) were united. After one more monarchical interlude, under the Emperor Faustin (1847–59), Haiti has been a republic. From 1915 to 1934 Haiti was under United States occupation.

Following a military *coup* in 1950, and subsequent uprisings, Dr François Duvalier was elected president on 22 Oct. 1957 and subsequently had himself declared president for life in 1964. After maintaining a régime of considerable barbarity, he died on 21 April 1971 and was succeeded as president for life by his son, Jean-Claude Duvalier who fled the country on 7 Feb. 1986. An interim military junta suspended presidential elections in 1987 while they were actually taking place. It permitted an election, widely regarded as a fraud, in 1988 and Prof. Leslie Manigat emerged as president.

Further Reading
Lundahl, M., *The Haitian Economy: Man, Land and Markets*. London, 1983

HONDURAS

In pre-Columbian times the area which is now Honduras was part of the Mayan empire. Discovered by Columbus in 1502, Honduras was ruled by Spain as part of the Captain-Generalcy of Guatemala. In 1821 Honduras gained its independence from Spain, and from 1823 was part of the Central American Federation. On 5 Nov. 1838 the country declared itself an independent sovereign state, free from the Federation. Political instability became the rule punctuated by a period of more serious administration from 1876 to 1891. The instability, with one period of US military occupation, continued until 1933. From 1933 to 1949 Gen. Tiburcio Carias Andino ruled as a dictator. There followed a disturbed period of presidential elections, depositions and military juntas. Dr Ramón Ernesto Cruz Velés was elected president in 1971, but a *coup* in 1972 led to his being superseded by Gen. López Arellano who ruled by decree until 1975 when he too was ousted by army officers in favour of Col. Melgar Castro. In 1978 a military junta took control, with the commander of the army, Gen. Policarpo Paz Garcia nominated as head of state.

The end of military rule seemed to come in 1981 when a general election gave victory to the more liberal and non-military party, PLH *(Partido Liberal de Honduras)*. The party's leader, Dr Roberto Svazo Cordova, became president. Considerable power, however, remained with the armed forces led by their commander-in-chief, Gen. Gustavo Alvarez. The armed forces became more free from government control, fought the left-wing guerrillas, and also seemed to be responsible for the disappearance of some of their political opponents.

In 1984 junior army officers forced Gen. Alvarez and other senior officers into exile, and Gen. Walter Lopez Reyes took over as commander-in-chief. There followed a period of less friendly relations with the USA and increasingly poor relations with Nicaragua since the anti Sandinista (contra) rebels maintain bases in Honduras.

The PLH narrowly won the presidential election held in Nov. 1985 and José Azcona Hoyo was sworn in as president on 27 Jan. 1986.

Further Reading
Morris, J. A., *Honduras: Caudillo Politics and Military Rulers*. Boulder, 1984

HONG KONG

Hong Kong Island and the southern tip of the Kowloon peninsula were ceded by China to Britain after the first and second Anglo-Chinese Wars respectively by the Treaty of Nanking 1842 and the Convention of Peking 1860. Northern Kowloon was leased to Britain for 99 years by China in 1898. Since then, Hong Kong has been under British administration, except from Dec. 1941 to Aug. 1945 during the Japanese occupation.

Hong Kong is administered by the Hong Kong government headed by the British Governor who is appointed by the Queen and advised by a series of Councils dealing with foreign, legislative, executive and urban affairs.

Talks began in Sept. 1982 between Britain and China over the future of Hong Kong after the lease expiry in 1997. On 19 Dec. 1984, the 2 countries signed a joint declaration whereby China would recover sovereignty over Hong Kong (including Hong Kong Island, Kowloon and the New Territories) from 1 July 1997 and establish it as a Special Administrative Region where the existing social and economic systems, and the present life-style, would remain unchanged for another 50 years.

Further Reading

Endacott, G. B., *A History of Hong Kong*. 2nd ed. OUP, 1973

HUNGARY

The Hungarians' name for themselves is 'Magyars'; 'Hungarian' derives from the Turkic name ('On ogur', i.e. ten arrows) of the tribal federation on the Don which Árpád and his horde left in order to settle the sparsely inhabited middle Danubian basin in 896, impelled by Pecheneg pressure from the east and at the request for military assistance by the Carolingian emperor in the west. Moravia was destroyed, Slovakia engulfed. The horde spread terror by its forays, but was pacified by defeat at the hands of the Germans at Augsburg in 955. In 1000 Stephen adopted Roman Catholicism and received a crown from the Pope. Stephen replaced the tribal structure with a system of counties administered by royal officials. As nomadism gave way to agriculture the mass of the population were attached to the soil, under a large class of nobility descended from the original conquerors and entitled to appear in general assembly. Transylvania was infiltrated by the Hungarians and imported colonies of Germans in the 11th century; King Kálmán acquired the Croatian throne in 1102. In 1222 an extravagant king was constrained to grant the Golden Bull, to which every king thereafter had to swear, granting the gentry certain rights against the royal prerogative.

In 1241 a Mongol horde invaded but did not stay, leaving massive devastation. In 1301 Árpád's line died out. Henceforth with 2 exceptions the throne was held by foreigners, sometimes holding other thrones simultaneously. The Angevin king, Lájos the Great (1342–82) was also king of Poland; under him Hungary attained a golden age of prosperity, civilization and international significance.

In the 15th century the expansionist Ottoman empire reached the southern borders of Hungary. This first incursion was repelled by János Hunyádi. His son Matthias Corvinus was elected king in 1458 and he ruled as an enlightened renaissance despot. In 1526 the Turks again advanced on the Hungarians who were defeated at the battle of Mohács and their king killed. Southern and central Hungary were annexed and turned into a desert. The western rump came under Habsburg rule, which was extended to most of Hungary with the expulsion of the Turks in 1699. A national rising in 1703 under Ferenc Rákoczi forced the crown to come to terms: Emperor Charles IV restored the constitution, and the Hungarian assembly recognized Charles's heirs' title to the Hungarian throne. The Habsburgs overtly or covertly imposed a centralizing Germanizing régime upon a Hungary economically stagnating under protective tariffs designed to restrict industrialization to Austria. Reform movements arose, linked with the cultural national revivalism of the early 19th century. The magnate Count Széchenyi argued for economic efficiency; he was overtaken by the radical democracy of the nationalist Lájos Kossuth, who set up a breakaway government in Debrecen during the 1848 revolutionary episode. Hungarian nationalists had their own nationalities to contend with, however; disaffected Croats fought for Vienna, and the Hungarian rebellion was soon put down with Russian help. Ruthless repression followed, but Austria's military defeats in Italy (1859) and against Prussia (1866) forced the emperor to moderate his absolutism. Under the Compromise *(Ausgleich)* of 1867 a Dual Monarchy was constituted; Hungary gained internal autonomy while foreign affairs and defence became joint Austro-Hungarian responsibilities.

Hungary entered the First World War on Austria's side, but as hostilities drew to a close the ideas of Mihaly Károlyi, who stood for peace and independence, grew in popularity. After the armistice of 3 Nov. 1918 a National Council under his chairmanship proclaimed an independent republic. Political and social unrest, however, were compounded by a Romanian invasion. On 21 March 1919 Károlyi was replaced by Béla Kun's Soviet republic, a reign of red terror which antagonized most of the population. Kun fled on 4 Aug. and a counter-revolutionary government annulled all his and Károlyi's legislation and appointed Admiral Horthy as regent. Hungary was drastically reduced in size by the Peace Treaty.

The 1920s under the premiership of István Bethlen were a period of consolidation, but Bethlen was forced to resign by the collapse of wheat prices in the world depression. Hungary's desire to revise the Versailles peace settlements brought her naturally into alignment with Germany in the 1930s, and this was reinforced by her growing economic dependence on Germany. In 1940 Hungary adhered to the Tripartite pact, and in June 1941 sent a force to join the German invaders of the Soviet Union. But pro-German sentiment was never wholehearted until Hitler occupied the country in March 1944. In Oct. Horthy was forced to abdicate in favour of a fascist 'Arrow Cross' government, but by then Soviet forces were well inside the frontiers.

The 4 democratic parties permitted by the Soviets formed a provisional government at Debrecen in Dec. 1944 which declared war on Germany and signed an armistice with the Allies. At the elections of Nov. 1945 the Communists polled only 17% of the vote; their way to power was to lie in their leader Rákosi's 'salami tactics' of divide and purge, backed up by their acquisition of key ministries under Soviet pressure. In Feb. 1949 Catholic opposition was weakened by the arrest of Cardinal Mindszenty, and all political parties were united in a People's Front whose single list of candidates gained 96% of the vote at the May 1949 elections and a Soviet-type constitution was adopted in Aug. Rákosi carried out a drastic purge of 'Titoists' and embarked on a programme of such ruthless collectivization and top-heavy industrialization that the post-Stalin Soviet leadership removed him from the premiership. As party leader, however, he intrigued against his successor Imre Nagy's more liberal 'new course', and took his place again in April 1955. Rákosi resigned the party leadership in July 1956, but popular discontent continued. On 23 Oct. the attempted suppression of a student demonstration sparked off a 13-day revolution. Nagy became prime minister and János Kádár party leader. Nagy declared Hungary's neutrality and withdrawal from the Warsaw pact. After some hesitation the Soviet army crushed the revolt on 4 Nov. and installed Kádár in power. Nagy was arrested and later executed; the gains of the uprising were harshly suppressed.

In the 1960s Kádár launched an 'alliance policy' to bring non-party people into administrative life; economic liberalization followed with the 'New Economic Mechanism' of 1968.

Further Reading

Ignotus, P., *Hungary*. London, 1972

ICELAND

It is possible that Mediterranean seafarers of the classical world knew of the existence of Iceland, but the earliest settlements on the island seem to be those of Irish hermits dating from the 9th century AD. These hermits are refuted to have fled upon the arrival of the pagan Norwegians (Vikings).

The first Norwegian settlement dates from 874 AD. By 930 the Icelandic Commonwealth had been formed with its *Althing* (parliament). Christianity arrived in the 10th century and by 1000 the entire country was Christian in faith. Norway attempted to control Iceland from the 10th century onwards and when internal difficulties resulted in Icelandic civil war the Icelandic nobles accepted Norwegian sovereignty. By the 'Old Treaty' of 1263 the country recognized the rule of the King of Norway; and in 1381 Iceland, along with Norway, came under the rule of the Danish kings. When in 1814 Norway was separated from Denmark, Iceland remained under the rule of the kings of Denmark. Since 1 Dec. 1918 Iceland has been acknowledged as a sovereign state, being united with Denmark only through the common sovereign. It was proclaimed an independent republic on 17 June 1944 after deciding by a referendum to sever all ties with the Danish Crown.

Further Reading

Magnússon, S. A., *Northern Sphinx: Iceland and the Icelanders from the Settlement to the Present*. London, 1977

INDIA

The Moghul emperors held power over most of north India and the Deccan (the central plateau of the Indian peninsula) by 1712, when the emperor Bahadur died and his sons weakened the dynasty by disputing the succession.

The power of the states within the empire then revived. The Mahratta rulers of central and western India were led by Shahu; it was he who created the hereditary office of chief minister *(peshwa)* and after his death in 1749 the *peshwas* became the effective rulers of the Mahratta states. In the Deccan, the Moghuls' viceroy of Hyderabad declared himself independent, becoming the founder of the Moslem dynasty of Nizams of Hyderabad. In the north-west in 1739 the Moghuls lost the Punjab to the Persians (who later lost it to the Afghans).

South of Hyderabad were the independent Hindu states of Mysore and Travancore, a number of small principalities and the territory around Madras where the British East India Company was the most powerful force. The Company had maintained a factory at Madras since 1639 and had since established other bases at Bombay (1668) and at Calcutta in Bengal.

In 1740 the Moghul governor *(nawab)* of Bengal rebelled successfully. In 1756, alarmed at the degree to which the Company (anticipating trouble with the French) was arming itself, he attacked and subdued the British base at Calcutta. In 1757 a large British force under Clive retaliated by defeating the Nawab at Plassey. The British were then able to install their own Nawab. Their hold on Bengal and Madras was soon complete and they defeated the French who presented the only serious European challenge. The East India Company thus became the rising power in India at the very time when Moghul power was in decline. Outside the remaining Moghul supremacy the other powers were the Mahrattas, the Punjab Sikhs (nominally under Afghan rule), Hyderabad and Mysore.

Mysore was a Hindu state until 1764 when the Moslem commander Hyder Ali usurped the throne. Having allied themselves to the Nizam of Hyderabad in 1766, the British attacked Mysore in 1767; war was intermittent until 1799 when Hyder Ali's successor Tippoo was defeated and the Hindu dynasty restored.

In 1775 a confederacy of Mahratta chiefs, led by the chief of Pune, united against the British power spreading from Bombay and were successful. Mahadaji Sindhia emerged from the war as the leader of a Mahratta empire, to which he added the former Moghul fief of Rajputana.

In 1784 the British government imposed tighter controls on the Company by means of the India Bill.

In 1794 Mahadaji Sindhia died. His successors entered into treaty relations with the British in 1805, by which time the Moghul emperor in Delhi was under Mahratta domination. British-Mahratta relations deteriorated, however, and in 1818 the British annexed the Mahratta states and became the 'protectors' of Rajputana. In 1826 they drove the Burmese out of Assam and in 1830 they occupied Mysore.

In the north-west the Sikh ruler Ranjit Singh had driven the Afghans out of the Punjab and Kashmir by 1819. He died in 1839. Within a short time his strong state and army were highly unstable. Mutual mistrust between Sikhs and British led in 1845–46 to war, ending in British annexation of some Sikh territory. In 1848–49 a second war was fought and the whole Punjab was annexed. Nagpur and Oudh were taken in 1853 and 1856.

Since 1818 the East India Company had been the greatest power in India. Within its territory change had been rapid, and the mass of the Hindu population felt threatened by European attitudes, laws and religion. In 1857–58 there was a general rebellion, beginning with a revolt of Indian troops in the Company's army. The excesses of rebels and suppressing forces made the rebellion a national trauma for the British.

The immediate result was the India Act 1858, which transferred the Company's authority and territory to the Crown. The territory (excluding areas now forming Pakistan and Bangladesh) consisted of the Madras and Bombay presidencies; Bengal (which included Assam until 1874 when it became a separate province; the United Provinces and Oudh; the Central Provinces; the Punjab; Ajmere-Merwara; Coorg; and the Andaman Islands. The central government consisted of a viceroy and his executive, and an administrative council in England. This area under direct British rule (British *Raj*) co-existed with the independent states ruled by Indian princes; the viceroy claimed the right to interfere in the latter in emergency, and often did so.

In 1885 the Indian National Congress was founded by A. O. Hume and others, to work for more representative government. In 1892 the first Indian Councils Act added nominated Indian members to the central and provincial legislative councils.

In 1905–11 the experimental partition of Bengal into Hindu and Moslem provinces aroused violent opposition among Hindu

Bengalis. This brought to the fore the question of national identity as opposed to religious identity. In 1906 the All-India Moslem League was founded to protect Moslem interests.

From 1909 there were further constitutional reforms, but the Congress thought them insufficient and began, especially after 1917, to work specifically for independence. The India Acts (1919 and 1935) defined and then revised the forms of parliamentary government. After 1930 Mohendas Gandhi led a campaign of civil disobedience for the end of British rule; his attempts at negotiation with Britain were abortive until the Second World War.

The war increased support for the independence movement, Congress being able to claim that Britain had involved India as a combatant state without consultation. In 1940, foreseeing a Hindu-dominated independent India, the Moslem League began to press for a separate Moslem state.

In June 1947 the scheme for partition was announced, after negotiations in which Gandhi had taken part. In Aug. India became independent within the Commonwealth, as a federal union of the former British provinces and the native states. Of the latter, Hyderabad had to be incorporated by force and was later dismembered.

Partition took place (see Pakistan), with mass movement of Hindus, Moslems and Sikhs, much violence and many deaths.

In 1950 India became a republic, within the Commonwealth, with Rajendra Prasad as the first president. In 1951 the Congress leader Pandit Nehru became prime minister, establishing a Congress domination which has lasted for all but brief periods. In 1966 his daughter Indira Gandhi became prime minister. She governed by Emergency Rule from 1975 but was defeated in the 1977 election, and re-elected again in 1979. Her son, Rajiv, succeeded her after her assassination by Sikh extremists on 31 Oct. 1984.

In 1956 the States Reorganization Act created a new structure of States and Territories with boundaries based on ethnic and language divisions.

There was an unresolved border war with China in 1962. But the status of Kashmir, disputed with Pakistan, has been the principal difficulty. The war of 1965, mediated at Tashkent by the USSR in 1966, left it divided between the two states. War again broke out when in Dec. 1971 India invaded East Pakistan and helped secure the independence of Bangladesh.

The Union was augmented by the annexation of Goa (a surviving Portuguese colony) in 1961 and of Sikkim in 1975. The main threat to the Union since then has come from Sikh demands for autonomy.

Further Reading

Majumdar, R. C., Raychandhuri, H. C., and Datta, K., *An Advanced History of India*. 2nd ed. London, 1950

INDIAN STATES

ANDHRA PRADESH

The state was first created in Oct. 1953 and consisted of the Telugu-speaking areas of the then state of Madras (now Tamil Nadu). In 1956 Andhra was enlarged by adding Telugu areas of the former state of Hyderabad; there was an exchange of territory with Madras in 1960.

'Andhra' is an alternative name for 'Telingana', the historic territory of a Telugu-speaking Buddhist nation which was at its most powerful from the 12th to 16th centuries AD.

ARUNACHAL PRADESH

Before independence the North East Frontier Agency of Assam was administered for the viceroy by a political agent working through tribal groups. After independence it became the North East Frontier Tract, administered for the central government by the Governor of Assam. In 1972 the area became the Union Territory of Arunachal Pradesh; statehood was achieved in Dec. 1986.

ASSAM

A kingdom once ruled by a Burmese dynasty, Assam was invaded by Burma in the early 19th century. The British drove out the Burmese by 1826 and established a protectorate. Between 1832 and 1839 they annexed it, attaching it to Bengal for administration. Mainly a hill-tribe territory, Assam then included the present areas of Meghalaya, Mizoram, Arunachal Pradesh, the Naga Hills and the Sylhet district of Bangladesh.

Assam was detached from Bengal in 1874 and was briefly united with East Bengal in 1905–11. The Sylhet district passed to East Pakistan at Partition in 1947. The Naga Hills became part of Nagaland in 1963, Meghalaya was separated in 1970 and Mizoram in 1972.

Under British rule tea was the leading industry; it is still important but oil-extraction is now equally so.

BIHAR

Bihar was part of Bengal under British rule until 1912 when it was separated together with Orissa. The two were joined until 1936 when Bihar became a separate province. As a state of the Indian Union it was enlarged in 1956 by the addition of land from West Bengal. There are three main Bihari languages: Maithili and Magahi (in the east) and Bhojpuri (used in the west).

GOA

The state was created on 30 May 1987 from the former Union Territory of Goa, Daman and Diu (the two latter remaining a Territory).

Coastal Goa was taken by the Portuguese in 1510. During the 18th century the inland area was added. Portuguese rule continued, until ended by Indian action in Dec. 1961.

GUJARAT

The Gujarati-speaking areas of India were part of the Moghul empire, coming under Mahratta domination in the late 18th century. In 1818 areas of present Gujarat around the Gulf of Cambay were annexed by the British East India Company. The remainder consisted of a group of small principalities, notably Baroda, Rajkot, Bhavnagar and Nawanagar. British areas became part of the Bombay Presidency.

At independence, all the area now forming Gujarat became part of Bombay State except for Rajkot and Bhavnagar which formed the state of Saurashtra until incorporated in Bombay in 1956.

In 1960 Bombay State was divided and the Gujarati-speaking areas became Gujarat.

HARYANA

The state was formed in Nov. 1966 and consists of the Hindi-speaking areas of the Punjab *(q.v.)*.

HIMACHAL PRADESH

Thirty small hill states were merged to form the Territory of

Himachal Pradesh in 1948; the state of Bilaspur was added in 1954 and parts of the Punjab in 1966. The whole territory became a state in Jan. 1971.

The state is a Himalayan area of hill-tribes, rivers and forests. Its main component areas are as follows:

Chamba, a former princely state, had been dominated in turn by Moghuls and Sikhs before coming under British influence in 1848.

Bilaspur was an independent Punjabi state until it was invaded by Gurkhas in 1814; the British East India Company forces drove out the Gurkhas in 1815.

Simla district developed around the town built by the Company near Bilaspur on land reclaimed from Gurkha troops; it was the summer capital of India from 1865 until 1939.

Mandi remained a princely state until 1948.

Kangra and Kulu districts were originally Rajput areas which had become part of the British-ruled Punjab; they were incorporated into Himachal Pradesh in 1966 when the Punjab was reorganized.

JAMMU AND KASHMIR

In 1756 the Afghans took Kashmir from the Moghul emperors. In 1819 they lost it to the Sikhs of the Punjab. The Sikhs had already taken Jammu, the neighbouring state, from the Rajputs in 1780, the Rajput royal house remaining as tributary rulers. In 1820 the Sikhs rewarded the service of the Rajput prince Gulab Singh by making him Raja of Jammu; this was the beginning of the Dogra dynasty.

In 1846 the British defeated the Sikhs in war and gave Kashmir to Gulab Singh. The area, ruled successively by Moslems, Sikhs and Hindus, had a mainly Moslem population.

At Partition in 1947, Moslem Pathan tribesmen invaded. They were met by Indian troops, called in by the then Maharajah who signed the treaty of accession to the Indian Union. The accession was not accepted by Pakistan. There was conflict until 1949, in 1965–66 and again in 1971. The Simla Agreement of 1972 established an agreed line of demarcation between areas under Indian and Pakistani control.

KARNATAKA

The state was founded in 1956 as Mysore, and consisted of the former states of Mysore and Coorg, and the Kannada-speaking areas of Bombay, Hyderabad and Madras. The name Karnataka was adopted in 1973.

Mysore was a Hindu kingdom apart from a short period under Moslem rulers (1764–99) and another under a British commissioner (1831–81). As Mysore, the state acceded to the Indian Union in 1947. The Kannada-speaking areas of other states were added to it in 1953 and 1956.

Coorg was an independent Hindu state until the arrival of British influence in 1834. It became a province of British India. Coorg was added to Mysore in 1953.

KERALA

The state was created in 1956, bringing together the Malayalam-speaking areas. It includes most of the former state of Travancore-Cochin and small areas from the state of Madras.

Cochin, an exceptionally safe harbour, was an early site of European trading in India. In 1795 the British took it from the Dutch and British influence remained dominant.

Travancore was a Hindu state which became a British protectorate in 1795, having been an ally of the British East India Company for some years.

Cochin and Travancore were combined as one state in 1947, reorganized and renamed Kerala in 1956.

MADHYA PRADESH

The state was formed in 1956 to bring together the Hindi-speaking districts of the area including most of the former state of Madhya Bharat, the former states of Bhopal and Vindhya Pradesh and a former Rajput enclave, Sironj.

This was an area which the Mahrattas took from the Moghuls between 1712 and 1760. The British overcame Mahratta power in 1818 and established their own Central Provinces. Nagpur became the Provinces capital and was also the capital of Madhya Pradesh until in 1956 boundary changes transferred it to Maharashtra.

The present capital, Bhopal, was the centre of a Moslem princely state from 1723. An ally of the British against the Mahrattas, Bhopal (with neighbouring small states) became a British-protected agency in 1818. After independence Bhopal acceded to the Indian Union in 1949. The states of Madhya Bharat and Vindhya Pradesh were then formed as neighbours, and in 1956 were combined with Bhopal and Sironj and renamed Madhya Pradesh.

MAHARASHTRA

The Bombay Presidency of the East India Company began with a trading factory, made over to the Company in 1668. The Presidency expanded, overcoming the surrounding Mahratta chiefs until Mahratta power was finally conquered in 1818.

After independence Bombay State succeeded the Presidency; its area was altered in 1956 by adding Kutch and Saurashtra and the Marathi-speaking areas of Hyderabad and Madhya Pradesh, and taking away Kannada-speaking areas (which were added to Mysore).

In 1960 the Bombay Reorganization Act divided Bombay State between Gujarati and Marathi areas, the latter becoming Maharashtra.

MANIPUR

The state was ruled by an independent Raja in the 18th century, but suffered frequent attacks from Burma, its neighbour to the south and east. These persisted until the British began their conquest of Burma in 1826.

During the 19th century there was frequent internal conflict as tribal rulers fought each other. British forces intervened after 1890 and again after 1917 when Manipur was administered from Assam by a political agent.

In 1947 negotiations began with the Government of India. The agency came to an end and Manipur became a territory ruled directly by the central government. Statehood was granted in 1972.

MEGHALAYA

The state was created under the Assam Reorganization Act 1969, but it remained a state-within-a-state until full independence in 1972. Meghalaya consists of the Garo Hills and the United Khasi and Jaintia Hills districts of Assam.

MIZORAM

The Mizo Hills district was separated from Assam and made into the Union Territory of Mizoram in Jan. 1972. Long disputes between the central government and the Mizo National Front were resolved in 1985. Statehood was granted by the State of Mizoram Act of July 1986.

NAGALAND

The state was created in 1961, effective 1963. It consisted of the Naga Hills district of Assam and the Tuensang Frontier Agency.

The agency was a British-supervized tribal area on the borders of Burma. Its supervision passed to the Government of India at independence, and in 1957 Tuensang and the Naga Hills became a Centrally Administered Area, governed by the central government through the Governor of Assam.

A number of Naga leaders fought for independence until a settlement was reached with the Indian Government at the Shillong Peace Agreement of 1975.

ORISSA

Orissa was divided between Mahratta and Bengal rulers when conquered by the British East India Company, the Bengal area in 1757 and the Mahratta in 1803. The area which now forms the state then consisted of directly controlled British districts and a large number of small princely states with tributary rulers.

The British districts were administered as part of Bengal until 1912 when, together with Bihar, they were separated from Bengal to form a single province. Bihar and Orissa were separated from each other in 1936.

In 1948 a new state government took control of the whole state, including the former princely states (except Saraikella and Kharswan which were transferred to Bihar, and Mayurbhanj which was not incorporated until 1949).

PUNJAB (INDIA)

The Punjab was part of the Moghul empire in the 18th century, although the Sikhs were already becoming a powerful force. Persian, and then Afghan, conquerors were driven out by 1809 when the Sikh ruler, Ranjit Singh, signed a treaty with the British as the ruler of the whole Punjab. When Ranjit Singh died in 1839, his kingdom fell into disarray and his powerful army into turbulence. In 1845–46 and 1848–49 there was war with the British, ending in British annexation of the Punjab.

In 1937 the Punjab was made an autonomous province. In 1947 the province was partitioned. West Punjab passed to Pakistan, East Punjab to India. The latter's name was changed to Punjab (India). In 1956 Patiala and East Punjab States Union were included. In 1966 the state was divided; Punjabi-speaking areas remained intact; Hindi-speaking areas became the new state of Haryana, or were assimilated in Himachal Pradesh.

Lahore, the capital, having passed to Pakistan, it was decided to build Chandigarh as a new capital. The city serves Haryana also, although ultimately it will serve only Punjab (India).

RAJASTHAN

The state is in the largely desert area formerly known as Rajputana. The Rajput princes were tributary to the Moghul emperors when they were conquered by the Mahrattas' leader, Mahadaji Sindhia, in the 1780s. In 1818 Rajputana became a British protectorate and was recognized during British rule as a group of princely states including Jaipur, Jodhpur and Udaipur.

After independence the Rajput princes surrendered their powers and in 1950 were replaced by a single state government. In 1956 the state boundaries were altered; small areas of the former Bombay and Madhya Bharat states were added, together with the neighbouring state of Ajmer.

Ajmer had been a Moghul power base; it was taken by the Mahrattas in 1770 and annexed by the British in 1818. In 1878 it became Ajmer-Merwara, a British province, and survived as a separate unit until 1956.

SIKKIM

A small Himalayan kingdom between Nepál and Bhután, Sikkim was independent in the 1830s although in continual conflict with larger neighbours. In 1839 the British took the Darjeeling district. British political influence increased during the 19th century, as Sikkim was the smallest buffer between India and Tibet. However, Sikkim remained an independent kingdom ruled by the 14th-century Namgyal dynasty.

In 1950 a treaty was signed with the Government of India, declaring Sikkim an Indian Protectorate. Indian influence increased from then on.

Internal political unrest came to a head in 1973, and led to the granting of constitutional reforms in 1974. Agitation continued until Sikkim became a 'state associated with the Indian Union' later that year. In 1975 the king was deposed and Sikkim became an Indian state, a change approved by referendum.

TAMIL NADU

The name was adopted in 1968 by the state of Madras.

In 1611 the British established their first trading factory in the area, followed by another at Madras itself in 1639. The British Madras Presidency grew from these, defeating rival powers until British rule was firmly established there by 1800. Even then the area included enclaves of French and Danish settlement under Indian princely rule; of the latter, the small state of Pudukottai was within the area of the present Tamil Nadu.

The Presidency included most of present Andhra Pradesh and extended across the peninsula to the Malabar Coast. In 1953, as the State of Madras, it lost the Telugu-speaking areas to Andhra Pradesh. The States Reorganization Act 1956 transferred the Malabar areas to Kerala in exchange for others. In 1960 there was an exchange of territory with Andhra Pradesh.

TRIPURA

The state was an independent principality with a Hindu dynasty of Maharajahs; nominal suzerainty had been exercised by the Moghuls until the late 18th century. Tripura was of strategic importance during the conflicts between Assam, the British in Bengal, and the Burmese. With the British ascendant, their suzerainty replaced that of the Moghuls.

Tripura acceded to the Indian Union in 1949. It became a territory in 1956 and a state in 1972.

UTTAR PRADESH

The area, formerly known as Hindustan, was under Moghul rule from the 16th century until the spread of British power from Bengal in the late 18th century. The British East India Company became dominant in Oudh after 1764 and in Agra in 1803; Agra was then in Mahratta hands, having been at times the Moghul capital (the Taj Mahal is there).

In 1833 the areas of Agra and Oudh were separated from Bengal and combined as one province, the Presidency of Agra. In 1836 the new presidency was divided into North West Province (Agra) and Oudh. The Indian Mutiny began at Meerut on 10 May 1857, and was largely caused by grievances in Oudh, where British control had become complete in 1856.

In 1902 the name 'United Provinces of Agra and Oudh' came into use, shortened to 'United Provinces' in 1935.

After independence the territory was enlarged by the addition of the small states of Rampur, Banaras and Tehri-Garwhal. In 1950 the Provinces became the state of Uttar Pradesh.

WEST BENGAL

Bengal was under the overlordship of the Moghul emperor and ruled by a Moghul governor *(nawab)* who declared himself independent in 1740. The British East India Company based at Calcutta was in conflict with the *nawab* from 1756 until 1757 when British forces defeated him at Plassey and installed their own *nawab* in 1760. The French were also in Bengal; the British captured their trading settlement at Chandernagore in 1757 and in 1794, restoring it to France in 1815.

The area of British Bengal included modern Orissa and Bihar, Bangladesh and (until 1833) Uttar Pradesh. Calcutta was the capital of British India from 1772 until 1912.

The first division into East and West took place in 1905–11 and was not popular. However, at Partition in 1947 the East (Moslem) chose to join Pakistan, leaving West Bengal as an Indian frontier state and promoting a steady flow of non-Moslem Bengali immigrants from the East. In 1950 West Bengal received the former princely state of Cooch Behar and, in 1954, Chandernagore. Small areas were transferred from Bihar in 1956.

INDONESIA

In the 16th century Portuguese traders settled in some of the islands which now comprise Indonesia, but were ejected by the British, who in turn were ousted by the Dutch in 1595. From 1602 the Netherlands East India Company conquered the area and ruled until the dissolution of the Company in 1798. The Netherlands government then ruled the colony from 1816 until 1941, when it was occupied by the Japanese until 1945. On 17 Aug. 1945 an independent republic was proclaimed by Dr Sukarno and Dr Hatta, the nationalist leaders. The republic was not, however, recognized by the Netherlands with whom negotiations and fighting continued until 1949. On 27 Dec. 1949 complete and unconditional sovereignty was transferred to the Republic of the United States of Indonesia.

A settlement of the New Guinea (Irian Jaya) question was, however, delayed until 15 Aug. 1962, when through the good offices of the UN, an agreement was concluded for the transfer of the territory to Indonesia on 1 May 1963.

In 1950 the federal form of government which had sprung up in 1946–48 was abolished, and Indonesia was again made a unitary state. On 5 July 1959, by presidential decree, the constitution of 1945 was reinstated.

On 12 Jan. 1960 President Sukarno issued a decree enabling him to control and dissolve the political parties. He also set up a mass organization, the National Front, and a supreme state body called the Provisional People's Consultative Assembly. On 6 March 1960 he prorogued parliament to be reorganized on the basis of the 1945 constitution with the local administrations nominating members to the new 'Mutual Co-operation House of Representatives'.

On 11–12 March 1966 the military commanders under the leadership of Lieut.-Gen. Suharto took over executive power while leaving President Sukarno as the head of state. The Communist party, which had twice attempted to overthrow the government and had killed six generals in 1965, was at once outlawed; the National Front was dissolved in Oct. 1966. On 22 Feb. 1967 Sukarno handed over all his powers to Gen. Suharto who has been continually re-elected president at five-year intervals, the last time being 1983.

Further Reading

McDonald, H., *Suharto's Indonesia*. Univ. Press of Hawaii, 1981

IRAN

Persia from the 16th century was ruled by the Shahs as an absolute monarchy until 30 Dec. 1906, when the first constitution was granted and a national assembly established. After a *coup* in 1921 Reza Khan began his rise to power which culminated in his deposing the last Shah of the Qajar Dynasty on 31 Oct. 1925. He was declared Shah as Reza Shah Pahlavi on 12 Dec. 1925 and the country's name was changed to Iran on 21 March 1935. When in the Second World War Iran supported Germany, the Allies occupied the country and forced Reza Shah to abdicate on 16 Sept. 1941 in favour of his son, Muhammad Reza Pahlavi.

Constant political unrest arose from Iran's oil industry and it was nationalized in March 1951. This was an important part of the policy of the National Front party, whose leader, Dr Muhammad Mussadeq, became prime minister in April 1951. He was opposed by the Shah, but although ousted in 1952, quickly regained power. The Shah fled the country temporarily until Aug. 1953 when monarchists staged a *coup* which led to Mussadeq finally being deposed.

The Shah's policy, which included the redistribution of land to small farmers and the enfranchisement of women, was opposed by the Shia religious scholars who considered it to be contrary to Islamic teaching. This group was considered responsible for the assassination of the prime minister, Hassan Ali Mansur, in 1965.

Despite economic growth, the country suffered considerable unrest because of opposition to the Shah's harsh repressive measures and his extensive use of Savak, the secret police. The opposition was widespread, and that led by Ayatollah Ruhollah Khomeini, the Shia Moslem spiritual leader who had been exiled in 1965, was successful. Following intense civil unrest in Tehrán the Shah left Iran with his family on 17 Jan. 1979 (and died in Egypt on 27 July 1980). The Ayatollah Khomeini returned from exile on 1 Feb. 1979 and appointed a provisional government on 5 Feb. The Shah's government resigned and parliament dissolved itself on 11 Feb. Following a referendum in March, an Islamic Republic was proclaimed on 1 April 1979. The constitution of the Islamic Republic, approved by a national referendum in Dec. 1979, gave supreme authority to a religious leader *(wali faqih)*, a position to be held by Ayatollah Khomeini for the rest of his natural life, and thereafter to be elected by the Moslem clergy. The chief executive is the president, to which post Abulhasan Bani-Sadr was elected in Jan. 1980. Unrest followed owing to the imposition of the Ayatollah's strict Moslem principles.

In Sept. 1980 war began with Iraq with the destruction of some Iranian towns and damage to the oil installations at Abadan. The war has since involved large land battles with heavy Iranian casualties, air strikes on urban centres and attacks on international shipping in the Gulf. This last development has led several nations to send naval forces in to the area in order to ensure the safe passage of their vessels. The 'Gulf War' was still in progress in 1988, Iran rejecting all peace proposals which do not include the removal of the Iraqi leader, Saddam Hussein.

Further Reading

Zabih, S., *Iran's Revolutionary Upheaval: An Interpretive Essay.* San Francisco, 1979.—*The Mosadegh Era: Roots of the Iranian Revolution.* Chicago, 1982.—*Iran since the Revolution.* London, 1982

IRAQ

Iraq, formerly Mesopotamia, was part of the Ottoman Empire from 1534 until it was captured by British forces in 1916. Under a League of Nations mandate, administered by Britain, Amir Faisal Ibn Hussain was crowned king in 1921. On 3 Oct. 1932 Britain's mandate expired, and Iraq became an independent country. The pro-British policy was continued, and in Jan. 1943 Iraq declared war on the Axis powers.

The ruling Hashemite dynasty was overthrown by an armed *coup* led by a group of army officers on 14 July 1958. King Faisal II and his uncle, the ex-Regent the Emir Abdul Ilah, and Nuri al Said, the prime minister, were killed. A republic was established, controlled by a military-led Council of Sovereignty under Gen. Qassim. The republican régime terminated the adherence of Iraq to the Arab Federation, which Iraq and Jordan had formed in Feb. 1958.

The Kurdish minority in the north-east of Iraq rose against the Iraqi authorities in 1962 and a bitter struggle was only ended in 1975 by an agreement between the Kurdish guerrillas and the Ba'athist regime.

In 1963 Qassim was overthrown, and Gen. Abdul Salam Aref became president, with a partial return to a civilian government. In 1966 Abdul Rahman Aref succeeded his brother as president, but on 17 July 1968 a successful *coup* was mounted by the Ba'th Party and Gen. Ahmed Al Bakr became president, prime minister, and chairman of a newly established ruling 9-member Revolutionary Command Council. In July 1969 Saddam Hussein, the vice-president, became president in a peaceful transfer of power.

During the 1980s Iraq's history has been dominated by her hostile relations with Iran. In Sept. 1980 Iraq invaded Iran in a dispute over territorial rights in the Shatt al-Arab waterway, being dissatisfied with the Treaty of 1975. In 1987 the UN proposed terms for a cease-fire, these were accepted by Iraq but rejected by Iran. The Gulf War was continuing in 1988.

Further Reading

Postgate, E., *Iraq: International Relations and National Development.* London, 1983

143

IRELAND

The Act of Union became law in 1801. Ireland was to be represented in the Westminster parliament by 28 Irish peers and four bishops elected for life by the whole Irish peerage. One hundred members were to represent Ireland in the British House of Commons.

Two bills for Home Rule were introduced in parliament in 1886 and 1893, but both were defeated. Home Rule reached the statute book in 1914 but because of the First World War the Act was suspended.

In April 1916 an insurrection against British rule took place and a republic was proclaimed. The armed struggle was renewed in 1919 and continued until 1921. The independence of Ireland was re-affirmed in Jan. 1919 by the National Parliament *(Dáil Éireann)*, elected in Dec. 1918.

In 1920 an Act was passed by the British Parliament, under which separate parliaments were set up for 'Southern Ireland' (composed of 26 of the 32 Irish counties) and 'Northern Ireland' (formed from the remaining 6 counties). The Unionists of the 6 counties accepted this scheme, and a Northern Parliament was duly elected on 24 May 1921. The rest of Ireland, however, ignored the Act.

On 6 Dec. 1921 a treaty was signed between Great Britain and Ireland by which Ireland accepted dominion status subject to the right of Northern Ireland to opt out. This right was exercised, and the border between *Saorstát Éireann* (26 counties) and Northern Ireland (6 counties) was fixed in Dec. 1925 as the outcome of an agreement between Great Britain, the Irish Free State (Eire) and Northern Ireland. The agreement was ratified by the 3 parliaments.

Subsequently the constitutional links between *Saorstát Éireann* and the UK were gradually removed by the *Dáil*. The remaining formal association with the British Commonwealth by virtue of the External Relations Act 1936 was severed when the Republic of Ireland Act 1948 came into operation on 18 April 1949.

Further Reading
Hickey, D. J. and Doherty, J. E., *A Dictionary of Irish History since 1800*. Dublin, 1980

ISRAEL

The area once designated as Palestine, of which Israel forms part, was formerly part of Turkey's Ottoman Empire. During the First World War, when Turkey was allied with Germany, the Arabs under Ottoman rule rebelled and Palestine was occupied by British forces. In 1917, the British Government issued the Balfour Declaration, stating that it viewed 'with favour the establishment in Palestine of a national home for the Jewish people'. In 1922, the League of Nations, recognized 'the historical connection of the Jewish people with Palestine' and 'the grounds for reconstituting their national home in that country,' and Britain assumed a mandate over Palestine, pending the establishment there of such a national home. In accordance with the mandate, Jewish settlers were admitted to Palestine, under the direction of Zionist settlement agencies, where the population had remained almost entirely Arab. There were anti-Zionist riots in 1921 and 1929. In the 1930s the Nazi persecution of the Jews led to their escalated immigration into Palestine. The Second World War postponed further developments.

In Nov. 1947 the UN General Assembly passed a resolution calling for the establishment of a Jewish and an Arab state in Palestine. On 14 May 1948 the British Government terminated its mandate, and the Jewish leaders proclaimed the State of Israel. No independent Arab state was established in Palestine. Instead the neighbouring Arab states invaded the new Israel on 15 May 1948. The Jewish state defended itself successfully, and the ceasefire in Jan. 1949 left Israel with one-third more land than had been originally assigned by the UN. The Suez crisis of 1956 saw Israel joined with Britain and France in a tripartite attack on Egypt in an effort to topple Nasser's régime which they each regarded as inimical to their own interests in the region.

In 1967, following some years of uneasy peace, local clashes on the Israeli-Syrian border were followed by Egyptian mass concentration of forces on the borders of Israel. The UN emergency force in Gaza was expelled and a blockade of shipping to and from Israel was imposed by Egypt in the Red Sea. Israel struck out at Egypt on land and in the air on 5–9 June 1967. Jordan joined in the conflict which spread to the Syrian borders. By 11 June the Israelis had occupied the Gaza Strip and the Sinai peninsula as far as the Suez Canal in

145

Egypt, West Jordan as far as the Jordan valley and the heights east of the Sea of Galilee, including Quneitra in Syria.

A further war broke out on 6 Oct. 1973 when Egyptian and Syrian offensives were launched. Following UN Security Council resolutions a ceasefire finally came into being on 24 Oct. In Dec. Egypt and Israel signed a disengagement agreement; as did Israel and Syria on 31 May 1974. A further disengagement agreement was signed between Israel and Egypt in Sept. 1975.

Developments in 1977 included President Sadat of Egypt's visit to Israel and peace initiative and in March 1978 Israeli troops entered southern Lebanon but later withdrew after the arrival of a UN peace-keeping force. In Sept. 1978 US President Carter convened the Camp David conference at which Egypt and Israel agreed on frameworks for peace in the Middle East with treaties to be negotiated between Israel and her neighbours. Negotiations began in the USA between Egypt and Israel in Oct. 1978 and a treaty was signed in Washington on 26 March 1979. Under this treaty Israel withdrew from the Sinai Desert in two phases; part was achieved on 26 Jan. 1980 and the final withdrawal by 26 April 1982.

In June 1982 Israeli forces once again invaded the Lebanon, this time in massive strength, and swept through the country, laying siege to and devastatingly bombing Beirut. On 16 Feb. 1985 the Israeli forces started a complete withdrawal, leaving behind an Israeli trained and equipped Christian Lebanese force to act as a control over and buffer against Moslem Shi'a or Palestinian guerrilla attacks.

Further Reading

Eban, A. B., *My Country: The Story of Modern Israel*. New York, 1972
Reich, B., *Israel: Land of Tradition and Conflict*. London, 1986

ITALY

From 1815 a strong movement grew throughout the Italian states for *risorgimento* (unification) and for independence from Austrian control. Victor Emmanuel II, King of Sardinia-Piedmont from 1849, his prime minister from 1852, Count Cavour, and Giuseppe Garibaldi, an Italian soldier, together achieved success for the movement. The first Italian parliament assembled in Feb. 1861, and on 17 March declared Victor Emmanuel to be King of Italy. The remaining part of the Papal States (the province of Rome), having been taken possession of by an Italian army on 20 Sept. 1870, was annexed to the new kingdom by plebiscite on 2 Oct. During the remaining years of the 19th century Italy acquired an African colonial empire composed of Eritrea, Somaliland and Libya. For her support of the allies in the First World War (1914–18) Italy gained the Trentino and the Istrian peninsula on the North Adriatic.

Fascism spread rapidly after the war and in 1922 Benito Mussolini, leader of the Fascist Party, was appointed prime minister. In 1924 he established himself as dictator with the title *Duce*. His internal policy, with a programme of public works, greater efficiency and better law and order was successful. In 1929 the Lateran Treaties with the Papacy ended over a century of tension between Church and State. However, his aggressive foreign policy as evinced by the invasion of Ethiopia in 1935, and his alliance with Nazi Germany in 1936, was eventually to lead to his downfall. During the Second World War (1939–45) British forces captured much of Italy's colonial empire, and in 1942 occupied Libya. The allies conquered Sicily and Mussolini was compelled to resign in July 1943. In 1945 he was captured and killed by Italian partisans.

June 1946 saw the end of the reign of the House of Savoy, whose kings had ruled over Piedmont for nine centuries and as Kings of Italy since 1861. The Crown Prince Umberto, son of King Victor Emmanuel III, had become Lieut.-Gen. (i.e. Regent) of the kingdom on 5 June 1944. Following the abdication and retirement to Egypt of his father on 9 May 1946, Umberto was declared King Umberto II, but his reign lasted only until 13 June when he left the country. Three days before, on 10 June 1946, Italy had become a republic following a referendum.

Trieste was ceded by Yugoslavia in 1954, although the Alto Adige is still a source of contention with Austria.

In the post-war years, Prime Minister de Gasperi, resisting the challenge of Togliatti's Communists, pursued a strongly pro-West and European policy. His Christian Democrat party held power from 1946 to 1963, but this was a time of constant changes of administrations because no government was successful in handling the poor economy, increasing lawlessness and corruption. After 1963 the coalition governments were no more successful. The Red Brigade terrorist movement was active after 1969 and strains arose from the economic growth of the north and stagnation in the south. The moderate Eurocommunist policies of the new communist leader, Enrico Berlinguer, helped the strong communist gains in the towns as the Party approached one-third of the national vote. Coalitions excluding the Communists continued into 1988.

Further Reading

Clark, M., *Modern Italy 1871–1982*. London, 1984
Spotts, F., and Wieser, T., *Italy: A Difficult Democracy*. CUP, 1986

JAMAICA

Jamaica was discovered by Columbus in 1494, and was occupied by the Spaniards from 1509 until 1655 when the island was captured by the English. Their possession was confirmed by the Treaty of Madrid of 1670. In 1661 a representative constitution was established consisting of a governor, privy council, legislative council and legislative assembly. The slave population introduced by the Spanish was augmented as sugar production increased in value and extent in the 18th century. The plantation economy collapsed with the abolition of the slave trade in the late 1830s. The 1866 Crown Colony government was introduced, with a legislative council consisting of official and unofficial members. In 1884 a partially elective legislative council was instituted. Women were enfranchised in 1919. By the late 1930s demands for self-government increased and the constitution of Nov. 1944 stated that the governor was to be assisted by a house of representatives of 32 elected members, a legislative council (the upper house) of 15 members, and an executive council. Every person over 21 years of age was granted the right to vote.

In 1958 Jamaica joined with Trinidad, Barbados, the Leeward Islands and the Windward Islands to create the West Indies Federation; but Jamaica withdrew in 1961. In 1959 internal self-government had been achieved, and in 1962 Jamaica became an independent state within the British Commonwealth.

The Jamaica Labour Party (JLP) was in office from 1962 to 1972, and the People's National Party (PNP) from 1972 to 1980. In 1980 the JLP, led by Edward Seaga, won 51 of the 60 house of representative seats, increasing this to all 60 in a 1983 election. The PNP did not contest the election because they considered inadequate notice had been given.

Further Reading
Floyd, B., *Jamaica: An Island Microcosm*. London, 1979
Manley, M., *Jamaica: Struggle in the Periphery*. London, 1983

JAPAN

The house of Yamato, from about 500 BC the rulers of one of several kingdoms, united the nation in about 200 AD. The present imperial family are their direct descendants. From 1186 until 1867 successive families of the military Shoguns exercised the temporal power. In 1867 the Emperor Meiji recovered the imperial power after the abdication on 14 Oct. 1867 of the fifteenth and last Tokugawa Shogun Keiki. In 1871 the feudal system *(Hōken Seido)* was abolished and in the early 1890s constitutional government was introduced by the Emperor.

Japan's victory over Russia in the war of 1904 prevented Russian expansion into Korea and consolidated Japan's position as the strongest military power in Asia. Japan used the pretext of the An-glo-Japanese alliance to attack Chinese territory during the First World War. Bad feelings over the terms of the subsequent peace treaty led to continuing hostility between the two countries.

Economic distress, population growth (from 30m. in 1868 to 65m. in 1930) and a sense of dissatisfaction with the 'unjapanese' system of constitutional government led to the emergence between the wars of extremist nationalist and militarist movements in Japan. Plots among the young army officers, a revolt in Manchuria, the assassination of two prime ministers (a third only escaped when his brother-in-law was shot by mistake) highlighted the weaknesses of the central government. In 1936 a military revolt in Tokyo gave the premiership to Konoe Fumimaro, a popular but ineffective figure, who failed to prevent further militarization of the country. In 1938 a national mobilisation law was passed and in 1940 all political parties merged into the Imperial Rule Assistance Association.

On 27 Sept. 1940 Germany, Italy and Japan signed a 10-year pact to assure their mutual co-operation in the establishment of a 'new world order', with Japanese leadership recognized in Asia. In 1940 Japan invaded North Indochina and on 7 Dec. 1941 attacked the United States (principally at Pearl Harbor) and British bases in the Pacific, and then declared war on these two countries. Japanese forces eventually surrendered in Aug. 1945 after the dropping of atomic bombs on Hiroshima and Nagasaki. The country was placed under US military occupation, and in a new constitution in 1947 the Japanese people renounced war and pledged themselves to uphold the ideas of democracy and peace. In the same constitution the

Emperor became a constitutional monarch instead of a divine ruler.

At San Francisco on 8 Sept. 1951 a Treaty of Peace was signed by Japan and representatives of 48 countries, and on 26 Oct. 1951 the Japanese Diet ratified the treaty by 307 votes to 47 with 112 abstentions. On the same day the Diet ratified a security treaty with the US by 289 votes to 71 with 106 abstentions. The treaty provided for the stationing of American troops in Japan until the latter was able to undertake its own defence. The peace treaty came into force on 28 April 1952, when Japan regained her sovereignty. Of the islands under US administration since 1945, the Bonin (Ogasawara), Volcano, and Daito groups and Marcus Island were returned to Japan in 1968, and the southern Ryukyu Islands (Okinawa) in 1972.

In the 1960s the country managed to exceed the objective set by Prime Minister Ikeda to double the national income in ten years. Government since 1955 has been in the hands of one or other faction of the Liberal Democratic Party.

Since Japanese recognition of the People's Republic of China in the early 1970s friendship with China has been seen as compatible with Japan's alliance with the US. Relations with the USSR have not improved, owing to Soviet refusal to discuss the future of the Kurile Islands, taken from Japan in 1945.

Further Reading

Sansom, G. B., *A History of Japan*. 3 vols, London, 1958–64

JORDAN

During the First World War (1914–18) the Arabs of Transjordan and Palestine rebelled against the suzerainty of Turkey which had become an ally of Germany. Britain supported the rebellion, occupied the areas and in 1920 was given a League of Nations mandate for Transjordan and Palestine. In April 1921 the Amir Abdullah Ibn Hussein (brother of King Feisal of Iraq) became the ruler of Transjordan, which was officially separated from Palestine in 1923. On 20 Feb. 1928 an agreement was signed between Transjordan and Britain whereby the latter (with the approval of the League of Nations) recognized the existence of an independent government in Transjordan under the rule of the Amir Abdullah.

By a treaty signed in London on 22 March 1946 Britain recognized Transjordan as a sovereign independent state. On 25 May 1946 the Amir Abdullah assumed the title of king; and when the treaty was ratified on 17 June 1949 the name of the territory was changed to that of the Hashemite Kingdom of Jordan. The legislature consists of a lower house of 60 members elected by universal suffrage, and a senate of 30 members nominated by the king.

In 1948–49 Jordanian forces occupied the West Bank, and formally annexed it in 1950; but the area was captured by Israel in 1967.

On 13 March 1957 the Anglo-Transjordan treaty of March 1948 was terminated by mutual consent, and all British troops were withdrawn.

King Hussein, who became king in 1953 at the age of 16 because his father was mentally unfit to rule, has remained in executive control in the face of attempted assassinations and constant changes of prime ministers. Although he has been able to control the guerrilla groups who tried to use Jordan as a base for their attacks on Israel, the Palestinian question, with the present occupation by Israel, remains a major issue for the king.

Further Reading
Toni, Y. T., and Mousa, S., *Jordan: Land and People*. Amman, 1973

KENYA

Prior to colonialism, the area covered by Kenya today comprised African farming communities, notably the Kikuyu and the Masai. From the 16th century through to the 19th, they were loosely controlled by the Arabic rulers of Oman (whose base moved to Zanzibar in the early 19th century). In 1895, the British declared some of the region the East Africa Protectorate, including the mainland dominions of the Sultan of Zanzibar as well as Mau, Kipini, the island of Lamu and all adjacent islands between the rivers Umba and Tana. The colony and the protectorate, formerly known as the East African Protectorate, were transferred on 1 April 1905 from the Foreign Office to the Colonial Office. In Nov. 1906 the protectorate, excluding the Sultan of Zanzibar's dominions, was placed under the control of a governor and annexed to the Crown, and known from 1920 as the Colony of Kenya. It was only in Dec. 1963 that the Sultan ceded his coastal strip to Kenya.

In the First World War the Germans in East Africa invaded the south of Kenya but the British army, under Gen. Smuts, counterattacked and captured much of German East Africa.

The influx of European settlers was resented by Africans not only for the whites' land holdings, but also for their exclusive political representation in the colonial Legislative Council. A state of emergency existed between Oct. 1952 and Jan. 1960 during the period of the Mau Mau uprising caused by discontent, particularly among the Kikuyu people, over colonial rule and land policy. Over 13,000 Africans and 100 Europeans were killed. The Kenya African Union was banned and its president, Jomo Kenyatta, imprisoned. When the state of emergency ended in 1960 political activity resumed, to pave the way to independence, and two political parties emerged.

On his release from imprisonment Jomo Kenyatta became president of the Kenya African National Union, while the Kenya African Democratic Union, which favoured a regional form of government, were led by Roland Ngala and Daniel Arap Moi.

Full internal self-government was achieved in 1962 and in Dec. 1963 Kenya became an independent member of the Commonwealth.

Before independence the East Africa High Commission had been administering services of an inter-territorial nature for Kenya,

Tanzania and Uganda and this continued after independence. The arrangement was changed to the East African Community in 1967. The Community practically ceased to function after 30 June 1977, chiefly because of the failure to agree a budget and the refusal of President Nyerere of Tanzania to negotiate with President Amin of Uganda.

In 1964 and 1965 constitutional amendments provided for Kenya to become a republic with a president as head of state, and a further change in 1966 required members who changed their parties to seek re-election. Later that year another amendment amalgamated the Senate and the House of Representatives to form a unicameral National Assembly.

In 1982 Kenya became a one-party state and in 1986 party preliminary elections were instituted to reduce the number of parliamentary candidates at general elections. Only those candidates obtaining over 30% of the preliminary vote were eligible to stand.

On the death of Kenyatta in Aug. 1978 David arap Moi, the vice-president, became acting president and was elected in 1979 and re-elected in 1983. An attempted *coup* in Aug. 1982 was unsuccessful.

Further Reading

Arnold, G., *Kenyatta and the Politics of Kenya*. London, 1974.—*Modern Kenya*. London, 1982

KIRIBATI

According to archaelogical discoveries, the islands that now constitute Kiribati were first settled by early Austronesian speaking peoples long before the 1st century AD. Fijians and Tongans arrived about the 14th century and subsequently merged with the older groups to form the traditional I-Kiribati Microneasian society and culture.

The Gilbert and Ellice Islands were proclaimed a British protectorate in 1892 and annexed (at the request of the native governments) as the Gilbert and Ellice Islands Colony on 10 Nov. 1915 (effective on 12 Jan. 1916). Formally part of the British Colony of Gilbert and Ellice Islands, which separated into two parts in 1976, the Gilberts achieved full independence as Kiribati in 1979. On 1 Oct. 1975 the former Ellice Islands severed its constitutional links with the Gilbert Islands and took a new name, Tuvalu.

Further Reading
Grimble, Sir Arthur, *A Pattern of Islands*. London, 1953

KOREA

Korea was united in a single kingdom under the Silla dynasty from 668. China, which claimed a vague suzerainty over Korea, recognized the latter's independence in 1895. Korea concluded trade agreements with the USA in 1882 and with Great Britain and Germany in 1883. After the Russo-Japanese war of 1904–5, Korea was virtually a Japanese protectorate. On 29 Aug. 1910 it was formally annexed by Japan, thus ending 600 years of Confucian rule under the Yi dynasty.

Following the collapse of Japan in 1945, American and Soviet forces entered Korea to enforce the surrender of the Japanese troops, dividing the country into portions separated by the 38th parallel of latitude. Negotiations between the Americans and the Russians regarding the future of Korea broke down in May 1946. In 1948 two separate states were proclaimed. In the south, Syngman Rhee, former president of the Korean government in exile, was elected president of the Republic of Korea, which was recognized by the UN as the only legal government of Korea. In the north, Kim Il-sung a major in the Red Army who had marched back into Korea with the Soviet forces, was proclaimed premier of the Democratic Peoples' Republic of Korea — which was recognized by the USSR as the only legal government of Korea.

The US occupation forces withdrew from South Korea in June 1949. Military equipment promised by the US as part of their aid programme was still on its way to Korea when the North Koreans launched, in June 1950, a full-scale invasion across the 38th parallel. The next day the Security Council of the UN approved a resolution condemning the invasion and asking all member-states to assist in the restoration of peace.

The war, in which North Korea received support from the Chinese army and South Korea from the UN forces and the US, lasted for three years, killed some 5m. people and destroyed an estimated 43% of Korea's industrial plant and 33% of her homes. It was concluded by an armistice signed on 27 July 1953 which implicitly recognized the 38th parallel and the *de facto* boundary between North and South Korea.

THE REPUBLIC OF KOREA

Twelve years of Syngman Rhee's authoritarian rule collapsed after student demonstrations brought the country to the brink of civil war in April 1960. There followed nine months of multi-party parliamentary government. A military *coup* in May 1961 led to the dissolution of the National Assembly, the introduction of martial law and the establishment of Gen. Park Chung Hee as president for the next 17 years. Park's assassination in Oct. 1979 threw the country again into a state of crisis. The prime minister, Choi Kyu Hah, became president until Aug. 1980. He was succeeded by Gen. Chun Doo Hwan who was re-elected under a revised constitution in March 1981 and retained his majority again in Feb. 1985. A new, more democratic, constitution, approved by both ruling and opposition parties in Sept. 1987 is to be the subject of a national referendum. Despite continuing military government and increasing public discontent, South Korea's economic progress has been remarkable, particularly in electronics and shipbuilding.

THE DEMOCRATIC PEOPLES' REPUBLIC

Kim Il-sung, prime minister and chairman of the Korean Workers' Party, has remained in power since the establishment of the Republic. He has maintained a highly authoritarian government under his personal control and has already named his son as his successor. Counting on both Soviet and Chinese help, Kim has successfully played the one off against the other in his foreign policy while remaining violently critical of the west and deeply opposed to South Korea, whose rapid economic growth contrasts with the continuing stagnation in the North.

Red Cross talks aimed at reuniting families divided by the Korean War broke down in Dec. 1977. Proposals for talks on reunification of North and South Korea began in 1980 but have repeatedly broken down. Relations between the two countries remain hostile and highly unstable.

Further Reading

Srivastava, M. P., *The Korean Conflict: Search for Unification*. New Delhi, 1982

NORTH KOREA

The Soviet army arrived in North Korea in Aug. 1945, one month ahead of the Americans, and established a Communist-led provisional government. The newly created Korean Workers' (i.e. Communist) party, with other pro-Communist groups and individuals formed the United Democratic front. On 25 Aug. 1948 the Communists organized elections for a Supreme People's Assembly, both in the Soviet-occupied north and the American-occupied south; some southern deputies went to the north and took their seats. A People's Democratic Republic was proclaimed on 9 Sept. 1948, and Kim Il Sung became premier, purging all rivals.

On 25 June 1950 North Korea invaded the south; its advance was stopped with the aid of UN forces. Chinese Communist 'volunteers' joined the war in Oct. 1950. Truce negotiations were begun in 1951 and concluded on 27 July 1953. A demilitarized zone was set up along the final battle line between North and South Korea.

Proposals for talks between North and South Korea on reunification began in 1980 but have repeatedly broken down.

Further Reading

Scalapino, R. A., and Lee, C.-S., *Communism in Korea*. Univ. of California Press, 1983

KUWAIT

The ruling dynasty was founded by Shaikh Sabah al-Awwal, who ruled from 1756 to 1772. In 1899 the then ruler Shaikh Mubarak concluded a treaty with Great Britain wherein, in return for the assurance of British protection, he undertook not to alienate any of his territory without the agreement of Her Majesty's Government. In 1914 the British Government recognized Kuwait as an independent government under British protection. On 19 June 1961 an agreement reaffirmed the independence and sovereignty of Kuwait and recognized the Government of Kuwait's responsibility for the conduct of internal and external affairs; the agreement of 1899 was terminated and Her Majesty's Government expressed their readiness to assist the Government of Kuwait should they request such assistance.

Further Reading
Sabah, Y. S. F., *The Oil Economy of Kuwait*. London, 1980

LAOS

The Kingdom of Laos, once called Lanxang (the Land of a Million Elephants) was founded in the 14th century. The kingdom has always depended on the maintenance of good relations with its more powerful neighbours, Thailand, Burma and Vietnam.

In 1893 Laos became a French protectorate and in 1907 acquired its present frontiers. In 1945, after French authority had been suppressed by the Japanese, an independence movement known as Lao Issara (Free Laos) set up a government under Prince Phetzarath, the viceroy of Luang Prabang. This government collapsed with the return of the French in 1946, its leaders fleeing to Thailand.

Under a new constitution of 1947 Laos became a constitutional monarchy under the Luang Prabang dynasty, and in 1949 became an independent sovereign state within the French Union. A few Lao Issara leaders remained in dissidence under Prince Souphanouvong who allied himself with the Vietminh and subsequently formed the 'Pathet Lao' (Lao state) rebel movement.

An almost continuous state of war began in 1953 between the Royal Lao Government, supported by American bombing and Thai mercenaries, and the Patriotic Front Pathet Lao, supported by North Vietnamese troops. Peace talks from 1972 resulted in an agreement on 21 Feb. 1973 providing for the formation of a provisional government of national union, and the withdrawal of foreign troops. A provisional coalition government was duly formed in 1974. However, after the Communist victories in neighbouring Vietnam and Cambodia in April 1975, the Pathet Lao took over the running of the whole country, maintaining only a façade of a coalition. On 29 Nov. 1975 HM King Savang Vatthana abdicated and the People's Congress proclaimed a People's Democratic Republic of Laos on 2 Dec. 1975. Prince Souphanouvong was appointed president and Laysone Phomvihane prime minister. In July 1977 Laos signed a series of wide-ranging military and economic agreements with Vietnam. The Lao People's Revolutionary Party, formed in 1955, now runs Laos as a one-party, Communist state.

Two opposition groups – one republican, one royalist – have grown up in exile in the 1980s.

Further Reading
Stuart-Cox, M., *Contemporary Laos*. Univ. of Queensland Press, 1983

LEBANON

The Ottomans invaded Lebanon, then part of Syria, in 1516–17 and held nominal control until 1918. After 20 years' French mandatory régime, Lebanon was proclaimed independent at Beirut on 26 Nov. 1941. On 27 Dec. 1943 an agreement was signed between representatives of the French National Committee of Liberation and of Lebanon, by which most of the powers and capacities exercised hitherto by France were transferred as from 1 Jan. 1944 to the Lebanese Government. The evacuation of foreign troops was completed in Dec. 1946.

In early May 1958 the opposition to President Chamoun, consisting principally (though not entirely) of Moslem pro-Nasserist elements, rose in insurrection; and for 5 months the Moslem quarters of Beirut, Tripoli, Sidon and the northern Bekaa were in insurgent hands. On 15 July the US Government acceded to President Chamoun's request and landed a considerable force of army and marines who re-established the authority of the Government.

Israeli attacks on Lebanon resulted from the presence and activities of armed Palestinian resistance units. Internal problems, which had long been latent in Lebanese society, were exacerbated by the politically active Palestinian population and by the deeply divisive question of the Palestine problem itself. An attempt to regulate the activities of Palestinian fighters through the secret Cairo agreement of 1969 was frustrated both by the inability of the Government to enforce its provisions and by an influx of battle-hardened fighters expelled from Jordan in Sept. 1970. A further attempt to control the guerrillas in 1973 also failed. From March 1975, Lebanon was beset by civil disorder causing considerable loss of life and economic life was brought to a virtual standstill.

By Nov. 1976 however, large-scale fighting had been brought to an end by the intervention of the Syrian-dominated Arab Deterrent Force which ensured sufficient security to permit Lebanon to establish quasi-normal conditions under President Sarkis. Large areas of the country, however, remained outside governmental control, including West Beirut which was the scene of frequent conflict between opposing militia groups. The south, where the Arab Deterrent Force could not deploy, remained unsettled and subject to frequent Israeli attacks. In March 1978 there was an Israeli invasion following a Palestinian attack inside Israel. Israeli troops eventually withdrew in June, but instead of handing over all their positions to UN Peacekeeping Forces they installed Israeli-controlled Christian Lebanese militia forces in border areas. Severe disruption continued in the south. In June 1982 Israeli forces once again invaded, this time in massive strength, and swept through the country, eventually laying siege to and devastatingly bombing Beirut. In Sept. Palestinian forces, together with the PLO leadership, evacuated Beirut. On 23 Aug. 1982 Bachir Gemayel was elected President of Lebanon. On 14 Sept. he was assassinated. His brother, Amin Gemayel, was elected in his place on 21 Sept. Since then there has been a state of 'no peace, no war' with intermittent clashes between the various *de facto* forces on the ground. Israeli forces started a complete withdrawal on 16 Feb. 1985. A peace agreement was signed by the leaders of the Druse, Amal and (Christian) Lebanese Forces to end the civil war on 28 Dec. 1985 but its terms were not implemented. Syrian forces were acting as a peacekeeping force between rival militias in early 1988.

Further Reading

Gordon, D. C., *The Republic of Lebanon: Nation in Jeopardy*. London, 1983

LESOTHO

The Basotho nation was constituted in the 19th century under the leadership of Moshoeshoe I, bringing together refugees from disparate tribes scattered by Zulu expansionism in southern Africa. War with land-hungry Boer settlers in 1856 (and again 1886) cost the Basotho significant territory, and Moshoeshoe appealed for British protection. This was granted in 1868, and in 1871 the territory was annexed to the Cape Colony (now the Republic of South Africa), but in 1883 it was restored to the direct control of the British government through the High Commissioner for South Africa. Basutoland declined to join the Union of South Africa both at the time of its establishment in 1910 and also later.

In 1955 the Basutoland Council which had been established in 1903, sought and obtained the right to pass its own laws for its internal affairs. In 1965 full internal self-government was achieved and the paramount chief became King Moshoeshoe II. On 4 Oct. 1966 Basutoland became an independent and sovereign member of the British Commonwealth as the Kingdom of Lesotho.

Chief Leabua Jonathan, leader of the Basotho National Party and prime minister from 1965, forced the king to refrain from trying to gain some executive power in 1967, and suspended the constitution when the elections of 1970 were declared invalid. Parliamentary rule, with a national assembly of nominated members, was reintroduced in April 1973; although there was subsequent talk of elections, these were constantly postponed.

On 20 Jan. 1986, after a border blockade by the Republic of South Africa, Chief Jonathan was deposed in a bloodless military *coup* led by Maj.-Gen. Justin Lekhanya who became the chairman of a newly formed military council, banned political parties, and granted significant powers to the king. South Africa embarked on a major scheme to develop Lesotho's water resources, and political activity by South African exiles in the country was severely curbed.

Further Reading
Spence, J. E., *Lesotho*. OUP, 1968

LIBERIA

Liberia is commonly associated with resettled American slaves, but it was originally populated between the 12th and 16th centuries by other people who indeed became victims of the slave trade in the 17th century. The Republic as such has its origins in the efforts of various American societies to establish freed American slaves in a colony on the West African coast, their intentions ranging from philanthropy to fear that the existence of freed Negroes in America threatened the system of slavery there. In 1822 a settlement was formed near the spot where Monrovia now stands. On 26 July 1847 the state was constituted as the Free and Independent Republic of Liberia. The new state was first recognized by Great Britain and France, and ultimately by other powers. However, this was not without a struggle against subsequent British, French and German claims on Liberian territory. US military bases were set up in the 1940s with the permission of Liberia's president William Tubman. When he died in 1971, he was succeeded by William Tolbert who had been vice-president since 1951.

On 12 April 1980, President Tolbert was assassinated; his government was overthrown and the constitution suspended. Tolbert's party, the True Whig Party, was formed in 1860 and had been in power since 1870. Recent economic decline and pressure for change had undermined the government. In March 1980, the newly formed People's Progressive Party was banned and its leaders arrested. The *coup* was led by Master-Sergeant Doe who was later installed as Head of State and Commander-in-Chief of the army.

Under Doe, a pro-Western orientation continued. A constitution was approved in 1984, and elections the following year saw Doe re-elected as president and surviving a *coup* attempt soon after.

Further Reading

Wilson, C. M., *Liberia: Black Africa in Microcosm*. New York, 1971

LIBYA

Tripoli fell under Ottoman domination in the 16th century, and though in 1711 the Arab population secured some measure of independence, the country came under the direct rule of Turkey in 1835. In 1911 Italy occupied Tripoli and in 1912, by the Treaty of Ouchy, Turkey recognized the sovereignty of Italy in Tripoli.

During the Second World War the British army expelled the Italians and their German allies, and Tripolitania and Cyrenaica were placed under British, and the Fezzan under French, military administration. This administration continued until 1950 under a UN directive. Libya became an independent, sovereign kingdom with the former Amir of Cyrenaica, Muhammad Idris al Senussi, as king, on 24 Dec. 1951.

King Idris was deposed in Sept. 1969 by a group of army officers, twelve of whom formed the Revolutionary Command Council which, chaired by Col. Muammar Qadhafi, proclaimed the Libyan Arab Republic.

Qadhafi favoured Arab unity, but his efforts in that direction have been abortive. The Federation of the Arab Republics formed in 1972 with Libya, Egypt and Syria as members; an agreement to merge Libya and Egypt in 1973; a proposed union with Tunisia in 1974; and a union with Syria in 1980, all proved unsuccessful.

In 1977 the country changed its name to the Socialist People's Libyan Arab Jamahiriya. At the same time the Revolutionary Command Council was superseded by a more democratic system of People's Congresses and Popular Committees. Qadhafi remained head of state.

Throughout the 1980s Libya has had constant disagreements with her neighbours, and her relations with the USA and other Western countries have deteriorated, culminating in the American bombing of the capital in April 1987, in an attempt to punish Qadhafi for his alleged support of international terrorism.

Further Reading
Wright, J., *Libya: A Modern History*. London, 1982

LIECHTENSTEIN

The Principality of Liechtenstein, situated between the Austrian province of Vorarlberg and the Swiss cantons of St Gallen and Graubunden, is a sovereign state whose history dates back to 3 May 1342, when Count Hartmann III became ruler of the county of Vaduz. Additions were later made to the count's domains, and by 1434 the territory had reached its present boundaries. It consists of the two former counties of Schellenberg and Vaduz (until 1806 immediate fiefs of the Roman Empire). The former in 1699 and the latter in 1712 came into the possession of the house of Liechtenstein and, by diploma of 23 Jan. 1719, granted by the Emperor Charles VI, the two counties were constituted as the Principality of Liechtenstein.

In 1862 the constitution established an elected diet which was to participate in the legislative process. After the First World War, Liechtenstein severed its treaties with Austria in 1919 and became orientated toward Switzerland, adopting Swiss currency in 1921 and being represented abroad by them since 1919. On 5 Oct. 1921 a new constitution based on that of Switzerland established more democratic privileges. It also stated that the head of government must be a Liechtenstein citizen.

In recent years proposals to change the constitution so that it embodies the equality of men and women have not been accepted.

Further Reading

Seger, O., *A Survey of Liechtenstein History*. 4th English ed. Vaduz, 1984

LUXEMBOURG

Luxembourg became a duchy in 1354, and formed part of the Holy Roman Empire (although it was annexed by Louis XIV from 1684 to 1697) until it was conquered by the French in 1795. In 1815 it became the Grand Duchy of Luxembourg under the house of Orange-Nassau. The Walloon-speaking area was joined to Belgium in 1839, but the eastern area remained under the Dutch king until 1890. Then, when there was no male heir to the house of Orange-Nassau, the personal union with the Netherlands ended with the accession of a member of another branch of the house of Nassau, Grand Duke Adolphe of Nassau-Weilburg.

The head of state takes part in the legislative process, exercises executive authority and plays a part in judicial decisions. The constitution leaves to the sovereign the right to organize the government.

In both world wars (1914–18 and 1939–45) Luxembourg was invaded and occupied by German forces. From May 1940 until Sept. 1944 the government carried on an independent administration in London.

In 1948 a customs union known as the Benelux was formed by Belgium, the Netherlands and Luxembourg to standardize prices, taxes and wages, and to allow free movement of labour between the three countries.

Further Reading

Newcomer, J., *The Grand Duchy of Luxembourg: The Evolution of Nationhood, 963 A.D. to 1983*. Washington, D.C., 1983

MADAGASCAR

Evidence of human inhabitants on Madagascar dates back 2,000 years, and the island was settled by people of African and Indonesian origin when it was visited by the Portuguese explorer, Diego Diaz, in 1500. The island was unified under the Imérina monarchy between 1797 and 1861, but French claims to a protectorate led to hostilities culminating in the establishment of a French protectorate on 30 Sept. 1895. The monarchy was abolished and Madagascar became a French colony on 6 Aug. 1896.

Madagascar became an Overseas Territory of France in 1946, and on 14 Oct. 1958, following a referendum, was proclaimed the autonomous Malagasy Republic within the French community, achieving full independence on 26 June 1960.

The government of Philibert Tsiranana, president from independence, resigned on 18 May 1972, and executive powers were given to Maj.-Gen. Gabriel Ramanantsoa, who replaced Tsiranana as president on 11 Oct. 1972. On 5 Feb. 1975, Col. Richard Ratsimandrava became head of state, but was assassinated six days later. A National Military Directorate under Brig.-Gen. Gilles Andriamahazo was established on 12 Feb. On 15 June it handed over power to a Supreme Revolutionary Council under Didier Ratsiraka. A new constitution was then approved by a referendum in Dec. 1975 and Madagascar became the Democratic Republic of Madagascar.

Executive power is vested in the president who is directly elected for seven years. There is a National People's Assembly of 137 members elected by universal suffrage for a five-year term. The intention is to have a single national party, and the *Front National pour la Défense de la Révolution Socialiste Malgache*, of which the *Avant-garde de la Révolution Malgache* was the original nucleus, presents a single list at elections. However, the *Mouvement National pour l'indépendence de Madagascar* has received support and there has been social and political discontent.

Ratsirake was re-elected in 1982, and the following year saw elections for the national assembly. Madagascar retains good relations with France and with the socialist countries.

Further Reading

Brown, M., *Madagascar Rediscovered*. London, 1978

MALAŴI

A powerful kingdom dominated much of Malaŵi and the surrounding area from the 15th to the 18th centuries, based on the Bantu-speaking people who began settling there 200 years earlier. However, by the beginning of the 19th century, this had disintegrated into many small entities, and occupation by Ngoni people from the south facilitated European control. The explorer David Livingstone reached Lake Nyasa, now Lake Malaŵi, in 1859 and it was the land along the lake's western shore that became, in 1891, the British Protectorate of Nyasaland. The name was changed to British Central Africa Protectorate in 1893 but reverted to Nyasaland in 1907.

In 1884 the British South Africa Company applied for a charter to trade. Within a few years the slavery and the slave trade had been suppressed. Pressure on land, the colour bar and other grievances about colonial rule generated Malaŵian resistance which was only checked by 1915. After the Second World War, the Nyasaland African Congress was formed to lead a new wave of resistance, particularly against the impending federation of the country to two neighbouring British colonies.

In 1953 Nyasaland was joined with Southern Rhodesia (Zimbabwe) and Northern Rhodesia (Zambia) to form the Federation of Rhodesia and Nyasaland, under British control. This union was dissolved in 1963 when Nyasaland was for a year self-governing, until on 6 July 1964 it became independent, adopting the name of Malaŵi. In 1966 Malaŵi was declared a republic and Dr Hastings Banda became the first president. Jailed in 1959–60 for his activities in the resistance, Banda had led the Malaŵi Congress Party to victory in elections in 1961. As president, he took strong measures against his opponents. In the 1970s he developed close ties with colonial Portugal and with the Republic of South Africa, where he paid a state visit in 1971.

Further Reading

Pachai, B., Smith, G. W., Tangri, R. K., (eds.) *Malawi Past and Present.* Blantyre, 1971

169

MALAYSIA

Malaysia is a federation consisting of the eleven States of Peninsular Malaysia and the two States of Sabah and Sarawak.

The Portuguese were the first Europeans to settle in the area and Malacca became a Portuguese possession in 1541. The Dutch took Malacca in 1641 and held it until 1794 when it was occupied by the British who had established three trading posts at the end of the 18th century. Although Malacca was returned to the Dutch in 1814, it was finally ceded to Britain in 1824. At the same time (1814–24) Stamford Raffles established a settlement and Singapore became British territory.

In 1826 Singapore and Malacca were incorporated with Penang to form the Straits Settlements. In 1896 Negri Sembilan, Penang, Perak and Selangor became the Federated Malay States; these were 'protected' states and were not part of the Straits Settlements. The remaining five Malay states became known as the Unfederated Malay States.

Singapore and what is now Malaysia were occupied by the Japanese from 1941 to 1945. Soon thereafter, in Jan. 1946, plans were published to create a Malayan Union excluding Singapore but including the four Federated and the five Unfederated Malay States and the Settlements of Penang and Malacca. The Union came into being in April 1946 but was soon abandoned in the face of opposition. However, in Jan. 1948 the Union was reconstituted as the Federation of Malaya.

From 1948 to 1960 a State of Emergency existed in order to counter a revolt by Malayan Communists aimed at the disruption of the country's economy. Commonwealth forces supported the Federation's own armed forces.

Following lengthy negotiations independence was granted to the Federation of Malaya on 31 Aug. 1957.

On 31 Aug. 1963 Malaysia was created from the Federation of Malaya, Singapore, North Borneo (now Sabah) and Sarawak. Brunei was also invited to join but no agreement could be reached. Singapore left Malaysia on 9 Aug. 1965 to become an independent sovereign state.

Further Reading

Milne, R. S. and Ratnam, K. J., *Malaysia, New States in a New Nation: Political Development of Sarawak and Sabah in Malaysia.* London, 1974

PENINSULAR MALAYSIA

Peninsular Malaysia consists of the States of Johore, Kedah, Kelantan, Malacca, Negri Sembilan, Pahang, Penang, Perak, Perlis, Selangor and Trengganu. In 1966 these States were known as West Malaysia but the name was later changed to Peninsular Malaysia. The Malaysian constitution established both a strong federal government and a measure of autonomy for the individual states, each of which has its own constitution and head of state.

SABAH

The territory now named Sabah, but until Sept. 1963 known as North Borneo, was in 1877–78 ceded by the Sultans of Brunei and Sulu and various other rulers to a British syndicate, which in 1881 was chartered as the British North Borneo (Chartered) Company. The territory obtained its boundaries in 1898. The Company's sovereign rights and assets were transferred to the Crown with effect from 15 July 1946. On that date, the island of Labuan (ceded to Britain in 1846 by the Sultan of Brunei) became part of the new Colony of North Borneo. On 16 Sept. 1963 North Borneo joined the new Federation of Malaysia and became the state of Sabah.

SARAWAK

The government of part of the present territory was obtained on 24 Sept. 1841 by Sir James Brooke from the Sultan of Brunei. Various accessions were made between 1861 and 1905. It was recognized as a separate state by 1850 and by Great Britain in 1864. In 1888 Sarawak was placed under British protection. On 16 Dec. 1941 Sarawak was occupied by the Japanese. After the liberation the Rajah took over his administration from the British military authorities on 15 April 1946. The Council Negeri, on 17 May 1946, authorized the Act of Cession to the British Crown by 19 to 16 votes, and the Rajah ceded Sarawak to the British Crown on 1 July 1946.

On 16 Sept. 1963 Sarawak joined the Federation of Malaysia.

MALDIVES

The Maldives, ruled by an elected Sultan, came under British protection in 1887, but with internal self-government. In 1948, 1953 and 1960 revised agreements were signed with Britain. Complete independence was achieved on 26 July 1965. The Maldives became a republic on 11 Nov. 1968, with the prime minister, Ibrahim Nasir, as its first president. In 1975 the post of prime minister was abolished.

The Republic of the Maldives became a 'special' member of the Commonwealth in 1982 and a full member in 1985.

In 1978 Maumoon Abdul Gayoom succeeded as president, and Nasir chose to live out of the country. Since then there have been rumours of plots, and of Nasir's implication in them, to overthrow the president. Gayoom was re-elected for his second term in 1983.

Further Reading

Bernini, F. and Corbin, G., *Maldive*. Turin, 1973

MALI

Mali's political organization and power reached their peak between the 11th and 13th centuries when its gold-based empire controlled much of the surrounding area. It declined thereafter and the French began invading from Senegal in the mid-19th century, fully annexing the country by 1904. The region became the territory of French Sudan as part of French West Africa. The Sudanese Union, led by Modibo Keita, gained strength in the 1950s and took over the internal running of the country after winning elections in 1957. The country became an autonomous state within the French Community on 24 Nov. 1958, and on 4 April 1959 joined with Senegal to form the Federation of Mali. The Federation achieved independence on 20 June 1960, but Sénégal seceded on 22 Aug. and Mali proclaimed itself an independent republic on 22 Sept. with Keita as president. Much later, in March 1982, Guinea and Mali were to agree to pursue gradual unification. The National Assembly was dissolved on 17 Jan. 1968 by President Modibo Keita, whose government was then overthrown by an army *coup* on 19 Nov. 1968; power was assumed by a Military Committee for National Liberation led by Lieut. (now Gen.) Moussa Traoré, who became president on 19 Sept. 1969. He ruled on the basis of tight control during the severe drought of the 1970s. Traoré formed a political party in 1976, the *Union démocratique du peuple malien* (UDPM), and was confirmed as president in elections in June 1979.

Further Reading
Decraene, P., *Le Mali*. Paris, 1980

MALTA

Malta was held in turn by Phoenicians, Carthaginians and Romans, and was conquered by Arabs in 870. In 1090 Count Roger of Sicily drove out the Arabs and the island was ruled by Sicily until 1530, when it was handed over to the Knights of St John, who ruled until dispersed by Napoleon in 1798. The Maltese rose in rebellion against the French and the island was subsequently blockaded by the British from 1798 to 1800. The Maltese people freely requested the protection of the British Crown in 1802 on condition that their rights and privileges be preserved. The islands were finally annexed to the British Crown by the Treaty of Paris in 1814 and became the base of the British Mediterranean fleet.

Malta was granted a measure of self-government under the constitution of 1947. On the resignation of the government led by Dom Mintoff in 1958 and the disturbances that followed, a state of emergency was declared on 30 April 1958 and the direct administration of the island was assumed by the Governor. In April 1959 the state of emergency was brought to an end and an interim constitution imposed. The 1961 constitution was introduced with the UK retaining responsibility for defence and external affairs.

On 15 April 1942, in recognition of the steadfastness and fortitude of the people of Malta during the Second World War, King George VI awarded the George Cross to the island.

Malta became independent on 21 Sept. 1964 and became a republic within the Commonwealth on 13 Dec. 1974.

British defence cuts in 1967 affected the island severely and in 1971 Malta began to follow a policy of strict non-alignment and closed the NATO base. Dom Mintoff, whose Labour Party had narrowly won the 1971 election, tried to widen foreign policy by overtures to the USSR and Libya. In March 1972 agreement was reached on the phasing out of the British military base which was closed down completely on 31 March 1979.

Further Reading

Blouet, B., *The Story of Malta*. Rev. ed. London, 1981

MAURITANIA

A political system dominated by Berber pastoralists characterized much of Mauritania's known history, surviving the pressures of the Ghanaian empire between the 10th and 13th centuries. Arabic penetration 200 years later led to the adoption of Islam by the inhabitants, and they became subjects of Arab emirates until French encroachment in the mid-19th century. Mauritania became a French protectorate in 1903 and a colony in 1920. It became an autonomous republic within the French Community on 28 Nov. 1958 and achieved full independence on 28 Nov. 1960. Under its first president, Moktar Ould Daddah, Mauritania became a one-party state in 1964, but following his deposition by a military *coup* on 10 July 1978, the ruling *Parti du peuple mauritanien* was dissolved and Lieut.-Col. Ould Salek seized power.

Following the Spanish withdrawal from Western Sahara on 28 Feb. 1976, Mauritania occupied the southern part (88,667 sq. km) of this territory and incorporated it under the name of Tiris el Gharbia. Along with Morocco, who had also seized part of the territory, Mauritania had to contend with resistance from the people living there led by the Polisario Front. When Salek resigned in June 1979, Lieut.-Col. Mohammed Louly succeeded him and made peace with Polisario. In Aug. 1979 Mauritania renounced sovereignty and withdrew from Tiris el Gharbia.

Following the *coup* of 10 July 1978, power was placed in the hands of a Military Committee for National Recovery (CMRN): the constitution was suspended and the 70-member National Assembly dissolved. On 6 April 1979 the CMRN was renamed the Military Committee for National Salvation (CMSN). A *coup* in Jan. 1980 installed Lieut.-Col. Mohammed Haidalla in power, and under his rule slavery was finally abolished in Mauritania. In Feb. 1984 he recognized Polisario's declaration of a Sahrawi Arab Democratic Republic. He was overthrown in Dec. 1984 that year when his prime minister, Lieut.-Col. Sid Ahmed Maaoya Taya, seized power.

Further Reading

Westebbe, R. M., *The Economy of Mauritania*. New York, 1971

MAURITIUS

Mauritius was known to Arab navigators probably not later than the 10th century. It was probably visited by Malays in the 15th century, and was discovered by the Portuguese between 1507 and 1512, but the Dutch were the first settlers in 1598, who named it after their stadtholder, Count Maurice. In 1710 they abandoned the island, which was occupied by the French under the name of Ile de France in 1715. The British occupied the island in 1810, and it was formally ceded to Great Britain by the Treaty of Paris, 1814.

The majority of the population were descendents of slaves brought by the French from Madagascar and East Africa, and indentured Indian labourers brought by Britain. European settlers unsuccessfully opposed independence, but the elections in Aug. 1967 which installed Seewoosagur Ramgoolam as prime minister provided an overwhelming mandate for independence. This was attained within the Commonwealth on 12 March 1968. In 1982, with the victory of the *Mouvement Militant Mauricien* (MMM) at the polls, Aneerood Jugnauth became prime minister. Divisions in the MMM led to the government's collapse, but Aneerood returned to power through alliances with other parties in 1983 and again in 1987.

In 1965 the Chagos Archipelago had been transferred to the British Indian Territory for military purposes. Both Mauritius and the Seychelles have campaigned for its return, calling for the Indian Ocean to become a 'zone of peace'.

Further Reading

Toussaint, A., *History of Mauritius*. London, 1978

MEXICO

Mexico's history falls into four epochs: the era of the Indian empires (before 1521), the Spanish colonial phase (1521–1810), the period of national formation (1810–1910), and the present period which began with the social revolution of 1910–21.

Mexico was conquered for Spain by Cortés in 1521, and became part of the viceroyalty of New Spain. In 1810 began the fight for independence which was eventually achieved in 1821. A substantial part of Mexico's territory (including the present state of California) was lost to the USA by the Mexican War of 1846–48. In the 1860s France, Britain and the USA declared war on Mexico; France invaded the country, and declared Maximilian, Archduke of Austria, to be Emperor of Mexico. When the French withdrew in 1867, Maximilian was executed by the Mexicans. The leader of the opposition to the French, Benito Juárez, again became president. In 1876 began the long presidency of Porfirio Díaz (1876–80, 1884–1911) which gave stability to the country, despite his establishing himself as a dictator.

The present period of Mexican history – regarded as one of social and national consolidation – began with the social revolution of 1910–21 led by Francisco Madero. The constitution of 1917 established a representative, democratic and federal republic, comprising 31 states and a federal district. There is a complete separation of legislative, executive and judicial powers. The president, who is the supreme executive authority, is directly elected for a single six-year term. Women were enfranchised in 1958.

Despite democratic elections, the PRI *(Partido Revolucionario Institucional)* has been in power for 60 years; in 1982 the PRI won all 64 seats in the Senate, and in 1985 289 of the 300 single-member seats in the Chamber of Deputies. The chief opposition party, PAN *(Partido de Acción Nacional)*, has caused civil disturbances, claiming illegalities in the elections.

The great homogeneity in the nature of successive administrations has brought relative political stability which has aided Mexico's rapid development since the Second World War.

Further Reading

Alba, V., *A Concise History of Mexico*. London, 1973

MONACO

Monaco is a small principality on the Mediterranean, surrounded by the French *département* of Alpes Maritimes except on the side towards the sea. From 1297 it belonged to the house of Grimaldi. In 1731 it passed into the female line, Louise Hippolyte, daughter of Antoine I, heiress of Monaco, marrying Jacques de Goyon Matignon, Count of Torigni, who took the name and arms of Grimaldi. The principality lay between the French Republic and the Kingdom of Sardinia under whose protection it was placed in 1815 by the Congress of Vienna. In 1861 in the border changes that were part of the creation of the Kingdom of Italy, it passed under French protection.

Monaco is a constitutional monarchy with a strong role assigned to the National Council in the constitution of 1962. There is a customs union with France that was revised in the French favour in May 1963 after complaints that French firms were using the principality to avoid French fiscal control.

MONGOLIA

Temujin became khan of Hamag Mongolia in 1190, and having united by conquest various Tatar and Mongolian tribes, was confirmed as 'Universal' ('Genghis', 'Chingiz') khan in 1206. The expansionist impulse of his nomadic empire (Beijing captured 1215; Samarkand, 1220) continued after his death in 1227, though the empire was by then administratively divided among his sons. Tamurlaine (died 1405) was the last of the conquering khans. In 1368 the Chinese drove the Mongols from Beijing, and for the next two centuries Sino-Mongolian relations alternated between war and trade. Lamaism spread from Tibet in the 16th century. The last Mongol khan, Ligden (1604–34), failed to stem the tide of Manchu expansion; southern (Inner) Mongolia was conquered in 1636 and Beijing in 1644. In 1691 Outer Mongolia accepted Manchu rule. The head of the Lamaist faith became the symbol of national identity, and his seat ('Urga', now Ulan Bator) was made the Mongolian capital.

When the Manchu dynasty was overthrown in 1911 Outer Mongolia declared its independence under its spiritual ruler and turned to Russia for support against China. 'Autonomy' (not independence) was agreed by the Sino-Russo-Mongolian agreement of May 1915. In 1919 China re-established central rule, but Soviet and Mongolian revolutionary forces set up a provisional government in March 1921. On the death of the spiritual ruler (the 'Urga Living Buddha') a people's republic and new constitution were proclaimed in May 1924.

With Soviet help Japanese invaders were fended off during the Second World War. The Mongols then took part in the successful Soviet campaign against Inner Mongolia and Manchuria. On 5 Jan. 1946 China recognized the independence of the People's Republic of Mongolia after the plebiscite stipulated by the Yalta agreement. In 1961 Mongolia finally gained admission to the UN. She now has diplomatic relations with 52 states.

Inner Mongolia has meanwhile been reorganized as an Autonomous Region within the Chinese People's Republic, and it is reported that the Chinese now greatly outnumber the native Mongolians.

Further Reading

Bawden, C. R., *The Modern History of Mongolia*. London, 1968

MONTSERRAT

Montserrat is an island dependency in the British Leeward group of islands in the West Indies/Caribbean. The island was discovered by Columbus in 1493, and colonized in 1632 by Britain with Irish settlers. The island formed part of the federal colony of the Leeward Islands from 1871 until 1956 when the Federation was dissolved. Montserrat then became a separate colony. The constitution came into force on 1 Jan. 1960 with an Administrator, from 1971 a Governor, as head of the government, and is responsible for external affairs, defence and internal security. The constitution also established an Executive Council with two-thirds of its members elected, and a Legislative Council with 7 of its 11 members elected.

Discussions about independence have taken place in the 1980s.

Further Reading

Fergus, H. A., *Montserrat: Emerald Isle of the Caribbean*. London, 1983

MOROCCO

From 1912 to 1956 Morocco was divided into three areas: a French protectorate, established by the Treaty of Fez of 1912 concluded between France and the Sultan; a Spanish protectorate, established by the Franco-Spanish Convention of 1912; and the international zone of Tangier which was established by France, Great Britain and Spain in 1923.

Gen. Lyautey, the first French resident-general, was responsible for much modernization and by 1934 had pacified the country. However, as tribesmen were defeated so nationalism in various forms developed.

On 2 March 1956 France and the Sultan terminated the Treaty of Fez and on 7 April 1956 Spain relinquished her protectorate. On 29 Oct. 1956 the international status of the Tangier Zone was abolished by common consent and Morocco became a kingdom on 18 Aug. 1957, with the Sultan taking the title Mohammed V.

The country became territorially complete when the northern strip of Spanish Sahara was ceded by Spain on 10 April 1958 and the former Spanish province of Ifni was returned to Morocco on 30 June 1969.

Crown Prince Moulay Hassan succeeded his father on 3 March 1961 as Hassan II. King Hassan tried to combine the various parties in government and he established an elected House of Representatives, but political unrest led him to discard any attempt at parliamentary government, and to rule autocratically from 1965 to 1977. In 1977 a new Chamber of Representatives was elected, and under the constitution Morocco became a constitutional monarchy with a single elective chamber.

For details of Sahrawi Arab Democratic Republic *see* WESTERN SAHARA.

Further Reading
Kinross, Lord, and Hales-Gary, D., *Morocco*. London, 1971

MOZAMBIQUE

Trading settlements were established by Arab merchants in the 15th century while inland various African tribes engaged in agriculture. Mozambique Island was visited by Vasco da Gama's fleet on 2 March 1498, and Sofala was occupied by the Portuguese in 1506. A century later, a harsh feudal system was introduced inland, while the slave trade became important along the coast. At first ruled as part of Portuguese India, a separate administration was created for the area in 1752. Rivalry with Britain led to full Portuguese occupation in 1895, although it took another 25 years for the Portuguese to suppress resistance to their rule. On 11 June 1951 Mozambique became an Overseas Province of Portugal.

A decade of guerrilla activity, along with other national liberation wars in Portugal's other African colonies, contributed to a *coup* in Portugal. The new government and the Mozambican nationalists jointly established a transitional government on 20 Sept. 1974. Independence was achieved on 25 June 1975. Samora Machel, leader of the combined nationalist groups, *Frente de Libertação Moçambique* (FRELIMO), became the first president.

Until the creation of Zimbabwe in 1980, Mozambique was the base for guerrillas fighting the Rhodesian régime; it still harbours the African National Congress banned from the Republic of South Africa. Since 1980 Mozambique, and especially its trade lines from its ports to the interior of Africa, has been constantly harrassed by the *Movimento Nacional da Resistência* (MNR) secretly supported by the Republic of South Africa. Under pressure of the war with the MNR and direct South African military raids, the Mozambican government signed a non-aggression pact with South Africa in March 1984. ANC activities were accordingly restricted, but South Africa escalated its support for the MNR. In 1985 Zimbabwe and Tanzania, and in 1987 Malaŵi, provided Mozambique with some military support. In Oct. 1986, President Machel was killed in a controversial air crash on South African soil.

Famine has resulted from a combination of drought, war and dislocation, and in 1987 nearly 5m. people were estimated to be facing starvation. Postponed elections to a People's Assembly were finally held in Dec. 1986.

Further Reading
Kaplan, I., (ed.) *Area Handbook of Mozambique*. Maputo, 1977

NAURU

Nauru is an island in the central Pacific Ocean, initially populated by people of Polynesian stock. The island was discovered by Capt. Fearn in 1798, annexed by Germany in Oct. 1888, and surrendered to the Australian forces in 1914. It was administered under a mandate, effective from 17 Dec. 1920, conferred on the British Empire and approved by the League of Nations until 1 Nov. 1947, when the United Nations General Assembly approved a trusteeship agreement with the governments of Australia, New Zealand and UK as a joint administering authority. Independence was gained in 1968.

The interests in the considerable phosphate deposits on the island were purchased in 1919 from the Pacific Phosphate Company by the governments of the UK, the Commonwealth of Australia and New Zealand at a cost of £Stg3·5m., and a Board of Commissioners representing the 3 governments was appointed to manage and control the working of the deposits. In May 1967, in Canberra, the British Phosphate Corporation agreed to hand over the phosphate industry to Nauru and on 15 June 1967 agreement was reached that the Nauruans could buy the assets of the B.P.C. for approximately $A20m. over 3 years. It is estimated that the deposits will be exhausted by 1993.

Further Reading
Pittman, G. A., *Nauru, the Phosphate Island*. London, 1959

NEPÁL

Nepál is an independent Himalayan Kingdom located between India and the Tibetan region of China. Until relatively recently, the history of Nepál was the struggle of rival chiefs for the consolidation of the surrounding area into a unified kingdom and its role as an asylum for refugees from the plains of India. Buddhism was introduced in about 639 AD.

From the 8th to the 11th centuries, many Buddhists fled to Nepál from India, which had been invaded by Muslims. In the 18th century Nepál was a collection of small principalities (many of Rajput origin) and the three kingdoms of the Malla dynasty: Káthmándu, Pátan and Bhádgaon. In central Nepál lay the principality of Gurkha (or Gorkha); its ruler after 1742 was Prithvi Náráyan Sháh, who conquered the small states which were his neighbours. Fearing his ambitions, in 1767 the Mallas brought in forces lent by the British East India Company to keep him in check. In 1769 these forces were withdrawn and Gurkha was then able to conquer the Malla kingdoms and unite Nepál as one state with its capital at Káthmándu.

Prithvi Náráyan also enlarged Nepál by annexing Sikkim and the Tarai, Kumáon, Garhwál and Simla areas of India. He died in 1775 and his successors were beset by internal rivalry. Most of the Indian annexations were lost to the British.

In 1846 the Ráná family became the effective rulers of Nepál, establishing the office of the prime minister as hereditary. In 1860 Nepál reached agreement with the British in India whereby Nepáli independence was preserved and the recruitment of Gurkhas to the British army was sanctioned.

In 1950 the Sháh royal family allied itself with Nepális abroad to end the power of the Ránás. The last Ráná prime minister resigned in Nov. 1951, the king having proclaimed a constitutional monarchy in Feb. 1951. A new constitution, approved in 1959, led to confrontation between the king and his ministers; it was replaced by one less liberal in 1962.

King Mahendra died in Jan. 1972 and was succeeded by his son Birendra Bir Bikram Sháh Dev.

Further Reading

Wadhwa, D. N., *Nepal.* [Bibliography] Oxford and Santa Barbara, 1986

THE NETHERLANDS

William of Orange (1533–84), as the German Count of Nassau, inherited vast possessions in the Netherlands and the Princedom of Orange in France. He was the initiator of the struggle for independence from Spain. The Revolt of the Netherlands began in 1568, and by the Union of Utrecht the more easily defensible seven provinces of the North – Holland, Zeeland, Utrecht, Overijssel, Groningen, Drenthe and Friesland – declared themselves independent. At the end of the Thirty Years War, by the Treaty of Westphalia (1648), Spain recognized the independence of the Republic of the United Netherlands. Members of the Orange-Nassau family became in succession the 'first servant of the Republic' with the title of 'Stadhouder' (governor). In 1689 Willem III acceded to the throne of England, becoming joint sovereign with his wife Mary. Willem III died in 1702 without issue, and there was no stadhouder until a member of the Frisian branch of Orange-Nassau was nominated hereditary stadhouder in 1747. His successor, Willem V, had, however, to take refuge in England in 1795 when the French army invaded. The country was freed from French domination in Nov. 1813.

The Congress of Vienna (1815) joined the Belgian provinces, called the 'Spanish' or the 'Austrian Netherlands' before the French Revolution, to the Northern Netherlands. The son of the former stadhouder, Willem V, was proclaimed King of the Netherlands as King Willem I on 16 March 1815. The union was dissolved by the Belgian revolution of 1830, and in 1839 Belgium and the Netherlands were recognized as two separate independent kingdoms.

In 1840 Willem I abdicated in favour of his son, Willem II, who was liberal in his outlook and who moved the Netherlands towards a constitutional monarchy, developing ministerial responsibility and electoral equality among direct tax payers. Willem II was succeeded by Willem III in 1849 under whom the liberal development continued. In 1890 Wilhelmina, the first of three successive queens, ascended to the throne (the Netherlands is a hereditary monarchy with the succession in the direct male or female line in the order of primogeniture).

The Netherlands followed a policy of non-participation in the European conflicts of the early 20th century and during the First World War remained neutral. In the Second World War, however, the Netherlands was occupied by Germany from 1940 until 1945. After liberation in 1945, the country abandoned its traditional policy of neutrality. In 1948 the Netherlands joined with Belgium and Luxembourg to form the Benelux economic union, in 1957 it was a founder member of the EEC, and in 1949 it joined NATO.

Since the Second World War the Netherlands has granted independence to her overseas possessions of Indonesia (in 1949 after much fighting) and Suriname (in 1975), leaving the Netherlands Antilles and Aruba as the only remaining Dutch dependencies.

Proportional representation has resulted in coalition governments. Recent politics has been dominated by economic problems and disagreement about the siting of NATO cruise missiles.

In April 1980 Queen Juliana, who had reigned since 1948, abdicated in favour of her daughter Beatrix.

Further Reading

Kossmann, E. H., *The Low Countries, 1780–1940*. Oxford, 1978
Newton, G., *The Netherlands: An Historical and Cultural Survey, 1795–1977*. Boulder, 1978
Pinder, D., *The Netherlands*. Folkestone, 1976

DUTCH DEPENDENCIES

ARUBA

Discovered by Alonzo de Ojeda in 1499, the island of Aruba was claimed for Spain but not settled. It was acquired by the Dutch in 1634, but apart from garrisons was left to the indigenous Caiquetios (Arawak) Indians until the 19th century. From 1828 Aruba formed part of the Dutch West Indies and, from 1845, part of the Netherlands Antilles, with which on 29 Dec. 1954 it achieved internal self-government.

Following a referendum in March 1977, the Dutch government announced on 28 Oct. 1981 that Aruba would proceed to independence separately from the other islands. Aruba was constitutionally separated from the Netherlands Antilles from 1 Jan. 1986, and full independence has been promised by the Netherlands after a 10-year period.

THE NETHERLANDS ANTILLES

The Netherlands Antilles comprise two groups of islands in the Caribbean, the Leeward group (Bonaire and Curaçao) and the Windward Islands. Bonaire and Curaçao islands, originally populated by Caiquetios Indians, were discovered in 1499 by Amerigo Vespucci and Alonso de Ojeda respectively, and claimed for Spain. They were settled in 1527, and the indigenous population exterminated and replaced by a slave-worked plantation economy. The three Windward Islands, inhabited by Caribs, were discovered by Columbus in 1493.

The two island groups were taken by the Dutch in 1632 (Saba and Sint Eustatius), 1634 (Curaçao and Bonaire) and 1648 (the southern part of Sint Maarten, with France acquiring the northern part). With Aruba, the islands formed part of the Dutch West Indies from 1828, and the Netherlands Antilles from 1845, with internal self-government being granted on 29 Dec. 1954. Aruba was separated from 1 Jan. 1986.

NEW ZEALAND

New Zealand comprises two main islands to the east of Australia. It was first called 'Aotearoa' by the Maori who arrived there from other northern islands in Polynesia sometime before the 14th century. The first European to discover New Zealand was Tasman in 1642. The coast was explored by Capt. Cook in 1769. From about 1800 onwards, New Zealand became a resort for whalers and traders, chiefly from Australia. By the Treaty of Waitangi in 1840, signed by Governor William Hobson and representatives of the Maori race, Maori landownership, fishing and forestry rights were formalized while the Maori chiefs ceded sovereignty to the British Crown, and the islands became a British colony. A steady stream of British settlers followed.

Between 1845 and 1848, and between 1860 and 1870, numerous conflicts over disputed rights over land led to war; peace was finally and permanently established in 1871, and thereafter a policy of assimilation began to introduce the Maori to Western culture.

The colony became a British dominion in 1907 and gained full independence by the Statute of Westminster in 1931. New Zealand troops played a significant part during the two world wars of 1914–18 and 1939–45.

During the 1970s and 1980s each of the two main political parties, the Labour Party and the National Party, have tended to win roughly equal support from the electorate.

Further Reading

Sinclair, K., *A History of New Zealand*. Rev. ed. London, 1980

FREELY ASSOCIATED STATES OF NEW ZEALAND

COOK ISLANDS

The Cook Islands were proclaimed a British protectorate in 1888. On 11 June 1901 they were annexed and proclaimed part of New Zealand. In 1965 the Cook Islands became a self-governing territory in free association with New Zealand. In Jan. 1986 the prime minister of Cook Islands declared the Islands to be a neutral country which would not be involved in any military relationship with a foreign country.

NIUE

The island was discovered by Capt. Cook in 1774 and became a British protectorate in April 1900. Niue was annexed to New Zealand in Sept. 1901 as part of the Cook Islands, but in 1904 it was granted a separate administration. Niue achieved internal self-government in Oct. 1974 in free association with New Zealand.

NICARAGUA

Active colonization of the Nicaraguan Pacific coast was undertaken by Spaniards from Panama, beginning in 1523. France and Britain however, and later the US have all tried to play a colonial or semi-colonial role in Nicaragua. Between 1740 and 1786 Britain attempted to organize a colony on the Miskito Coast and from 1848 to 1860 the British occupied the port of San Juan de Norte. After links with other Central American territories and with Mexico, Nicaragua became an independent republic in 1838. Its independence was often threatened by US intervention. William Wolber, the filibuster from Tennessee conquered the country and declared himself President in 1856–57. And between 1910 and 1930 the country was under almost continuous US military occupation.

In 1914 the Bryan-Chamarro Treaty between Nicaragua and the USA was signed, under which the US, in return for US$3m. acquired a permanent option for a canal route through Nicaragua, a 99-year option for a naval base in the Bay of Fonseca on the Pacific coast, and the Corn Islands on the Atlantic coast. The Bryan-Chamarro Treaty was ratified in 1916 and was not abrogated until 14 July 1970 and the Corn Islands returned to Nicaragua in 1971.

The Somoza family held political domination of Nicaragua from 1933 to 1979. Through a brutal dictatorship imposed through the National Guard, they secured for themselves a large share of the national wealth. In 1962 the radical Sandinista National Liberation Front was formed with the object of overthrowing the Somozas. After 17 years of civil war the Sandinistas triumphed. On 17 July 1979 President Somoza was overthrown and fled into exile. A Government Junta of National Reconstruction was established by the revolutionary government on 20 July, and a 51-member Council of State was later created.

Since this revolution the USA, especially under the presidency of Ronald Reagan, has tried to unseat the revolutionary government. The US has supported the Contras (counter-revolutionary forces) since 1981, and has tried to destabilize the Nicaraguan régime through economic boycott and in other ways. In March 1984 the Nicaraguan government filed a case against the USA in the International Court of Justice; the court's subsequent ruling was, however, ignored by the USA.

The elections that were expected after the 1979 revolution did not take place until Nov. 1984. The Government Junta of National Reconstruction and the Council of State were dissolved on 10 Jan. 1985 following the presidential and legislative elections; the Constituent Assembly which replaced them drew up a constitution within two years as instructed. On 9 Jan. 1987 the Sandinista president, Daniel Ortega, signed the new constitution, but immediately reimposed a state of emergency, suspending many of the liberties granted under the constitution.

The state of emergency was lifted early in 1988 as part of the Central American peace process.

Further Reading

Weber, H., *Nicaragua: The Sandinista Revolution*. London and New York, 1981

NIGER

Occupied by France between 1883 and 1899, Niger was in 1901 constituted a military territory which became part of French West Africa in 1904. On 18 Dec. 1958 it became an autonomous republic within the French Community and achieved full independence on 3 Aug. 1960. Hamani Diori was elected president and pursued a policy of good relations with France. He was twice re-elected before being overthrown in a military *coup* on 15 April 1974, led by Lieut.-Col. Seyni Kountché, who suspended the constitution, dissolved the national assembly and banned political groups.

Kountché has remained as president in the face of political plots and of serious droughts. More civilian members have been brought into the government; in 1983 a system of elected Development Councils was created, culminating in a 150-member National Development Council with limited legislative powers charged with drafting a new constitution.

In 1984 ex-president Diori was released from house arrest, although this restriction was re-imposed a year later following political troubles.

Further Reading

Fugelstad, F., *A History of Niger, 1850–1960*. OUP, 1984

NIGERIA

Farming communities settled in the area of present-day Nigeria 4,000 years ago, which was previously occupied by hunter-gatherers. They developed the large centralized state of Kanem-Bornu in the 8th century, based on control of trans-Saharan trade. Adjacent states, notably the Hausa, Oyo and Benin empires arose later, and became caught up in the slave trade by the 18th century. British occupation aimed at enforcing the abolition of the trade.

The port of Lagos was captured by Britain in 1851 and annexed in Aug. 1861, administered first from Sierra Leone and then from the Gold Coast. Growing British involvement in the Lagos hinterland and in the Niger Delta led to the establishment of protectorates in the former in Jan. 1886 with Lagos itself becoming a separate colony, and in the latter, known as the Oil Rivers Protectorate, in June 1885. British commercial interests among the Moslem emirates of the north led in July 1886 to the chartering of the Royal Niger Company which established its own political administration over a wide territory.

In 1893 the Oil Rivers Protectorate was expanded and renamed the Niger Coast Protectorate. On 1 Jan. 1900 the Royal Niger Company transferred its territory to the British Crown, and the southern parts of this were amalgamated with the Niger Coast Protectorate to form the Protectorate of Southern Nigeria (to which the colony and protectorate of Lagos was added in Feb. 1906), while the remainder was constituted as the Protectorate of Northern Nigeria. On 1 Jan. 1914 the two territories were merged to form the 'colony and protectorate of Nigeria'.

Through the system of indirect rule, Africans were excluded from political power until the end of the Second World War. A constitution was promulgated in 1947, and on 1 Oct. 1954 Nigeria vested in a federal system of government comprising Eastern, Western and Northern Regions; the first two of these secured internal self-government in 1956 and the Northern Region in 1959. Full independence was achieved by the Federation of Nigeria on 1 Oct. 1960 and it became a republic on 1 Oct. 1963. Instability characterized the period, relating to election disputes.

The republic was overthrown by a military *coup* on 15 Jan. 1966, and a military government established. In May 1967 a decree replaced the existing regions by 12 new states. Ethnic and regional conflict ensued, with Hausa northerners fearing domination by the Ibo people from the east of the country. Aguiyi-Ironsi was killed in an army mutiny and replaced by Lieut.-Col. Yakubu Gowon. He restored the federal system, but the Eastern Region decided to secede as the Republic of Biafra in May 1967. This set off a bloody civil war, prolonged by international involvement, and a severe famine developed. Federal forces re-established control in Jan. 1970. Besides the political problems, Gowon also faced economic problems related to Nigeria's new oil wealth, and he was ousted in a *coup* on 27 July 1975. He was succeeded by Brig. Murtala Muhammed who was, however, assassinated the following year. Lieut.-Gen. Olusegun Obasanjo replaced him, and returned the country (now organized in 19 states) to civilian rule in Oct. 1979 when Shehu Shagari was elected president. Shagari was re-elected in Sept. 1983, but overthrown by the military later that year. In Aug. 1985, Maj.-Gen. Ibrahim Babangida replaced Maj.-Gen. Muhammadu Buhari as head of the Armed Forces Ruling Council. In 1986, he announced that 1990 would see a return to civilian government.

Further Reading

Crowder, M., and Abdullahi, G., *Nigeria: An Introduction to its History.* London, 1979

NORWAY

Norway was under Danish domination from the 14th century. By a treaty of 14 Jan. 1814, the King of Denmark ceded Norway to the King of Sweden, but the Norwegian people declared themselves independent and elected Prince Christian Frederik of Denmark as their king. The foreign powers refused to recognize this election, and on 14 Aug. a convention proclaimed the independence of Norway in a personal union with Sweden. This was followed on 4 Nov. by the election of Karl XIII (II) as King of Norway. Norway declared this union dissolved on 7 June 1905 and Sweden agreed to the repeal of the union on 26 Oct. 1905. The throne was offered to a prince of the reigning house of Sweden, who declined. After a plebiscite, Prince Carl of Denmark was formally elected king on 18 Nov. 1905, and he took the name of Haakon VII, reigning for 52 years, after which he was succeeded by his son.

From 1940 to 1944, during the Second World War, Norway was occupied by the Germans who set up a widely resented pro-German government under Vidkun Quisling, a Norwegian.

Apart from this wartime episode, the Labour Party held office, and the majority in the Storting (parliament), from 1935 to 1965. From 1965 coalitions of minority governments held power until a Labour government again took office on 9 May 1986, succeeding a Conservative and Centre coalition. In 1949 Norway became a member of NATO, but membership of the EEC was rejected by a referendum in 1972.

NORWEGIAN DEPENDENCIES

SVALBARD

On Svalbard the lucrative whale hunting caused rival Dutch, British and Danish-Norwegian claims to sovereignty, as did the discovery of coalfields in the 20th century. By a treaty signed on 9 Feb. 1920, Norway's sovereignty over the archipelago was recognized and on 14 Aug. 1925 the archipelago was officially incorporated in Norway.

JAN MAYEN

The name Jan Mayen derives from the Dutch whaling captain, Jan Jacobsz May, who discovered the island in 1614 when it was uninhabited. On 8 May 1929 Jan Mayen was officially proclaimed as incorporated in the Kingdom of Norway.

BOUVET ISLAND

Bouvet Island was discovered in 1739 by a French naval officer, Jean Baptiste Bouvet, but the British were the first to hoist a flag on the island. In 1928 Britain waived its claim to the island in favour of Norway. A law of 27 Feb. 1930 declared Bouvet Island (Bouvetøya) a Norwegian dependency.

PETER I ISLAND

The Norwegian flag was first hoisted on Peter I Island in 1929. On 1 May 1931 Peter I Island was placed under Norwegian sovereignty, and on 24 March 1933 it was incorporated in Norway as a dependency.

QUEEN MAUD LAND

Queen Maud Land was ownerless until the Norwegians explored it, and on 14 Jan. 1939 the Norwegian cabinet placed it under Norwegian sovereignty. In 1957 Queen Maud Land was given the status of a Norwegian dependency.

Further Reading

Derry, T. K., *A History of Modern Norway, 1814–1972*. OUP, 1973.—*A History of Scandinavia*. London, 1979

OMAN

Oman was dominated by Portugal from 1507–1649. The Al-Busaid family assumed power in 1744 and have ruled to the present day. The Sultanate of Oman, known as the Sultanate of Muscat and Oman until 1970, is an absolute monarchy ruled by the Sultan by decree without a constitution.

On 23 July 1970 Said bin Taimur was deposed by his son Qaboos who pronounced reforms and has developed communications, housing, education and health services. In 1981 a 45-member state advisory council was established.

Further Reading

Peterson, J. E., *Oman in the Twentieth Century*. London and New York, 1978

PAKISTAN

The state of Pakistan was created on 14 Aug. 1947 by the Partition of India and consisted of the former East Bengal (with a district of Assam), the North West Frontier, Sind, the West Punjab and Baluchistan. Kashmir was disputed between Pakistan and India.

Pakistan was a deliberate creation, formed in order to provide Indian Moslems with their own state. This aim had been expressed by the All-India Moslem League since 1940 and was successfully pressed by Mohammad Ali Jinnah (1876–1948) despite initial strong opposition from the predominantly Hindu Indian National Congress.

East Bengal acceded to Pakistan in 1947 and seceded after civil war in Dec. 1971 when it became the independent republic of Bangladesh *(q.v.)*.

The North West Frontier was created by the government of British India as a military buffer zone to protect its Indian empire from Tsarist Russian expansion through central Asia; it was administered as a tribal agency, and included parts of the Punjab across the Indus River, the Peshawar valley and the mountain areas between Chitrál and the Vihowa River. The people were Moslem Pathan hill tribes; government contact with them was often difficult, but essential in order to protect the vital routes across the province through the Khyber, Kuram, Tochi and Gomal passes. The centre was Peshawar, an ancient city on a caravan route.

Sind was a tributary state of the Mughal empire from 1592, its people having previously come under Persian and Arabian influence. The British took Sind in 1843 and governed it as part of the Bombay Presidency, developing Karachi as a supply port.

The western Punjab was part of the Sikh homeland annexed by the British in 1849 (*see* India).

Baluchistan was an independent state which entered into treaty relations with British India in 1854 and 1876. The British then obtained a small area around Quetta, British Baluchistan. They also received the right to fortify and administer Quetta and Bolan, and to bring troops into the territory of the paramount Baluch chief, the Khan of Kalat, who in return received a subsidy. Outside Quetta, Bolan and British Baluchistan there was Kalat as an independent state and an independent northern area which was not ruled by the khan and was mainly Pathan. In 1887 British Baluchistan was incorporated into British India.

In 1947 Pakistan came into being, with Jinnah as its first governor-general. The state incorporated the whole of Baluchistan, an action which is still the cause of unrest. Pakistan's status was that of a Dominion within the Commonwealth; it became a republic in 1956 and left the Commonwealth in 1972.

The first of several periods of martial law began in 1958, followed by the rule of Field Marshal Mohammad Ayub Khan (until 1969) and Maj.-Gen. Agha Mohammad Yahya Khan (until 1971).

During the latter's term, differences between East and West Pakistan came to a head. The East Pakistan Awami League won the majority of seats in the general election of 7 Dec. 1970, pressing for autonomy. Martial law continued while attempts were made to negotiate, but civil war broke out in March 1971 and ended in Dec. 1971 with the creation of Bangladesh. President Yahya Khan resigned and was succeeded by Zulfiqar Ali Bhutto.

A new constitution came into force on 14 Aug. 1973, providing a federal parliamentary government with a president as head of state and a prime minister as head of the government. Mr Bhutto became prime minister, relinquishing the post of president. His government was thought by traditionalists to be too Western and not sufficiently Islamic. There was an army *coup* led by Gen. Mohammad Zia ul-Haq in July 1977. Gen. Zia ul-Haq became president in 1978.

The constitution of 1973 was held in abeyance and national elections were not held until Feb. 1985. The president set up a National Security Council to control the elected government in March 1985; in April 1985 this was replaced by a Federal Cabinet. Martial law ended on 30 Dec. 1985.

The Constitution (Ninth Amendment) Bill, 1986, confirmed that Islamic teaching is the basis of national law.

The invasion of neighbouring Afghánistán by the USSR in 1979 caused a flow of Afghan refugees into Pakistan. By 1987 they numbered about 3m., most in the North West Frontier Province which still functions as a military buffer zone.

Further Reading

Hasan, M., (ed.) *Pakistan in a Changing World*. Karachi, 1978

PANAMA

A revolution, inspired by the USA, led to the separation of Panama from the United States of Colombia and the declaration of its independence on 3 Nov. 1903. The *de facto* government was recognized by the USA on 5 Nov., and soon afterwards by the other major powers. Diplomatic relations between Colombia and Panama were finally established on 8 May 1924.

On 18 Nov. 1903 a treaty between the USA and the Republic of Panama was signed making it possible for the USA to build and operate a canal connecting the Atlantic and Pacific oceans through the Isthmus of Panama. The treaty granted the US in perpetuity the use, occupation and control of a Canal Zone, in which the USA would possess full sovereign rights. In return the USA guaranteed the independence of the republic and agreed to pay the republic $10m. and an annuity of $250,000. The USA purchased the French rights and properties – the French had been labouring from 1879 to 1899 in an effort to build the Canal – for $40m. and in addition paid private landholders within what would be the Canal Zone a mutually agreeable price for their properties.

The US domination of Panama has provoked frequent anti-American political actions. In 1968 a more independently minded president, Col. Omar Torryas Herrera, took power in a *coup* and attempted to negotiate a more advantageous treaty with the USA. Two new treaties between Panama and the USA were agreed on 10 Aug. and signed on 7 Sept. 1977. One deals with the operation and defence of the canal until the end of 1999 and the other guarantees permanent neutrality.

The USA maintains operational control over all lands, waters and installations, including military bases, necessary to manage, operate and defend the canal until 31 Dec. 1999. Until 1990 the canal administrator will be a US citizen and the deputy will be Panamanian. After that date the position will be reversed.

Six months after the exchange of instruments of ratification Panama assumed general territorial jurisdiction over the former Canal Zone and became able to use portions of the area not needed for the operation and defence of the canal. In 1986 a tripartite commission formed by Japan, Panama and the USA began studies on alternatives to the Panama Canal. Options are: to build a sea-level canal, to enlarge the existing canal with more locks, to improve

the canal alongside upgraded rail and road facilities, or to continue
with the existing facilities.

Torryas vacated the presidency in 1978 but maintained his power
as head of the National Guard until his death in an air crash in 1981.
Since then, under several presidents Gen. Noriega, Torryas'
successor as head of the National Guard, has been the strong man of
the régime: His position has, however, been threatened in 1988 by
some internal political opposition and economic pressure applied
by the USA.

Further Reading
Jorden, W. J., *Panama Odyssey*. Univ. of Texas Press, 1984

PAPUA NEW GUINEA

New Guinea, especially the eastern half, Irian Jaya, was known to Indonesian and Asian seafarers centuries before it was known to the Europeans. In 1512 the Portuguese sighted the New Guinea coast but made no landing until 1527. Spanish first claimed the island in 1545 but the first attempt at colonization was made in 1793 by the British. The Dutch however, claimed the west half of the island as part of the Dutch West Indies in 1828.

In order to prevent that portion of the island of New Guinea not claimed by the Netherlands or Germany from passing into the hands of another foreign power, the Government of Queensland annexed Papua in 1883. This step was not sanctioned by the Imperial Government, but on 6 Nov. 1884 a British Protectorate was proclaimed over the southern portion of the eastern half of New Guinea, and in 1887 Queensland, New South Wales and Victoria undertook to defray the cost of administration, and the territory was annexed to the Crown the following year. By 1884 the south-east of New Guinea had been annexed to Britain and the German New Guinea Company took over the north-east of the country. The Australian federal government took over control in 1901; the political transfer was completed by the Papua Act of the federal parliament in Nov. 1905, and on 1 Sept. 1906 the Governor-General of Australia declared that British New Guinea was to be known henceforth as the Territory of Papua. The northern portion of New Guinea was a German colony until 1914 when Australian armed forces occupied it and it remained under their administration for the next seven years. It became a League of Nations mandated territory in 1921, administered by Australia, and later a UN Trust Territory (of New Guinea).

The Papua New Guinea Act 1949–72 provides for the administration of the UN Australian Trust Territory of New Guinea in an administrative union with the Territory of Papua, under the title of Papua New Guinea. Australia granted Papua New Guinea self-government on 1 Dec. 1973, and on 16 Sept. 1975 Papua New Guinea became a fully independent state.

Further Reading

Hasluck, P., *A Time for Building*. Melbourne Univ. Press, 1976

PARAGUAY

A landlocked territory bordered by Brazil, Argentina and Bolivia, Paraguay was occupied by the Spanish in 1537 and became a Spanish colony as part of the viceroyalty of Peru. The Guaraní-speaking population gained some protection from the powerful Jesuit mission stations until the expulsion of the Jesuits in 1767. In 1776 the area became part of the viceroyalty of Rio de la Plata, gaining its independence from Spain, as the Republic of Paraguay, on 14 May 1811. Since 1814 Paraguay has been ruled by a succession of dictators, the first being Dr José Gaspar Rodriguez de Francia who was elected dictator in 1814 by the national assembly and became perpetual dictator in 1816; he died in 1840. In 1844 a new constitution was adopted under which Carlos Antonio López (nephew of Dr Francia) and his son, Francisco López, ruled until 1870.

During a devastating war, fought from 1865 to 1870, between Paraguay and a coalition of Argentina, Brazil and Uruguay, Paraguay's population was reduced from about 600,000 to 233,000 and the economy seriously damaged. In 1942 Argentina, and in 1943 Brazil, cancelled reparations which Paraguay had never paid.

Further severe losses were incurred during the war with Bolivia (1932–35) over territorial claims in the Chaco inspired by the unfounded belief that minerals existed in the territory.

The dictatorship of Gen. Higinio Moringo was ended following a civil war in which the right-wing party *(Partido Colorado)* defeated the Liberals. A period of unrest ensued until Gen. Alfredo Stroessner Mattianda, the C.-in-C. of the Army, assumed power in a military *coup* in 1954.

A new constitution took effect in Feb. 1968 under which executive power is discharged by an executive president. In 1977 the constitution was amended to enable the president to stand for more than two consecutive terms of office. Gen. Stroessner was, in fact, re-elected 7 times between 1958 and 1988.

The state of siege in force since 1947 – associated with the suspension of civil liberties and widespread violation of human rights – was allowed to lapse on 8 April 1987.

Further Reading

Lewis, P. H., *Paraguay under Stroessner*. Univ. of North Carolina Press, 1980

PERU

The Incas of Peru were conquered by the Spanish in the 16th century, and subsequent Spanish colonial settlement made Peru the most important of the Spanish viceroyalties in South America. On 28 July 1821 Peru declared its independence, but it was not until after a war which ended in 1824 that the country gained its freedom. The two presidential terms served by Gen. Ramón Castilla (1845–51 and 1855–62) were prosperous ones for Peru; but in a disastrous war with Chile (1879–83) Peru's capital, Lima, was captured and she lost some of her southern territory to Chile under the peace treaty. Tacna remained in Chilean control from 1880 until 1929.

In 1924 Dr Victor Raúl Haya de la Torre founded the *Alianza Popular Revolucionaria Americana* to oppose the dictatorial government then in power. Although this party was banned between 1931 and 1945 and between 1948 and 1956, and although its leader failed regularly in the presidential elections it was at times the largest party in Congress.

In Oct. 1948 Gen. Manuel Odria deposed President José Luis Bustamante y Rivera and became president in 1950. He was succeeded by an elected president, Dr Manuel Prado y Ugarteche in 1956; but the closeness of the 1962 elections led Gen. Ricardo Pérez Godoy, Chairman of the Joint Chiefs-of-Staff, to seize power. A *coup* led by Gen. Nicolás Lindley López deposed him in 1963. There followed, after elections, a period of civilian rule under President Fernando Belaúnde Terry, who enacted important legislation and measures to promote agrarian reforms. The military staged yet another *coup* in 1968, and the Army Chief-of-Staff, Gen. Juan Velasco Alvarado, usurped the presidency and dissolved Congress. He in turn was overthrown and superseded by Gen. Francisco Morales Bermudez in 1975. In 1978–79 a constituent assembly drew up a new constitution, after which a civilian government was installed and President Fernando Belaúnde Terry again took office on 28 July 1980. He was succeeded in a constitutional process of election by President Alan Garcia Pérez in July 1985.

Further Reading
McClintock, C. and Lowental, A. F. (eds.), *The Peruvian Experiment Reconsidered*. Princeton Univ. Press, 1983

THE PHILIPPINES

Discovered by Magellan in 1521, the Philippine islands were conquered by Spain in 1565 and named after the Spanish king, Philip. The independence of the Philippines was declared in June 1898 but in Dec. 1898 at the signing of the Treaty of Paris, following the Spanish-American War, the Philippines were ceded to the USA. A four-year war followed with considerable loss of life of Filopinos.

The Philippines acquired self-government as a Commonwealth of the USA by Act of Congress signed by President Roosevelt in March 1934. This Act provided for complete independence after a ten-year transitional period. The islands were occupied by the Japanese from 1942 to 1945. Independence was achieved in July 1946. From independence until 1972 the Philippines were governed under a constitution based largely on the US pattern consisting of a president with a fixed four-year term of office, a bicameral legislature and an independent judiciary. Two political parties dominated the political scene during this period, the Liberals and the Nationalists.

In 1971 changes were planned for the constitution. However, in Sept. 1972 before the constitution could be ratified President Ferdinand Marcos declared martial law. His action was motivated in part by concern at the growing strength of Communists, but it was also felt that the president wished to remain in power after 1973 which would not have been possible under the new constitution. A succession of referenda approved extensions to the president's term of office.

Following the sentence of death being passed on Benigno Aquino, Jr, the main opposition leader, in Nov. 1977, criticism of Marcos increased. A stay of execution was allowed and in May 1980 Aquino was released from prison to go to the USA for medical treatment.

Jan. 1981 saw the lifting of martial law and in Aug. 1983 Aquino returned to the Philippines after three years' exile and was shot dead on arrival at Manila airport. This action united the opposition parties against Marcos.

Under pressure as much from the USA as from political and economic situations within the Philippines, Marcos agreed to presidential elections in Feb. 1986. Although the National Assembly announced that Marcos had a majority, the elections proved to be fraudulent and Marcos fled the country on 26 Feb.

1986. On the same day Corazan Aquino (widow of Benigno Aquino) was sworn in as president.

On 25 March 1986 the president suspended the constitution and declared a provisional government.

A new constitution was ratified by referendum in 1987 with 78·5% of the voters endorsing it. It aimed 'to secure to ourselves and our posterity the blessings of independence and democracy under the rule of law and a régime of truth, justice, freedom, love, equality and peace.'

Further Reading

Bresnan, J., *Crisis in the Philippines: The Marcos Era and Beyond.* Princeton Univ. Press, 1986

Lightfort, K., *The Philippines.* London, 1973

PITCAIRN ISLAND

The island, an isolated volcanic formation in the south Pacific Ocean, was discovered by Carteret in 1767, but remained uninhabited until 1790, when it was occupied by 9 mutineers of HMS *Bounty*, with 12 women and 6 men from Tahiti. Nothing was known of their existence until the island was visited in 1808. In 1856 the population having become too large for the island's resources, the inhabitants (194 in number) were, at their own request, removed to Norfolk Island; but 43 of them returned in 1859–64.

Pitcairn was brought within the jurisdiction of the High Commissioner for the Western Pacific in 1898 and transferred to the Governor of Fiji in 1952. When Fiji became independent in Oct. 1970, the British High Commissioner in New Zealand was appointed Governor.

Further Reading

A Guide to Pitcairn. Rev. ed. Pitcairn Island Administration, Auckland, 1982

POLAND

Poland takes its name from the Polanie ('plain dwellers'), whose ruler Mieszko I had achieved a federation by 966, a date taken as that of the foundation of the Polish state. He placed Poland under the Roman Holy See around 990. His son Bolesław I (992–1025) continued his father's territorial expansionism until by the time of his coronation in 1024 Poland's boundaries were much as they are today. The tendency of this state to fragment under German pressure was formalized by Bolesław III (1102–38), whose sons divided the kingdom into 3 duchies. In the 13th century Poland was laid waste by incursions from the pagan proto-Prussians and Mongols. In 1320 Władysław of Kraków succeeded in being crowned king of Poland. The work of unification was consolidated by his son, Kazimierz III (1333–70), whose reign brought prosperity and administrative efficiency. A descendant of his married the pagan duke of Lithuania, Jagiełło, who was converted to Catholicism and became king of Poland in 1386, uniting Poland and Lithuania in a vast multi-ethnic empire which was able to break the power of the Teutonic Knights at Tannenberg in 1410.

The Jagiełłonian period to 1572 is regarded as an economic and cultural 'golden age'. In 1648 a Cossack revolt in the Ukraine resulted in a Russian victory and acquisition of territory; immediately afterwards Sweden occupied and devastated the whole country. Turkish inroads were only finally quelled by King Jan Sobieski's victory at Vienna in 1683. Poland's involvement in the Russo-Swedish wars of 1700–09 brought not only further economic ruin but also the political dependence of the Polish king on the might of Peter the Great. In 1701 the Hohenzollern prince Frederick assumed the title of King of Prussia; his descendant, Frederick the Great, brought Prussia to the position of European power. In the 'First Partition' of 1772 Russia and Prussia in conjunction with Austria took over a third of Poland's territory on the pretext of a Polish uprising at Bar (1768). Poland was wiped off the map by the Second and Third partitions (1793, 1795), except for a brief independent interlude under Napoleon.

Risings in 1830, 1846, 1848 and 1863 were unsuccessful. Thereafter nationalist efforts were channelled more into cultural and economic development. Political parties were formed: the National Democrats under Roman Dmowski campaigned for autonomy; the

Socialists under Józef Piłsudski joined the 1905 uprising in search of independence. With the impending collapse of the partitioning powers in the First World War, a Polish National Committee was formed in Paris in 1917 and recognized by the Allies. The thirteenth of President Woodrow Wilson's 'Fourteen Points' guaranteed Poland's independence and access to the sea. A Polish army was organized in France in 1918. Inside Poland Piłsudski had formed a fighting force of his own, the 'Polish legions', and he set up a rival government. The breach was healed by the appointment to the premiership of the neutral pianist, Jan Paderewski, with Piłsudski remaining chief of state.

A constitution was voted in March 1921. Poland's frontiers were not established until 1923, after plebiscites in Silesia and East Prussia and a war with Soviet Russia in 1920 which Poland nearly lost. Piłsudski took power in a *coup* in May 1926. His dictatorship endured until 1935. In foreign affairs Poland attempted to maintain a balance between Germany and the USSR, but after Munich she accepted a British guarantee of her independence in April 1939. In Aug. Hitler signed a non-aggression pact with Stalin which provided for a partition of Poland; this took place a few days after the outbreak of war.

Poland was rapidly overrun, but Polish forces were able to reform on Allied soil under a government-in-exile. Moscow broke off relations with the 'London' Poles in 1943 and recognized the Polish Committee of National Liberation (the 'Lublin committee') which proclaimed itself the sole legal government when Lublin was liberated in July 1944. In Aug. and Sept. the Soviet army stopped short of the city while the resistance forces were destroyed in the Warsaw uprising. At the Yalta conference Stalin agreed that the Lublin government should be extended to include non-Communists, and the 'London' Polish leader Mikolajczyk with 3 colleagues joined the cabinet in July 1945.

Elections were held on 19 Jan. 1947. Of the 12·7m. votes cast, 9m. were given for the Communist-dominated 'Democratic Bloc'. After riots in Poznań in June 1956 nationalist anti-Stalinist elements gained control of the Communist Party, under the leadership of Władysław Gomułka.

In 1970 the Federal Republic of Germany recognized Poland's western boundary as laid down by the Potsdam Conference of 1945 (the 'Oder-Neisse line').

In Dec. 1970 strikes and riots in Gdańsk, Szczecin and Gdynia led to the resignation of a number of leaders including Gomułka. He was replaced by Edward Gierek.

The raising of meat prices on 1 July 1980 resulted in a wave of strikes which broadened into generalized wage demands and eventually by mid-Aug. acquired a political character. Workers in Gdańsk, Gdynia and Sopot elected a joint strike committee, led by Lech Wałęsa demanding the right to strike and to form independent trade unions, the abolition of censorship, access to the media and the release of political prisoners.

On 31 Aug. the government and Wałęsa signed the 'Gdańsk Agreements' permitting the formation of independent trade unions.

On 5 Sept. Gierek suffered a heart attack and retired from the party leadership. On 17 Sept. various trade unions decided to form a national confederation ('Solidarity') and applied for legal status, which was granted on 24 Oct. after some government resistance.

In Feb. the Defence Minister, Gen. Wojciech Jaruzelski took over the premiership. At Solidarity's national congress (Sept.–Oct. 1981) Wałęsa was re-elected chairman and a radical programme of action was adopted. On 18 Oct. Jaruzelski took over the party leadership and imposed martial law. Solidarity was proscribed and its leaders detained. Wałęsa was released in Nov. 1982. Martial law was lifted in July 1983.

Further Reading

Davies, N., *Heart of Europe: A Short History of Poland*. OUP, 1984

PORTUGAL

Portugal has been an independent state since the 12th century apart from one period of Spanish rule (1580–1640). It became a kingdom in 1139 under Alfonso I.

During the 15th century with considerable encouragement from Henry the Navigator (1415–61), Portugal played a leading role in oceanic exploration, opening up new trade routes and establishing colonies. Portuguese influence spread in Guinea, Brazil, the Indies and on the African coast.

The Braganza family came to the throne when Portugal rebelled against Spain in 1640 after 60 years of Spanish domination.

In 1807, during the Napoleonic wars, the Spaniards again invaded Portugal, but were driven out by the Duke of Wellington and Portuguese guerrillas during the Peninsular War. Brazil, where the king had fled during the French invasion, became independent in 1822.

During much of the 19th century liberal governments, led by financial and agrarian oligarchs and chosen by an electorate composed of fewer than one per cent of the population, were in office. The excluded nationalistic republicans finally deposed King Manuel II on 5 Oct. 1910. Another *coup* on 28 May 1926 removed the unstable parliamentary republic which had fought from 1916 on the Allied side in the First World War. The military government established on 1 June 1926 was succeeded in 1932 when Dr Antonio de Oliveira Salazar became Prime Minister. The corporatist constitution of the New State was adopted on 19 March 1933 under which a civil dictatorship governed in a one-party state. The Iberian Pact with Spain was signed on 17 March 1939.

In the 1960s Portugal faced economic stagnation at home and rebellion in her colonies. Goa was seized by India in 1961. War raged in the African colonies, which gained eventual independence in 1974–75. In Sept. 1968 Salazar was succeeded by Dr Caetano, but the government party, from 1970 called the *Acçao Nacional Popular*, remained in power.

There was a fresh *coup* on 25 April 1974, establishing a junta of National Salvation. Gen. Antonio Ribeiro de Spinola became president. When he resigned in Sept. he was succeeded by Gen. Francisco de Costa Gomes. During 1974–75 most of the Portuguese overseas possessions gained independence.

Following an attempted revolt on 11 March 1975, the junta was dissolved and a Supreme Revolutionary Council formed which ruled until 25 April 1976 when constitutional government was resumed. The Supreme Revolutionary Council was renamed the Council of the Revolution, becoming a consultative body chaired by the president.

The transition to full civilian government was completed in 1982 when the constitution of 1976 was revised so as to abolish the Council of the Revolution and to reduce the powers of the president. Since 1976 Mario Soares's Socialists have been the largest party though all governments have been coalitions. Portugal had been a founder member of EFTA and entered the European Community on 1 Jan. 1986.

Further Reading

Gallagher, T., *Portugal: A Twentieth Century Interpretation*. Manchester Univ. Press, 1983

MACAO

Macao is an overseas territory of Portugal on the southern China Coast. It was visited by Portuguese traders from 1513 and trade with China was placed on an official basis in 1553. It became a Portuguese colony in 1557 and was soon a principal entrepôt for international trade with China and Japan. Initially sovereignty remained vested in China, with the Portuguese paying an annual rent. In 1848–49 the Portuguese declared Macao a free port and established jurisdiction over the territory. A Sino-Portuguese treaty of 1 Dec. 1887 confirmed Portuguese rights to the territory. Diversion of its trade to Hong Kong, and the opening of the treaty ports by China, left Macao handling only local distributive trade, although its entrepôt role was briefly revived during the closure of the Hong Kong/China border in 1939. It was an Overseas Province of Portugal from 1951–74. In 1976 it became a Territory under Portuguese administration. On 6 Jan. 1987 Portugal agreed to return Macao to China in 1999 under a plan in which it would become a special administrative zone of China, with considerable autonomy.

QATAR

Qatar became part of the Ottoman Empire in 1872 but was evacuated by Turkey in 1914. By a treaty of 3 Nov. 1916 Qatar became a British protectorate ruled by Shaikh Abdullah-Al-Thani, with internal self-government. A further treaty was signed in 1934. Having failed to form a federation of states, Britain withdrew its forces from Qatar in 1971 and the State of Qatar declared itself independent from Britain on 3 Sept. 1971, the ruler taking the title of emir. A treaty of friendship was also signed between the two countries.

The emir rules as an absolute monarch with neither a legislative body nor political parties.

Further Reading
El Mallakh, R., *Qatar: The Development of an Oil Economy.* New York, 1979

ROMANIA

The Romanians cherish their Latin origins and language, which date from Trajan's occupation of Dacia. The foundation of the feudal 'Danubian Principalities' of Wallachia and Moldavia in the late 13th and early 14th centuries marks the beginning of an era. (Transylvania also part of modern Romania by this time was in the hands of the Magyars). The Orthodox church and quarrelsome nobility were nearly as powerful as the princes, a balance of power which the expansionist Turks were able to manipulate after the 14th century. Wallachia and Moldavia became tribute-paying vassals without ever being formally incorporated into the Ottoman empire. The nobility acted as the Turks' agents until 1711 when, their bribery funds exhausted and suspected of pro-Russian sentiments (Peter the Great was on their northern doorstep), they were replaced by Greek merchant adventurers, the Phanariots.

The Phanariot period of ruthless extortion and corruption was ameliorated by Russian interference. Bessarabia was annexed and Russian support after the rebellion of Tudor Vladimirescu in 1821 brought about a restoration of Romanian princes. Between 1829 and 1834 the foundations of the modern state were laid under a Russian protectorate, but in the revolutionary episode of 1848 Russian interference became repressive. After the Crimean War Bessarabia was restored to Moldavia, and under the auspices of the great powers elections were held in both principalities which resulted in the election of Alexandru Cuza to both thrones in Jan. 1859; the Moldavian and Wallachian assemblies were fused in 1862. Cuza's reforms brought him into conflict with the nobility, who deposed him in 1866. Carol of Hohenzollern was brought to the throne, and a constitution adopted based on that of Belgium of 1831. Romania was formally declared independent by the Treaty of Berlin of 1878, and became a kingdom (the 'Old Kingdom') in 1881. Romania regained Bessarabia by the Treaty, and gained Dobrudja from Bulgaria in the Balkan wars of 1913.

This was a period of expansion for an economy firmly in the hands of the landowners (represented by the Conservative party) and nascent industrialists (of the Liberal party). The condition of the peasantry remained miserable, and the rebellion of 1907 was an expression of their discontent. Romania joined the First World War on the allied side in 1916. The spoils of victory brought Transylvania (with large Hungarian and German populations), Bessarabia, Bukovina and Dobrudja into union with the 'Old Kingdom'. The centralizing constitution of 1923 reduced the autonomy of the Transylvanian Romanians; the National Peasant party of Iuliu Maniu was formed in 1926 in protest. The Liberals had broken the power of the Conservatives by the land reform of 1920, and continued in office until the (relatively fair) elections of 1928, at which the Peasants gained 330 seats to the Liberals' 13. Carol II's advent to the throne was delayed by a sexual scandal; when he acceded in 1930 Maniu resigned. Hit by the world recession, Romania was increasingly drawn into Germany's economic orbit. Against this background the fascist Iron Guard arose, which assassinated the Liberal leader in 1934. Carol himself adopted increasingly totalitarian modes of rule, banning political parties by his constitution of 1938. Following Nazi and Soviet annexations of Romanian territory in 1940 he abdicated in favour of his son Michael. The government of the fascist Ion Antonescu declared war on the USSR on 22 June 1941. On 23 Aug. 1944 Michael with the backing of a bloc of opposition parties deposed Antonescu and switched sides.

The armistice of Sept. 1944 gave the Soviet army control of Romania's territory. This, and the 'spheres of influence' diplomacy of the Allies, predetermined the establishment of communism in Romania. A government under the pro-communist peasant leader Petru Groza was installed in March 1945. Transylvania was restored to Romania (though it lost Bessavabic and Southern Dobrudja), and large estates were broken up for the benefit of the peasantry. Elections in Nov. 1946 were held in an atmosphere of intimidation and fraudulence; the communist bloc received 376 seats, the Peasants 33, the Liberals 3. In 1947 the latter parties were abolished, Michael was forced to abdicate and a people's republic was proclaimed. The communist leader, Gheorghe Gheorghiu-Dej purged himself of his fellow leaders in the early 1950s. His successor, Nicolae Ceausescu, has developed Dej's tendencies to economic autarky and foreign policy independence, and has established a form of dynastic rule.

Further Reading

Seton-Watson, R. W., *A History of the Roumanians from Roman Times to the Completion of Unity.* CUP, 1934, reprinted 1963

RWANDA

From the 16th century, Rwanda was organized as part of the wider Tutsi kingdom encompassing present-day Burundi. It was taken as part of German East Africa in 1890, and passed to Belgium after the German defeat in the First World War. Administered with Burundi as a League of Nations mandate and later a UN trust territory, the Tutsi feudal hierarchy was maintained until an uprising of the Hutu in 1959. The Tutsi ruler, Mwami Kigeri V, went into exile. Elections and a referendum under the auspices of the UN in Sept. 1961 resulted in an overwhelming majority for the republican party, the Parmehutu *(Parti du Mouvement de l'Emancipation du Bahutu)*, and the rejection of the institution of the Mwami. The republic proclaimed by the Parmehutu on 28 Jan. 1961 was recognized by the Belgian administration (but not by the UN) in Oct. 1961. Internal self-government was granted on 1 Jan. 1962, and by decision of the General Assembly of the UN the Republic of Rwanda became independent on 1 July 1962.

Conflict between the Hutu and Tutsi in 1963 was renewed, and again trouble broke out, with much bloodshed, in 1972–73. A *coup* on 5 July 1973 deposed the first president, Gregoire Kayibanda, and a military government was established. The military leader of this *coup*, Gen. Juvénal Habyarimana, became president. There was gradual return to civilian rule. In 1978 a new constitution was accepted by a national referendum. President Habyarimana was confirmed in office in elections in 1978 and again in 1983, when candidates from the country's sole political party, the National Revolutionary Democratic Movement, were also returned. Over the past ten years the country has contended with the problem of refugees fleeing repression and war in neighbouring Uganda.

Further Reading
Lemarchand, R., *Rwanda and Burundi.* London, 1970

ST CHRISTOPHER (ST KITTS) –NEVIS

The islands of St Christopher (known also as St Kitts and to its Carib inhabitants as Liamuiga) and Nevis in the north eastern Caribbean were discovered and named by Columbus in 1493. When Columbus visited the islands they were occupied by the warlike cannibalistic Caribs, who had driven the more peaceful Arawaks from most of the lesser Antilles (islands). British settlers arrived in 1623, and French settlers in 1624, so ownership was disputed until 1713. The island of St Christopher was ceded to Britain by the Treaty of Utrecht (1713). However, fighting with the French continued, and the island was finally restored to Britain by the Treaty of Versailles in 1783. Nevis also suffered from French and Spanish attacks in the 17th and 18th centuries. Most of the present inhabitants are decendants of black Africans brought to the islands as slaves.

St Christopher and Nevis formed part of the Leeward Island Federation from 1871 to 1956, and part of the Federation of the West Indies from 1958 to 1962. In Feb. 1967 the former colony of St Kitts, Nevis and Anguilla became an Associated State with the UK responsible only for foreign policy and defence, while the islands were given full internal self-government. The Administrator became the Governor, and a House of Assembly replaced the Legislative Council. Anguilla separated from the colony, which was formally effected in Dec. 1980 (*see* ANGUILLA).

St Christopher–Nevis became fully independent on 19 Sept. 1983 when the new constitution described the country as a 'sovereign democratic federal state'. At the same time Nevis was given its own Island Assembly and the right of secession from St Christopher.

Further Reading
Gordon, J., *Nevis: Queen of the Caribees*. London, 1985

ST HELENA

This remote island in the South Atlantic was administered by the East India Company from 1659. In 1673 nearly half the inhabitants were imported slaves. Napoleon Bonaparte was exiled there from 1815 until his death in 1821. In 1834 St Helena was established as a British Colony.

After 1869, with the opening of the Suez Canal, St Helena was no longer on a main shipping trade route and since then the island has been heavily dependent on economic aid from Britain.

On 1 Jan. 1967 a constitution was promulgated and this established a Legislative Council consisting of the Governor, the Secretary, the Treasurer and 12 elected members. The constitution also established an Executive Council.

ST LUCIA

An island state of the lesser Antilles in the eastern Caribbean, St Lucia is believed to have been settled by the Arawaks, Amerindians who were subsequently driven out by the warlike Caribs. The island was probably discovered by Columbus in 1502. An unsuccessful attempt to colonize by the British took place in 1605, and again in 1638 when the settlers were soon murdered by the Caribs who peopled the island. France claimed the right of sovereignty, and ceded it to the French West India Company in 1642. The French settlers fought constant battles with the Caribs until peace was established in 1660. St Lucia regularly and constantly changed hands between Britain and France, until it was finally ceded to Britain in 1814 by the Treaty of Paris.

Since 1924 the island has had representative government. It was a part of the federal government of the Windward Islands until, in Jan. 1960, along with the colonies in the group, it was given its own Administrator. In March 1967 St Lucia gained full control of its internal affairs while Britain remained responsible for foreign affairs and defence; the Administrator became the Governor, and a House of Assembly replaced the Legislative Council. On 22 Feb. 1979 St Lucia achieved independence, opting to remain in the British Commonwealth.

Further Reading

Ellis, G., *St Lucia: Helen of the West Indies*. London, 1985

ST VINCENT AND THE GRENADINES

These islands in the eastern Caribbean were originally inhabited by the Carib tribes. St Vincent was discovered by Columbus on 22 Jan. (St Vincent's Day) 1498. British and French settlers occupied parts of the islands after 1627.

In 1773 the Caribs by a treaty recognized British sovereignty and agreed to a division of territory between themselves and the British. Resentful of British rule, the Caribs rebelled in 1795, aided by the French, but the revolt was subdued within a year. Most of the Carib population was deported to islands in the Gulf of Honduras and the surviving population was further reduced by eruptions of the volcano Santiere in 1812 and 1902.

The islands were part of the federal government of the Windward Islands until, in Jan. 1960, along with the other colonies in the group, they were given their own Administrator. Universal adult suffrage had been in existence on the islands since 1951. On 27 Oct. 1969 St Vincent became an Associated State with the UK responsible only for foreign policy and defence, while the islands were given full internal self-government. The Administrator became the Governor, and a House of Assembly replaced the Legislative Council. On 27 Oct. 1979 the colony acquired full independence as St Vincent and the Grenadines.

SAN MARINO

San Marino is a small republic situated on the Adriatic side of central Italy. According to tradition, St Marinus and a group of Christians settled there to escape persecution. By the 12th century San Marino had developed into a commune ruled by its own statutes and consul. Unsuccessful attempts were made to annex the republic to the papal states in the 18th century when Napoleon invaded Italy in 1797 he respected the rights of the republic and even offered to extend its territories.

In 1815 the Congress of Vienna recognized the independence of the republic. On 22 March 1862 San Marino concluded a treaty of friendship and co-operation, including a *de facto* customs union, with the Kingdom of Italy, thus preserving its ancient independence although completely surrounded by Italian territory. This treaty was renewed in 1872, 1879 and 1939, with several amendments between 1942 and 1985.

Further Reading
Matteini, N., *The Republic of San Marino*. San Marino, 1981

SÃO TOMÉ AND PRINCIPE

The islands of São Tomé and Principe off the west coast of Africa were colonized by Portugal for 5 centuries after being first visited by Portuguese navigators on 21 Dec. 1470. There may have been a few African inhabitants or visitors earlier, but most of the population arrived during the centuries when the islands served as an important slave-trading depot for South America and some slaves were kept on the islands to work on the sugar plantations. In the 19th century the islands became the first parts of Africa to grow cocoa. Although in 1876 Portugal abolished slavery in name, in practice it continued thereafter with many Angolans, Mozambicans and Cape Verdians being transported to work on the cocoa plantations. Because the slave-descended population was cut off from African culture, São Tomé had a higher proportion than other Portuguese colonies of *assimilados* (Africans acquiring full Portuguese culture and certain rights).

After becoming an Overseas Province of Portugal in 1951, São Tomé saw serious riots against Portuguese rule in 1953. From 1960 a Committee for the Liberation of São Tomé and Principe operated from neighbouring African territories. There was, however, no armed resistance on the islands, where in 1970 Portugal introduced some reforms and formed a 16-member legislative council and a provincial consultative council. Following the Portuguese revolution of 1974, the Movement for the Liberation of São Tomé and Principe, headed by Manoel Pinto da Costa, held talks with Portugal. A transitional government was formed later that year and, after a period of tension due to landowners' resistance to decolonization and the temporary retention of Portuguese troops, independence came on 12 July 1975. Pinto da Costa became the first president and was re-elected for a further five years in 1985.

Independent São Tomé and Principe officially proclaimed Marxist-Leninist policies, but it maintained a non-aligned foreign policy and has received aid from Portugal.

SAUDI ARABIA

In the 18th century, Nejd was an autonomous region governed from Diriya, the stronghold of the Wahhabis, a puritanical Islamic sect. It subsequently fell under the Turkish rule, but in 1913 Abdul Aziz Ibn Saud defeated the Turks and also captured the Turkish province of al Hasa. In 1920 he captured the Asir, and in 1921 by force of arms he added to his dominions the Jebel Shammar territory of the Rashid family. In 1925, he completed the conquest of the Hejaz.

The Kingdom of Saudi Arabia is a union of the two regions, Nejd and Hejaz. Great Britain recognized Abdul Aziz Ibn Saud as an independent ruler, King of the Hejaz and of Nejd and its dependencies, by the Treaty of Jiddah on 20 May, 1927. The name was changed to the Kingdom of Saudi Arabia in Sept. 1932.

Ibn Saud ruled as king until his death in Nov. 1953. The king is also the prime minister and the religious leader; there is no legislative body and no political parties.

During King Ibn Saud's reign there was considerable development of the oil resources of the country. Although begun before the Second World War, oil exploitation grew greatly with the support of the USA after 1945.

Abdul Ibn Saud has been succeeded by his sons, Saud, Faisal, Khalid and Fahd. Saud succeeded to the throne in 1953 but in March 1964 abdicated in favour of Faisal Ibn Abdul Aziz who had carried considerable power during the older brother's reign, being for a time prime minister with control over foreign and economic policy. Faisal was assassinated in 1975, and was succeeded by his brother, Khalid Ibn Abdul Aziz. On Khalid's death in 1982, Fahd Ibn Abdul Aziz became king. The kingdom has always maintained friendly relations with the USA, owing to the oil connection, and, since 1970, has attempted to act as a moderating, conservative force in inter-Arab politics.

Further Reading
Anderson, N., *The Kingdom of Saudi Arabia*. Rev. ed. London, 1982

SENEGAL

The major ethnic groups of Senegal are the Wolof, Serer, Tukulor (or Toucouleur), Soninke (or Sarakolle), Mandinka and Diola peoples. Some of them had important traditional kingdoms. In Fouta Toro in the east there was the state of Tekrur and then an Islamic state founded in 1776 by Muslim Tukulors. Islam reached the Senegal river valley by the 11th century, and later the Fulanis (whose migration all over West Africa began from Senegal) and the related Tukulors helped spread Islam over a large area.

For several centuries starting in the 14th the Wolofs had a supreme ruler, the Bourba Jolof, and several important kingdoms under him, notably the kingdom of Kayor (Kajoor) ruled by 30 kings or *damels* from the 16th century to 1886. The last *damel*, the Muslim Lat Dior, was famous for his resistance to French rule.

While in the mid-1400s the Portuguese were the first Europeans to reach the area around the Senegal river estuary, in succeeding centuries the French became the dominant Europeans on the coast in that area, except for the Gambia where the British were installed. The French founded St Louis in 1659 and also occupied the island of Goree, an important slave-trading depot. By the 18th century St Louis had an important small elite community, partly African, called the *habitants*. In the 19th century French rule, interrupted earlier by occasional British occupation, was confirmed over St Louis and Goree. Free Africans received the vote in 1833, and the franchise was further extended in 1848 when slavery was abolished in all French colonies. The Africans in St Louis and Goree, and also in Dakar and Rufisque, were in the 19th century called the *originaires* and had the rights of French citizens. They elected a deputy to the French National Assembly and voted for local government councils (or *communes*).

From the late 1870s France, which had begun expansion inland earlier, began a sustained push up the river and into the interior where groundnuts were already being grown for export to France, but where African monarchs still ruled including the new Islamic conqueror El Hadj Umar and, after his death in 1864, his son Ahmadu. There was strong resistance to the French, notably that led by Lat Dior from 1882 until his death in action in 1886. French rule was established by the mid-1890s, while the British then consolidated their rule inland in The Gambia; French efforts to obtain cession of that territory, entirely surrounded by Senegal, did not succeed.

The normal French colonial system prevailed, one of its features being the breaking up of traditional kingdoms (completed in Senegal by the 1920s). Senegal was part of French West Africa *(Afrique Occidentale Française)*, whose seat of government was at Dakar. In 1920 a Colonial Council was created.

Blaise Diagne, in 1914 the first African to be elected deputy for Senegal, was the political leader for many years; others followed, as party politics and a free press flourished except during the Second World War. The Vichy régime ruled from 1940 to 1942 and drove off an Allied and Free French attack in 1940. Post-war reforms in the French empire led to the granting of rights to other Africans, including those of the interior of Senegal. African nationalist politics then developed over the whole area of Senegal, with the *Bloc Démocratique Sénégalais* (BDS), founded in 1948 and led by Léopold Senghor, becoming the major party.

In elections leading to partial self-government in 1957 the *Bloc Populaire Sénégalais*, formed by the BDS and other groups, was victorious. In 1958 another merger led to formation of the *Union Progressiste Sénégalais* (UPS) which won elections to a national assembly in 1959. In that year Senegal and French Sudan were united to form the Mali Federation, which became independent on 22 June 1960. Two months later, however, the 2 countries split up again, to form the separate independent republics of Mali (ex-French Sudan) and Senegal.

After President Diouf of Senegal helped restore President Jawara of The Gambia following a *coup d'état* there in July 1981, the two governments agreed to join their countries in a Confederation of Senegambia, which came into being on 1 Feb. 1982. There is a Confederal Assembly (one-third Gambian), and an agreement was signed in 1983 on integration of the armed forces. But the two countries still remain separate sovereign states. President Diouf was re-elected in 1983.

Further Reading

Gellar, S., *Senegal*. Boulder, 1982

SEYCHELLES

The Seychelles were first colonized by the French in 1756 in order to establish plantations for growing spices to compete with the Dutch monopoly. The islands were captured by the English in 1794. During discussions before the Treaty of Paris was signed, Britain offered to return Mauritius and its dependencies which included the Seychelles to France if that country would renounce all claims to her possessions in India. France refused and the Seychelles were formally ceded to Britain as a dependency of Mauritius. In Nov. 1903 the Seychelles archipelago became a separate British Crown Colony. Internal self-government was achieved on 1 Oct. 1975, and independence as a republic within the British Commonwealth on 29 June 1976.

The first president, James Mancham, was deposed in a *coup* on 5 June 1977 and replaced by his prime minister, Albert René. The National Assembly was dissolved and the constitution suspended. A new constitution came into force on 5 June 1979, under which the Seychelles People's Progressive Front became the sole legal party and nominates all candidates for election. There is a unicameral People's Assembly and an executive president directly elected for a five-year term. In 1979 and in 1984 Albert René was the only candidate in the presidential elections. Under René the Seychelles has campaigned for the demilitarization of the British Indian Ocean Territory and refused entry to ships carrying nuclear weapons.

Further Reading
Franda, M., *The Seychelles: Unquiet Islands*. Boulder, 1982
Lionnet, G., *The Seychelles*. Newton Abbot, 1972

SIERRA LEONE

The colony of Sierra Leone originated in 1787 with the sale by native chiefs to English settlers of a piece of land intended as a home for natives of Africa who were waifs in London. The land was later used as a settlement for Africans rescued from slave-ships. The hinterland was declared a British protectorate on 21 Aug. 1896.

The first constitution was introduced in 1951 and this removed the political component from the privileged status of the Creoles of the colony by giving power to the majority. Sierra Leone became independent as a member state of the British Commonwealth on 27 April 1961. In a general election in March 1967, Dr Siaka Stevens's All People's Congress came to power and was installed despite a military *coup* to prevent his taking office. Sierra Leone became a republic on 19 April 1971, with Dr Siaka Stevens as executive president.

Following a referendum in June 1978, a new constitution was instituted under which the ruling All People's Congress became the sole legal party.

Stevens remained president until 1985 when he handed over to Maj.-Gen. Dr Joseph Saidu Momoh, the army C.-in-C., who was the only candidate in the presidential election that year and received 99% of the votes cast. The new president appointed an entirely civilian cabinet, reappointing a number of his predecessor's ministers.

Further Reading

Fyfe, C., *A History of Sierra Leone*. OUP, 1962
Kup, A. P., *Sierra Leone*. Newton Abbot, 1975

SINGAPORE

Singapore Island became part of the Javanese Majapahit Empire in the 14th century. The Portuguese established hegemony in the area in the 16th century, followed by the Dutch a hundred years later. In 1819 Sir Thomas Stamford Raffles, the British East India Administrator, established a trading settlement there. The original lease of the site of a factory to the British East India Company by the Sultan of Johore was followed by the treaty of 2 Aug. 1824 ceding the entire island in perpetuity to the company. In 1826 Penang, Malacca and Singapore were combined as the Straits Settlements in an Indian presidency. On 1 April 1867 the settlements were transferred from the control of the Indian government to that of the British Secretary of State for the Colonies. With the opening of the Suez Canal in 1869 and the advent of the steamship, an era of prosperity began for Singapore. Growth continued with the export of tin and rubber from the Malay peninsula.

Thought to be impregnable by land, Singapore fell to the Japanese in 1942 and the Japanese occupation continued until the end of the Second World War. In 1945 Singapore became a Crown Colony, being separated from Penang and Malacca. In June 1959 the state was granted complete internal self-government. When the Federation of Malaysia was formed in Sept. 1963, Singapore became one of the 14 states of the newly created country.

On 7 Aug. 1965, by agreement with the Malaysian government, Singapore left the Federation of Malaysia and became an independent sovereign state. The name of the state was changed to 'Republic of Singapore' with a president as its head. Singapore and Malaysia agreed to enter into a treaty for external defence and mutual assistance. The British military presence was withdrawn from Singapore in 1971. Continuing economic prosperity has made Singapore a powerful influence in ASEAN. In domestic as in international politics, the country's dominant voice since independence has been that of its first prime minister, Lee Kuan Yew, leader of the People's Action Party.

Further Reading

Turnbull, C. M., *A History of Singapore, 1819–1975*. OUP, 1977

SOLOMON ISLANDS

The Solomon Islands were discovered in 1568 by the Spanish explorer Alvaro de Mendana on a voyage of discovery from Peru; 200 years passed before European contact was again made with the Solomons. The southern Solomon Islands were placed under British protection in 1893, and further islands were added in 1898 and 1899. Santa Isabel and the other islands to the north were ceded by Germany in 1900. Following the Second World War, British rule was opposed by the Marching Rule movement. Full internal self-government was achieved in 1976 and independence on 7 July 1978.

Further Reading

Kent, J., *The Solomon Islands*. Newton Abbot, 1972

SOMALIA

The origins of the Somali people can be traced back 2,000 years when they migrated to the region, displacing and absorbing an earlier Arabic people. They converted to Islam in the 10th century and were organized in loose Islamic states by the 19th century. The northern part of Somaliland was created a British protectorate in 1884. The southern part belonged to two local rulers who, in 1889, accepted Italian protection for their lands. The Italian invasion of Ethiopia in 1935 was launched from Somaliland and in 1936 Somaliland was incorporated with Eritrea and Ethiopia to become Italian East Africa. In 1940 Italian forces invaded British Somaliland but in 1941 the British, with South African and Indian troops, recaptured this territory as well as occupying Italian Somaliland. A military government then ruled the two Somalilands. After the Second World War British Somaliland reverted to its colonial status and ex-Italian Somaliland became the UN Trust Territory of Somaliland, administered by Italy.

The independent Somali Republic came into being on 1 July 1960 as a result of the merger of the British Somaliland Protectorate, which first became independent on 26 June 1960, and the Italian Trusteeship Territory of Somaliland. Aden Abdullah Osman was elected president of the new republic, and the legislatures of the two territories were merged to create a single national assembly.

On 21 Oct. 1969 Maj.-Gen. Mohammed Siyad Barre, the C.-in-C. of the armed forces, took power in a *coup*. He suspended the constitution and formed a Supreme Revolutionary Council to administer the country, which was renamed the Somali Democratic Republic.

A new constitution was approved by a referendum on 25 Aug. 1979. The sole legal party since 1 July 1976 is the Somali Revolutionary Socialist Party, administered by a 51-member central committee. The executive president is nominated by the central committee.

In 1977 Somalia invaded Ethiopia, seeking to capture the Ogaden desert. It lost the ensuing war. Border fighting continues, although talks with Ethiopia were initiated in 1985. In 1977, Soviet advisers were expelled from the country, and a re-alignment with Western interests took place. Barré's presidency was confirmed in elections in 1986.

Further Reading
Legum, C. and Lee, B., *Conflict in the Horn of Africa.* London, 1977

REPUBLIC OF SOUTH AFRICA

The Dutch first established a trading post at the Cape in 1652. The hinterland was then inhabited by the Khoisan peoples and further east and north by Bantu-speaking peoples. There was some white settlement over the next century. During the Napoleonic Wars, Britain took possession of the Cape and later many Boer (Dutch) settlers migrated north-east in the Great Trek. In the mid-19th century Britain ruled the Cape Colony and Natal along the coast of southern Africa, while in the interior the Afrikaners or Boers, descendants of Dutch settlers, had established their own independent republics in the Transvaal and the Orange Free State. Some Bantu African peoples remained unconquered, notably the Xhosas east of the Cape Colony and, north of Natal, the Zulus, whose leader Shaka (died 1828) had formed a powerful kingdom in a great political and demographic upheaval called the *Mfecane*. The Sothos, who formed another new state under Moshoeshoe, resisted the Boers' encroachment on their land, until in 1868 Britain granted Moshoeshoe's request for a protectorate over Basutoland. Meanwhile British settlers had emigrated to Cape Colony and Natal in the 19th century, and from the 1860s many Indians were brought to Natal as indentured labourers on the sugar plantations. The population of the Cape Colony included many Afrikaners as well as the 'Coloured' community, descendants of Dutch settlers and indigenous Khoisan women and of Malay slaves. Most Coloureds spoke Afrikaans, the offshoot of Dutch spoken by the Boers.

Britain annexed the Transvaal in 1877, and fought in 1879 with the Zulus, who under King Ketshwayo won a victory at Isandhlwana but were then defeated at Ulundi. Britain restored independence to the Transvaal (South African Republic) in 1884 but annexed Zululand in 1887. Both the British and the Boers fought African resistance for many years, the last major rising being in Natal in 1906. However, the British and Boers were also rivals for supremacy, especially after the discovery of diamonds at Kimberley in 1867 and of gold in the Transvaal in 1884. This led to an economic boom and wealth for many, of whom Cecil Rhodes, for a time prime minister of the Cape, was the dominant entrepreneurial figure.

In the South African War of 1899–1902 the British defeated and annexed the Boer republics. The Boer republics were given self-government again in 1907, and on 31 May 1910 Cape Colony, Natal, the Transvaal and the Orange Free State combined to form the Union of South Africa, a self-governing dominion under the British Crown. The Union was ruled by the white minority; the franchise accorded to some non-whites in Cape Colony was kept, but not extended to the other three provinces.

The Union's economy was based on gold and diamond mining, for which there was organized recruitment of migrant African labourers from Union territory and other parts of Africa. Senior positions in the mines were reserved for Whites and the 'job reservation' system was in force by the 1920s. By then, too, the Pass Laws were in operation, controlling Africans' movements in the towns and industrial areas, where they were regarded officially as temporary residents and segregated in 'townships'. By an Act of 1913 87% of the land was reserved for white ownership only, much of it being owned by white farmers while Africans farmed as tenants or squatters.

African protests at segregation and lack of political rights were led from 1912 by the South African Native National Congress, founded in that year and in 1925 renamed the African National Congress (ANC). From 1918 there were also many African labour protests. African rights were further suppressed after the coming to power in 1924 of the Afrikaner Nationalist Party. Founded in 1914 and led by J. B. Hertzog, this party voiced Afrikaner protests against past British policy, present British political and economic hegemony, and the rule of Prime Minister Jan Smuts (1919–24). After coming to power, Hertzog's government secured recognition of full independence for South Africa by the Statute of Westminster on 11 Dec. 1931. It also promoted the status of the Afrikaans language and introduced new segregation measures. These policies continued after the formation of a Hertzog-Smuts coalition to deal with the economic crisis in 1933–34. In 1936 the African voters in Cape Province were removed from the common electoral roll. However, some Afrikaner Nationalists remained dissatisfied and formed a 'purified' National Party under Dr D. F. Malan.

When the Second World War began the cabinet split over South Africa's participation; it did participate, on the Allied side, under Jan Smuts who remained prime minister until 1948. The revived Afrikaner National Party won the elections of 1948 and has held power ever since. The ANC also revived in the 1940s and international attention began to be directed at South Africa, partly because it continued to rule the former German colony of South-West Africa without converting it from a Mandated to a Trust territory, and partly because the Indians' protests at segregation had backing from India.

From 1948 the National Party government reinforced the segregation system, developing it into the system of Apartheid. Among other measures, it introduced strict area segregation in the 1950 Group Areas Act, outlawed African trade unionism, and reinforced job reservation. Strong protests were led by the ANC, whose leader then was Albert Luthuli, and which with other bodies drew up a Freedom Charter in 1955. A long treason trial of Luthuli and others (1956–61) led to their acquittal. Internal and foreign protests were, however, ignored as the Apartheid system was enforced under prime ministers Malan (1948–54), Strijdom (1954–58), Verwoerd (1958–66) and Vorster (1966–78). The shooting by police of protesters against the Pass Laws at Sharpeville on 21 March 1960 led to a major crisis from which, however, the government emerged only stronger. The ANC and the Pan African Congress were banned, and their leaders forced to operate from exile after internal ANC leaders, including Nelson Mandela, were gaoled in 1964.

On 31 May 1961 South Africa became a Republic outside the Commonwealth.

From 1959 the policy of developing African self-government in the original tribal areas (called 'Bantustans or Homelands') was developed, until on 26 Oct. 1976 Transkei was granted independence which, however, was recognized only by South Africa. Other 'independent homelands' (Bophuthatswana in 1977, Venda in 1979, and Ciskei in 1981) have similarly been refused recognition by the outside world. Pressure has been maintained on South Africa to give up Namibia (South-West Africa). But in the 1980s South Africa proceeded with its own devolution measures there, leading to a transitional government on 17 June 1985. In Namibia guerrillas of SWAPO have fought since the 1960s, and in South Africa itself from the late 1970s some guerrilla attacks have been staged by the ANC's military wing, *Umkhonto we Sizwe*, and in the mid-1970s the régime was shaken by urban revolt centred on the township of Soweto, near Johannesburg.

The Republic's efforts to counter foreign criticism involved secret financial dealings which emerged in the 'Information Scandal' of 1978–79; during this affair Vorster resigned first as prime minister in 1978 and then, after his rôle was criticized, as state president in 1979. P. W. Botha succeeded him as prime minister. Under Botha, a number of elements of the Apartheid system were modified or ended in the 1980s; Africans were allowed to form legal trade unions, creation of Black local government authorities in cities was enacted, and the Acts banning marriage and sexual relations between people of different races were repealed. These changes were enough to make some Afrikaners leave the National Party and form in 1982 the

Conservative Party of South Africa. But they did not satisfy African opponents of Apartheid, who formed the United Democratic Front (UDF) in 1983.

A new constitution, approved in a referendum of white voters on 2 Nov. 1983 and in force from 3 Sept. 1984, created a new three-part parliament, with a House of Assembly for the Whites, a House of Representatives for the Coloureds, and a House of Delegates for the Indians; Africans remained without representation. At the same time an executive presidency was created, to which Botha was elected. Boycotts ensured low polls in the elections for the Coloured and Indian houses held on 22 and 28 Aug. 1984 respectively. The Whites retained their House of Assembly as elected in 1981 with its massive National Party majority.

From late 1984 Blacks in the cities and industrial areas staged large-scale protests, including strikes. Largely spontaneous – though the gaoled ANC leader Mandela was seen as the Africans' hero – the protests involved large-scale violence. In June 1986 a state of emergency was imposed. Foreign condemnation of this led to the first economic sanctions against South Africa imposed by a number of countries including the USA. In May 1987 a whites-only election returned the National Party with an increased majority but saw the defeat of the Progressive parties and the emergence of the ultra-conservative Afrikaner parties as the main parliamentary opposition.

Further Reading

Davenport, T. R. H., *South Africa: A Modern History.* 3rd ed. CUP, 1987

CAPE PROVINCE

When European travellers first reached the Cape of Good Hope in the late 15th century, the inhabitants of the area were Khoi and San (Khoisan), known as Hottentots and Bushmen, living by hunting and gathering. European settlement began in 1652 with the arrival of Dutch settlers who founded what became Cape Town. Over the next two centuries there grew up a community of Dutch-descended people called Boers and later Afrikaners, and a community of mixed descent (the offspring of the Dutchmen and Khoisan women, and of the slaves of the Dutch) called the 'Cape Coloureds'. Both used – and still use – the Dutch-derived Afrikaans language.

Cape Colony was occupied by Britain 1795–1803 and again in 1806, and formally annexed under the Convention of London on 13 Aug. 1814. British settlers started arriving soon afterwards. The Boers objected to aspects of British rule, such as the abolition of slavery in 1834, and in 1836 many of them headed inland in the 'Great Trek'. Other Boers, however, remained in Cape Colony with the Coloured community. British rule expanded eastwards against strong opposition from Bantu Africans who had been coming from the north-east for centuries. The Xhosa were finally subjugated after they had killed their own cattle under the influence of a diviner.

By Letters Patent of 1850 Cape Colony was given a Legislative Council and a House of Assembly. Local politics was dominated by white people including Cecil Rhodes (1853–1902), Cape prime minister as well as a major profiteer from the diamond mines at Kimberley (in an area annexed to Cape Colony in 1880). Because of restrictive property or income qualifications, few non-whites had the vote. Africans were nevertheless politically active, Tengo Jabavu (1859–1921) being for many years the most prominent figure.

On 31 May 1910 Cape Colony became Cape Province of the Union of South Africa, and thenceforth the parliament of South Africa met at Cape Town. Although the non-racial franchise was entrenched into the constitution, Afrikaner Nationalist governments managed to alter it in 1936, when Africans were removed from the common electoral roll, and 1956, when the Coloureds were also removed. Anti-Apartheid protests in Cape Province have included those surrounding the Crossroads settlement at Cape Town.

Areas of Cape Province became the states of Transkei (1976) and Ciskei (1979); and some smaller areas became parts of Bophuthatswana (1977).

NATAL

In the early 19th century a succession of wars and mass migrations (called the Mfecane) among the Nguni peoples led to the creation of a powerful Zulu state by Shaka which, from the 1830s, clashed with the Boers to the west. To the south, Britain annexed territory called by the old Portuguese name of Natal to Cape Colony in 1844, put it under separate administration in 1845, and on 15 July 1856 established it as a separate colony. White settlers came and, from the 1860s, many Indians were brought in as labourers. Most of the Indians of South Africa still live in Natal.

Following the Zulu war of 1879, and Britain's annexation of Zululand in 1887, Zululand was added to Natal on 30 Dec. 1897, which had obtained responsible government in 1893. The districts of Vryheid, Utrecht and part of Wakkerstroom, formerly belonging to Transvaal, were added to Natal in Jan. 1903. The last major African uprising until recent times in South Africa, the Bambata rising, took place in Natal in 1906. On 31 May 1910 Natal became a province of the Union.

Zululand was constituted a homeland, KwaZulu, in 1973. Its chief minister, Chief Gatsha Buthelezi, heads the powerful *Inkatha* movement and is a major figure in South Africa. He has refused independence for KwaZulu, but is accused by his opponents in the United Democratic Front of collaborating with the white régime.

In April 1978 East Griqualand was transferred from Cape Province to Natal.

TRANSVAAL

Boers leaving Cape Colony in the Great Trek occupied Transvaal from the late 1830s. They established a state recognized as independent by Britain by the Sand River Treaty in 1852, and called the South African Republic from 1853. The Boers of the Transvaal fought with the Zulus to the east, and with Africans within the Transvaal. These included the Venda and the Ndebele, the latter being one of the Nguni peoples who migrated in the Mfecane upheaval (others went on to what became Zimbabwe).

The South African Republic was annexed by Britain in 1877 but revolted in 1881 and, after its forces defeated the British at Majuba Hill, was recognized as semi-independent again although with some restrictions and subject to British suzerainty. By the London Convention of 1884 the British suzerainty was removed and some of the restrictions lifted, but the British government retained the right of approval of Transvaal's foreign relations, except with the other Boer republic, the Orange Free State.

Gold was discovered on the Witwatersrand in 1886 and Johannesburg grew rapidly as a boom town as foreigners rushed to exploit the world's richest seams of gold. Relations between these new immigrants and the Transvaal government under President Paul Kruger were strained. This tension was partly responsible for the war between Britain and the Transvaal which began in 1899. The South African War ended in the Treaty of Vereeniging on 31 May 1902, by which the Transvaal and the Orange Free State surrendered their independence. Five years of Crown Colony administration followed before responsible government was granted to Transvaal on 12 Jan. 1907. On 31 May 1910 Transvaal became a province of the Union of South Africa, whose seat of government was placed there, at Pretoria.

The Rand gold mines have remained the mainstay of the whole country's economy. The problems and tensions of the urban-industrial areas of South Africa have often been at a peak in Transvaal, as for example in 1976 when hundreds died in rioting in Soweto, the great African township of Johannesburg. Parts of Transvaal were incorporated into Bophuthatswana, declared independent in 1977, while another independent homeland, Venda, was created out of Transvaal in 1979. Transvaal also includes another homeland, Kwandebele.

ORANGE FREE STATE

The Orange river was first crossed by Europeans in the mid-18th century, and some settlements were made in areas north of the upper Orange between 1810 and 1820. Many more Afrikaners moved to the area in the late 1830s after the Great Trek. At that time the local African people, notably the Sothos, were in the turmoil of wars and mass migrations called the Mfecane. A Sotho kingdom was formed by Moshoeshoe and fought for years with the Boers.

In 1848 Sir Harry Smith proclaimed the territory between the upper Orange and Vaal a British possession, the Orange River Sovereignty. But in 1854, by the Convention of Bloemfontein, Britain recognized the independence of the Orange Free State. Wars with Lesotho continued until in 1866, by the Treaty of Thaba Bosiu, large areas of Sotho population came under Orange Free State rule. Lesotho then became a British protectorate (as Basutoland) in 1868, and in the following year the Treaty of Aliwal North restored some areas to Lesotho, though others remained under the Orange Free State. Griqualand West, including the Kimberley area and its diamonds, was later claimed by the Orange Free State but annexed to Cape Colony.

Linked by treaty with the South African Republic (Transvaal), the Orange Free State fought the British in the Boer War of 1899–1902, and was annexed on 28 May 1900 as the Orange River Colony. Crown Colony government continued until 1907, when responsible government was restored. On 31 May 1910 the Orange Free State became a province of the Union of South Africa; Bloemfontein is the judicial capital of South Africa.

Qwaqwa, a Black homeland, is within the Orange Free State, and an area of the province was made part of Bophuthatswana when it was declared independent in 1977.

SOUTH WEST AFRICA (NAMIBIA)

The sparse population of the area between the Orange and Cunene rivers in the 19th century included the Hottentots or Namas, San or Bushmen, Hereros, and Damaras. They had contact with Protestant missionaries and European traders, and on 12 March 1878 Walvis Bay was annexed by Britain. The rest of the area, called South West Africa, was annexed by Germany in 1884–85. After a few years' rule by the German South West Africa Colonial Company, the Imperial German government took over control in 1888. The Hereros and other Africans resisted strongly, notably in the great Herero and Witboii risings in 1904. White settlement and mining began under German rule and expanded later.

South West Africa was occupied by South African forces fighting for the Allies in 1915, and allotted to South Africa as a League of Nations Mandated Territory by the Treaty of Versailles. The terms of the Mandate were laid down in Dec. 1920 and an Administrator was appointed in 1921. The seat of government was at Windhoek. There was some African resistance, notably the rising in 1922 of the Hottentot clan of the Bondelswarts which was harshly suppressed. In 1926 an all-white legislative assembly was set up.

After the Second World War and the end of the League of Nations, South Africa refused to turn its Mandated Territory into a UN Trust Territory (as had been undertaken by other Mandates). From 1949 it treated South West Africa in many ways as a part of South Africa, applying there new laws under the Apartheid system. Some distinct status was maintained, however. In 1960 Ethiopia and Liberia brought a case against South Africa before the International Court of Justice, for violating the terms of the Mandate. Although on 18 July 1966 the Court ruled that they had no standing to bring the case, in Oct. of the same year the UN General Assembly voted to end the Mandate over South West Africa.

The territory then came nominally under the rule of the UN, which created a Council for South West Africa in 1967 and in 1968 changed the territory's name to Namibia. In fact South Africa continued to rule and proceeded for a time with plans for separate homelands as in South Africa proper. But African opposition grew from the 1950s; there was major unrest at Windhoek in 1959, and thereafter the Ovamboland People's Organization spread over the territory, becoming in 1964 the South West African People's Organization (SWAPO). This became the leading nationalist party and launched guerrilla operations from the late 1960s. These were aided by the independence of Angola in 1976, but South Africa, in turn, attacked SWAPO bases in Angola, as for example in a major raid on Kassinga in 1978. SWAPO was recognized by the UN, which appointed a High Commissioner for Namibia in 1973, as sole representative of Namibia pending free elections. South Africa rejected this as it also rejected an advisory opinion by the International Court of Justice in 1971, stating South African rule was illegal.

South Africa talked for years with the UN and with a group of five Western powers about changes to lead to independence for Namibia, but no agreement was reached. UN Security Council Resolution No. 435, of 27 July 1978, represented an apparently agreed programme of elections and independence, but it has not been implemented. Instead South Africa has sponsored developments on its own initiative within Namibia. A multi-racial advisory council was appointed in 1973. Representatives of all ethnic groups, meeting at the Turnhalle in Windhoek in 1975–76, agreed on 17 August 1976 on a programme for independence which was rejected by the 'Contact Group'. On 4–8 Dec. 1978 elections, boycotted by SWAPO, were held to a constituent assembly and were won by the Democratic Turnhalle Alliance (DTA). On 1 July 1980 a 12-member council of ministers was set up, headed by the DTA leader, Dirk Mudge. In Sept. 1981 the council was enlarged to 15 and given power over all matters except constitutional issues, foreign affairs and security. While many features of Apartheid were ended from the mid-70s onwards, South Africa proceeded with plans for ethnic self-government, and on 11–13 Nov. 1980 elections were held to second-tier representative authorities for ethnic groups. The constituent assembly was turned, with addition of 15 members to the 50 elected, into a national assembly.

In Jan. 1983 the assembly and the council of ministers were dissolved. A multi-party conference was installed in Sept. 1983 as a new representative body, but it seemed at first more dependent on the South African administrator-general than the DTA had been. In April 1984 there were talks in Lusaka between South Africa, the multi-party conference and SWAPO. Neither this nor a visit by the UN Secretary-General to Windhoek in Aug. 1983 led to any progress, and by 1985 the Contact Group had ceased its work.

On 17 June 1985 a transitional government was announced, with representatives of six political groups. In opposition to it, there were massive legal demonstrations in support of SWAPO in Windhoek in mid-1986. Despite the high cost of a big military presence to contain SWAPO guerrillas, South Africa seems likely to remain in control for some time.

Further Reading

Jaster, R., *South Africa in Namibia: The Botha Strategy.* Univ. Press of America, 1985

SOUTH AFRICAN HOMELANDS

BOPHUTHATSWANA

Bophuthatswana, which was declared independent on 6 Dec. 1977, was the first to obtain self-government under the Bantu Homelands Constitution Act of 1971. The homeland of some of the Tswana people – others live in nearby independent Botswana – Bophuthatswana consisted of six separate portions of land in Cape Province and Transvaal, and an enclave in Orange Free State. At the time of independence, recognized only by the Republic of South Africa, President Mangope protested about the South Africans' refusal to consolidate these scattered parts of the homeland.

TRANSKEI

Transkei, the homeland of the Xhosa people, was granted self-government in 1963 and on 26 Oct. 1976 became the first of the Bantu Homelands to obtain independence. This was not recognized by any other country except the Republic of South Africa, even though Transkei broke off relations with South Africa from 1978 to 1980 because of a claim to white-owned land in East Griqualand. Transkei remains economically dependent on South Africa where over 1·5m. Transkeians live and work although they have ceased legally to be South African citizens.

Two *coups* occurred in Sept. and Dec. 1987, and in Jan. 1988 Gen. Holomisa assumed the role of government and military leader. Martial law was declared and all political activity banned.

VENDA

Venda, in northern Transvaal, became on 13 Sept. 1979, the third Black Homeland to be granted independence, having obtained self-government in 1973. Recognized as independent only by the Republic of South Africa, Venda is the homeland of the Vhavenda people. The smallest of all the independent homelands in area and population, it is totally dependent on South Africa.

CISKEI

Ciskei was declared independent on 4 Dec. 1981 but only recognized by the Republic of South Africa. The Xhosa people have been divided between Transkei and Ciskei and this has produced considerable opposition from Transkei. The people of Ciskei lost their South African citizenship at independence.

SOUTH GEORGIA AND
SOUTH SANDWICH ISLANDS

South Georgia was probably first sighted by a London merchant, Antonio de la Roche, and then in 1756 by a Spanish captain, Gregorie Jerez. The first landing and exploration was undertaken by Capt. James Cook, who formally took possession in the name of George III on 17 Jan. 1775. British sealers arrived in 1788 and American sealers in 1791. Sealing reached its peak in 1800. A German team was the first to carry out scientific studies there in 1882–83. Whaling began in 1904 when the Compania Argentina de Pesca formed by C. A. Larsen, a Norwegian, established a station at Grytviken. Six other stations were established up to 1912. Whaling ceased in 1966 and the civil administration was withdrawn. Argentine forces invaded South Georgia on 3 April 1982. A British naval task force recovered the island on 25 April 1982. Under the constitution, on 3 Oct. 1985 the Territories ceased to be dependencies of the Falkland Islands.

Further Reading

Headland, R. K., *The Island of South Georgia*. OUP, 1985

SPAIN

The modern Spanish state was founded with the marriage in 1469 of the heirs of the crowns of Castile and Aragón, respectively Isabel I and Fernando V. Under their joint reign Spain recovered Granada, the last Islamic territory in the Iberian peninsula, and sponsored the modern discovery of America, both events in 1492. This dynasty ended in 1700 and subsequently the French Bourbon dynasty was enthroned, with Felipe V as its first king; the present monarch, Juan Carlos I, installed in 1975, is his direct descendant.

Queen Isabel II, who came to the throne in 1833, was deposed and exiled in 1868 by a liberal revolution. A provisional government, headed by the Duke de la Torre, established universal male suffrage and convened a constituent election for Jan. 1869. The Cortes (Parliament) approved a new constitution, and the deputies chose as the new king Amadeo I, of the then reigning Italian dynasty of Savoy. He reigned as a scrupulous democrat from 2 Jan. 1871, but unable to adapt to the peculiar Spanish political habits, abdicated on 11 Feb. 1873. The Cortes immediately proclaimed a republic.

The first brief republican experience saw great instability. On 29 Dec. 1874, in Sagunto, Gen. Martínez Campos led a *coup* and restored the Bourbon monarchy, with Alfonso XII as king, the son of the exiled Queen Isabel II. A general election took place early in 1876 and the new Cortes approved a constitution which was effective until 1923. This period, known as the Restoration, saw the reimposition of a restricted suffrage (the universal one was not re-established until 1890), and was dominated by two parties, Conservative and Liberal, led respectively by A. Cánovas del Castillo and P. M. Sagasta, both of whom served as prime minister several times in the last quarter of the 19th century.

Alfonso XII died in 1885. His wife, María Cristina of Hapsburg, was regent till their son, Alfonso XIII, reached his majority in 1902.

During the period of the Restoration, Spain still had a very backward economy and very low standards of living. At the same time Spain was embroiled in external conflicts, with wars in northern Morocco and in the remaining colonies of Cuba and the Philippines. The US intervention led to the cession of Philippines, Puerto Rico and Guam, and also of Cuba which formally became independent in 1901.

Spain was neutral in the First World War, leading to a boom in industry and trade. A new industrial working class was then emerging, amongst a climate of industrial unrest and with a growing opposition to conscription for the war in the north of Morocco.

In Sept. 1923 Gen. Primo de Rivera led a *coup* and abolished the 1876 constitution, closed down the Cortes and governed by decree until his resignation in Jan. 1930. During his dictatorship the war in the Spanish Protectorate in Morocco came to an end.

An interim period followed until the municipal elections of 12 April 1931, which were won by a republican–socialist coalition in Madrid, provincial capitals and other urban areas. Two days later Alfonso XIII exiled himself and the republic was proclaimed a second time. In June a new Cortes was elected; it drafted a new constitution, which was in force by Dec. 1931. Complete religious freedom and an agrarian reform were the significant landmarks of this period. An election in 1932, for the first time with female suffrage, established a very conservative coalition government, which resulted in serious rioting in Oct. 1934. An election in Feb. 1936 gave power to the Popular Front, a coalition of all left parties, including the then tiny Communist party.

On 18 July 1936 the colonial army in northern Morocco, led by Gen. Francisco Franco, and some other military units rebelled against the government. The rebellion was crushed in a few days in Madrid, Barcelona, Valencia and almost all industrial and mining areas. But the rural regions were easily controlled by the rebels who received substantial help in men, tanks and aircraft from Germany, Italy and Portugal. The government, however, suffered from the 'non-intervention' policy declared by the democracies, notably Britain and France. The International Brigades, a volunteer force, and conditional aid from the USSR were the only significant foreign support received by the Spanish Republic. Franco's forces finally overcame all resistance and the war ended on 1 April 1939.

Gen. Franco was chief of state till his death on 20 Nov. 1975. His brutal régime was modelled on those of the Axis countries. Nevertheless, Franco's Spain did not take part in the Second World War. The 15 years following the Civil War saw extremely depressed economic conditions. But a rapid boom began in the 1950s. A nominal monarchy existed from 1947, but with a vacant throne until the francoist state accepted in 1969 the future succession in favour of Juan Carlos de Borbón, grandson of Alfonso XIII. Franco recognized also the independence of Morocco in 1956 and ceded the small Spanish protectorate to the Moroccon Government. Spain also withdrew from Equatorial Guinea in 1968 but continued to occupy Western Sahara until 1976.

On 22 Nov. 1975, following Gen. Franco's death, Juan Carlos was proclaimed king. A gradual return to democracy began. A referendum held in Dec. 1976 endorsed some key reforms in the legal system of the dictatorship, making possible a free election on 15 June 1977. The elected bicameral Cortes drafted a new constitution which came into force on 29 Dec. 1978. New elections followed in 1979, 1982 and 1986. Since Oct. 1982 the cabinet has been headed by Felipe González, leader of the Spanish Workers Socialist Party.

Spain joined NATO in 1982 and the European Communities in 1986.

Further Reading

Livermore, H. V., *A History of Spain*. 2nd ed. London, 1966

WESTERN SAHARA

The colony of Spanish Sahara became a Spanish province in July 1958 following resistance to Spanish rule which was suppressed in 1957. Spanish Sahara only became of economic importance when phosphates started to be exploited in the early 1970s. On 14 Nov. 1975 Spain, Morocco and Mauritania reached agreement on the transfer of power over Western Sahara to Morocco and Mauritania on 28 Feb. 1976. Morocco occupied al-Aiaún in late Nov. and on 12 Jan. 1976 the Spanish army withdrew from Western Sahara which had ceased to be a Spanish province on 31 Dec. 1975. The country was partitioned by Morocco and Mauritania on 28 Feb. 1976; Morocco reorganized its sector into three provinces. In Aug. 1979 Mauritania withdrew from the territory it took over in 1976. The area was taken over by Morocco and reorganized into a fourth province.

A liberation movement, *Frente Polisario*, launched an armed struggle against Spanish rule on 20 May 1973 and, in spite of occupation of all western centres by Moroccan troops, Saharawi guerrillas based in Algeria continue to attempt to liberate their country. They have renamed it the Saharawi Arab Democratic Republic and hold most of the desert beyond a defensive line built by Moroccan troops encompassing Smara, Bu Craa and Laayoune.

In 1982 the Saharawi Arab Democratic Republic became a member of the Organization of African Unity.

Further Reading

Thompson, V. and Adloff, R., *The Western Saharans: Background to Conflict*. London, 1980

SRI LANKA

In the 18th century the central kingdom, Kandy, was the only surviving independent state on the island of Ceylon. The Dutch, who had obtained their first coastal possessions in 1636, had driven out the preceding Portuguese interests and become the dominant power in most of the island.

The Dutch attacked Kandy but were unable to hold it. The interior terrain was mountainous and thickly forested and the king of Kandy's forces were well-trained to make use of it as guerrillas.

The king attracted British attention by asking for help against the Dutch. In 1796 the British East India Company sent a naval force to Ceylon (as the British then called it). The Dutch surrendered their possessions, which left the British in control of the maritime areas surrounding Kandy. These areas were at first attached to the Madras Presidency of India, whence the naval force had come, but in 1802 they were constituted a separate colony under the Crown.

Once the British began to develop their new territory they came to see Kandy as a threat. An attack in 1803 failed, but by 1815 the chiefs of Kandy were discontented with their king who was of alien (south Indian) stock and a despot. The chiefs approached the British, who invaded Kandy with their help. The king was deposed and the British crown succeeded him as sovereign.

The Kandyan Convention of 1815 annexed Kandy to British Ceylon while recognizing most of the traditional rights of the chiefs. However, in 1817, dissatisfied with the terms, the chiefs rebelled. The rebellion was suppressed and the rights established by the Convention were abolished.

Ceylon was then united for the first time since the 12th century. The British (like the preceding Dutch and Portuguese) built up a plantation economy. Coffee was dominant until an outbreak of *Hoemilia vastatrix* fungus destroyed the plants in 1870. Spices, cocoa and rice all followed but tea became the main cash crop after successful experiments in the 1880s.

Foreign rule served to subdue the traditional hostility between northern Tamils and southern Singhalese, providing as it did a new frame of reference to an alien culture. The Ceylon National Congress, formed in 1919, contained both Sinhalese and Ceylon Tamil groups. (The Indian Tamils brought in as a labour force for the tea estates were a separate community.) Tamil national feeling, however, was expressed over the issue of the use of Tamil languages in schools.

On 4 Feb. 1948 the Ceylon Independence Act took effect, and Ceylon became a Dominion of the Commonwealth. UK defence forces were to be allowed to remain as mutually agreeable, although it was later decided that all UK bases should be transferred or withdrawn by 1962.

In 1956 Solomon Bandaranaike became prime minister at the head of the People's United Front, advocating neutral foreign policy and the promotion of Singhalese national culture at home. In Sept. 1959 he was murdered; his widow Sirima Bandaranaike succeeded him in July 1960 at the head of an increasingly socialist government. Agreements were made with India (in 1964 and 1974) for the repatriation of Indian nationals. In May 1972 Ceylon became a republic and adopted the name Sri Lanka.

In July 1977 Mrs Bandaranaike's government fell, mainly because of economic failures and the repression of non-Singhalese elements. The United National Party (dominant until 1956) returned to power and in 1978 a new constitution provided a presidential system with the United National Party leader Junius Jayawardene as the first executive president. Economic problems were approached through large-scale investment of foreign capital.

The problem of communal unrest remained unsolved and Tamil separatists were active. There was violence in 1981. In 1983 the Tamil United Liberation Front members of parliament were asked to renounce their object of a separate Tamil state. They refused and withdrew from parliament. Militant Tamils then began armed action which developed into civil war.

The government of India viewed the war with concern and made known its sympathy for the Tamil community. In July 1987 an agreement was reached between the Tamil guerrilla leader, the Indian government and President Jayawardene; it provided a degree of Tamil autonomy and an Indian-Sri Lankan peace-keeping force during the period of adjustment. In October 1987, massacres of Singhalese provoked fierce fighting between the Tamil guerrillas and the Indian force.

Further Reading

de Silva, K. M. A., *A History of Sri Lanka*. London, 1982

SUDAN

In 1821 the area that is now Sudan was conquered by the Egyptians. In 1881 Muhammad Ahmad, proclaiming himself the Mahdi, led an uprising and gained control until, in 1899, an Anglo-Egyptian army defeated the Mahdi and established an Anglo-Egyptian condominium.

On 19 Dec. 1955 the Sudanese parliament passed unanimously a declaration that a fully independent state should be established forthwith, and that a Council of State should assume the duties of head of state. The UK and Egypt gave their assent on 31 Dec. 1955 and on 1 Jan. 1956 Sudan was proclaimed a sovereign independent republic.

In 1958 there was a *coup* that established a military government until the end of 1964 when a civilian government was re-established. On 8 July 1965 the Constituent Assembly elected Ismail al Azhari as President of the Supreme Council, but the government was faced with constant difficulties from the southern provinces which considered themselves dominated by the north. Rebellions began in 1955.

On 23 April 1969 the prime minister, Muhammad Ahmed Mahgoub resigned; and on 25 May the government was taken over by a 10-man Revolutionary Council under Col. Jaafar al Nemery. The Council was dissolved in 1972, and a new constitution was introduced in 1973. Legislative power was placed with a National Assembly, an elected body; and some measure of self-government was granted to the southern provinces. However, discontent in these latter provinces continued, and in addition Nemery met considerable opposition in his attempts to make Sudan a formal Islamic state. On 6 April 1985 he was deposed in a military *coup* led by Gen. Abel-Rahman Swar al-Dahab, who established a Military Council to which the Cabinet was responsible prior to the promised re-establishment of civilian rule. Elections were held, although they were suspended in parts of the southern provinces, in April 1986 for the 301-seat National Assembly. A new constitution was being drafted in 1987.

Further Reading

Holt, P. M., *A Modern History of the Sudan*. 3rd ed. New York, 1979

SURINAME

The first Europeans to reach the area were the Spanish in 1499, but it was the British who established a colony there in 1650. At the peace of Breda (1667) between Great Britain and the United Netherlands, the area known as Suriname was assigned to the Netherlands in exchange for the colony of New Netherland in North America, and this was confirmed by the treaty of Westminster of Feb. 1674. Suriname was twice in British possession during the Napoleonic Wars in 1799–1802 (when it was restored to the Batavian Republic at the peace of Amiens) and 1804–16, when it was returned to the Kingdom of the Netherlands according to the convention of London of 13 Aug. 1814, confirmed at the peace of Paris of 20 Nov. 1815.

On 25 Nov. 1975, Suriname gained full independence and was admitted to the UN on 4 Dec. 1975. On 25 Feb. 1980 the government was ousted in a *coup*, and a National Military Council (NMC) established. A further *coup* on 13 Aug. replaced several members of the NMC, and the State President. Other attempted *coups* took place in 1981 and 1982, with the NMC retaining control.

In Oct. 1987 a new constitution was approved by referendum and following elections in Nov. Suriname returned to democracy in Jan. 1988.

Further Reading
Van de Polle, W., *Surinam, the Country and its People*. London, 1951

SWAZILAND

The Swazi migrated into the country to which they have given their name, in the last half of the 18th century. They settled first in what is now southern Swaziland, but moved northwards under their chief, Sobhuza – known also to the Swazi as Somhlolo. Sobhuza died in 1838 and was succeeded by Mswati. The further order of succession has been Mbandzeni and Bhunu, whose son, Sobhuza II, was installed as King of the Swazi nation in 1921 after a long minority.

The independence of the Swazis was guaranteed in the conventions of 1881 and 1884 between the British Government and the Government of the South African Republic. In 1890, soon after the death of Mbandzeni, a provisional government was established representative of the Swazis, the British and the South African Republic Governments. In 1894 the South African Republic was given powers of protection and administration. In 1902, after the conclusion of the Boer War, a special commissioner took charge, and under an order-in-council in 1903 the Governor of the Transvaal administered the territory, through the special commissioner. Swaziland became independent on 6 Sept. 1968.

On 25 April 1967 the British Government gave the country internal self-government. It changed the country's status to that of a protected state with the Ngwenyama, Sobhuza II, recognized as King of Swaziland and head of state. King Sobhuza died on 21 Aug. 1982. On 25 April 1986, King Mswati III was installed as King of Swaziland. Despite a secret pact with the Republic of South Africa concluded in 1982 and providing for joint operations against guerrillas fighting apartheid, the South Africans launched an armed raid into Swaziland in August 1986 aimed at the (South African) African National Congress. There is conflict within the Swazi government over the role of the royal family and relations with the Republic of South Africa.

Further Reading
Matsebula, J. S. M., *A History of Swaziland*. London, 1972

SWEDEN

Sweden was organized as an independent unified state in the 10th century, when the Swedes in the north of the country and the Goths in the south were united by Olof. Finland was acquired in the 13th century. In the 14th century Sweden was joined with Norway and Denmark in the Kalmar Union; however, under Gustav I, Sweden regained her independence in 1523.

Sweden became a constitutional monarchy in 1809, in which year she also ceded Finland to Russia. Norway was united with Sweden in 1815, but the former country became independent in 1905. Sweden remained neutral during the two world wars of 1914–18 and 1939–45.

In 1975 a new constitution came into force replacing that of 1809 and making Sweden a representative and parliamentary democracy. The king remains head of state, but has very limited power. Executive power lies with the cabinet *(Regeringen)* which is responsible to parliament *(Riksdag)* which since 1971 has been unicameral. The prime minister is nominated by the speaker of the *Riksdag* and then is confirmed in office by the whole parliament. From 1932 until 1976 when welfare state costs caused its defeat, Sweden was governed by the Social Democratic Party. However, in 1981 the party's leader, Olaf Palme, became prime minister with support from the Communist Party. On 28 Feb. 1986 Palme was assassinated in Stockholm by unknown assailants; Ingvar Carlsson succeeded him as prime minister.

Further Reading

Derry, T. K., *A History of Scandinavia*. Univ. of Minnesota Press, 1979
Scott, F. D., *Sweden: The Nation's History*. Univ. of Minnesota Press, 1983

SWITZERLAND

On 1 Aug. 1291 the men of Uri, Schwyz and Unterwalden entered into a defensive league. In 1353 the league included 8 members and in 1513, 13. Various territories were acquired either by single cantons or by several in common, and in 1648 the league became formally independent of the Holy Roman Empire. No addition was made to the number of cantons until 1798, in which year, under the influence of France, the unified Helvetic Republic was formed. This failed to satisfy the Swiss, and in 1803 Napoleon Bonaparte, in the Act of Mediation, gave a new constitution, and out of the lands formerly allied or subject increased the number of cantons to 19. In 1815 the perpetual neutrality of Switzerland and the inviolability of her territory were guaranteed by Austria, France, Great Britain, Portugal, Prussia, Russia, Spain and Sweden, and the Federal Pact, which included 3 new cantons, was accepted by the Congress of Vienna. In 1848 a new constitution was passed. The 22 cantons set up a federal government (consisting of a federal parliament and a federal council) and a federal tribunal. This constitution, in turn, was on 29 May 1874 superseded by the present constitution, which also combines the federal principle with a national and local use of referendums. Though women constitute a third of the work-force, female franchise dates only from Feb. 1971. In a national referendum held in Sept. 1978, 69·9% voted in favour of the establishment of a new canton, Jura, which was established on 1 Jan. 1979.

Switzerland was neutral in both world wars. After the First World War, it joined the League of Nations, which was based in Geneva. After the Second World War the same policy pointed to non-membership of the UN, though Switzerland participates in its agencies and since 1948 has been a contracting party to the Statute of the International Court of Justice.

Further Reading

Martin, W., *Switzerland from Roman Times to the Present*. London, 1971
Steinberg, J., *Why Switzerland?* London, 1980

SYRIA

Syria was under Turkish control from the 12th century, and part of the Ottoman Empire from the 16th century until the First World War. Following the defeat of the Turks in that war, the League of Nations granted to France a mandate for Syria from 1920. On 27 Sept. 1941, Gen. Catroux, the Free French C.-in-C., in the name of the Allies, proclaimed the independence of Syria at Damascus. On 27 Dec. 1943 an agreement was signed between representatives of the French National Committee of Liberation and of Syria, by which most of the powers and capacities exercised hitherto by France under mandate were transferred as from 1 Jan. 1944 to the Syrian government. The evacuation of all foreign troops in April 1946 marked the complete independence of Syria, but the political situation was unsettled and military *coups* were staged in Dec. 1949 and in Feb. 1954.

Syria merged with Egypt to form the United Arab Republic from 2 Feb. 1958 until 29 Sept. 1961, when Syrian independence was resumed following a *coup* the previous day. Following the fifth *coup* of the decade, Lieut.-Gen. Hafez al Assad became prime minister on 13 Nov. 1970, and assumed the presidency on 22 Feb. 1971. President Assad was re-elected in 1978 and 1985 for 7-year terms.

A new constitution, approved by plebiscite on 12 March 1973, confirmed the Arab Socialist Renaissance (Ba'ath) Party as the 'leading party in the state and society'.

Further Reading

Devlin, J. F., *Syria: Modern State in an Ancient Land*. Boulder, 1983

TANZANIA

At the end of the 17th century the inhabitants of Zanzibar drove out the Portuguese with the assistance of the Arabs of Oman. Thereafter an Arab governor from Oman was sent to Zanzibar, but the government of the interior remained in the hands of a local ruler. In 1832 Seyyid Said bin Sultan, ruler of Oman, established his capital at Zanzibar. Arab merchants explored the mainland in search of slaves and ivory and soon the whole of that island and the island of Pemba together with a large strip of the east African mainland coast came under his effective rule. Seyyid Said died in 1856. Five years later his former African possessions were, under an arbitration award made by the British Governor-General of India, declared to be independent of Oman. In 1887 the Sultan of Zanzibar handed over the administration of his possessions to the north of Vanga on the African continent to the British East Africa Association. These territories eventually passed to the British government and are now part of Kenya. In 1888 a similar concession was granted to the German East Africa Association of the Sultan's mainland territories between the River Umba and Cape Delgado. In 1890 the German government bought these territories outright for 4m. marks. In 1892 the administration of the Benadir Ports (which had in 1889 been conceded to the British East Africa Association) was, with the consent of the Sultan, transferred to the Italian government in consideration of a quarterly payment of Rs 40,000. In 1886 the Sultan renounced in favour of Portugal all claims to the coast to the south of Cape Delgado.

German East Africa was conquered by the Allies in the First World War and subsequently divided between the Belgians, the Portuguese and the British. Ruanda and Urundi went to the Belgians, the Kionga triangle to Portugal, and Tanganyika to Britain. The country was administered as a League of Nations mandate until 1946, and then as a UN trusteeship territory until 9 Dec. 1961.

Tanganyika achieved responsible government in Sept. 1960 and full self-government on 1 May 1961. On 9 Dec. 1961 Tanganyika became a sovereign independent member state of the Commonwealth of Nations. The first prime minister, Dr Julius Nyerere, resigned in Jan. 1962; but on 9 Dec. 1962 the country adopted a republican form of government (still within the British Commonwealth), and Dr Nyerere was elected as the first president.

Before independence the East Africa High Commission had been administering services of an inter-territorial nature for Kenya, Tanzania and Uganda and this continued after independence. The arrangement was changed to the East African Community in 1967. The Community practically ceased to function after 30 June 1977, chiefly because of the failure to agree a budget and the refusal of President Nyerere to negotiate with President Amin of Uganda.

On 24 June 1963 Zanzibar became an internal self-governing state, and on 9 Dec. 1963 she became independent from British rule. On 12 Jan. 1964 her sultanate was overthrown and the Sultan sent into exile by a revolt of the Afro-Shirazi Party leaders who established the People's Republic of Zanzibar. Also in Jan. 1964 there was an attempted *coup* against Nyerere, who had to seek British military help to suppress it. On 26 April 1964 Tanganyika, Zanzibar and Pemba combined to form the United Republic of Tanganyika and Zanzibar. On 29 Oct. 1964 this union was renamed Tanzania. Tanzania became a member of the East African community in 1967. The community ceased to function after June 1977 due to the difficulties of negotiating with Uganda's President Idi Amin. In 1978 President Amin attacked Tanzania and the following year Tanzania invaded Uganda, overthrew the Amin régime and remained in occupation until 1981.

Dr Nyerere was re-elected president in 1965, 1970, 1975 and 1980, but did not offer himself in 1985, when Ndugu Ali Hassan Mwinyi (President of Zanzibar) was elected.

THAILAND

The Thais migrated to the present territory from Nan Chao in the Yunnan area of China in the 8th and 9th centuries. Thais today look back to the state of Sukhothai, a Buddhist kingdom which grew up in the central plain of Thailand in the 13th century, as their first historical state. A hundred years later Sukhothai was succeeded by the new kingdom of Ayutthaya, which served until the Burmese invasion of 1767. After some years of confusion Thailand's leading general, Chao Phraya Chakkri, assumed the throne in 1782, thus establishing the dynasty which still heads the Thai state.

Siam, as Thailand was called until 1939, remained an independent state ruled by an absolute monarchy until 24 June 1932. Discontented with the social, political and economic stagnation of the country a group of rebels, calling themselves the Peoples' Party and headed by a young lawyer, Pridi Phanomyong, precipitated a bloodless *coup*. The rebels seized control of the army, imprisoned many royal officials and persuaded the king to accept the introduction of constitutional monarchy.

When, the following year, the king tried to dissolve the newly appointed General Assembly the army moved to prevent him, thus becoming the dominant force behind the government which they have remained ever since. Nationalism dominated political life through the 1930s. In 1939 Field Marshall Pibul Songgram became premier and embarked on a pro-Japanese irridentist policy that eventually brought Thailand into the Second World War on Japan's side.

Since 1945 political life has been characterized by periods of military rule interspersed with rather short attempts at democratic, civilian government. Thus three years of civilian rule from 1945 to 1948 were brought to an end when Songgram came back to power for a nine-year period. In 1957 power was seized from him by another army leader, Sarit Thanarat, who abolished the constitution and ruled without outside intereference until his death in 1963, when he was replaced by the new Commander-in-Chief, Thano Kittikachon. Democratic government was reintroduced for a short time after 1973, when 100 students were killed in clashes with the army and again from 1969–71 when another successful military *coup* was staged aimed at checking the high crime rate and the growth of Communist insurgence.

A new, moderately democratic constitution was introduced in 1978 which paved the way for elections in 1979. Government according to the new constitution is by two houses of the National Assembly, the Senate whose members are appointed by the king and the House of Representatives whose members are elected by the people. The king remains head of state and of the armed forces and is responsible for appointing the prime minister. His person is held to be sacred and inviolable and the royal family continues to be seen as the central symbol of Thai unity.

In the general election of 1987 16 political parties competed for office. The majority rests with a coalition of the Democrats, Chart Thai, Social Action and Rassadoru. Thailand is a member of ASEAN (Association of South East Asian Nations) and pursues a moderate, non-aligned foreign policy.

Further Reading

Morrell, D. and Samudavanija, C., *Political Conflict in Thailand.* Cambridge, Mass., 1981

TOGO

The Africans of Togo are of several tribes, including the Ewes of the south (also living in Ghana and Benin), and the Kabres, Dagombas, Tyokossis and others in the north. They had small pre-colonial states but were dominated by the powerful kingdoms of Ashanti to the west and Dahomey to the east. Europeans, beginning with the Portuguese who first visited the area in 1471–72, traded on the coast for centuries, especially in slaves, but the area between the Gold Coast forts and Whydah was for long relatively unimportant for them. In the 19th century, however, palm oil exports flourished at Anecho, Agoue and Porto Seguro, where British, French and German traders operated. Several prominent Togolese families of partly Brazilian or Portuguese origin, still important among the coastal African élite, arose at that time. Protestant and Catholic missions began working before the establishment of colonial rule. Despite the important rival influences of Britain and France in the area, it was Germany that established colonial rule on the coast in 1884.

German control was then extended inland but encountered strong resistance from the Kabres, Konkombas and other peoples, and only in 1912 was the colony fully subdued.

German Togo was overrun by the Allies in 1914. It was partitioned in 1919 into British and French Mandated Territories under the League of Nations. After the Second World War, when Vichy France held Togo at first, reforms in the whole French empire were applied to Togo, whose people acquired French citizenship and voting rights, choosing African deputies to the French National Assembly. In 1946 French Togo and British Togoland became Trust Territories under the United Nations.

From 1945 to 1952 the *Comité de l'unité togolaise* (CUT) led by Sylvanus Olympio was the leading African political party in French Togo; then the *Parti togolais du peuple* (PTP) under Nicolas Grunitzky was dominant for some years. Meanwhile some Ewe leaders called for unification of their people, split up by the colonial borders. In British Togoland a referendum was held on 9 May 1956, in which a majority voted for union with Gold Coast, although most people in the south voted for union with French Togo. The whole territory was merged with what soon afterwards became independent Ghana, but many Togolese, including Ewe reunificationists, objected. In French Togo partial self-government was granted in 1956 and Grunitzky became prime minister. Fuller self-government came in 1958. On 27 April 1960 the country became independent and Sylvanus Olympio was elected president.

President Olympio faced domestic opposition which was encouraged by President Nkrumah of Ghana, who was hostile to him. He also faced problems with Togolese soldiers discharged from the French forces. Some of them, including an NCO named Etienne Eyadema, killed Olympio on 13 Jan. 1963. Grunitzky became president, but on 13 Jan. 1967 the army seized power under Eyadema.

Eyadema, now a general and since 1974 renamed Gnassingbe Eyadema during a move to introduce African forenames, has ruled the country since 1967. He rules with the support of the army, mostly composed of Kabres like himself, and his régime, in which northerners are prominent, has faced opposition from the coastal élite, notably the exiled sons of Olympio. There have been several plots, and on 23–24 Sept. 1986 an insurgent force attempted to overthrow Eyadema. French and Zairean troops helped suppress the challenge.

Emergency rule was formally ended with the enactment of a new constitution in Dec. 1979. President Eyadema was re-elected then, and again in Dec. 1986. Multi-candidate elections were held in July 1987.

Further Reading

Cornevin, R., *Histoire du Togo.* 3rd ed. Paris, 1969

TONGA

The Tongatapu group of islands in the south western Pacific Ocean was discovered by Tasman in 1643. Tonga was inhabited at least 3,000 years ago by Austronesian-speaking peoples. A stratified social system headed by a paramount ruler was developed by the Tongans and in the 13th century their dominion extended as far as Hawaii. The Kingdom of Tonga attained unity under Taufa'ahau Tupou (George I) who became ruler of his native Ha'apai in 1820, of Vava'u in 1833 and of Tongatapu in 1845. By 1860 the kingdom had become converted to Christianity (George himself having been baptized in 1831). In 1862 the king granted freedom to the people from arbitrary rule of minor chiefs and gave them the right to the allocation of land for their own needs. These institutional changes, together with the establishment of a parliament of chiefs, paved the way towards the democratic constitution under which the kingdom is now governed, and provided a background of stability against which Tonga was able to develop her agricultural economy.

The kingdom continued up to 1899 to be a neutral region in accordance with the Declaration of Berlin of 6 April 1886. By the Anglo-German Agreement of 14 Nov. 1899 subsequently accepted by the USA, the Tonga Islands were left under the Protectorate of Great Britain. A protectorate was proclaimed on 18 May 1900, and a British Agent and Consul appointed. The Protectorate was dissolved on June 4 1970 when Tonga, the only ancient kingdom surviving from the pre-European period in Polynesia, achieved complete independence within the Commonwealth.

Further Reading
Luke, Sir Harry, *Queen Salote and Her Kingdom*. London, 1954

TRINIDAD AND TOBAGO

Officially the Republic of Trinidad and Tobago, these islands lie just off the coast of Venezuela in the Caribbean Sea. When Columbus visited Trinidad in 1498 the island was inhabited by Arawak Indians. Tobago was occupied by the Caribs. Trinidad remained a neglected Spanish possession for almost 300 years until it was surrendered to a British naval expedition in 1797. The main crop on the island was tobacco. Slaves were imported for labour to replace the original Indian population that had been worked to death by the Spanish.

The British first attempted to settle Tobago in 1721 but the French captured the island in 1781 and transformed it into a sugar producing colony. In 1802 the British acquired Tobago and in 1899 it was administratively combined with Trinidad. When slavery was abolished in the late 1830s, the British subsidized immigration from India to replace plantation labourers.

Sugar and cocoa, which were the basis of the economy, declined towards the end of the 19th century and oil and asphalt have been the dominant source of income since then.

Under the Bases Agreement concluded between the governments of the UK and the USA on 27 March 1941, and the concomitant Trinidad-US Bases Lease of 22 April 1941, defence bases were leased to the US Government for 99 years. On 8 Dec. 1960 the USA agreed to abandon 21,000 acres of leased land and the US has since given up the remaining territory, except for a small tracking station. From 1958–61 the territory was a member of the short-lived Federation of the West Indies.

On 31 Aug. 1962 Trinidad and Tobago became an independent member state of the British Commonwealth. A republican constitution was adopted on 24 Sept. 1976.

The first political party to be formed was the People's National Movement, founded in 1956 and headed by Dr Eric Williams. Gradually a left-wing opposition has grown from four parties uniting in 1986 under the name National Alliance for Reconstruction.

Further Reading
Williams, E., *History of the People of Trinidad and Tobago*. London, 1964

TUNISIA

Settled by the Phoenicians, this area of the north African coast developed into the Carthaginian Empire and was later incorporated into the Roman Empire. It became a powerful state under the dynasty of the Berber Hafsids (1207–1574).

Tunisia was nominally a part of the Ottoman Empire from the end of the 17th century and descendants of the original Ottoman ruler remained Beys of Tunis until the modern state of Tunisia was established. A French protectorate since 1883, Tunisia saw considerable anti-French activity in the late 1930s including a general strike in 1938 led by the *Néo-Destour* party (renamed *Parti Socialiste Destourien* – PSD – in 1964) under Habib Bourguiba. Tunisia did, however, support the Allies in the Second World War and was the scene of heavy fighting.

France granted internal self-government in 1955 and Tunisia became fully independent on 20 March 1956. A constitutional assembly was established and Habib Bourguiba became prime minister. A republic was established in 1957, the Bey deposed and the monarchy was abolished; Bourguiba became president. In 1975 the constitution was changed so that Bourguiba could be made President-for-life.

Tunisia was a one-party (PSD) state until 1981. When elections were held on 2 Nov. 1986 all seats in the national assembly were won by *Front National*, an alliance of the PSD and the *Union générale des travailleurs tunisiens*. All other parties boycotted the elections.

On 7 Nov. 1987 Habib Bourguiba was removed from office on grounds of ill health. His successor as president is Zine El Abidine Ben Ali.

Further Reading

Ling, D. L., *Tunisia: From Protectorate to Republic*. Indiana Univ. Press, 1967

TURKEY

In the 13th century the kingdom of Othman I became the dominant power in Asia Minor (now the Asian part of Turkey). In 1453 the Turks captured Constantinople and destroyed the Eastern Roman Empire. Thereafter, the Ottoman Empire expanded to include an area from Morocco to Persia and westwards into the Balkans. From the 17th century, however, the Empire began to decline, its power weakening rapidly in the 19th century.

The Turkish War of Independence (1919–22), following the disintegration of the Ottoman Empire, was led and won by Mustafa Kemal (Atatürk) on behalf of the Grand National Assembly which first met in Ankara on 23 April 1920. On 20 Jan. 1921 the Grand National Assembly voted a constitution which declared that all sovereignty belonged to the people and vested all power, both executive and legislative, in the Grand National Assembly. The name 'Ottoman Empire' was later replaced by 'Turkey'. On 1 Nov. 1922 the Grand National Assembly abolished the office of Sultan and Turkey became a republic on 29 Oct. 1923.

Religious courts were abolished in 1924, Islam ceased to be the official state religion in 1928, women were given the franchise and western-style surnames were adopted in 1934.

On 27 May 1960 the Turkish Army, directed by a National Unity Committee under the leadership of Gen. Çemal Gürsel, overthrew the government of the Democratic Party. The Grand National Assembly was dissolved and party activities were suspended. Party activities were legally resumed on 12 Jan. 1961. A new constitution was approved in a referendum held on 9 July 1961 and general elections were held the same year.

On 12 Sept. 1980, the Turkish armed forces overthrew the Demirel Government (Justice Party). Parliament was dissolved and all activities of political parties were suspended. The Constituent Assembly was convened in Oct. 1981, and prepared a new constitution which was enforced after a national referendum on 7 Nov. 1982.

Further Reading
Weiker, W., *The Modernization of Turkey*. New York, 1981

TURKS AND CAICOS ISLANDS

The Turks and Caicos Islands consist of two small groups of islands in the West Indies. There is evidence that a primitive culture once existed on these islands but at the time of their discovery by the Spanish 1512, the islands were uninhabited. They remained unoccupied until 1678, when British settlers from Bermuda established a salt-panning industry. After a long period of French and Spanish claims, the islands were eventually secured to the British Crown by the appointment in 1766 of a Resident British Agent. Towards the end of the 18th century the Bahamas Government laid claims to the islands and in 1804 by Order in Council the legislature of the Bahamas Government was extended to them despite protests from the Bermuda salt-rakers. In 1874 the islands became a dependency of Jamaica until 1962. The islands became a separate colony in that year.

The Governor retains responsibility for external affairs, internal security, defence and certain other matters; otherwise the islands are governed by an Executive Council and a Legislative Council.

The Progressive National Party (PNP) has won the elections held since 1980, and it does not favour independence.

TUVALU

Formally known as the Ellice Islands, Tuvalu is a group of nine islands in the western central Pacific. Traditions recorded by missionaries in the 19th century indicate Samoa or Tonga as the original home of Tuvalu's first Polynesian settlers. Tuvaluan language supports this and genealogical data suggests settlement dates back to 1325. A number of castaways and beachcombers settled and intermarried with the Tuvaluans during 1820–70, when whalers frequented the surrounding seas.

In 1892 when the British established the Gilbert Islands Protectorate, the Tuvalu islanders were encouraged to join. They became the Gilbert and Ellice Islands colony in 1916.

After the Japanese occupied the Gilberts in 1942, US forces occupied the Ellice Islands and built air strips on three islands. Many Tuvaluans emigrated to Tarawa in the Gilberts after the Second World War for employment rivalry between them and the Kiribatians set the stage for separation. On the recommendation of a commissioner, appointed by the British Government, to consider requests that the island group be separated from the Gilbert Islands, a referendum was held in 1974. There was a large majority in favour of separation and this took place in Oct. 1975. Independence was achieved on 1 Oct. 1978. Early in 1979 the US signed a treaty of friendship with Tuvalu and relinquished its claim to the four southern islands in return for access to its Second World War bases, and the right to veto any other nation's request to use any of Tuvalu's islands for military purposes.

UGANDA

The Luo (a Nilotic-speaking people) invaded the territory of present-day Uganda in the late 15th and 16th centuries, and while assimilating with the existing Bantu-speaking inhabitants, also founded several strong centralized kingdoms. Buganda was the most prominent of these and prospered through the 19th century, assisting British forces in the conquest of its neighbours. Uganda became a British Protectorate in 1894, the province of Buganda being recognized as a native kingdom under its Kabaka. In 1961 Uganda was granted internal self-government with federal status for Buganda.

Uganda became a fully independent member of the Commonwealth on 9 Oct. 1962 after nearly 70 years of British rule. Full sovereign status was granted by the Uganda Independence Act 1962, and the constitution is embodied in the Uganda (Independence) Order in Council 1962. The post of Governor-General was on 9 Oct. 1963 replaced by that of President as head of state, elected by the National Assembly for a five-year term. Uganda became a republic on 8 Sept. 1967.

Before independence the East Africa High Commission had been administering services of an inter-territorial nature for Kenya, Tanzania and Uganda and this continued after independence. The arrangement was changed to the East African Community in 1967. The Community practically ceased to function after 30 June 1977; the main reasons were the failure to agree a budget and the refusal of President Nyerere of Tanzania to negotiate with President Amin of Uganda.

President Milton Obote set about returning land given to the Buganda by the British in 1900 to its original Bunyoro owners. He also abolished Buganda's federal status and autonomy in the country. A rebellion by Buganda was quelled, but in 1971 Obote was overthrown by troops under Gen. Idi Amin. Amin's rule was characterized by widespread repression and the expulsion of Asian residents in 1972.

In April 1979 a force of the Tanzanian Army and Ugandan exiles advanced into Uganda taking Kampala on 11 April. Amin fled into exile. On 14 April Dr Yusuf Lule was sworn in as president and the country was administered, initially, by the Uganda National Liberation Front.

The former Attorney-General, Godfrey Lukonwa Binaisa QC,

was appointed president by the National Consultative Council on 20 June 1979. Dr Lule subsequently left the country. Dr Binaisa was overthrown in May 1980 by the Military Commission, the military arm of Uganda National Liberation Front.

In Dec. 1980 following elections Dr Obote again became president, but on 27 July 1985 he was overthrown, the constitution suspended, and the borders closed. Lieut.-Gen. Tito Okello became head of state on 29 July but on the following day the National Resistance Army (NRA) stated that it was not prepared to co-operate with the new régime. A ceasefire between the NRA, under Yoweri Museveni, and government forces was agreed on 17 Dec. 1985.

NRA troops took Kampala on 26 Jan. 1986, and Yoweri Museveni was inducted as president. He set up a joint military and civilian government, suspended political parties and postponed elections. Various rebel forces were organized against his government, but suffered heavy losses in 1987.

Further Reading

Jørgensen, J. J. *Uganda: A Modern History*, London, 1981

UNION OF SOVIET SOCIALIST REPUBLICS

Until 12 March 1917 the territory now forming the USSR, together with that of Finland, Poland and certain tracts ceded in 1918 to Turkey, but less the territories then forming part of the German, Austro-Hungarian and Japanese empires – East Prussia, Eastern Galicia, Transcarpathia, Bukovina, South Sakhalin and Kurile Islands – which were acquired during and after the Second World War, was constituted as the Russian Empire. It was governed as an autocracy under the tsar, with the aid of ministers responsible to himself and a State Duma with limited legislative powers, elected by provincial assemblies chosen by indirect elections on a restricted franchise.

On 8 March 1917 a revolution broke out. The Duma parties, on 12 March, set up a Provisional Committee of the State Duma, while the factory workmen and the insurgent garrison of Petrograd elected a Council (Soviet) of Workers' and Soldiers' Deputies. Soviets were also elected by the workmen in other towns, in the Army and Navy and, as time went on, by the peasantry. On 15 March 1917 Tsar Nicholas II abdicated, and the Provisional Committee, by agreement with the Petrograd Soviet, appointed a Provisional Government and, on 14 Sept., proclaimed a republic. However, a political struggle went on between the supporters of the Provisional Government – the Mensheviks and the Socialist Revolutionaries – and the Bolsheviks who advocated the assumption of power by the Soviets. When they had won majorities in the Soviets of the principal cities and of the armed forces on several fronts, the Bolsheviks organized an insurrection through a Military-Revolutionary Committee of the Petrograd Soviet. On 7 Nov. 1917 the Committee arrested the Provisional Government and transferred power to the second All-Russian Congress of Soviets. This elected a new government, the Council of People's Commissars, headed by Lenin.

On 25 Jan. 1918 the third All-Russian Congress of Soviets issued a Declaration of Rights of the Toiling and Exploited People, which proclaimed Russia a Republic of Soviets of Workers', Soldiers' and Peasants' Deputies; and on 10 July 1918 the fifth Congress adopted a constitution for the Russian Soviet Federal Socialist Republic (RSFSR). In the course of the following civil war other Soviet republics were set up in the Ukraine, Belorussia and Transcaucasia.

267

These first entered into treaty relations with the RSFSR and then, in 1922, joined with it in a closely integrated Union.

The Union of Soviet Socialist Republics (USSR) was formed by the union of the RSFSR, the Ukrainian Soviet Socialist Republic, the Belorussian Soviet Socialist Republic and the Transcaucasian Soviet Socialist Republic; the Treaty of Union was adopted by the first Soviet Congress of the USSR on 30 Dec. 1922. In Oct. 1924 the Uzbek and Turkmen Autonomous Soviet Socialist Republics and in Dec. 1929 the Tadzhik Autonomous Soviet Socialist Republic were declared constituent members of the USSR, becoming Union Republics.

From about 1929 Stalin's authority was supreme. Resistance to agricultural collectivization was ruthlessly suppressed. A series of Five-Year Plans (1928, 1933, 1937, 1946 and 1951) transformed the USSR into a powerful industrial state. Opposition in party and government was crushed by the purges of 1933 and 1936–38.

At the eighth Congress of the Soviets, on 5 Dec. 1936, a new constitution of the USSR was adopted. The Transcaucasian Republic was split up into the Armenian Soviet Socialist Republic, the Azerbaijan Soviet Socialist Republic and the Georgian Soviet Socialist Republic, each of which became constituent republics of the Union. At the same time the Kazakh Soviet Socialist Republic and the Kirghiz Soviet Socialist Republic, previously autonomous republics within the RSFSR, were proclaimed constituent republics of the USSR.

In Sept. 1939 (under a secret clause of the 10-year non-aggression signed with Nazi Germany on 23 Aug. 1939) Soviet troops occupied eastern Poland as far as the 'Curzon line', which in 1919 had been drawn on ethnographical grounds as the eastern frontier of Poland, and incorporated it into the Ukrainian and Belorussian Soviet Socialist Republics. In Feb. 1951 some districts of the Drogobych Region of the Ukraine and the Lublin Voivodship of Poland were exchanged.

On 31 March 1940 territory ceded by Finland was joined to that of the Autonomous Soviet Socialist Republic of Karelia to form the Karelo-Finnish Soviet Socialist Republic, which was admitted into the Union as the 12th Union Republic. On 16 July 1956 the Supreme Soviet of the USSR altered the status of the Karelo-Finnish Republic from that of a Union Republic of the USSR to that of an Autonomous (Karelian) Republic within the RSFSR.

On 2 Aug. 1940 the Moldavian Soviet Socialist Republic was constituted as the 13th Union Republic. It comprised the former Moldavian Autonomous Soviet Socialist Republic and Bessarabia (44,290 sq. km, ceded by Romania on 28 June 1940), except for the districts of Khotin, Akerman and Izmail, which, together with Northern Bukovina (10,440 sq. km), were incorporated in the Ukrainian Soviet Republic. The Soviet-Romanian frontier thus constituted was confirmed by the peace treaty with Romania, signed on 10 Feb. 1947. On 29 June 1945 Ruthenia (Sub-Carpathian Russia, 12,742 sq. km) was by treaty with Czechoslovakia incorporated into the Ukrainian Soviet Socialist Republic.

On 3, 5 and 6 Aug. 1940 Lithuania, Latvia and Estonia were incorporated in the Soviet Union as the 14th, 15th and 16th Union Republics respectively. The change in the status of the Karelo-Finnish Republic reduced the number of Union Republics to 15.

After the defeat of Nazi Germany it was agreed by the governments of the UK, the USA and the USSR that part of East Prussia should be embodied in the USSR. The area (11,655 sq. km), which includes the towns of Konigsberg (renamed Kaliningrad), Tilsit (renamed Sovyetsk) and Insterburg (renamed Chernyakhovsk), was joined to the RSFSR by decree of 7 April 1946.

By the peace treaty with Finland, signed on 10 Feb. 1947, the province of Petsamo (Pechenga), ceded to Finland on 14 Oct. 1920 and 12 March 1946, was returned to the Soviet Union. On 19 Sept. 1955 the Soviet Union renounced its treaty rights to the naval base of Porkkala-Udd and on 26 Jan. 1956 completed the withdrawal of its forces from Finnish territory.

In 1945, after the defeat of Japan, the southern half of Sakhalin (36,000 sq. km) and the Kurile Islands (10,200 sq. km) were, by agreement with the Allies, incorporated in the USSR. However, Japan has since asked for the return of the Etorofu and Kunashiri Islands as not belonging to the Kurile Islands proper. The Soviet government informed Japan on 27 Jan. 1960 that the Habomai Islands and Shikotan would be handed back to Japan on the withdrawal of American troops from Japan.

N. Khruschev, Secretary-General of the Party, criticized the régime of Stalin who died in 1953 at the Twentieth Party Congress in 1956. This encouraged a liberalizing of the Russian-backed communist régimes of Hungary and Poland, and later Czechoslovakia (1968) which the USSR crushed with its forces and those of the Warsaw Pact (established 1955). A policy of 'peaceful co-existence' with the West, especially after the war scare with the USA in 1962 over Cuban missiles, led to years of strained relations with China. Since 1985, M. Gorbachev has been Secretary-General of the Communist Party and a new period of *glasnost* (openness) and *perestroika* (reconstruction) has been inaugurated.

Further Reading

Riasanovsky, N. V., *A History of Russia*. 4th ed. OUP, 1984

CONSTITUENT REPUBLICS OF THE USSR

RUSSIAN SOVIET FEDERAL SOCIALIST REPUBLIC

Autonomous Soviet Republics within the RSFSR

Bashkir Autonomous Soviet Socialist Republic

Bashkiria was annexed to Russia in 1557. It was constituted as an Autonomous Soviet Republic on 23 March 1919.

Buriat Autonomous Soviet Socialist Republic

The area was penetrated by the Russians in the 17th century and finally annexed from China by the treaties of Nerchinsk (1689) and Kyakhta (1727). It adopted the Soviet system on 1 March 1920. The name was changed from Buriat-Mongol on 7 July 1958.

Checheno-Ingush Autonomous Soviet Socialist Republic

After 70 years of almost continuous fighting, the Chechens and Ingushes were conquered by Russia in the late 1850s. In 1918 each nationality separately established its 'National Soviet' within the Terek Autonomous Republic, and in 1920 (after the Civil War) were constituted areas within the Mountain Republic. The Chechens separated out as an Autonomous Region on 30 Nov. 1922 and the Ingushes on 7 July 1924. In Jan. 1934 the two regions were united, and on 5 Dec. 1936 constituted as an Autonomous Republic. This was dissolved in 1944, but reconstituted on 9 Jan. 1957; 232,000 Chechens and Ingushes returned to their homes in the next two years.

Chuvash Autonomous Soviet Socialist Republic

The territory was annexed by Russia in the middle of the 16th century. On 24 June 1920 it was constituted as an Autonomous Region, and on 21 April 1925 as an Autonomous Republic.

Dagestan Autonomous Soviet Socialist Republic

Annexed from Persia in 1723, Dagestan was constituted an Autonomous Republic on 20 Jan. 1921.

Kabardino-Balkar Autonomous Soviet Socialist Republic

Annexed to Russia in 1557. The republic was constituted on 5 Dec. 1936.

Kalmyk Autonomous Soviet Socialist Republic

The Kalmyks migrated from western China to Russia (Nogai Steppe) in the early 17th century. The territory was constituted an Autonomous Region on 4 Nov. 1920, and an Autonomous Republic on 22 Oct. 1935; this was dissolved in 1943. On 9 Jan. 1957 it was reconstituted as an Autonomous Region and on 29 July 1958 as an Autonomous Republic once more.

Karelian Autonomous Soviet Socialist Republic

Before 1917, Karelia (then known as the Olonets Province) was noted chiefly as a place of exile for political and other prisoners.

After the November Revolution of 1917, Karelia formed part of the RSFSR. In June 1920 a Karelian Labour Commune was formed and in July 1923 this was transformed into the Karelian Autonomous Soviet Socialist Republic (one of the autonomous republics of the RSFSR). On 31 March 1940, after the Soviet-Finnish war, practically all the territory (with the exception of a small section in the neighbourhood of the Leningrad area) which had been ceded by Finland to the USSR was added to Karelia and the Karelian Autonomous Republic was transformed into the Karelo-Finnish Soviet Socialist Republic as the 12th republic of the USSR. In 1946, however, the southern part of the republic, including its whole seaboard and the town of Viipuri (Vyborg) and Keksholm, was attached to the RSFSR and in 1956 the republic reverted to ASSR status with the RSFSR.

Komi Autonomous Soviet Socialist Republic

Annexed by the princes of Moscow in the 14th century and occupied by British and American forces in 1918–19, the territory was constituted as an Autonomous Region on 22 Aug. 1921 and as an Autonomous Republic on 5 Dec. 1936.

Mari Autonomous Soviet Socialist Republic

The Mari people were annexed to Russia, with other peoples of the Kazan Tatar Khanate, when the latter was overthrown in 1552. On 4 Nov. 1920 the territory was constituted as an Autonomous Region, and on 5 Dec. 1936 as an Autonomous Republic.

Mordovian Autonomous Soviet Socialist Republic

By the 13th century the Mordovian tribes had been subjugated by the Russian princes of Ryazan and Nizhni-Novgorod. In 1928 the territory was constituted as a Mordovian Area within the Middle-Volga Territory, on 10 Jan. 1930 as an Autonomous Region and on 20 Dec. 1934 as an Autonomous Republic.

North Ossetian Autonomous Soviet Socialist Republic

The Ossetians, known to antiquity as Alani (who were also called by their immediate neighbours 'Ossi' or 'Yassi'), were annexed to Russia after the latter's treaty of Kuchuk-Kainardji with Turkey, and in 1784 the key fortress of Vladikavkaz was founded on their territory (given the name of Terek region in 1861). On 4 March 1918 the latter was proclaimed an Autonomous Soviet Republic, and after the Civil War this territory with others was set up as the Mountain Autonomous Republic (20 Jan. 1921), with North Ossetia as the Ossetian (Vladikavkaz) Area within it. On 7 July 1924 the latter was constituted as an Autonomous Region and on 5 Dec. 1936 as an Autonomous Republic.

Tatar Autonomous Soviet Socialist Republic

From the 10th to the 13th centuries this was the territory of the flourishing Volga-Kama Bulgar State; conquered by the Mongols, it became the seat of the Kazan (Tatar) Khans when the Mongol Empire broke up in the 15th century, and in 1552 was conquered again by Russia. On 27 May 1920 it was constituted as an Autonomous Republic.

Tuva Autonomous Soviet Socialist Republic

The Tuvans are a Turkic people, formerly ruled by hereditary or elective tribal chiefs. Tuva was incorporated in the USSR as an Autonomous Region on 13 Oct. 1944 and became an Autonomous Republic on 10 Oct. 1961.

Udmurt Autonomous Soviet Socialist Republic

The Udmurts (formerly known as Votyaks) were annexed by the Russians in the 15th and 16th centuries. On 4 Nov. 1920 the Votyak Autonomous Region was constituted (the name was changed to Udmurt, used by the people themselves, in 1932), and on 28 Dec. 1934 became an Autonomous Republic.

Yakut Autonomous Soviet Socialist Republic

The Yakuts were subjugated by the Russians in the 17th century. The territory was constituted an Autonomous Republic on 27 April 1922.

UKRAINE

The Ukrainian Soviet Socialist Republic was proclaimed on 25 Dec. 1917 and was finally established in Dec. 1919. In Dec. 1920 it concluded a military and economic alliance with the RSFSR and on 30 Dec. 1922 formed, together with the other Soviet Socialist Republics, the Union of Soviet Socialist Republics. On 1 Nov. 1939 Western Ukraine (about 88,000 sq. km) was incorporated in the Ukrainian SSR. On 2 Aug. 1940 Northern Bukovina (about 6,000 sq. km) ceded to the USSR by Romania 28 June 1940, and the Khotin, Akkerman and Izmail provinces of Bessarabia were included in the Ukrainian SSR, and on 29 June 1945 Ruthenia (Sub-Carpathian Russia, covering about 7,000 sq. km) was also incorporated. From the new territories two new regions were formed, Chernovits and Izmail.

BELORUSSIA

The Belorussian Soviet Socialist Republic was established on 1 Jan. 1919. It forms one of the constituent republics of the USSR.

AZERBAIJAN

The 'Mussavat' (Nationalist) party, which dominated the National Council or Constituent Assembly of the Tatars, declared the independence of Azerbaijan on 28 May 1918, with a capital, first at Ganja (Elizavetpol) and later at Baku. On 28 April 1920 Azerbaijan was proclaimed a Soviet Socialist Republic. From 1922, with Georgia and Armenia it formed the Transcaucasian Soviet Federal Socialist Republic. In 1936 it assumed the status of one of the Union Republics of the USSR.

Nakhichevan Autonomous Soviet Socialist Republic

The population, mainly Azerbaijanis, had a chequered history for 1,500 years under the ancient Persians, Arabs, Seljuk Turks,

Mongols, Ottoman Turks and modern Persians before being annexed by Russia in 1828. On 9 Feb. 1924 it was constituted as an Autonomous Republic within Azerbaijan.

Nagorno-Karabakh Autonomous Region

A separate khanate in the 18th century, it was established on 7 July 1923 as an Autonomous Region within Azerbaijan.

GEORGIA

The independence of the Georgian Social Democratic Republic was declared at Tiflis on 26 May 1918 by the National Council, elected by the National Assembly of Georgia on 22 Nov. 1917. The independence of Georgia was recognized by the USSR on 7 May 1920. On 12 Feb. 1921 a rising broke out in Mingrelia, Abkhazia and Adjaria, and Soviet troops invaded the country, which, on 25 Feb. 1921, was proclaimed the Georgian Soviet Socialist Republic. At the first Transcaucasian Soviet Congress on 15 Dec. 1922, Georgia, together with Armenia and Azerbaijan, united to form the Transcaucasian Soviet Federal Socialist Republic, and a federal constitution was adopted and published 10 Jan. 1923. In 1936 the Georgian Soviet Socialist Republic became one of the constituent republics of the USSR.

Abkhazian Autonomous Soviet Socialist Republic

This area, the ancient Colchis, included Greek colonies from the 6th century BC onwards. From the 2nd century BC onwards, it was a prey to many invaders – Romans, Byzantines, Arabs, Ottoman Turks – before accepting a Russian protectorate in 1810. However, from the 4th century AD a West Georgian kingdom was established by the Lazi princes in the territory (known to the Romans as 'Lazica') and by the 8th century the prevailing language was Georgian and the name Abkhazia. In March 1921 a congress of local Soviets proclaimed it a Soviet Republic, and its status as an Autonomous Republic, within Georgia, was confirmed on 17 April 1930.

Adjarian Autonomous Soviet Socialist Republic

After a history similar to that of Abkhazia, this area fell under Turkish rule in the 17th century, and was annexed to Russia (rejoining Georgia) after the Berlin Treaty of 1878. On 16 July 1921 the territory was constituted as an Autonomous Republic within the Georgian SSR.

South Ossetian Autonomous Region

This area was populated by Ossetians from across the Caucasus (North Ossetia), driven out by the Mongols in the 13th century. The region was set up within the Georgian SSR on 20 April 1922.

ARMENIA

On 29 Nov. 1920 Armenia was proclaimed a Soviet Socialist Republic. The Armenian Soviet Government, with the Russian Soviet Government, was a party to the Treaty of Kars (March 1921) which confirmed the Turkish possession of the former Government of Kars and of the Surmali District of the Government of Yerevan. From 1922 to 1936 it formed part of the Transcaucasian Soviet Federal Socialist Republic. In 1936 Armenia was proclaimed a constituent republic of the USSR.

MOLDAVIAN SOVIET SOCIALIST REPUBLIC

The republic was formed by the union of part of the former Moldavian Autonomous Soviet Socialist Republic (organized 12 Oct. 1924), formerly included in the Ukrainian Soviet Socialist Republic, and the areas of Bessarabia (ceded by Romania to the USSR, 28 June 1940) with a mainly Moldavian population.

ESTONIA

The workers' and soldiers' Soviets in Estonia took over power on 8 Nov. 1917, were overthrown by the German occupying forces in March 1918, and were restored to power as the Germans withdrew in Nov. 1918, establishing the 'Estland Labour Commune'. It was overthrown with the assistance of British naval forces in May 1919, and a democratic republic proclaimed. In March 1934 this régime was, in turn, overthrown by a fascist *coup*.

The secret protocol of the Soviet-German agreement of 23 Aug. 1939 assigned Estonia to the Soviet sphere of interest. An ultimatum (16 June 1940) led to the formation of a government acceptable to the USSR; on 21 July the State Duma proclaimed the establishment of an Estonian Soviet Socialist Republic and applied to join the USSR, and on 6 Aug. the Supreme Soviet accepted the application. The incorporation has been accorded *de facto* recognition by the British Government, but not by the US Government, which continues to recognize an Estonian consul-general in New York.

LATVIA

In the part of Latvia unoccupied by the Germans, the Bolsheviks won 72% of the votes in the Constituent Assembly elections of Nov. 1917. Soviet power was proclaimed in Dec. 1917, but was overthrown when the Germans occupied all Latvia (Feb. 1918). Restored when they withdrew (Dec. 1918), it was overthrown once more by combined British naval and German military forces (May–Dec. 1919), and a democratic government set up. This régime was in turn replaced when a fascist *coup* took place in May 1934.

The secret protocol of the Soviet-German agreement of 23 Aug. 1939 assigned Latvia to the Soviet sphere of interest. An ultimatum (16 June 1940) led to the formation of a government acceptable to the USSR. On 21 July a People's Diet proclaimed the establishment of the Latvian Soviet Socialist Republic and applied to join the USSR, whose Supreme Soviet accepted the application on 5 Aug. The incorporation has been accorded *de facto* recognition by the British Government, but not by the US Government, which continues to recognize the Chargé d'Affaires in Washington, D.C., USA.

LITHUANIA

In 1914–15 the German army occupied the whole of Lithuania. On its withdrawal (Dec. 1918) Soviets were elected in all towns and a Soviet republic was proclaimed. In the summer of 1919 it was overthrown by Polish, German and nationalist Lithuanian forces, and a democratic republic established. In Dec. 1926 this régime was in turn overthrown by a fascist *coup*.

The secret protocol of the Soviet-German frontier treaty of 28 Sept. 1939 assigned the greater part of Lithuania to the Soviet sphere of influence. In Oct. 1939 the province and city of Vilnius (in Polish occupation 1920–39) were ceded by the USSR. An ultimatum (16 June 1940) led to the formation of a government acceptable to the USSR. A People's Diet, elected on 14–15 July, proclaimed the establishment of the Lithuanian Soviet Socialist Republic on 21 July and applied for admission to the USSR, which was effected by decree of the USSR Supreme Soviet on 3 Aug. and included also those parts of Lithuania which had been reserved for inclusion in Germany. This incorporation has been accorded *de facto* recognition by the British Government, but not by the US Government, which continues to recognize a Lithuanian Chargé d'Affaires in Washington, D.C., USA.

SOVIET CENTRAL ASIA

Soviet Central Asia embraces the Kazakh Soviet Socialist Republic, the Uzbek Soviet Socialist Republic, the Turkmen Soviet Socialist Republic, the Tadzhik Soviet Socialist Republic and the Kirghiz Soviet Socialist Republic.

Turkestan (by which name part of this territory was then known) was conquered by the Russians in the 1860s. In 1866 Tashkent was occupied and in 1868 Samarkand, and subsequently further territory was conquered and united with Russian Turkestan. In the 1870s Bokhara was subjugated, the emir, by an agreement of 1873, recognizing the suzerainty of Russia. In the same year Khiva became a vassal state to Russia. Until 1917 Russian Central Asia was divided politically into the Khanate of Khiva, the Emirate of Bokhara and the Governor-Generalship of Turkestan.

In the summer of 1919 the authority of the Soviet Government became definitely established in these regions. The Khan of Khiva was deposed in Feb. 1920, and a People's Soviet Republic was set up, the medieval name of Khorezm being revived. In Aug. 1920 the Emir of Bokhara suffered the same fate, and a similar régime was set up in Bokhara. The former Governor-Generalship of Turkestan was constituted an Autonomous Soviet Socialist Republic within the RSFSR on 11 April 1921.

In the autumn of 1924 the Soviets of the Turkestan, Bokhara and Khiva Republics decided to redistribute the territories of these republics on a nationality basis; at the same time Bokhara and Khiva became Socialist Republics. The redistribution was completed in May 1925, when the new states of Uzbekistan, Turkmenistan and Tadzhikistan were accepted into the USSR as Union Republics. The remaining districts of Turkestan populated by Kazakhs were united with Kazakhstan which was established as an ASSR in 1925 and became a Union Republic in 1936. Kirghizia, until then part of the RSFSR, was established as a Union Republic in 1936.

UNITED ARAB EMIRATES

From Sha'am, 35 miles south-west of Ras Musam dam, for nearly 400 miles to Khor al Odeid at the south-eastern end of the peninsula of Qatar, the coast, formerly known as the Trucial Coast, of the Gulf (together with 50 miles of the coast of the Gulf of Oman) belongs to the rulers of the 7 Trucial States. In 1820 these rulers signed a treaty prescribing peace with the British Government. This treaty was followed by further agreements providing for the suppression of the slave trade and by a series of other engagements, of which the most important were the Perpetual Maritime Truce (May 1853) and the Exclusive Agreement (March 1892). Under the latter, the sheikhs, on behalf of themselves, their heirs and successors, undertook that they would on no account enter into any agreement or correspondence with any power other than the British Government, receive foreign agents, cede, sell or give for occupation any part of their territory save to the British Government.

British forces withdrew from the Gulf at the end of 1971 and the treaties whereby Britain had been responsible for the defence and foreign relations of the Trucial States were terminated, being replaced on 2 Dec. 1971 by a treaty of friendship between Britain and the United Arab Emirates. The United Arab Emirates (formed 2 Dec. 1971) consists of the former Trucial States: Abu Dhabi, Dubai, Sharjah, Ajman, Umm al Qawain, Ras al Khaimah (joined in Feb. 1972) and Fujairah. The small state of Kalba was merged with Sharjah in 1952.

Further Reading

Zahlan, R. S., *The Origins of the United Arab Emirates*. London, 1978

UNITED KINGDOM

Great Britain became a political unit when England and Wales united with Scotland in a single parliament in 1707.

By 1790 British government was conducted by an effective cabinet subject to royal intervention. For historical reasons the Church of England was privileged and Nonconformists and Roman Catholics penalized, the latter heavily because they were considered politically dangerous.

Ireland was governed by English law through a nominally independent parliament. The people, mainly Catholic, rebelled in 1798. The settlement proposed was legislative union and Catholic emancipation; the latter was delayed until 1828–29 (when Nonconformists also received full civil rights) but the union took effect in 1801, as the United Kingdom of Great Britain and Ireland.

In 1793 revolutionary France declared war, and was not finally defeated until 1815. The demands of war stimulated the new, steam-powered industries. After 1815 there was frequent unrest as an increasingly urban and industrial society found its interests poorly represented by a parliament composed of landowners.

The Reform Act of 1832 improved representation in Parliament, and further acts (1867, 1884, 1918 and 1928) led gradually to universal adult suffrage. Early industrial development produced great national wealth but its distribution was extremely uneven and the condition of the poor improved slowly. Legislation to improve working conditions, education and public health did not keep pace with the growth of industrial cities. The 1840s saw much immigration from Ireland (where there was famine) and from areas of political unrest in continental Europe; a second wave of immigration from the continent occurred after 1880, including Jewish refugees.

Abroad, there was war with Russia in the Crimea (1854–56); most wars, however, were fought to conquer or pacify colonies. The 19th century empire included India, Canada, Australasia, and vast territories in Africa and Eastern Asia. After 1870 the Suez Canal enabled Britain to control the empire more effectively; she became a 40% shareholder in 1875 and the controlling power in Egypt in 1882.

The most serious imperial wars were the Boer Wars of 1881 and 1899–1902. British opinion was deeply divided, and the Liberal government elected in 1905 negotiated a Union of South Africa, by which South Africa enjoyed the same autonomy which had been agreed for Canada (1867), Australia (1901) and later New Zealand (1907). The 'dominion status' of these countries was clarified by the Statute of Westminster (1931).

Whereas early Victorian reforms were responses to obvious distress, governments after 1868 were more inclined towards preventive state action. The budget of 1910 was designed largely to finance a programme of welfare; its rejection in parliament by the House of Lords led to the Parliament Act (1911) which ended the Lords' power to veto bills.

On 3 Aug. 1914 Germany invaded Belgium and Britain was obliged by treaty to retaliate by declaring war.

During the war with Germany a rebellion was staged in Ireland, born of the failure of successive attempts to agree a formula for Irish Home Rule. The issue was complicated by factional disagreement in southern Ireland and the wish of northern Ireland to remain in the United Kingdom. In 1920 after four years' conflict the Government of Ireland Act partitioned the country. The northern six counties remained British, a parliament was created and a Unionist government took office. The southern 26 counties moved by stages to complete independence as the Republic of Ireland.

The First World War ended in Nov. 1918; the cost in men and morale had been very great and there followed a long period of economic decline and industrial difficulty. There was an unsuccessful General Strike in 1926. In 1931 an emergency coalition National Government was formed to deal with the impact of world depression.

The UK has no written constitution. Since the death of George IV in 1830 there had been steady progress to a fully constitutional monarchy, pragmatically developed, and though George V (1910–36) ruled actively he always adhered to this principle. His son Edward VIII abdicated in Dec. 1936 because his proposed marriage was incompatible with his constitutional role.

Germany revived as a military power in the 1930s, and invaded Poland on 1 Sept. 1939. Britain, bound once more by treaty, declared war.

The Second World War ended with German and Japanese defeat in 1945. It was a time of great social upheaval. In the 1945 election a Labour government was returned with a large majority and a socialist programme. Subsequent governments modified but generally accepted the changes then introduced; since 1980, however, Conservative governments have reversed much of this legislation.

In 1949 Britain became a member of the North Atlantic Treaty Organization.

Beginning with the independence and partition of India and Pakistan in 1947, a policy was pursued of rapid progress to independence of the colonies. The new concept adopted was of a Commonwealth of freely-associated states, recognizing the British monarch as symbolic Commonwealth head (some states chose to retain the monarch as head of state). Immigration to Britain from former colonies, however, increased as constitutional ties were loosened.

In 1961 an application to join the European Economic Community failed; it was controversial at home and was anyway vetoed by France. A second application in 1973 was successful; membership was endorsed by referendum in 1975.

Further Reading

Ensor, R., *England 1870–1914*. OUP, 1936
Taylor, A. J. P., *English History 1914–1945*. OUP, 1965

NORTHERN IRELAND

Home Rule was opposed in Northern Ireland by the majority Protestant population who feared becoming a minor part of a mainly Roman Catholic independent country. In 1920 an Act was passed by the British Parliament under which separate parliaments were set up for 'Southern Ireland' (composed of 26 counties) and 'Northern Ireland' (formed from the remaining 6 counties). Only the Protestant Ulster Unionists of 'Northern Ireland' accepted the scheme, and a Northern Parliament was duly elected on 24 May 1921.

The Roman Catholic minority in Northern Ireland has never been content with these arrangements. What began ostensibly as a Civil Rights campaign in 1968 escalated into a full-scale terrorist campaign designed to overthrow the State. This campaign was originally mounted by an illegal organization, the Irish Republican Army (the IRA, and not to be confused with the legitimate Army of the Republic of Ireland). At times counter-measures have required the services of over 20,000 regular troops, in addition to the Royal Ulster Constabulary, the RUC Reserve and the part-time Ulster Defence Regiment.

As the violence increased and terrorist acts were committed on the mainland of Britain by the Provisional IRA, leading to retaliatory actions by the Protestant Loyalists, the British Parliament assumed direct rule in 1972 and the Northern Ireland Parliament was prorogued. In 1973 a Northern Ireland Executive, with Protestant and Catholic representatives, was established and was to be responsible to an Assembly. This agreement soon collapsed and in 1974 direct rule by the Secretary of State for Northern Ireland was imposed. The Constitutional Convention then established, and other conferences since, have failed to devise an acceptable form of government. Violence between the 2 religious groups, and attacks on the police and on British troops have continued. In 1988 warnings were given of the probability of increasing violence with more sophisticated weapons likely to be used by the IRA. *See* Ireland.

Further Reading

Wallace, M., *British Government in Northern Ireland: From Devolution to Direct Rule.* Newton Abbot, 1982

ISLE OF MAN

The Isle of Man was first inhabited by Celts and the island became attached to Norway in the 9th century. In 1266 it was ceded to Scotland, but it came under English control in 1406 when possession was granted to the Stanley family (the Earls of Derby) and was later purchased by the British.

The Isle of Man has been a British Crown possession since 1828, with the British government responsible for its defence and foreign policy. Otherwise it has extensive right of self-government and is administered in accordance with its own laws by the Court of Tynwald, consisting of the Lieut.-Governor (appointed by the Crown), the Legislative Council (mainly selected from the House of Keys), and the House of Keys (24 members chosen on adult suffrage).

A special relationship exists between the Isle of Man and the European Economic Community providing for free trade and adoption by the Isle of Man of the EEC's external trade policies with third countries. The island remains free to levy its own system of taxes.

Further Reading

Kinvig, R. H., *History of the Isle of Man.* Oxford, 1945.—*The Isle of Man: A Social, Cultural and Political History.* Liverpool Univ. Press, 1975

CHANNEL ISLANDS

The islands of Jersey and Guernsey, with the dependencies of the latter (Alderney, Sark and other small islands), were an integral part of the Duchy of Normandy at the time of the Norman Conquest of England in 1066. Since then they have belonged to the British Crown and are not part of the UK. The islands have created their own form of self-government, with the British government at Westminster being responsible for defence and foreign policy. The Lieut.-Governors of Jersey and Guernsey, appointed by the Crown, are the personal representatives of the Sovereign as well as being the commanders of the armed forces. The legislature of Jersey is 'The States of Jersey', and that of Guernsey is 'The States of Deliberation'.

From 1940 to 1945 the islands were left undefended and were the only British territory to fall to the Germans.

Further Reading

Coysh, V., *Alderney*. Newton Abbot, 1974

THE UNITED STATES
OF AMERICA

In 1775 white settlement in America was located in 13 British colonies on the east coast and in Spanish colonial territory in the south and south-west. The rest was Indian land, where former French claims to control had been given up in 1763. Spain succeeded to those claims in land west of the Mississippi and Britain in land east of it. Britain designated such land as Indian territory and forbade colonial expansion west of the Appalachians.

Britain's colonial subjects rebelled against her taxation and trading exploitation. The colonies declared their independence on 4 July 1776, provoking war with Britain which lasted until 1783 when Britain acknowledged the independent United States of America.

The Union extended south to the border of Florida (Spanish) and west to the Mississippi. A permanent constitution came into force in 1789, providing for a federal government. The rights of states to nullify federal laws if they contradicted state policies became a source of dispute, especially in relation to the slave-owning southern states which feared the Union preference for abolition.

In 1800 France bought back from Spain her title to 'Louisiana', the territory west of the Mississippi. In 1803 the US bought it from France.

In 1812–14 the US fought an inconclusive war with Britain on the grounds that Britain, operating from Canada, was encouraging Indian resistance; at sea, Britain was using her conduct of the Napoleonic War to harrass American shipping.

Westward movement began almost with independence, increasing after the Homestead Act of 1832 and the removal of Indians to reservations during the 1830s.

The Spanish empire in the Americas had ended in 1821, and the north American territories had passed to Mexico, except for Florida which the US acquired. In 1836 Texas broke away from Mexico, surviving as an independent republic until 1845 when the US, seeing strategic danger in its vulnerability, annexed it. This provoked war with Mexico which the US won in 1848, receiving the Mexican territories in the south-west including the present states of California, Arizona, Colorado, Utah, Nevada and New Mexico.

In the north-west, the Oregon Trail attracted thousands of migrants in the 1840s. In 1846 a long dispute with Britain was resolved, confirming the US title to the Oregon Territory. Westward migration was further stimulated by the California gold rush of 1848.

In the east and mid-west, tension over the question of slavery led to the secession of the southern states in 1860–61, and their formation as the Confederacy. Civil war broke out, ending in northern victory in 1865. Slavery was abolished and a period of radical reconstruction began for the South. Many reforms then implemented were cancelled after 1877, when the northern military presence was withdrawn and southern whites regained their political power, enforcing segregation and curtailing black civil and political rights.

During the late 19th century eastern and mid-western industrialization expanded rapidly. Growing cities attracted thousands of poor European immigrants, many of whom were escaping religious or political persecution as well as looking for work. This inward flow of labour continued into the 1930s and was matched by a flow of Asians to the west coast. A similar northward movement of Spanish-speakers from the Caribbean and Mexico, and of black workers from southern states, continues.

In the west there were Indian wars. The Apache and Navajo wars of the south-west lasted intermittently from 1861 until 1886. The Comanche fought for decades to protect their plains hunting grounds from settlement, as did the Cheyenne and Sioux. The latter's victory under Sitting Bull in 1876 only produced an increase in military action against them. Indian resistance ended after some 200 Sioux were shot at Wounded Knee in 1890.

In the Spanish-American war of 1898 the US succeeded in replacing Spanish influence in the Caribbean with her own. She also replaced it in the Philippines, and acquired Guam in the western Pacific as a strategic base.

The US entered the First World War in 1917, and afterwards reacted with an isolationist policy. In 1929 the stock market collapsed and serious economic depression lasted through the 1930s. The country turned to policies of government intervention in the economy; recovery began, but only became rapid when the Second World War necessitated a huge increase in production.

The war and subsequent victory led to active participation in the affairs of Europe and to a state of 'cold war' mistrust between the US and the USSR. The US Marshall Plan financed the recovery of much of European industry. At the same time it appeared prudent to aid other nations where instability might admit Communist influence; this policy governed relations with Caribbean and Central American countries, and involved the US in war against Communist forces in Korea (1950–53) and Vietnam (1961–73).

At home, the Civil Rights Movement in the 1960s campaigned for the end of segregation in southern states; many of the segregation laws passed by state governments since 1877 were challenged in court and declared unconstitutional.

The Union consisted of 48 states until the admission of Alaska and Hawaii in 1959.

Further Reading

Morison, S. E., *et al, The Growth of the American Republic.* OUP, 1980

STATES OF THE USA

ALABAMA

In the 16th century the main powers were the Creeks, Choctaws, Chickasaws and Cherokees. The first European explorers were Spanish, including Hernando de Soto in 1540, but the first permanent European settlement was French, as part of French Louisiana after 1699. During the 17th and 18th centuries the British, Spanish and French all fought for control of the territory; it passed to Britain in 1763 and thence to the US in 1783, except for a Spanish enclave on Mobile Bay, which lasted until 1813. Alabama was organized as a Territory in 1817 and was admitted into the Union as a state on 14 Dec. 1819.

The economy was then based on cotton, grown in white-owned plantations by black slave labour imported since 1719. Alabama seceded from the Union at the beginning of the Civil War (1861) and joined the Confederate States of America; its capital Montgomery became the Confederate capital. After the defeat of the Confederacy the state was readmitted to the Union in 1878. Attempts made during the reconstruction period to find a role for the newly-freed black slaves – who made up about 50% of the population – largely failed, and when whites regained political control in the 1870s a strict policy of segregation came into force.

At the same time Birmingham began to develop as an important centre of iron- and steel-making. Most of the state was still rural. In 1915 a boll-weevil epidemic attacked the cotton and forced diversification into other farm produce. More industries developed from the power schemes of the Tennessee Valley Authority in the 1930s.

The black population remained mainly rural, poor and without political power. During the 1950s and 1960s there were confrontations on the issue of civil rights, which produced some reforms.

Further Reading

Wiggins, S. W., (ed.) *From Civil War to Civil Rights 1860–1960.* Univ. of Alabama Press, 1987

ALASKA

In the 18th century there were a number of Indian, Eskimo and Aleut tribes. Russian fur-traders made the first European contact after Russian expeditions, led by Vitus Bering, had discovered the Alaskan coast in 1741. After 1799 the territory was administered by the Russian-American Company and was known as Russian America, its capital after 1806 being at Sitka.

The company's charter was due to expire in 1861 and the US began negotiations to buy Alaska in 1859 until dealings were interrupted by the Civil War. The territory was administered by a Russian governor until 1867 when the purchase was completed on 30 March.

American settlement was stimulated by gold-rushes during the 1880s. In 1884 the territory was organized as a District governed by the laws of the neighbouring state of Oregon. On 24 Aug. 1912 the District became an Incorporated Territory. The first legislature sat in 1913 at Juneau, which had become the capital in 1906.

During the Second World War the Federal Government acquired large areas for defence purposes and for the construction of the strategic Alaska Highway. In the 1950s oil was found. Alaska became the 49th state of the Union on 3 Jan. 1959.

In the 1970s new oilfields were discovered and the Trans-Alaska pipeline was opened in 1977. The state obtained most of its income from petroleum by 1985.

Questions of land-use predominate; there are large areas with valuable mineral resources, other large areas held for the native peoples and some still held by the Federal Government. The population increased by over 400% between 1940 and 1980.

Further Reading

Hunt, A. R. *Alaska: A Bicentennial History.* New York, 1976

ARIZONA

Spaniards looking for sources of gold or silver entered Arizona in the 16th century, finding there nomadic tribes of Navajo and Apache. The first Spanish Catholic mission was founded in 1692 by Father Eusebio Kino, settlements were made in 1752 and a Spanish army headquarters was set up at Tucson in 1776. The area was governed by Mexico after the collapse of Spanish colonial power. Mexico ceded it to the US after the Mexican-American war (1848). Arizona was then part of New Mexico; the Gadsden Purchase (of land south of the Gila River) was added to it in 1853. The whole was organized as the Arizona Territory on 24 Feb. 1863.

Years of war between Indian and immigrant populations began when troops were withdrawn to serve in the Civil War. The Navajo surrendered in 1865, but the Apache continued to fight a series of wars, under Geronimo and other leaders, until 1886. After the wars the area settled to Mexican-style ranching. Arizona was admitted to the Union as the 48th state in 1912.

In the 20th century, and especially after 1920, irrigated farming began to replace ranching as the main activity. Large areas, however, were retained as Indian reservations and other large areas by the Federal Government to protect the exceptional desert and mountain landscape. In recent years this landscape and the Indian traditions have been used to attract tourist income. In 1980 about 16% of the population was Spanish-speaking and about 6% was Indian.

Further Reading

Faulk, O. B., *Arizona: A Short History*. Univ. of Oklahoma Press, 1970

ARKANSAS

In the 16th and 17th centuries, French and Spanish explorers entered Arkansas, finding there tribes of Chaddo, Osage and Quapaw. The first European settlement was French, at Arkansas Post in 1686, and the area became part of French Louisiana. The US bought Arkansas from France as part of the Louisiana Purchase in 1803, it was organized as a Territory in 1819 and entered the Union on 15 June 1836 as the 25th state.

The eastern plains by the Mississippi were settled by white plantation-owners who grew cotton with black slave labour. The rest of the state attracted a scattered population of small farmers. The plantations were the centre of political power. Arkansas seceded from the Union in 1861 and joined the Confederate States of America. At that time the slave population was about 25% of the total.

In 1868 the state was readmitted to the Union. Attempts to integrate the black population into state life achieved little, and a policy of segregation was rigidly adhered to until the 1950s.

In 1957 federal law ordered that segregation in a public high school must end. The state governor ordered the state militia to prevent desegregation; there was rioting, and federal troops were called to Little Rock, the capital, to restore order. School segregation ended within the following 10 years. In 1980 the black population was about 16% of the total.

The main industrial development followed the discovery of large reserves of bauxite, but half the population was still rural in 1980.

CALIFORNIA

There were many small Indian tribes, but no central political power, when the area was discovered in 1542 by the Spanish navigator Juan Cabrillo. The Spaniards did not begin to establish missions until the 18th century, when the Franciscan friar Junipero Serra settled at San Diego in 1769. The missions became farming and ranching villages with large Indian populations. When the Spanish empire collapsed in 1821, the area was governed from newly-independent Mexico.

The first wagon-train of American settlers arrived from Missouri in 1841. In 1846, during the war between Mexico and the US, Americans in California proclaimed it to be part of the US. The territory was ceded by Mexico on 2 Feb. 1848 and became the 31st state of the Union on 9 Sept. 1850.

Gold was discovered in 1848–49 and there was an immediate influx of population. The state remained isolated, however, until the development of railways in the 1860s. From then on the population doubled on average every 20 years. The sunny climate attracted fruit-growers, market-gardeners and wine producers. In the early 20th century the bright light and cheap labour attracted film-makers to Hollywood, Los Angeles.

Southern California remained mainly agricultural with an Indian or Spanish-speaking labour force until after the Second World War. By 1980, 91·3% of the population was urban, and the main manufacture was electronic equipment, much of it for the defence and aerospace industries.

The state's position on the Pacific coast was of strategic importance during the Second World War and has also attracted many immigrants from China, Japan and elsewhere in south-east Asia.

Further Reading

Bean, W., and Rawl, J. J., *California: An Interpretive History*. New York, 1982

COLORADO

Spanish explorers claimed the area for Spain in 1706; it was then the territory of the Arapaho, Cheyenne, Ute and other Plains and Great Basin Indians. Eastern Colorado, the hot, dry plains, passed to France in 1802 and then to the US as part of the Louisiana Purchase in 1803. The rest remained Spanish, becoming Mexican when Spanish power in the Americas ended. In 1848, after war between Mexico and the US , Mexican Colorado was ceded to the US. A gold rush in 1859 brought a great influx of population, and in 1861

Colorado was organized as a Territory. The Territory officially supported the Union in the Civil War of 1861–65, but its settlers were divided and served on both sides.

Colorado became a state in 1876. Mining and ranching were the mainstays of the economy. In the 1920s the first large projects were undertaken to exploit the Colorado River. The Colorado River Compact was agreed in 1922, and the Boulder Dam (now Hoover Dam) was authorized in 1928. Since then irrigated agriculture has overtaken mining as an industry and is as important as ranching. In 1945 the Colorado-Big Thompson project diverted water by tunnel beneath the Rocky Mountains to irrigate 700,000 acres (284,000 hectares) of northern Colorado. By 1980, however, 80% of the population was urban, and most engaged in trade and service industries, especially tourism.

Settlement developed mainly in the towns of central Colorado (the Piedmont) which held about 70% of the population by 1985.

Further Reading

Sprague, M., *Colorado: A History*. New York, 1976

CONNECTICUT

Formerly territory of Algonquian-speaking Indians, Connecticut was first colonized by Europeans during the 1630s, when English Puritans moved there from Massachusetts Bay. Settlements were founded in the Connecticut River Valley at Hartford, Saybrook, Wethersfield and Windsor in 1635. They formed an organized commonwealth in 1637. A further settlement was made at New Haven in 1638 and was united to the commonwealth under a royal charter in 1662. The charter confirmed the commonwealth constitution, drawn up by mutual agreement in 1639 and called the Fundamental Orders of Connecticut.

The area was agricultural and its population of largely English descent until the early 19th century. After the War of Independence Connecticut was one of the original 13 states of the Union. Its state constitution came into force in 1818 and survived with amendment until 1965 when a new one was adopted.

In the early 1800s a textile industry was established using local water power. By 1850 the state had more employment in industry than in agriculture, and immigration from the continent of Europe – and especially from southern and eastern Europe – grew rapidly throughout the 19th century. Some immigrants worked in whaling and iron-mining, both now extinct, but most sought industrial employment. Settlement has been spread over a large number of relatively small cities, with no single dominant centre.

Yale University was founded at New Haven in 1701. The US Coastguard Academy was founded in 1876 at New London, a former whaling port.

Further Reading
Van Dusen, A. E., *Connecticut*. New York, 1981

DELAWARE

Delaware was the territory of Algonquian-speaking Indians who were displaced by European settlement in the 17th century. The first settlers were Swedes who came in 1638 to build Fort Christina (now Wilmington), and colonize what they called New Sweden. Their colony was taken by the Dutch from New Amsterdam in 1655. In 1664 the British took the whole New Amsterdam colony, including Delaware, and called it New York.

In 1682 Delaware was granted to William Penn, who wanted access to the coast for his Pennsylvania colony. Union of the two colonies was unpopular, and Delaware gained its own government in 1704, although it continued to share a royal governor with Pennsylvania until the War of Independence. Delaware then became one of the 13 original states of the Union and the first to ratify the federal constitution (on 7 Dec. 1787).

The population was of Swedish, Finnish, British and Irish extraction. The land was low-lying and fertile, and the use of slave labour was legal. There was a significant number of black slaves, but Delaware was a border state during the Civil War (1861–65) and did not leave the Union.

The main 19th century immigrants were European Jews, Poles, Germans and Italians. The north became industrial and densely populated, becoming more so after the Second World War with the rise of a petrochemical industry. Industry in general profited from the opening of the Chesapeake and Delaware Canal in 1829; it was converted to a toll-free deep channel for ocean-going ships in 1919.

Further Reading
Hoffecker, C. E., *Delaware: A Bicentennial History*. New York, 1977

DISTRICT OF COLUMBIA

The District was organized in 1790 as the proposed seat of government for the USA and for that purpose land was ceded by the states of Maryland and Virginia. The District was established by Acts of Congress approved on 16 July 1790 and 3 March 1791. The new capital was laid out after designs by Pierre-Charles L'Enfant, and construction began in 1793. The Federal Government moved there from Philadelphia in 1800 and the District was confirmed as under federal authority in 1801. The city of Washington grew to be co-extensive with it.

In 1814 Washington was abandoned briefly following an invasion by British forces under Admiral Sir George Cockburn during which the White House, the Capitol and the Navy Arsenal were burnt.

In 1846 the small area ceded by Virginia was returned to that state.

The rebuilding of the Capitol Dome was ordered by President Lincoln as a symbol of united national endeavour during the Civil War of 1861–65.

From 1878 until 1967 the District was governed as a corporation by a board of commissioners appointed by the president. From 1967 until 1973 there was a Mayor Council government still with appointed officers. In 1973 the latter was replaced by elected officers and full legislative power in local matters was granted in 1974. Congress retained a right of supervision and veto of the Council's acts, and the right to legislate for the District itself. Citizens received the right to vote in national elections in 1961.

The black population was less than half the size of the white in 1930, but larger by a third in 1960 and more than double the white population in 1980.

FLORIDA

There were French and Spanish settlements in Florida in the 16th century, of which the Spanish, at St Augustine in 1565, proved permanent. Florida was claimed by Spain until 1763 when it passed to Britain. Although regained by Spain in 1783, the British used it as a base for attacks on American forces during the war of 1812. Gen. Andrew Jackson in 1818 captured Pensacola for the US. In 1819 a treaty was signed which ceded Florida to the US with effect from 1821 and it became a Territory of the US in 1822.

Florida had been the home of Apalachee and Timucua Indians. After 1770 groups of Creek Indians began to arrive as refugees from the European-Indian wars. These 'Seminoles' or runaways attracted other refugees including slaves, the recapture of whom was the motive for the first Seminole War of 1817–18. A second war followed in 1835–42, when the Seminoles retreated to the Everglades swamps. After a third war in 1855–58 most Seminoles were forced or persuaded to move to reserves in Oklahoma.

Florida became a state in 1845. About half of the population were black slaves. At the outbreak of Civil War in 1861 the state seceded from the Union.

During the 20th century Florida continued to grow fruit and vegetables, but real-estate development (often for retirement) and the growth of tourism and the aerospace industry have prevented it from remaining a typical ex-plantation state. There has been some recent immigration from Caribbean states, notably Cuba and Haiti.

Further Reading

Tebeau, C. W., *A History of Florida*. Rev. ed. Univ. of Miami Press, 1980

GEORGIA

Originally the territory of Creek and Cherokee tribes, Georgia was first settled by Europeans in the 18th century. James Oglethorpe founded Savannah in 1733, intending it as a colony which offered a new start to debtors, convicts and the poor. Settlement was slow until 1783, when growth began in the cotton-growing areas west of Augusta. The Indian population was cleared off the rich cotton land and moved beyond the Mississippi. Georgia became one of the original 13 states of the Union.

A plantation economy developed rapidly, using slave labour. In 1861 Georgia seceded from the Union and became an important source of supplies for the Confederate cause, although some northern areas never accepted secession and continued in sympathy with the Union during the Civil War. At the beginning of the war 56% of the population were white, descendants of British, Austrian and New England immigrants; the remaining 44% were black slaves. By 1980 the state was still about 40% black.

The city of Atlanta, which grew as a railway junction, was destroyed during the war but revived to become the centre of southern states during the reconstruction period. The daily newspaper *Atlanta Constitution* was important in this context. Also in Atlanta were developed successive movements for black freedom in social, economic and political life. Atlanta was confirmed as state capital in 1877.

Racial confrontation continued through the 20th century. The Southern Christian Leadership Conference, led by Martin Luther King (assassinated 1968), was based in King's native city of Atlanta.

Further Reading

Georgia History in Outline. Univ. of Georgia Press, 1978

HAWAII

The islands of Hawaii were settled by Polynesian immigrants, probably from the Marquesas Islands, about AD 400. A second major immigration, from Tahiti, occurred around 800–900. In the late 18th century all the islands of the group were united into one kingdom by Kamehameha I. Western exploration began in 1778, and Christian missions were established after 1820. Europeans called Hawaii the Sandwich Islands. The main foreign states interested were the US, Britain and France. Because of the threat imposed by their rivalry, Kamehameha III placed Hawaii under US protection in 1851. US sugar-growing companies became dominant in the economy and in 1887 the US obtained a naval base at Pearl Harbor. A struggle developed between forces for and against annexation by the US. In 1893 the monarchy was overthrown. The republican government agreed to be annexed to the US in 1898, and Hawaii became a US Territory in 1900.

The islands and the naval base were of great strategic importance during the Second World War, when the Japanese attack on Pearl Harbor brought the US into the war.

Hawaii became the 50th state of the Union in 1959. The 19th century plantation economy led to much immigration of workers, especially from China and Japan. At the same time the Hawaiians fell victim to foreign diseases and their laws, religion and culture were gradually adapted to foreign models. By 1980 the population was about 12% Hawaiian.

Sugar-cane is still important, as is pineapple-growing and the tourist industry.

Further Reading

Kuykendall, R. S., and Day, A. G., *Hawaii, a History*. Rev. ed. New Jersey, 1961

IDAHO

The original people of Idaho were Kutenai, Kalispel, Nez Percé and other tribes, living on the Pacific watershed of the northern Rocky Mountains. European exploration began in 1805, and after 1809 there were trading posts and small settlements. The area was disputed between Britain and the US until 1846 when British claims were dropped. In 1860 gold and silver were found, and there was a rush of immigrant prospectors. The newly enlarged population needed organized government. An area including that which is now Montana was created a Territory in March 1863. Montana was separated from it in 1864. Population growth continued, stimulated by refugees from the Confederate states after the Civil War and by settlements of Mormons from Utah.

Fur-trapping and mining gave way to farming, especially of potatoes, wheat and sugar-beet, as the main economic activity. Idaho became a state in 1890, with its capital at Boise. The Territorial capital, Idaho City, had been a gold-mining boom town whose population (about 40,000 at its height) declined to 1,000 by 1869.

During the 20th century the Indian population has shrunk to 1% (by 1980). The Mormon community has grown to include much of south-eastern Idaho and more than half the church-going population of the state.

Industrial history has been influenced by the development of the Snake River of southern Idaho for hydro-electricity and irrigation, especially at the American Falls and reservoir. Processing food, minerals and timber have become important to the economy. The population, however, remains sparse and mainly rural.

ILLINOIS

Territory of a group of Algonquian-speaking tribes, Illinois was explored first by the French in 1673. France claimed the area until 1763 when, after the French and Indian War, it was ceded to Britain along with all the French land east of the Mississippi. In 1783 Britain recognized the US' title to Illinois, which became part of the North West Territory of the US in 1787, and of Indiana Territory in 1800. Illinois became a Territory in its own right in 1809, and a state in 1818.

Settlers from the eastern states moved on to the fertile farmland, immigration increasing greatly with the opening in 1825 of the Erie Canal from New York along which settlers could move west and their produce back east for sale. Chicago was incorporated as a city in 1837 and quickly became the transport, trading and distribution centre of the middle west. Once industrial growth had begun there, a further wave of immigration took place in the 1840s, mainly of European refugees looking for work. This movement continued with varying force until the 1920s, when it was largely replaced by immigration of black work-seekers from the southern states.

During the 20th century the population has been largely urban (83% in 1980) and heavy industry has been established along an intensive network of rail and waterway routes. Chicago recovered from a destructive fire in 1871 to become the hub of this network and the second largest American city.

Many of the European immigrant communities in Illinois have retained their national characteristics.

Further Reading

Howard, R. P., *Illinois: A History of the Prairie State*. Grand Rapids, 1972

INDIANA

The area was inhabited by Algonquian-speaking tribes when the first European explorers (French) laid claim to it in the 17th century. They established some fortified trading posts but there was little settlement. In 1763 the area passed to Britain, with other French-claimed territory east of the Mississippi. In 1783 Indiana became part of the North West Territory of the US; it became a separate territory in 1800 and a state in 1816. Until 1811 there had been continuing conflict with the Indian inhabitants, who were then defeated at Tippecanoe.

Early farming settlement was by families of British and German descent, including Amish and Mennonite communities. Later industrial development offered an incentive for more immigration from Europe, and, later, from the southern states. In 1906 the town of Gary was laid out by the United States Steel Corporation and named for its chairman, Elbert H. Gary. The industry flourished on navigable water midway between supplies of iron ore and of coal. Trade and distribution in general benefitted from Indiana Port on Lake Michigan, especially after the opening of the St Lawrence Seaway in 1959. The Ohio River has also been exploited for carrying freight.

Indianapolis was laid out after 1821 and became the state capital in 1825. Natural gas was discovered in the neighbourhood in the late 19th century, and this stimulated the growth of a motor industry, celebrated with the Indianapolis 500 race, held annually since 1911.

In 1980 manufacturing industries were still the base of the economy and the steel industry the most important of them.

IOWA

Originally the territory of the Iowa Indians, the area was explored by the Frenchmen Marquette and Joliet in 1673. French trading posts were set up, but there was little other settlement. In 1803 the French sold their claim to Iowa to the US as part of the Louisiana Purchase. The land was still occupied by Indians but, in the 1830s, the tribes sold their land to the US government and migrated to reservations. Iowa became a US Territory in 1838 and a state in 1846.

The state was settled by immigrants drawn mainly from neighbouring states to the east. Later there was more immigration from Protestant states of northern Europe. The land was extremely fertile and most immigrants came to farm. Not all the Indian population had accepted the cession and there were some violent confrontations, notably the murder of settlers at Spirit Lake in 1857.

The population is still mainly rural and farming predominates, especially livestock farming with its associated stockfeed crops. Most industry is based on agriculture, either as food-processing or agricultural engineering.

The capital, Des Moines, was founded in 1843 as a fort to protect Indian rights. It expanded rapidly with the growth of a local coal field after 1910.

KANSAS

The area was explored from Mexico in the 16th century, when Spanish travellers found groups of Kansa, Wichita, Osage and Pawnee tribes. The French claimed Kansas in 1682 and they established a valuable fur trade with local tribes in the 18th century. In 1803 the area passed to the US as part of the Louisiana Purchase and became a base for pioneering trails further west. After 1830 it was 'Indian Territory' and a number of tribes displaced from eastern states were settled there. In 1854 the Kansas Territory was created and opened for white settlement. The early settlers were farmers from Europe or New England, but the Territory's position brought it into contact with southern ideas also. Until 1861 there were frequent outbursts of violence over the issue of slavery. Slavery had been excluded from the future Territory by the Missouri Compromise of 1820, but the 1854 Kansas-Nebraska Act had affirmed the principle of 'popular sovereignty' to settle the issue, which was then fought out by opposing factions throughout 'Bleeding Kansas'.

Kansas finally entered the Union (as a non-slavery state) in 1861; the part of Colorado which had formed part of the Kansas Territory was then separated from it.

The economy developed through a combination of cattle-ranching and railways. Herds were driven to the railheads and shipped from vast stockyards, or slaughtered and processed in rail-head meat-packing plants. Wheat and sorghum also became important once the plains could be ploughed on a large scale.

Further Reading

Zornow, W. F., *Kansas: A History of the Jayhawk State*. Norman, Oklahoma, 1957

KENTUCKY

Lying west of the Appalachians and south of the Ohio River, the area was the meeting place and battle-ground for the eastern Iroquois and the southern Cherokees. Northern Shawnees also penetrated. The first successful white settlement took place in 1769 when Daniel Boone reached the Bluegrass plains from the eastern, trans-Appalachian, colonies. After 1783 immigration from the east was rapid, settlers travelling by river or crossing the mountains by the Cumberland Gap. The area was originally attached to Virginia but became a separate state in 1792.

Large plantations dependent on slave labour were established, as were small farms worked by white owners. The state became divided on the issue of slavery, although plantation interests (mainly producing tobacco) dominated state government. In the event the state did not secede in 1861, and the majority of citizens supported the Union. Public opinion swung round in support of the south during the difficulties of the reconstruction period.

The eastern mountains became an important coal-mining area, tobacco-growing continued and the Bluegrass plains produced livestock, including especially fine thoroughbred horses.

The Negro population was 236,000 out of a total of 1,321,011 in 1860. In 1980 it was 259,477 out of 3,660,777. The relative decline reflects a general drift to the northern industrial cities from the rural south, Kentucky being still a predominantly rural state.

Further Reading

Lee, L. G., *A Brief History of Kentucky and Its Counties*. Berea, 1981

LOUISIANA

Originally the Territory of Choctaw and Caddo tribes, the whole area was claimed for France in 1682. The French founded New Orleans in 1718 and it became the centre of a crown colony in 1731. During the wars which the European powers fought over their American interests, the French ceded the area west of the Mississippi (most of the present state) to Spain in 1762 and the eastern area, north of New Orleans, to Britain in 1763. The British section passed to the US in 1783, but France bought back the rest from Spain in 1800, including New Orleans and the mouth of the Mississippi. The US, fearing to be excluded from a strategically important and commercially promising shipping area, persuaded France to sell Louisiana again in 1803. The present states of Missouri, Arkansas,

Iowa, North Dakota, South Dakota, Nebraska and Oklahoma were included in the purchase.

The area became the Territory of New Orleans in 1804 and was admitted to the Union as a state in 1812. The economy at first depended on cotton and sugar-cane plantations. The population was of French, Spanish and black descent, with a growing number of American settlers. Plantation interests succeeded in achieving secession in 1861, but New Orleans was occupied by the Union in 1862. Planters re-emerged in the late 19th century and imposed rigid segregation of the black population, denying them their new rights.

The state has become mainly urban industrial, with the Mississippi ports growing rapidly. There is petroleum and natural gas, and a strong tourist industry based on the French culture and Caribbean atmosphere of New Orleans.

Further Reading

The History and Government of Louisiana. Baton Rouge, 1975

MAINE

Originally occupied by Algonquian-speaking tribes, the Territory was disputed between different groups of British settlers, and between the British and French, throughout the 17th and most of the 18th centuries. After 1652 it was governed as part of Massachusetts, and French claims finally failed in 1763. Most of the early settlers were English and Protestant Irish, with many Quebec French.

The Massachusetts settlers had gained control when the original colonist, Sir Ferdinando Gorges, supported the losing royalist side in the English civil war. Their control was questioned during the English-American war of 1812, when Maine residents claimed that the Massachusetts government did not protect them against British raids. Maine was separated from Massachusetts and entered the Union as a state in 1820.

Maine is a mountainous state and even the coastline is rugged, but the coastal belt is where most settlement has developed. In the 19th century there were manufacturing towns making use of cheap water-power, and the rocky shore supported a shell-fish industry. The latter still flourishes, together with intensive horticulture, producing potatoes and fruit. The other main economic development has been in exploiting the forests for timber, pulp and paper.

The capital is Augusta, a river trading post which was fortified against Indian attacks in 1754, incorporated as a town in 1797 and chosen as capital in 1832.

MARYLAND

The first European visitors found groups of Algonquian-speaking tribes, often under attack by Iroquois from further north. The first white settlement was made by the Calvert family, British Roman Catholics, in 1634. The settlers received some legislative rights in 1638. In 1649 their assembly passed the Act of Toleration, granting freedom of worship to all Christians. A peace treaty was signed with the Iroquois in 1652, after which it was possible for farming settlement to expand north and west. The capital (formerly at St Mary's City) was moved to Annapolis in 1694. Baltimore, which became the state's main city, was founded in 1729.

The first industry was tobacco-growing, which was based on slave-worked plantations. There were also many immigrant British small farmers, tradesmen and indentured servants.

At the close of the War of Independence the Treaty of Paris was ratified in Annapolis. Maryland became a state of the Union in 1788. In 1791 the state ceded land for the new federal capital, Washington, and its economy has depended on the capital's proximity ever since. Baltimore also grew as a port and industrial city, attracting much European immigration in the 19th century. Although strong sympathy for the south was expressed, Maryland remained within the Union in the Civil War albeit under the imposition of martial law.

By 1980 the population was about 80% urban and 23% black. Most people lived in the Baltimore and Washington metropolitan areas.

MASSACHUSETTS

The first European settlement was at Plymouth, when the *Mayflower* landed its company of English religious separatists in 1620. In 1626–30 more colonists arrived, the main body being a large company of English Puritans who founded a Puritan commonwealth. This commonwealth, of about 1,000 colonists led by John Winthrop, became the Massachusetts Bay Colony and was founded under a company charter. Following disagreement between the English government and the colony the charter was withdrawn in 1684, but in 1691 a new charter united a number of settlements under the name of Massachusetts Bay. The colony's government was rigidly theocratic.

Shipbuilding, iron-working and manufacturing were more important than farming from the beginning, the land being poor. The colony was Protestant and of English descent until the War of

Independence. The former colony adopted its present constitution in 1780 and became the 6th state of the Union in 1788, having been the scene of many early developments in the war. The state acquired its present boundaries (having previously included Maine) in 1820.

During the 19th century, industrialization and immigration from Europe both increased and Catholic Irish and Italian immigrants began to change the population's character. The main inland industry was textile manufacture, the main coastal occupation was whaling; both have now gone. Boston has remained the most important city of New England, attracting a large black population since 1950.

Further Reading

Hart, A. B. (ed.), *Commonwealth History of Massachusetts, Colony, Province and State*. 5 vols. New York, 1966

MICHIGAN

The French were the first European settlers, establishing a fur trade with the local Algonquian Indians in the late 17th century. They founded Sault Ste Marie in 1668 and Detroit in 1701. In 1763 Michigan passed to Britain, along with other French territory east of the Mississippi, and from Britain it passed to the US in 1783. Britain, however, kept a force at Detroit until 1796, and recaptured Detroit in 1812. Regular American settlement did not begin until later. The Territory of Michigan (1805) had its boundaries extended after 1818 and was admitted to the Union as a state (with its present boundaries) in 1837.

During the 19th century there was rapid industrial growth, especially in mining and metalworking. Many groups of immigrants from Poland, Italy, Holland and Scandinavia came to settle as miners, farmers and industrial workers. The motor industry became dominant, especially in Detroit. Lake Michigan ports shipped bulk cargo, especially iron-ore and grain.

Detroit was the capital until 1847, when that function passed to Lansing. Detroit remained, however, an important centre of flour-milling and shipping, and during the First World War its industrial growth accelerated, especially in making assembly-line vehicles. At the same time it began to attract a large black population, which it still has (63% in 1980).

Since 1970 the economy has diversified wherever possible, the motor industry having proved very vulnerable to increases in the price of oil and in concern over atmospheric pollution.

Further Reading

Dunbar, W. F., and May, G. S., *Michigan: A History of the Wolverine State.* Grand Rapids, 1980

MINNESOTA

Minnesota remained an Indian territory until the middle of the 19th century, the main groups being Chippewa and Sioux, many of whom are still there. In the 17th century there had been some French exploration, but no permanent settlement. After passing under the nominal control of France, Britain and Spain, the area became part of the Louisiana Purchase and so was sold to the US in 1803.

Fort Snelling was founded in 1819. Early settlers came from other states, especially New England, to exploit the great forests. Lumbering gave way to homesteading, and the American settlers were joined by Germans, Scandinavians and Poles. Agriculture, mining and forest industries became the mainstays of the economy. Minneapolis, founded as a village in 1856, grew first as a lumber centre, processing the logs floated down the Minnesota River, and then as a centre of flour-milling and grain marketing. St Paul, its twin city across the river, became Territorial capital in 1849 and state capital in 1858. St Paul also stands at the head of navigation on the Mississippi, which rises in Minnesota.

The Territory (1849) included parts of North and South Dakota, but at its admission to the Union in 1858, the state of Minnesota had its present boundaries. The state contributed a force to the Union armies during the Civil War and was also concerned, for some time, with repelling Indian attacks from the Dakota Territory.

Further Reading

Lass, W. B., *Minnesota: A Bicentennial History.* New York, 1977

MISSISSIPPI

Mississippi was one of the territories claimed by France since the 17th century and ceded to Britain in 1763. The indigenous people were Choctaw and Natchez. French settlers at first traded amicably with them, but in the course of three wars (1716, 1723 and 1729) the French allied with the Choctaw to drive the Natchez out. During hostilities the Natchez massacred the settlers of Fort Rosalie, which the French had founded in 1716 and which was later renamed Natchez.

In 1783 the area passed to the US except for Natchez which was under Spanish control until 1798. The US then made it the capital of the Territory of Mississippi. The boundaries of the Territory were extended in 1804 and 1812. In 1817 it was separated in two, the western part becoming the state of Mississippi. (The eastern part became the state of Alabama in 1819). The city of Jackson was laid out in 1822 as the new state capital.

A cotton plantation economy developed, based on black slave labour, and by 1860 the majority of the population was black. Mississippi joined the Confederacy during the Civil War. After defeat and reconstruction there was a return to rigid segregation and denial of black rights. This situation lasted until the 1960s. There was a black majority until the Second World War, when out-migration began to change the pattern. By 1980 about 35% of the population was black, and manufacture (especially clothing and textiles) had become the largest single employer of labour.

Further Reading
Bettersworth, J. K., *Mississippi: A History*. Rev. ed. Austin, 1964

MISSOURI

Territory of several Indian groups, including the Missouri, the area was not settled by European immigrants until the 18th century. The French founded Ste Genevieve in 1735, partly as a lead-mining community. St Louis was founded as a fur-trading base in 1764. The area was nominally under Spanish rule from 1770 until 1800 when it passed back to France. In 1803 the US bought it as part of the Louisiana Purchase.

St Louis was made the capital of the whole Louisiana Territory in 1805, and of a new Missouri Territory in 1812. In that year American immigration increased markedly. The Territory became a state in 1821, but there had been bitter disputes between slave-owning and anti-slavery factions, with the former succeeding in obtaining statehood without the prohibition of slavery required of all other new states north of latitude 36° 30′; this was achieved by the Missouri Compromise of 1820. The Compromise was repealed in 1854 and declared unconstitutional in 1857. During the Civil War the state held to the Union side, although St Louis was placed under martial law.

With the development of steamboat traffic on the Missouri and Mississippi rivers, and the expansion of railways, the state became the transport hub of all western movement. Lead and other mining remained important, as did livestock farming. European settlers came from Germany, Britain and Ireland. Since 1940 the industries and commerce of St Louis and Kansas City have attracted many from the southern states.

Further Reading
Foley, W. E., et al., History of Missouri. 4 vols. Univ. of Missouri Press, 1971–86

MONTANA

Originally the territory of many groups of Indian hunters including the Sioux, Cheyenne and Chippewa, Montana was not settled by American colonists until the 19th century. The area passed to the US with the Louisiana Purchase of 1803, but the area west of the Rockies was disputed with Britain until 1846. Trappers and fur-traders were the first immigrants, and the fortified trading post at Fort Benton (1846) became the first permanent settlement. Colonization increased when gold was found in 1862. Montana was created a separate Territory (out of Idaho and Dakota Territories) in 1864. In 1866 large-scale grazing of sheep and cattle was allowed, and this provoked violent confrontation with the indigenous people whose hunting lands were invaded. Indian wars led to the defeat of federal forces at Little Bighorn in 1876 and at Big Hole Basin in 1877, but the Indians could not continue the fight and they had been moved to reservations by 1880. Montana became a state in 1889.

Helena, the capital, was founded as a mining town in the 1860s. In the early 20th century there were many European immigrants who settled as farmers or in the mines, especially in copper-mining at Butte. Mining has remained important as has farming, especially of stock, cereals and sugar-beet. Billings, the largest city, began as a railway junction in 1882 but survives as the service centre of an irrigated cropland.

Further Reading
Malone, M. P., and Roeder, R. B., Montana, a History of Two Centuries. Univ. of Washington Press, 1976

NEBRASKA

The area was occupied by various Indian groups, farming in the east and hunting on the western plains. By 1803, when the US bought the land from France as part of the Louisiana Purchase, there had been some exploration by Europeans but little settlement. During the 1840s the Platte River valley became an established trail for thousands of pioneers' wagons heading for Oregon and California.

The need to serve and protect the trail led to the creation of Nebraska as a Territory in 1854. In 1862 the Homestead Act opened the area for settlement, but colonization was not very rapid until the Union Pacific Railroad was completed in 1869. The largest city, Omaha, developed as the starting point of the Union Pacific and became one of the largest railway towns in the country.

Nebraska became a state in 1867, with approximately its present boundaries except that it later received small areas from the Dakotas. Many early settlers were from Europe, brought in by railway-company schemes, and settling as farmers. From the late 1880s eastern Nebraska suffered catastrophic drought but crop and stock farming recovered. The climate remains dry, and crop growing was only established in the west by means of irrigation.

Most of the state's surface area is now classified as agricultural, but by 1980 43% of the population lived in the metropolitan areas of Omaha and the capital, Lincoln.

Further Reading

Olson, J. C., *History of Nebraska*. Univ. of Nebraska Press, 1955

NEVADA

Nevada was inhabited by Shoshoni, Mohave and other Indian groups and was visited in the 18th century by Spanish missionaries from Mexico. The area was part of Spanish America until 1821, when it became part of the newly-independent state of Mexico. Following a war between Mexico and the US, Nevada was ceded to the US as part of California in 1848. Settlement began in 1849, and the area was separated from California and joined with Utah Territory in 1850. In 1859 a rich deposit of silver was found in the Comstock Lode. Virginia City was founded as a mining town and immigration increased rapidly. Nevada Territory was formed in 1861. During the Civil War the Federal Government, allegedly in order to obtain the wealth of silver for the Union cause, agreed to admit Nevada to the Union as the 36th state. Areas of Arizona and Utah Territories were added to it in 1866–67.

The silver boom lasted until 1882, by which time cattle ranching had become equally important in the valleys where the climate is less arid. Carson City, the capital, developed in association with the nearby silver-mining industry. The largest cities, Las Vegas and Reno, grew most in the 20th century with the building of the Hoover Dam, the introduction of legal gambling and of easily obtained divorce.

After 1950 much of the desert area was adopted by the Federal

Government for weapons testing and other military purposes. By 1980 about 80% of the land area was federally owned, 85% of the population was urban and 82% lived in the metropolitan areas of Las Vegas and Reno.

Further Reading

Laxalt, R., *Nevada: A History*. New York, 1977

NEW HAMPSHIRE

The area was part of a grant by the English crown made to John Mason and fellow-colonists, and was first settled in 1623. In 1629 an area between the Merrimack and Piscatagua rivers was called New Hampshire. More settlements followed, and in 1641 they were taken under the jurisdiction of the governor of Massachusetts. New Hampshire became a separate colony in 1679.

After the War of Independence New Hampshire became one of the 13 original states of the Union, drawing up its constitution in 1784 and revising it on accession to the Union in 1792.

Early settlement was of Protestants from Britain and Northern Ireland. They developed manufacturing industries, especially shoemaking, textiles and clothing, to which large numbers of French Canadians were attracted after the Civil War.

Portsmouth, originally a fishing settlement and now a naval base, was the colonial capital and is the only seaport. In 1808 the state capital was moved to Concord (having had no permanent home since 1775), Concord produced the Concord Coach which was widely used on the stagecoach routes of the West until at least 1900.

The economy is now based on diverse manufacturing and on tourism.

Further Reading

Squires, J. D., *The Granite State of the United States: A History of New Hampshire from 1623 to the Present*. 4 vols. New York, 1956

NEW JERSEY

Originally the territory of the Delaware Indians, the area was first settled by immigrant colonists in the early 17th century, when Dutch and Swedish traders established fortified posts on the Hudson and Delaware rivers. The Dutch took control but lost it to the English in 1664. In 1676 the English divided the area in two; the eastern portion was assigned to Sir George Carteret and the western granted to Quaker settlers. This division lasted until 1702 when New

Jersey was united as a colony of the Crown and placed under the jurisdiction of the governor of New York. It became a separate colony in 1738.

During the War of Independence crucial battles were fought at Trenton, Princeton and Monmouth. New Jersey became the third state of the Union in 1787. Trenton, the state capital since 1790, began as a Quaker settlement and became an iron-working town. Industrial development grew rapidly, there and elsewhere in the state, after the opening of canals and railways in the 1830s. Princeton, also a Quaker settlement, became an important post on the New York road; the College of New Jersey (Princeton University) was transferred there from Newark in 1756.

The need for supplies in the Civil War stimulated industry and New Jersey became a manufacturing state, which it still is. The growth beyond its borders of New York and Philadelphia, however, produced a pattern of commuting to employment in both centres. By 1980, about 60% of the state's population lived within 30 miles of New York. The 4 largest New Jersey cities were the industrial centres of Newark, Jersey City, Paterson and Elizabeth, all of which lie across the Hudson river from New York. The largest ethnic group is of Italian descent.

Further Reading

Kull, I. S. (ed.), *New Jersey, a history*. 4 vols. New York, 1930

NEW MEXICO

The land supported various groups of agriculturists, who were invaded by nomadic, hunting Apaches and Navajos from the north. The 16th-century Spanish treasure-seekers who penetrated the area from Mexico established a Spanish claim to the land and were followed by missionaries. The first permanent settlement by Spanish colonists was a mission at Santa Fe in 1610. Spanish settlement increased during the 18th century.

In 1821 Mexico became independent of Spain and New Mexico became part of the new state. Ceded to the US in 1848 after war between the US and Mexico, the area was organized as a Territory in 1850, by which time its population was Spanish and Indian. There was frequent conflict, especially between new settlers and raiding parties of Navajo and Apaches. The Indian wars lasted from 1861 until 1886, and from 1864–68 about 8,000 Navajo were imprisoned at Bosque Redondo.

The boundaries were altered several times when land was taken into Texas, Utah, Colorado and lastly (1863) Arizona. New Mexico became a state in 1912.

Settlement proceeded by means of irrigated crop-growing and Mexican-style ranching. During the Second World War the desert areas were brought into use as testing zones for atomic weapons; this use continues and has produced associated industries. Mineral extraction also developed, especially after the discovery of uranium and petroleum.

By 1980 the population was about 37% Spanish-speaking, and about half of these were from Mexico. The Indian population was about 8%, mainly on reservations.

Further Reading

Beck, W., *New Mexico: A History of Four Centuries*. Univ. of Oklahoma, 1979

NEW YORK STATE

The first European immigrants came in the 17th century, when there were two powerful Indian groups in rivalry: the Iroquois confederacy (Mohawk, Oneida, Onondaga, Cayuga and Seneca) and the Algonquian-speaking Mohegan and Munsee. The Dutch made settlements at Fort Orange (now Albany) in 1624 and at New Amsterdam in 1625, trading with the Indians for furs. In the 1660s there was conflict between the Dutch and the British in the Caribbean; as part of the concluding treaty the British in 1664 received Dutch possessions in the Americas, including New Amsterdam, which they renamed New York.

In 1763 the Treaty of Paris ended war between the British and the French in North America (in which the Iroquois had allied themselves with the British). Settlers of British descent in New England then felt confident enough to expand westward into the area. The climate of northern New York being severe, most settled in the Hudson river valley. After the War of Independence New York became the 11th state of the Union (1788), having first declared itself independent of Britain in 1777.

The economy depended on manufacturing, shipping and other means of distributing goods, and trade. During the 19th century New York City became the most important city in the US. Its manufacturing industries, especially clothing, attracted thousands of European immigrants. Industrial development spread along the Hudson-Mohawk valley, which was made the route of the Erie Canal (1825) linking New York with Buffalo on Lake Erie and thus with the developing farmlands of the middle west.

New York City has retained its importance in the 20th century, especially as the national centre of finance and of news and entertainment media. In 1980 the state's population was beginning to decline after waves of immigration, but density was still 354 per sq. mile (137 per sq. km).

Further Reading

Ellis, D. M., *History of New York State*. Cornell Univ. Press, 1967

NORTH CAROLINA

The early people were Cherokees. European settlement was attempted in 1585–87, following an exploratory visit by Sir Walter Raleigh, but this failed. Settlers from Virginia came to the shores of Albemarle Sound after 1650, and in 1663 Charles II chartered a private colony of Carolina. In 1691 the north was put under a deputy governor who ruled from Charleston in the south. The colony was formally separated into North and South Carolina in 1712. In 1729 control was taken from the private proprietors and vested in the Crown, whereupon settlement grew, and the boundary between north and south was finally fixed (1735).

After the War of Independence North Carolina became one of the original 13 states of the Union. The city of Raleigh was laid out as the new capital. Having been a plantation colony North Carolina continued to develop as a plantation state, growing tobacco with black slave labour. It was also an important source of gold before the western gold-rushes of 1848.

In 1861 at the outset of the Civil War North Carolina seceded from the Union, but General Sherman occupied the capital unopposed. A military governor was appointed in 1862, and civilian government restored with readmission to the Union in 1868.

Manufacturing, forest industries and mineral extraction all became important. Opportunities for emancipated slaves were inadequate, and there was a steady movement of the black population away from the state.

By 1980 the population growth-rate was high but the proportion of black residents had dropped to 22% (from about 30% in 1910).

Further Reading

Lefler, H. T., and Newsome, A. R., *North Carolina: The History of a Southern State*. Univ. of North Carolina, 1963

NORTH DAKOTA

The original people were various groups of Plains Indians. French explorers and traders were active among them in the 18th century, often operating from French possessions in Canada. France claimed the area until 1803, when it passed to the US as part of the Louisiana Purchase, except for the north-eastern part which was held by the British until 1818.

Trading with the Indians, mainly for furs, continued until the 1860s, with American traders succeeding the French. In 1861 the Dakota Territory (North and South) was established. In 1862 the Homestead Act was passed (allowing 160 acres of public land free to any family who had worked and lived on it for 5 years) and this greatly stimulated settlement. Farming settlers came on to the wheat lands in great numbers, many of them from Canada, Norway and Germany.

Bismarck, the capital, began as a crossing-point on the Missouri and was fortified in 1872 to protect workers building the Northern Pacific Railway. There followed a gold-rush nearby, and the town became a service centre for prospectors. In 1889 North and South Dakota were admitted to the Union as separate states, and Bismarck became the Northern capital. The largest city is Fargo which was also a railway town, named after William George Fargo the express-company founder.

The population grew rapidly until 1890 and steadily until 1930 by which time it was about one-third European in parentage. Between 1930 and 1970 there was a steady population drain, increasing whenever farming was affected by the extremes of the continental climate. The state is still mainly agricultural although oil was discovered in 1951 and manufacturing has since increased.

Further Reading
Robinson, E. B., *History of North Dakota*. Univ. of Nebraska Press, 1966

OHIO

The land was inhabited by Delaware, Miami, Shawnee and Wyandot Indians. It was explored by French and British traders in the 18th century and confirmed as part of British North America in 1763. After the War of Independence it became part of the Northwest Territory of the new United States. Former American soldiers of the war came in from New England in 1788 and made the first permanent white settlement at Marietta, at the confluence of the Ohio and Muskingum rivers. In 1803 Ohio was separated from the rest of the Territory and admitted to the Union as the 17th state.

During the early 19th century there was steady immigration from Europe, mainly of Germans, Swiss, Irish and Welsh. Industrial growth began from the processing of local farm, forest and mining products; it increased rapidly with the need to supply the Union armies in the Civil War of 1861–65.

As the industrial cities grew, so immigration began again, with many whites from eastern Europe and the Balkans and blacks from the southern states looking for work in Ohio.

The largest city is Cleveland, which developed rapidly as a Lake Erie port after the opening of commercial waterways to the interior and the Atlantic coast (1825, 1830 and 1855). It first became an iron-and-steel town during the Civil War. Columbus, planned in 1812 and capital since 1816, is the second largest city.

Population growth almost stopped between 1970 and 1980, by which time the black population was about 10% of the whole state and 44% of the city of Cleveland.

Further Reading

Rosebloom, E. H., and Weisenburger, F. P., *A History of Ohio*. Columbus, 1953

OKLAHOMA

Francisco Coronado led a Spanish expedition into the area in 1541, claiming the land for Spain. There were several Indian groups, but no strong political unit. In 1714 Juchereau de Saint Denis made the first French contact. During the 18th century French fur-traders were active, and France and Spain struggled for control, a struggle that was resolved by the French withdrawal in 1763. France returned briefly in 1800–03, and the territory then passed to the US as part of the Louisiana Purchase.

In 1828 the Federal Government set aside the area of the present state as Indian Territory, that is, a reservation and sanctuary for Indian tribes who had been driven off their lands elsewhere by white settlement. About 70 tribes came, among whom were Creeks, Choctaws and Cherokees from the south-eastern states, and Plains Indians.

In 1889 the government took back about 1m. hectares of the Territory and opened it to white settlement. About 10,000 homesteaders gathered at the site of Oklahoma City on the Santa Fe Railway in the rush to stake their land claims. The settlers' area, and others subsequently opened to settlement, were organized as the Oklahoma Territory in 1890. In 1907 the Oklahoma and Indian

Territories were combined and admitted to the Union as a state. Indian reservations were established within the state.

The economy first depended on ranching and farming, with packing stations on the railways. A mining industry grew in the 1870s attracting foreign immigration, mainly from Europe. In 1901 oil was found near Tulsa, and the industry grew rapidly.

By 1980 there was a varied population, 6% Indian and 7% black, with a high growth rate.

Further Reading

Gibson, A. M., *The History of Oklahoma*. Rev. ed. Univ. of Oklahoma, 1984

OREGON

The area was divided between many Indian groups including the Chinook, Tillamook, Cayuse and Modoc. In the 18th century English and Spanish visitors tried to establish national claims, based on explorations of the 16th century. The US also laid claim by right of discovery when an expedition entered the mouth of the Columbia River in 1792.

Oregon was disputed between Britain and the US. An American fur company established a trading settlement at Astoria in 1811, which the British took in 1812. The Hudson Bay Company were the most active force in Oregon until the 1830s when American pioneers began to migrate westwards along the Oregon Trail. The dispute between Britain and the US was resolved in 1846 with the boundary fixed at 49° N. lat. Oregon was organized as a Territory in 1848 but with wider boundaries; it became a state with its present boundaries in 1859.

Early settlers were mainly American. They came to farm in the Willamette Valley and to exploit the western forests. Portland developed as a port for ocean-going traffic, although it was 100 miles inland at the confluence of the Willamette and Columbia rivers. Industries followed when the railways came and the rivers were exploited for hydro-electricity. The capital of the Territory from 1851 was Salem, a mission for Indians on the Willamette river; it was confirmed as state capital in 1864. Salem became the processing centre for the farming and market-gardening Willamette Valley.

By 1980 most of the population was concentrated in the western valleys and particularly in the metropolitan areas of Portland, Salem, Eugene and Medford.

Further Reading

Dodds, G. B., *Oregon: A Bicentennial History*. New York, 1977

PENNSYLVANIA

Pennsylvania was occupied by 4 powerful groups in the 17th century: Delaware, Susquehanna, Shawnee and Iroquois. The first white settlers were Swedish, arriving in 1643. The British became dominant in 1664, and in 1681 William Penn, an English Quaker, was given a charter to colonize the area as a sanctuary for his fellow Quakers. Penn's ideal was peaceful co-operation with the Indians and religious toleration within the colony. Several religious groups were attracted to Pennsylvania because of this policy, including Protestant sects from Germany and France. During the 18th century, co-operation with the Indians failed as the settlers pushed into more territory and the Indians resisted.

During the War of Independence the Declaration of Independence was signed in Philadelphia, the main city. Pennsylvania became one of the original 13 states of the Union. In 1812 Harrisburg, which began as a trading post and ferry point on the Susquehanna river, was chosen as the state capital. The new state's southern boundary was the Mason and Dixon Line, which became the dividing line between free and slave states during the conflict leading to the Civil War. During the war crucial battles were fought in the state, including Gettysburg. Industrial growth was rapid after the war. Pittsburgh, founded as a British fort in 1761 during war with the French, had become an iron-making town by 1800 and grew rapidly when canal and railway links opened in the 1830s. The American Federation of Labor was founded in Pittsburgh in 1881, by which time the city was of national importance in producing coal, iron, steel and glass.

In the 20th century, industry attracted immigration from Italy and eastern Europe. In farming areas the early sect communities survive, notably Amish and Mennonites. (The Pennsylvania 'Dutch' are of German extraction.)

Further Reading

Klein, P. S., and Hoogenboom, A., *A History of Pennsylvania*. New York, 1973

RHODE ISLAND

The earliest white settlement was founded by Roger Williams, an English Puritan who was expelled from Massachusetts because of his dissident religious views and his insistence on the land-rights of the Indians. At Providence he bought land from the Narragansetts and founded a colony there in 1636. A charter was granted in 1663. The colony was governed according to policies of toleration, which attracted Jewish and nonconformist settlers; later there was French Canadian settlement also.

Shipping and fishing developed strongly, especially at Newport and Providence; these two cities were twin capitals until 1900, when the capital was fixed at Providence.

Significant actions took place in Rhode Island during the War of Independence. In 1790 the state accepted the federal constitution and was admitted to the Union.

Early farming development was most successful in dairying and poultry. Early industrialization was mainly in textiles, beginning in the 1790s, and flourishing on abundant water power. Textiles dominated until the industry began to decline after the First World War. British, Irish, Polish, Italian and Portuguese workers settled in the state, working in the mills or in the shipbuilding, shipping, fishing and naval ports. The crowding of a new population into cities led to the abolition of the property qualification for the franchise in 1888.

The population was predominantly industrial and urban in 1980, and population density was the highest in the country.

Further Reading
McLoughlin, W. G., *Rhode Island: a History*. Norton, 1978

SOUTH CAROLINA

Originally the territory of Yamasee Indians, the area attracted French and Spanish explorers in the 16th century. There were attempts at settlement on the coast, none of which lasted. Charles I of England made a land grant in 1629, but the first permanent white settlement began at Charles Town in 1670, moving to Charleston in 1680. This was a proprietorial colony including North Carolina until 1712; both passed to the Crown in 1729.

The coastlands developed as plantations worked by slave labour. In the hills there were small farming settlements and many trading posts, dealing with Indian suppliers.

After active campaigns during the War of Independence, South Carolina became one of the original states of the Union in 1788.

In 1793 the cotton gin was invented, enabling the speedy mechanical separation of seed and fibre. This made it possible to grow huge areas of cotton and meet the rapidly growing needs of new textile industries. Plantation farming spread widely, and South Carolina became hostile to the anti-slavery campaign which was strong in northern states. The state first attempted to secede from the Union in 1847, but was not supported by other southern states until 1860, when secession led to civil war.

At that time the population was about 703,000, of whom 413,000 were black. During the reconstruction period there was some political power for black citizens, but control was back in white hands by 1876. The constitution was amended in 1895 to disenfranchise most black voters, and they remained with hardly any voice in government until the Civil Rights movement of the 1960s.

Columbia became the capital in 1786, and grew into the largest town. By 1980 most of the population was concentrated in towns, the main industries being textiles, chemicals and paper. The black population has declined to about 30%.

Further Reading

Jones, L., *South Carolina: A Synoptic History for Laymen*. Lexington, 1978

SOUTH DAKOTA

The area was part of the hunting grounds of nomadic Dakota (Sioux) Indians. French explorers visited the site of Fort Pierre in 1742–43, and claimed the area for France. In 1763 the claim fell and, together with French claims to all land west of the Mississippi, passed to Spain. Spain held the Dakotas until defeated by France in the Napoleonic Wars, when France regained the area and sold it to the US as part of the Louisiana Purchase in 1803.

Fur-traders were active, but there was no settlement until Fort Randall was founded on the Missouri river in 1856. In 1861 North and South Dakota were organized as the Dakota Territory, and the Homestead Act of 1862 stimulated settlement, mainly in the southeast until there was a gold-rush in the Black Hills of the west in 1875–76. Colonization developed as farming communities in the east, miners and ranchers in the west. Livestock farming predominated, attracting European settlers from Scandinavia, Germany and Russia.

In 1889 the North and South were separated and admitted to the Union as states. The capital of South Dakota is Pierre, founded as a railhead in 1880, chosen as temporary capital and confirmed as permanent capital in 1904. It faces Fort Pierre, the former centre of the fur trade, across the Missouri river. During the 20th century there have been important schemes to exploit the Missouri for power and irrigation.

In 1980 the population was still mainly rural, but farming areas suffer a drain of young population as agriculture suffers from the extremes of the mid-continental climate.

Further Reading

Milton, John R., *South Dakota: A Bicentennial History*. New York, 1977

TENNESSEE

Bordered on the west by the Mississippi, Tennessee was part of an area inhabited by Cherokee. French, Spanish and British explorers penetrated the area up the Mississippi and traded with the Cherokee in the late 16th and 17th centuries. French claims were abandoned in 1763, colonists from the British colonies of Virginia and Carolina then began to cross the Appalachians westwards, but there was no organized Territory until after the War of Independence. In 1784 there was a short-lived, independent state called Franklin. In 1790 the South West Territory (including Tennessee) was formed, and Tennessee entered the Union as a state in 1796.

The state was active in the war against Britain in 1812. After the American victory, colonization increased and pressure for land mounted. The Cherokee were forcibly removed during the 1830s and taken to Oklahoma, a journey on which many died.

Tennessee was a slave state and seceded from the Union in 1861, although eastern Tennessee was against secession. There were important battles at Shiloh, Chattanooga, Stone River and Nashville. In 1866 Tennessee was readmitted to the Union.

Nashville, the capital since 1843, Memphis, Knoxville, and Chatanooga all developed as river towns, Memphis becoming an important cotton and timber port. Growth was greatly accelerated by the creation of the Tennessee Valley Authority in the 1930s, producing power for a manufacturing economy. Industry increased to the extent that, by 1970, the normal southern pattern of emigration and population loss had been reversed.

Further Reading

Corlew, R. E., *Tennessee: A Short History*. 2nd ed. Univ. of Tennessee Press, 1981

TEXAS

A number of Indian groups occupied the area before French and Spanish explorers arrived in the 16th century. In 1685 La Salle established a French colony at Fort St Louis, but Texas was confirmed as Spanish in 1713. Spanish missions increased during the 18th century with San Antonio (1718) as their headquarters.

In 1820 a Virginian colonist, Moses Austin, obtained permission to begin a settlement in Texas. In 1821 the Spanish empire in the Americas came to an end, and Texas, together with Coahuila, formed a state of the newly independent Mexico. The Mexicans agreed to the Austin venture, and settlers of British and American descent came in.

The settlers became discontented with Mexican government and declared their independence in 1836. Warfare, including the siege of the Alamo fort in Feb.–March, ended with the foundation of the independent Republic of Texas, which lasted until 1845. During this period the Texas Rangers were organized as a policing force and border patrol.

Texas was annexed to the Union in Dec. 1845, as the Federal Government feared its vulnerability to Mexican occupation. This led to war between Mexico and the US from 1845 to 1848. In 1861 Texas left the Union and joined the southern states in the Civil War, being readmitted in 1869.

Ranching and cotton-growing were the main activities before the discovery of oil in 1901 altered the state's economy completely.

By 1980 the growth rate of population was more than twice the national average; about 20% of the population was of Spanish origin, most of them Mexican; about 12% was black.

Further Reading
Fehrenbach, T. R., *A History of Texas and the Texans*. New York, 1986

UTAH

Spanish Franciscan missionaries explored the area in 1776, finding Shoshoni Indians. Spain laid claim to Utah and designated it part of Spanish Mexico. As such it passed into the hands of the Mexican Republic when Mexico revolted against Spain and gained independence in 1821.

In 1848, at the conclusion of war between the US and Mexico, the US received Utah along with other south-western territory. Settlers had already arrived in 1847 when the Mormons (the Church of Jesus Christ of Latter-day Saints) arrived, having been driven on by local hostility in Ohio, Missouri and Illinois. Led by Brigham Young, they entered the Great Salt Valley and colonized it. In 1849 they applied for statehood but were refused. In 1850 Utah and Nevada were joined as one Territory. The Mormon community continued to ask for statehood but this was only granted in 1896, after they had renounced polygamy and disbanded their People's Party.

Mining, especially of copper, and livestock farming were the base of the economy. Settlement had to adapt to desert conditions, and the main centres of population were in the narrow belt between the Wasatch Mountains and the Great Salt Lake. Salt Lake City, the capital, was founded in 1847 and laid out according to Joseph Smith's plan for the city of Zion. It was the centre of the Mormons' provisional 'State of Deseret' and Territorial capital from 1856 until 1896, except briefly in 1858 when federal forces occupied it during conflict between territorial and Union governments.

By 1980 the state's population was growing at about 3 times the national average, mostly from immigration. Over two-thirds of the population is Mormon.

Further Reading
Petersen, C. S., *Utah, a History*. New York, 1977

VERMONT

The original Indian hunting grounds of the Green Mountains and lakes was explored by the Frenchman Samuel de Champlain in 1609 who reached Lake Champlain on the north-west border. The first attempt at permanent settlement was also French, on Isle la Motte in 1666. In 1763 the British gained the area from the French by the Treaty of Paris. The Treaty, which also brought peace with the Indian allies of the French, opened the way for settlement, but in a mountain state transport was slow and difficult. Montpelier, the state capital from 1805, was chartered as a township site in 1781 to command the main pass through the Green Mountains.

During the War of Independence Vermont declared itself an independent state, to avoid being taken over by New Hampshire and New York. In 1791 it became the 14th state of the Union.

Most early settlers were New Englanders of British and Protestant descent. After 1812 a granite-quarrying industry grew around the town of Barre, attracting immigrant workers from Italy and Scandinavia. French Canadians also settled in Winooski. When textile and engineering industries developed in the 19th century these brought more European workers.

Vermont saw the only Civil War action north of Pennsylvania, when a Confederate raiding party attacked from Canada in 1864.

During the 20th century the textile and engineering industries have declined but paper and lumber industries flourish and so does printing. Settlement is still mainly rural or in small towns, farming is pastoral.

Further Reading
Morrissey, C. T., *Vermont: A Bicentennial History*. New York, 1981

VIRGINIA

In 1607 a British colony was founded at Jamestown, on a peninsula in the James River, to grow tobacco. The area was marshy and unhealthy but the colony survived and in 1619 introduced a form of representative government. The tobacco plantations expanded and African slaves were imported. Jamestown was later abandoned, but tobacco-growing continued and spread through the eastern part of the territory. The west was hilly and forested, and not suitable.

In 1624 control of the colony passed from the Virginia Company of London to the Crown. Growth was rapid during the 17th and 18th centuries. The movement for American independence was strong in Virginia; George Washington and Thomas Jefferson were both Virginians, and crucial battles of the War of Independence were fought there.

When the Union was formed, Virginia became one of the original states, but with reservations regarding the constitution because of its attachment to slave-owning. In 1831 there was a slave rebellion. The tobacco plantations began to decline, and plantation owners turned to the breeding of slaves. While the eastern plantation lands seceded from the Union in 1861, the small farmers and miners of the western hills refused to secede and remained in the Union as West Virginia.

Richmond, the capital, became the capital of the Confederacy. Much of the Civil War's decisive conflict took place in Virginia, with considerable damage to the economy. After the war the position of the black population remained extremely difficult, despite Booker T. Washington's movement for black education. Blacks remained without political or civil rights until the 1960s, and their numbers declined from about one-half of the population (1860) to about one-fifth (1980).

Tobacco and its products are still important, although it no longer dominates farming, in which livestock has become more important.

Further Reading
Rubin, L. D., Jr., *Virginia: A Bicentennial History*. Norris, 1977

WASHINGTON

The strongest Indian tribes in the 18th century were Chinook, Nez Percé, Salish and Yakima. The area was designated by European colonizers as part of the Oregon Country. Between 1775 and 1800 it had been claimed by explorers for Spain, Britain and the US; the dispute between the two latter nations was not settled until 1846.

The first small white settlements were Indian missions and fur-trading posts. In the 1840s American settlers began to push west-wards along the Oregon Trail, making a speedy solution of the dispute with Britain necessary. When this was achieved the whole area was organized as the Oregon Territory in 1848, and Washington was made a separate Territory in 1853.

Apart from trapping and fishing, the important industry was log-ging, mainly to supply building timbers to the new settlements of California. After 1870 the westward extension of railways helped to stimulate settlement. Statehood was granted in 1889. The early population was composed mainly of Americans from neighbouring states to the east, and Canadians. Scandinavian immigrants followed. Seattle, the chief city, was laid out in 1853 as a saw-milling town and named after the Indian chief who had ceded the land and befriended the settlers. It grew as a port during the Alaskan and Yukon gold-rushes of the 1890s.

During the 20th century the economy has been greatly expanded by exploiting the Columbia River for hydro-electric power.

Further Reading

Avery, M. W., *Washington, a History of the Evergreen State*. Univ. of Washington Press, 1965

WEST VIRGINIA

In 1861 the state of Virginia seceded from the Union over the issue of slave-owning. The 40 western counties of the state were composed of hilly country, settled by miners and small farmers who were not slave-owners. In 1862 these counties ratified an ordinance providing for the creation of a new state. On 20 June 1863 West Virginia became the 35th state of the Union.

The nature of the west had always been different from the rest of Virginia, and there had been campaigns for separation in 1769 and 1776.

The capital, Charleston, was an 18th-century fortified post on the early westward migration routes across the Appalachians. In 1795 local brine wells were tapped and the city grew as a salt town. Coal, oil, natural gas and a variety of salt brines were all found in due course. Huntington, the next largest town, developed as a railway terminus serving the same industrial area, and also providing trans-port on the Ohio river.

Three-quarters of the state is forest and settlement has been concentrated in the mineral-bearing Kanawha valley, along the Ohio river and in the industrial Monongahela valley of the north. In 1980 the population was about 2m. of which 1·2m. were still classified as rural. The traditional small farms and small hill-mines, however, support few, and the majority of rural dwellers commute to industrial employment.

Further Reading

Williams, J. A., *West Virginia: A Bicentennial History*. New York, 1976

WISCONSIN

The French were the first European explorers of the territory; Jean Nicolet landed at Green Bay in 1634, a mission was founded in 1671 and a permanent settlement at Green Bay followed. In 1763 French claims were surrendered to Britain. In 1783 Britain ceded them to the US, which designated the Northwest Territory, of which Wisconsin was part. In 1836 a separate Territory of Wisconsin was organized, including the present Iowa, Minnesota and parts of the Dakotas.

Territorial organization was a great stimulus to settlement. In 1836 James Duane Doty founded the town site of Madison and successfully pressed its claim to be the capital of the Territory even before it was inhabited. In 1848 Wisconsin became a state, with its present boundaries.

The city of Milwaukee was founded, on Lake Michigan, when Indian tribes gave up their claims to the land in 1831–33. It grew rapidly as a port and industrial town, attracting Germans in the 1840s, Poles and Italians 50 years later. Germans are still the most numerous group in the state, followed by those of Scandinavian, Polish and British descent.

The Lake Michigan shore was developed as an industrial area; the rest of the south proved suitable for dairy farming; the north, mainly forests and lakes, has remained sparsely settled except for tourist bases.

There is a Menominee Indian reservation in the north-east, where many of the 29,000 remaining Indians live. Since the Second World War there has been black immigration from the southern states to the industrial lake-shore cities.

Further Reading

Current, R. N., *Wisconsin. A History*. New York, 1977

WYOMING

The territory was inhabited by Plains Indians (Arapahoes, Sioux and Cheyenne) in the early 19th century. There was some trading between them and white Americans, but very little white settlement. In the 1840s the great western migration routes, the Oregon and the Overland Trails, were made through the territory, Wyoming offering mountain passes accessible to wagons. Once migration became a steady flow it was necessary to protect the route from Indian attack, and forts were built.

In 1867 coal was discovered. In 1868 Wyoming was organized as a separate Territory, and in 1869 the Sioux and Arapaho were confined to reservations. At the same time the route of the Union Pacific Railway was laid out, and working settlements and railway towns grew up in southern Wyoming. Settlement of the north was delayed until after the final defeat of hostile Indians in 1876.

The economy of the settlements at first depended on ranching. Cheyenne had been made Territorial capital in 1869, and also functioned as a railway town moving cattle. Casper, on the site of a fort on the Pony Express route, was also a railway town on the Chicago and North Western. Laramie started as a Union Pacific construction workers' shanty town in 1868.

In 1890 oil was discovered at Casper, and Wyoming became a state in the same year.

During the 20th century mineral extraction became the leading industry, as natural gas, uranium, bentonite and trona were exploited as well as oil and coal. Pastoral farming of cattle and sheep continues, but most of the population is classified as urban, and about a quarter live in Cheyenne, Casper and Laramie. Indians, who make up about 2% of the total population, still live on the Wind River reservation.

Further Reading

Larsen, T. A., *History of Wyoming*. Rev. ed. Univ. of Nebraska, 1979

OUTLYING TERRITORIES

GUAM

The island of Guam (also called Guajan or Guahan) was claimed by Spain in 1565 and ceded to the US after the Spanish-American War (1898). Its main function was to act as a military outpost in the Pacific. During the Second World War it was occupied by Japanese forces.

The US Navy Department administered Guam until 1950, when control was transferred to the Interior Department and full citizenship was conferred on the inhabitants. A civil governor was elected for the first time in 1970, and a single-chamber elected parliament has some legislative power.

The economy depends on the US military bases and on tourism.

Further Reading

Carano, P., and Sanchez, P. C., *Complete History of Guam*. Rutland, Vt., 1964

FREELY-ASSOCIATED STATES

NORTHERN MARIANAS

Under the Treaty of Versailles (1919) Japan was appointed mandatory to the former German possessions north of the equator. In 1946 the USA agreed to administer the former Japanese-mandated islands of the Caroline, Marshall and Mariana groups (except Guam) as a trusteeship for the United Nations; the trusteeship agreement was approved by the Security Council on 27 April 1947 and came into effect on 18 July 1947. The Trust Territory was administered by the US Navy until 1951, when, except for Tinian and Saipan in the Marianas, all the islands were transferred to the Secretary of the Interior. In 1962 the Interior Department assumed responsibility for Tinian and Saipan also. On 17 June 1975 the voters of the Northern Mariana Islands, in a plebiscite observed by the UN, adopted a covenant to establish a Commonwealth of the Northern Mariana Islands in Union with the USA. In April 1976 the US government approved the covenant and separated the administration of the Northern Marianas from that of the rest of the Trust Territory. The rest was constituted as 3 entities, each with its own constitution: the Marshall Islands, the Federated States of Micronesia (Yap, Kosrae, Truk and Pohnpei) and the Republic of Palau. In 1985–86 the US Congress agreed compacts of free association with all except Palau; free association gives the USA the authority to control military and defence activities in return for federal government assistance and budget supports to the otherwise autonomous constitutional governments. Palau did not vote in favour of the new status until Aug. 1987, when the previous requirement of a 75% vote was dropped, and a simple majority became sufficient. The USA was to ratify the decision in early 1988.

AMERICAN SAMOA

In the 1880s Samoa was an independent kingdom in which the US, Britain and Germany all had interests. In 1889 the 3 powers signed a treaty proclaiming Samoa to be a neutral territory. Ten years later Britain and Germany renounced their interests in the eastern islands of the group, where the USA remained the protective power. In 1900 the High Chiefs of Tutuila and Aunu'u ceded their islands to the US; the Chiefs of the Manu'a group followed suit in 1904. Congress formally accepted the islands in 1929, the US having annexed Swain's Island (to the north-north-west) in 1925.

The islands formed an 'unincorporated territory' of the USA. A bicameral parliament was established in 1948 and given some legislative power in 1960.

PUERTO RICO

Puerto Rico, a Spanish dependency since the 16th century, was ceded to the US in 1898 after the Spanish defeat in the Spanish-American War. The island's name was then Porto Rico. A US military government was installed, being replaced by a civil government in 1900.

In 1917 the Organic Act of Congress defined the territorial government and conferred US citizenship on the inhabitants. In 1932 the name was changed to Puerto Rico.

In 1952 Puerto Rico was proclaimed a commonwealth, with representative government and a directly-elected governor.

The economy has depended on sugar, tobacco and rum, and on emigration to work in the eastern United States.

Further Reading

Falk, P. S., (ed.) *The Political Status of Puerto Rico*. Lexington, Mass., 1986

VIRGIN ISLANDS OF THE UNITED STATES

The islands were claimed by Spain from the 16th century, but a French force occupied St Croix in 1651 and a Danish force St Thomas in 1666. Denmark acquired the whole island group by

1754, in which year it came under the control of the Danish Crown. The Danes imported African slaves until 1803, when the trade was abolished. They held the islands (with two short periods of British occupation in 1801–02 and 1807–15) until 1917, when the US bought them for $25m.

Since the islands' value was strategic, they were administered by the US Navy Department until 1931. Citizenship was conferred in 1927, and control passed to the US Department of the Interior in 1932. In 1954 a single-chamber assembly was given some legislative power, and there is an elected governor. The islands remain an 'unincorporated territory' of the USA; four attempts to introduce greater autonomy have been defeated by the electorate at referenda.

Further Reading

Dookhan, I., *A History of the Virgin Islands of the United States*. Caribbean Univ. Press, 1974

URUGUAY

Uruguay was the last colony settled by Spain in the Americas. Part of the Spanish viceroyalty of Rio de la Plata until revolutionaries expelled the Spanish in 1811, and subsequently a province of Brazil, Uruguay declared its independence 25 Aug. 1825 which was recognized by the treaty between Argentina and Brazil signed at Rio de Janeiro on 27 Aug. 1828. The first constitution was adopted on 18 July 1830. In the 1830s two political parties, the *blancos* (conservatives) and the *colorados* (liberals), emerged and conflict between the parties in 1865–70 precipitated the War of the Triple Alliance. In 1903, peace and prosperity were restored under President José Battle y Ordónezo. Since 1904 Uruguay has been unique in her constitutional innovations, all designed to protect her from the emergence of a dictatorship. The favourite device of the group known as the 'Batllistas' (a *colorado* faction) which, until defeated at the 1958 elections, held a parliamentary majority for over 90 years, has been the collegiate system of government, in which the two largest political parties were represented.

The early part of the 20th century saw the development of a welfare state in Uruguay which encouraged fairly extensive immigration.

In 1919 a new constitution was adopted providing for a colegiado – plural executive based on the Swiss pattern. However, the system was abolished in 1933 and replaced by presidential government, with quadrennial elections. From 1951 to 1966 a collective form of leadership again replaced the presidency. During the 1960s, following a series of strikes and riots, the Army became increasingly influential, repressive measures such as censorship of the press were adopted and presidential government was restored in 1967. The Tupamaro, Marxist urban guerrillas, sought violent revolution but were finally defeated by the Army in 1972. In 1984 the military permitted presidential elections, although several candidates were banned.

The return to civilian rule came on 12 Feb. 1985 when Gen. Alvarez resigned as president and was succeeded by Dr Julio Maria Sanguinetti, who established a government of National Unity and ordered the release of all political prisoners.

Further Reading

Finch, M. H. J., *A Political Economy of Uruguay Since 1870*. London, 1981

VANUATU

Vanuatu occupies the group of islands, formerly known as the New Hebrides, in the south western Pacific Ocean. Many of the northern islands have been inhabited by Melanesian peoples for at least 3,000 years. The islands which comprise the Republic of Vanuatu were first discovered in 1606 by the Portuguese. They were rediscovered by the French in 1768 and charted and named the New Hebrides by Captain Cook in 1774. Captain Bligh and his companions, cast adrift by the *Bounty* mutineers, sailed through part of the island group in 1789. Sandalwood merchants and European missionaries came to the islands in the mid 19th century and were then followed by cotton planters — mostly French and British — in 1868.

Complaints by missionaries regarding the activities of slave traders induced Britain to establish legislation to protect the islanders. Shortly thereafter British and French settlers began to arrive and French influence increased. In response to Australian calls to annex the islands, Britain and France agreed on joint supervision, initially through an 1888 Joint Naval Commission and subsequently through a Condominium Government, established in 1906, which was superseded by an Anglo-French Protocol in 1914. Joint sovereignty was held over the indigenous Melanesia people, but each nation retained responsibility for its own nationals according to the protocol of 1914. The island group escaped Japanese invasion during the Second World War and became an Allied base. After the war, local political initiatives originated as there was growing concern over land-ownership.

In 1972, the New Hebrides National Party, now known as the Vanuaaku Pati, was formed. The Vanuaaku Pati was instrumental in winning agreement from the condominium powers for independence and on 30 July 1980 New Hebrides became an independent nation under the name of Vanuatu, meaning 'Our Land Forever'.

Further Reading

Brookfield, H. C., *Colonialism, Development and Independence. The Case of the Melanesian Islands in the South Pacific*, 1972

VATICAN CITY STATE

For many centuries the Popes held temporal sway over a territory stretching across mid-Italy from sea to sea and comprising some 17,000 sq. miles, with a population finally of over 3m. In 1859–60 and 1870 the Papal States were incorporated into the Italian Kingdom. The consequent dispute between Italy and successive Popes was only settled on 11 Feb. 1929 by three treaties between the Italian Government with the Vatican: a political treaty, which recognized the full and independent sovereignty of the Holy See in the city of the Vatican; a concordat, to regulate the condition of religion and of the Church in Italy; and a financial convention, in accordance with which the Holy See received 750m. lire in cash and 1,000m. lire in Italian 5% state bonds. This sum was to be a definitive settlement of all the financial claims of the Holy See against Italy in consequence of the loss of its temporal power in 1870. The treaty and concordat were ratified on 7 June 1929. The treaty has been embodied in the constitution of the Italian Republic of 1947. A revised concordat between the Italian Republic and the Holy See was subsequently negotiated and came into force on 3 June 1985.

The Vatican City State is governed by a commission appointed by the Pope. The reason for its existence is to provide an extra-territorial, independent base for the Holy See, the government of the Roman Catholic Church.

Further Reading
Hebblethwaite, P., *In the Vatican*. London, 1986

VENEZUELA

Columbus sighted Venezuela in 1498 and it was visited by Alonzo de Ojeda and Amerigo Vespucci in 1499 who named it Venezuela (Little Venice). It was part of the Spanish colony of New Granada until 1821 when it became independent, at first in union with Colombia and then as a separate independent republic from 1830.

Between 1830 and 1945 the country was governed mainly by dictators. In 1945 a three-day revolt against the reactionary government of Gen. Isaías Medina led to Romulo Betancourt assuming the presidency. Betancourt produced constitutional and economic reforms but he was replaced by Gen. Marcos Pérez Jiménez who seized power in 1952. Jiménez was himself overthrown by a military junta in a revolution in 1958, led by Adm. Wolfgang Larrazabal. Betancourt again became president.

In 1961 a new constitution was promulgated which provided for a presidential election every five years, a national congress, and state and municipal legislative assemblies. Since that date all presidents have completed their term of office.

Betancourt's progressive policies were continued by his successor, Dr Raúl Leoni. There was an abortive military uprising in 1963. In 1969 Dr Rafael Caldera Rodríguez became the first Christian Democratic president and in 1978 Dr Luis Herrera became president but as his party, the *Partido Social-Christiano* (COPEI), failed to obtain an overall majority in congress he was forced to form alliances with smaller parties in order to make legislative progress.

Twenty political parties participated in the 1983 elections. Of 13 presidential candidates, Dr Jaime Lusinchi was elected with 57% of the votes.

Further Reading

Ewell, J., *Venezuela: A Century of Change*. London, 1984

VIETNAM

Vietnam was conquered by the Chinese in 111 BC, and though it broke free of Chinese domination in 939 AD, at many subsequent periods it was a nominal Chinese vassal.

By the end of the 15th century the Vietnamese had conquered most of the Kingdom of Champa (now Vietnam's central area), and by the end of the 18th century had acquired Cochin-China (now its southern area). At the end of the 18th century France helped to establish the Emperor Gia-Long (with whom Louis XVI had signed a treaty in 1787) as ruler of a unified Vietnam, known then as the Empire of Annam. French influence increased with a series of treaties between 1874 and 1884, the establishment of French protectorates over Tonkin and Annam, and the formation of the French colony of Cochin-China. By a Sino-French treaty of 1885 the Empire of Annam ceased to be a tributary to China. Cambodia had become a French protectorate in 1863, and in 1899 after the extension of French protection to Laos in 1893, the Indo-Chinese Union was proclaimed.

In 1940 Vietnam was occupied by the Japanese. In 1941 a nationalist coalition of nationalist, revolutionary and Communist organizations, known as the Vietminh League, was founded by the Communists. On 9 March 1945 the Japanese interned the French authorities and proclaimed the independence of Indo-China. In Aug. 1945 they allowed the Vietminh movement to seize power, dethrone the Emperor of Annam and establish a republic known as Vietnam. On 6 March 1946 France recognized 'the Democratic Republic of Vietnam' as a 'Free State within the Indo-Chinese Federation'. On 19 Dec. Vietminh forces made a surprise attack on Hanoi, the signal for nearly eight years of hostilities. An agreement on the cessation of hostilities in Vietnam was reached on 20 July 1954 at the Geneva Conference. The French withdrew and by the Paris Agreement of 29 Dec. 1954 completed the transfer of sovereignty to Vietnam.

The conference divided Vietnam along the 17th parallel into Communist North Vietnam and non-Communist South Vietnam. From 1959 the North promoted insurgency in the south and from 1961 the USA came to the aid of the south and a full-scale guerrilla war developed.

In 1963 the South Vietnamese president, Diem, was overthrown;

Nguyen Van Thieu took power as chairman of a national leadership committee in 1965, becoming president in 1967.

In Paris on 27 Jan. 1973 an agreement was signed ending the war in Vietnam. After the US withdrawal in that year, however, hostilities continued between the North and the South until the latter's defeat in 1975. Between 150,000 and 200,000 South Vietnamese fled the country, including the former President Thieu.

After the collapse of Thieu's régime the provisional revolutionary government established an administration in Saigon. A general election was held on 25 April 1976 for a national assembly representing the whole country. Voting was by universal suffrage of all citizens of 18 or over, except former functionaries of South Vietnam undergoing 're-education'. The unification of North and South Vietnam into the Socialist Republic of Vietnam finally took place on 2 July 1976. Following the signing of a treaty of friendship with the USSR in 1978 relations with China correspondingly deteriorated. Vietnam invaded Cambodia in Dec. 1978 and China attacked Vietnam in consequence. Thailand's relations with Vietnam worsened considerably in view of Vietnam attacks on guerrilla bases along the Thai border.

The many refugees escaping in small boats across the South China Sea have become known as the 'boat people'.

Further Reading

Harrison, J. P., *The Endless War: Fifty Years of Struggle in Vietnam*. New York, 1982

Karnow, S., *Vietnam: A History*. New York, 1983

BRITISH VIRGIN ISLANDS

The Virgin Islands were discovered by Columbus on his second voyage in 1493, who named them Las Virgenes. The British Virgin Islands were settled first by the Dutch in 1648 and then in 1666 by a group of British planters. The islands were officially annexed by Britain in 1672. From 1872 they were a part of the Federation of the British Leeward Islands Colony, and when this federation was dissolved in 1956 the British Virgin Islands became a British Crown colony. However, they did not have their own Administrator until 1960. The title Governor was adopted in 1971. Although the constitutions of 1967 and 1977 gave an increasing amount of self-government to the islands, the Governor remains responsible for defence, internal security, external affairs, the public service and the courts.

Further Reading
Pickering, V. W., *Early History of the British Virgin Islands*. London, 1983

WESTERN SAMOA

Polynesians settled in the Samoan group of islands in the southern Pacific from about 1000 BC. Shortly before European arrival, stratified society with paramount chiefs and fortified settlements developed. Although probably sighted by the Dutch in 1722, the first European visitor was French in 1768. Treaties were signed between the Chiefs and European nations in 1838–39.

Continuing strife among the chiefs was compounded by British, German and US rivalry for influence. In the Treaty of Berlin 1889 the three powers agreed to Western Samoa's independence and neutrality. When strife continued, the treaty was annulled and the Samoan group was annexed.

Western Samoa became a German protectorate until in 1914 it was occupied by a New Zealand expeditionary force. The island was administered by New Zealand from 1920 to 1961, at first under a League of Nations Mandate and from 1946 under a United Nations Trusteeship Agreement. In May 1961 a plebiscite held under the supervision of the UN on the basis of universal adult suffrage voted overwhelmingly in favour of independence as from 1 Jan. 1962, on the basis of the constitution which a Constitutional Convention had adopted in Aug. 1960. In Oct. 1961 the General Assembly of the United Nations passed a resolution to terminate the trusteeship agreement as from 1 Jan. 1962, on which date Western Samoa became an independent sovereign state.

Under a treaty of friendship signed on 1 Aug. 1962 New Zealand acts, at the request of Western Samoa, as the official channel of communication between the Samoan Government and other governments and international organizations outside the Pacific islands area. Liaison is maintained by the New Zealand High Commissioner in Apia.

The constitution provides for a head of state known as 'Ao o le Malo', which position from 1 Jan. 1962 was held jointly by the representatives of the two royal lines of Tuiaana/Tuiatua and the Malietoa. On the death of HH Tupua Tamasese Mea'ole, CBE, on 5 April 1963, HH Malietoa Tanumafili II, CBE, became, as provided by the constitution, the sole head of state for life. Future heads of state will be elected by the Legislative Assembly and hold office for five-year terms.

Further Reading

Fox, J. W. (ed.), *Western Samoa*. Univ. of Auckland, 1963

YEMEN ARAB REPUBLIC

The area was ruled from 897 AD by Moslem religious leaders (imams) of the Zaydi sect but it became part of the Ottoman Empire from 1520 until 1918 when the Imam regained full control. Although the Imam Yahya was assassinated in 1948 together with two of his sons, his eldest son, Ahmed, succeeded.

In 1958 Yemen became part of the United Arab Republic together with Egypt and Syria, but this lasted only until 1961 when Syria defected.

On 18 Sept. 1962 the Imam Ahmed died and was succeeded by his son Badr. Army officers seized power on 26–27 Sept., deposed Badr and declared a republic. The republican régime was supported by Egyptian troops, whereas the royalist tribes received aid from Saudi Arabia. On 24 Aug. 1965 President Nasser and King Faisal signed an agreement according to which the two powers were to support a plebiscite to determine the future of the Yemen. A conference of republican and royalist delegates met at Haradh on 23 Nov. 1965 without agreement. At a meeting of the Arab heads of state in Aug. 1967 Nasser and Faisal agreed to disengage themselves from the civil war in Yemen. At the time there were still about 50,000 Egyptian troops in the country, holding San'a, Ta'iz, Hodeida and the plains, whereas the mountains were in the hands of the royalists. During 1967 the Egyptians totally withdrew. In Nov. 1967 President Sallal was deposed and a republican council took over the government; but in 1974 a military *coup* gave control to Col. Ibrahim al-Hamadi. However, he was assassinated in 1977 and his successor, Col. Ahmed ibn Hussein al-Ghashmi, was assassinated in 1978. Col. Ali Abdullah Saleh was then elected as president, and in 1983 he was re-elected for a second five-year term.

There have been talks regarding forming a union with the People's Democratic Republic of Yemen (Southern Yemen) and the first session of the council for unification took place in Aug. 1983.

Further Reading

Bidwell, R., *The Two Yemens*. Boulder and London, 1983

THE PEOPLE'S DEMOCRATIC REPUBLIC OF YEMEN

The area was part of the Ottoman Empire from 1520 until 1918, when the Empire was dissolved. In 1839 the British East India Company captured Aden from the Turks, and well into the early 20th century made treaties with local rulers around Aden so as to protect trade. Thus the Protectorate of South Arabia came into being. In 1963 the Federation of South Arabia was formed by Aden and neighbouring members of the Protectorate.

Between Aug. and Oct. 1967 the 17 sultanates of the Federation of South Arabia were overrun by the forces of the Marxist National Liberation Front (NLF). The rulers were deposed, resigned or fled. At the same time the rival organization of FLOSY (Front for the Liberation of Occupied South Yemen) fought a civil war against the NLF, and harassed the British forces and civilians in Aden. In Nov. 1967 the United Arab Republic withdrew its support from FLOSY, and with the backing of the Army the NLF took over throughout the country. The last British troops left Aden on 29 Nov. 1967, and on 30 Nov. the Southern Yemen People's Republic was proclaimed. Qaltan ash-Sha'abi became president, but was compelled to resign in 1969 when a Presidential Council, with a prime minister, took control.

In 1970 the name of the country was changed to the People's Democratic Republic of Yemen, and the new constitution established a single legislature of 101 (later 111) members called the Supreme People's Council. The elected presidium of this council chooses a chairman who is also the head of state.

Despite border clashes from 1971–72 and again in 1979, between the People's Democratic Republic of Yemen (Southern Yemen) and The Yemen Arab Republic (North Yemen), there have been regular discussions proposing a union between the two Yemens.

On 13 Jan. 1986 there was a *coup* attempt against President Ali Nasser Mohammed which developed into virtual civil war. By 24 Jan. the rebel forces had taken control of the capital, Aden, and at a meeting of the Socialist Party Central Committee the presidium of the Supreme People's Council announced that the Acting President was Heidar al-Attas. He was elected president on 6 Nov. 1986.

Further Reading

Stookey, R. W., *South Yemen: A Marxist Republic in Arabia*. Boulder and London, 1982

YUGOSLAVIA

On 28 June 1914 Archduke Franz Ferdinand of Austria was assassinated in Bosnia by a young nationalist. Though Serbia complied with most of the terms of Austria's subsequent ultimatum, Austria declared war on 28 July, thus precipitating the First World War. In the winter of 1915–16 the Serbian army was forced to retreat to Corfu, where the government, under Prime Minister Pašić, was established. Montenegro capitulated in 1916 and its king fled. Exiles from Croatia and Slovenia had formed a 'Yugoslav Committee' in 1914 whose aim was South Slav federation. This was not compatible with Pašić's goal of a centralized, Serb-run state, but the Committee and the government managed to contrive a joint 'Corfu Declaration' in July 1917 demanding a 'constitutional, democratic, parliamentary monarchy headed by the Karadjordjevićs'. This was accepted by the Allies as the basis for the new state. The Croats were forced by the pressure of events to join Serbia and Montenegro on 1 Dec. 1918. From 1918–29 the country was known as the Kingdom of the Serbs, Croats and Slovenes.

Boundary disputes with Italy and other neighbouring countries lasted into the 1920s. A constitution of 1921 established an assembly under King Alexander, but the trappings of parliamentarianism could not bridge the gulf between Serbs and Croats. The Croat peasant leader Radić was assassinated in 1928; his successor, Vlatko Maček, set up a separatist assembly in Zagreb. On 6 Jan. 1929 the king suspended the constitution and established a royal dictatorship, redrawing provincial boundaries without regard for ethnicity. In Oct. 1934 he was murdered by a Croat extremist while on an official visit to France.

During the 1930s Yugoslavia had become heavily dependent on the German economy. During the regency of Prince Paul, Prime Minister Stojadinović pursued a pro-fascist line. On 25 March 1941 Paul was induced to adhere to the Axis Tripartite Pact. On 27 March he was overthrown by military officers in favour of the boy king Peter. Germany invaded on 6 April. Within 10 days Yugoslavia surrendered; king and government fled to London. Two resistance movements came into being, a royalist group, under Draža Mihailović, and the communist-dominated partisans of Josip Broz, nicknamed Tito. The latter were imbued with revolutionary as well as liberationist aims. The movements often fought each other, and

Mihailović collaborated to some extent with the Germans. Allied support was switched from him to Tito in 1944.

Tito succeeded in liberating Yugoslavia largely by his own efforts. The partisan Liberation Committee formed the nucleus of the post-war provisional government. A constituent assembly was elected in Nov. 1945 from a single list of People's Front candidates. A people's republic was proclaimed with a Soviet-type constitution. Tito embarked on a programme of enthusiastic Sovietization, but was too independent for Stalin, who sought to topple him by excommunicating Yugoslavia in 1948–49. However, Tito survived by the support of his people and a *rapprochement* with the west, and it was the Soviet Union under Khrushchev which had to extend the olive branch in 1956. As a spin-off from this schism Yugoslavia has evolved its 'own road to socialism'. Collectivization of agriculture was abandoned; the principles of 'industrial self-management' were developed, and extended into the whole of the representative process; and Yugoslavia has become a champion of international 'non-alignment'. A collective presidency came into being with the death of Tito in 1980.

Further Reading

Singleton, F., *A Short History of the Yugoslav Peoples*. CUP, 1985

THE REPUBLICS OF YUGOSLAVIA

BOSNIA

The Slavs who have inhabited this area since the 7th century do not have the same clearly defined national identity as Serbs or Croats, being an admixture of both. Their original clan system evolved between the 12th and 14th centuries into a principality under a *ban*. During this time the neo-Manichean Bogomil heresy became entrenched there and was embraced by Ban Kulin (1180–1204). Although Kulin was forced to recant under Hungarian pressure, the creed revived in the 14th century. Bosnia was conquered by the Turks in 1463 and the majority of Bogomils converted to Islam.

In 1875 a revolt broke out against Turkish tax collectors and rapidly spread. Austria-Hungary proposed a programme of supervized reforms to Turkey, but Serbia and Montenegro invaded Bosnia. A ceasefire was agreed in Nov. 1876. By the Treaty of Berlin (1878), Bosnia and Herzegovina were assigned to Austrian administration under Turkish suzerainty. Austria annexed them outright in 1908.

CROATIA

Croatia includes Slavonia and Dalmatia. The Croats migrated to their present territory in the 6th century and were converted to Roman Catholicism after accepting the suzerainty of the Holy Roman Emperor, Charlemagne, in 803. In 924 a kingdom was established under Tomislav, originally based in Dalmatia, where Venice also established a presence after 1000 which lasted until Napoleonic times. In 1102 the nobility recognized the king of Hungary as king of Croatia also, with control over defence and foreign affairs. Croatia retained a chief executive *(ban)*, an assembly and a legal system. The degree of Croatian autonomy remained a source of contention until 1918. In 1493 the flower of the Croatian nobility were massacred by the Turks at Krbavsko Polje. When Hungary fell to the Turks the Croatian assembly elected Ferdinand of Hapsburg as king in 1527. Ferdinand created a military frontier, manned by mercenaries and Serbian refugees, which remained in being until 1881, a defence not only against the Turks but also against rebellious Croat and Hungarian nobles. Much of Croatia did undergo Turkish occupation, however, until the Turkish tide was turned by the Treaty of Karlovac in 1699.

During the Napoleonic wars Croats were united with Slovenes and Serbs in the 'Illyrian Provinces' for 4 years. The Congress of Vienna (1815) returned these to Austria, together with Dalmatia and the hitherto independent Ragusa (now Dubrovnik). The Austro-Hungarian compromise *(Ausgleich)* of 1867 restored Croatia to Hungary. Hungary recognized Croatia as semi-autonomous under its own assembly, but in fact embarked thereafter on a programme of repressive magyarization.

In April 1941 a puppet Independent State of Croatia was established by Hitler under Ante Pavelić and his *Ustaša* movement, who pursued a campaign of ruthless atrocities against Serbs and dissidents.

MACEDONIA

Christian Slavs who had settled in Macedonia in the 6th century were conquered by the non-Slav Bulgars in the 7th century and in the 9th century formed a Macedo-Bulgarian empire, the western part of which survived until Byzantine conquest in 1014. In the 14th century it fell to Serbia, and in 1355 to the Turks. After the Balkan Wars of 1912–13 Turkey was ousted, and Serbia received the greater part of the territory, the rest going to Bulgaria and Greece. In 1918 Yugoslav Macedonia was incorporated into Serbia as South Serbia.

MONTENEGRO

Montenegro is an essentially Serbian Orthodox state which emerged as a separate entity on the break-up of the Serbian empire in 1355. Owing to its mountainous nature it was never effectively subdued by the Turks. During the absence of the ruler it became the practice for the bishop to take charge of the government, a practice which became permanent in 1516 when the bishop-princes took over on the extinction of the princely line. A royal house (of Njegoš) was refounded in 1851.

The Treaty of Berlin (1878) recognized the full independence of Montenegro and doubled the size of its territory.

SERBIA

The Serbs received Orthodox Christianity from the Byzantines in 891, but shook off the latter's secular suzerainty to form a prosperous state, firmly established under Stevan Nemanja (1167–96). A Serbian Patriarchate was established at Peć during the reign of Stevan Dušan (1331–55). Dušan planned the conquest of Constantinople, but he was forestalled by incursions of Turks. After he died many Serbian nobles accepted Turkish vassalage; the reduced Serbian state under Prince Lazar received the *coup de grace* at Kosovo on St Vitus's day, 1389. Turkish preoccupations with a Mongol invasion and wars with Hungary, however, postponed the total incorporation of Serbia into the Ottoman empire until 1459.

The Turks permitted the Orthodox church to practice, though the Patriarchate was abolished in 1766. The native aristocracy was eliminated and replaced by a system of fiefdoms held in return for military or civil service. Local self-government based on rural extended family units *(zadruga)* continued. In its heyday the Ottoman system probably bore no harder on the peasantry than the Christian feudalism it had replaced, but with the gradual decline of Ottoman power, corruption, oppression and reprisals led to economic deterioration and social unrest.

In 1804 murders carried out by mutinous Turkish infantry provoked a Serbian rising under Djordje Karadjordje, a meat trader. The Sultan's army disciplined the mutineers, but was then defeated by the intransigent Serbs. By the Treaty of Bucharest (1812), however, Russia agreed that Serbia, known as Servia until 1918, should remain Turkish. The Turks reoccupied Serbia with ferocious reprisals. A new rebellion broke out in 1815 under Miloš Obrenović which, this time with Russian support, won autonomy for Serbia within the Ottoman empire. Miloš had Karadjordje murdered in

1817. In 1838 he was forced to grant a constitution establishing an appointed state council, and abdicated in 1839. In 1842 a *coup* overthrew the Obrenovićs and Alexander Karadjordjević was elected as ruler. He was deposed in 1858.

During the reign of the western-educated Michael Obrenović (1860 until his assassination in 1868) the foundations of a modern centralized and militarized state were laid, and the idea of a 'Great Serbia', first enunciated in Prime Minister Garašanin's *Draft Programme* of 1844, took root. Milan Obrenović proclaimed formal independence in 1882. He suffered defeats against Turkey (1876) and Bulgaria (1885), and abdicated in 1889. Alexander Obrenović was assassinated in 1903, and replaced by Peter Karadjordjević, who brought in a period of stable constitutional rule.

In her foreign policy, Serbia's striving for an outlet to the sea was consistently thwarted by Austria, who annexed Bosnia in 1908, and forced the Serbs to withdraw from the Adriatic after the first Balkan war (1912).

SLOVENIA

The lands settled in the 6th century by the Slovenes were incorporated into his kingdom by Charlemagne, who proceeded to their Christianization. After the battle of Marchfeld (1278) the Slovenes gradually came under Hapsburg rule. Austro-German nobility, clergy and settlers were imposed on a Slovene peasantry. In the early 16th century Protestantism made considerable headway until crushed by the Counter-Reformation. Administratively and economically part of Austria, Slovenia developed a prosperous and educated Slovene-speaking middle class which was fertile ground for the seeds of nationalism inspired by the Napoleonic administration of 1809–13.

ZAÏRE

Until the middle of the 19th century the territory drained by the Congo River was practically unknown to Europeans. However, it had a long history, involving the powerful and extensive kingdoms of Kongo, Kuba, Luba and Lunda. But these states were unable to survive European intrusion, beginning with the advent of the Portuguese in the 16th century. When the explorer, Henry Morton Stanley reached the mouth of the Congo in 1877, King Leopold II of the Belgians recognized the immense possibilities of the Congo Basin and took the lead in exploring and exploiting it. The Berlin Conference of 1884–85 recognized King Leopold II as the sovereign head of the Congo Free State. He had formed the *Association Internationale Africaine* in 1876. A commission of inquiry in 1905 revealed serious maladministration and abuses which led to the annexation of the state to Belgium by the treaty of 28 Nov. 1907. The law of 18 Oct. 1908, called the Colonial Charter (last amended in 1959), provided for the government of the Belgian Congo, until the country became independent on 30 June 1960. The country's name was changed from Congo (Congo-Kinshasa) to Zaïre in Oct. 1971.

The departure of large numbers of Belgian administrators, teachers and doctors on the day of independence left a vacuum which speedily resulted in complete chaos. Neither Joseph Kasavubu, the leader of the Abako Party, who on 24 June 1960 had been elected head of state, nor Patrice Lumumba, leader of the Congo National Movement, who was the prime minister of an all-party coalition government, could establish his authority. Lumumba found his main support in the Oriental and Kivu provinces. Personal, tribal and regional rivalries led to the breakaway of Katanga province under premier Moïse Tshombe. Early in July the *Force Publique* mutinied and removed all its Belgian officers. Lumumba and Kasavubu called for intervention by the United Nations as well as by the USSR. The UN Secretary-General dispatched a military force of about 20,000, composed of contingents of African and Asian countries. Lumumba was kidnapped by Katanga tribesmen and, in early Feb. 1961, murdered; his place was taken by Antoine Gizenga, who set up a government in Stanleyville.

On 15 Aug. 1961 the UN recognized the government of Cyrille

Adoula as the central government, and in mid-Sept. UN forces invaded Katanga.

On 15 Jan. 1962 the forces of Gizenga in Stanleyville surrendered to those of the central government, and on 16 Jan. Adoula dismissed Gizenga. UN forces again invaded Katanga in Dec. 1962 and by the end of Jan. 1963 had occupied all key towns; Tshombe left the country. The UN troops left the Congo by 30 June 1964.

The Gizenga faction started a fresh rebellion and after the capture of Albertville (19 June) and Stanleyville (5 Aug.) proclaimed a People's Republic on 7 Sept. 1964. Government troops, Belgian paratroopers and a mercenary contingent captured Stanleyville on 24 Nov. after the rebels had massacred thousands of black and white civilians. The last rebel strongholds were captured at the end of April 1965.

In 1977 an Angolan-based invasion of Shaba (formerly Katanga) province was reported and in 1978 a full-scale conflict developed. This invasion was repulsed with French intervention, however it brought about reforms under President Mobutu including the holding of direct elections. In 1987, there were reports of Zaïre continuing its long standing support for rebels opposing Angola's MPLA government, despite talks with the Angolans in 1985 and again in 1987.

Further Reading

Young, C., and Turner, T., *The Rise and Decline of the Zaïrian State*. Univ. of Wisconsin Press, 1985

ZAMBIA

The early history of Zambia is obscure. The first expedition of real geographical value was Livingstone's missionary journey of 1851 during which he discovered the Victoria Falls.

The great majority of the present African population of the area is of Bantu origin, descended from invaders who swept over the country. There are more than 70 different tribes, the most important being the Bemba and the Bgoni in the north-east, and there are also about 30 different dialects in use. The chief invaders of the early 19th century were the Arabs from the north, the Ngoni Zulus fleeing from Shaka, and the Kololo, who fought their way from the south across the Zambezi and founded a kingdom with a high degree of social organization. One of the more successful of the invading tribes was the Lozi under Lewanika, who asked for and obtained the protection of the British government in 1891. In 1900 the chartered company acquired certain trading and mining rights over Lewanika's territory. In 1899 and 1900 orders in council established the company's administration of the western and north-eastern portions of the country. These 2 territories were amalgamated in 1911 under the name of Northern Rhodesia, and in 1924 the Crown took over the administration of Northern Rhodesia from the British South Africa Company.

In 1953, following a referendum in Southern Rhodesia, the Federation of Rhodesia and Nyasaland, of which Northern Rhodesia was a component part, was created. Federation brought great economic benefits to Northern Rhodesia, but it was from the outset bitterly opposed by the African leaders there. Kenneth Kaunda led a sustained campaign against Federation, and after elections held under a new constitution of 1962, his United National Independence party gained wide success. In March 1963 Britain agreed in principle to Northern Rhodesia's right to secede from the Federation, which was duly dissolved at the end of the year. In Jan. 1964 full internal self-government was attained. On 24 Oct. Northern Rhodesia became an independent republic within the Commonwealth, changing its name to Zambia. Kaunda became its first president, and led the efforts to break the foreign hold on Zambia's mineral resources.

Further Reading

Roberts, A., *A History of Zambia*. London, 1977

343

ZIMBABWE

Shona-speaking people lived in Zimbabwe hundreds of years before Europeans arrived. It was a major commercial centre in the 14th and 15th centuries, although the ruins of Great Zimbabwe date back to the 8th century. It became increasingly secondary to the Kingdom of Mwanamutapa which arose in the north. By backing rival kings, Portuguese traders managed to destroy Mwanamutapa by 1700. The Shona inhabitants were unable to repel the invasion of Ndebele people under Mzilikazi who settled in the south west of current day Zimbabwe and treated the Shona as vassals. When Lobengula succeeded Mzilikazi in 1870, the Ndebele had a very powerful state. However, it was not strong enough to defeat European settlers who forcibly acquired Shona lands in 1890 and turned to Ndebele territory in 1893. Revolts by both peoples several years later were also defeated.

The territory which now forms Zimbabwe was administered by the British South Africa Company from the beginning of European colonization in 1890 until 1923 when it was granted the status of a self-governing colony. In 1911 it had been divided into Southern and Northern Rhodesia (*see* Zambia).

In 1953 Southern and Northern Rhodesia were again united, along with Nyasaland to form the Federation of Rhodesia and Nyasaland. When this federation was dissolved on 31 Dec. 1963 Southern Rhodesia reverted to the status of a self-governing colony within the British Commonwealth.

Ian Smith, prime minister from April 1964, had discussions about independence on three occasions with two British prime ministers during 1964 and 1965. On 11 Nov. 1965 Smith and his government issued a unilateral declaration of independence (UDI). Thereupon the Governor dismissed Smith and his cabinet, and the British government reasserted its own formal responsibility for Rhodesia; but effective internal government was carried on by the Smith cabinet.

The UN Security Council on 20 Nov. called upon all member states to break off economic relations with Rhodesia. Only Portugal and the Republic of South Africa did not impose an embargo. From 1–3 Dec. Harold Wilson, the British prime minister, and others met Smith on board H.M.S. *Tiger* and drafted a 'Working Document' on the procedure for progress towards legal independence. This statement was approved by the British cabinet, but rejected by the Smith government. As a result the British government approached the UN and on 16 Dec. 1966 the Security Council voted for mandatory sanctions including oil: France and the USSR abstained. Further talks based on the *Tiger* proposals were held between the British prime minister and Smith aboard H.M.S. *Fearless* on 10–13 Oct. 1968. On 2 March 1970 the Smith government declared Rhodesia a republic and adopted a new constitution.

On 24 Nov. 1971 an agreement was signed between Britain and Rhodesia with terms for the recognition of independence on condition that these should be acceptable to the people of Rhodesia as a whole. A commission sent to Rhodesia in 1972 found that the proposals were not acceptable. A new move towards a constitutional conference was begun in 1974 between the Rhodesian government and leaders of the Rhodesian African Council, but was ruined by increased terrorist activity. A further constitutional conference between the same two parties in Aug. 1975 also broke down. In Dec. 1976 a conference in Geneva was adjourned until an unspecified date. During 1977 three further efforts were made by the British government to present proposals, but to no avail.

On 3 March 1978 Smith signed a constitutional agreement with the internationally-based black nationalist leaders. It decreed independence, as Zimbabwe, on 31 Dec. 1978. Smith was to retain his constitutional position as elected prime minister but act as co-equal with Abel Muzorewa, Ndabaningi Sithole and Jeremiah Chirau. This agreement was rejected by the Patriotic Front and opposed by the Organization of African Unity and the UN Security Council. In Nov. 1978 the government considered it was impossible to meet the independence date. A draft constitution was published in Jan. 1979 and was accepted by the white electorate in a referendum. In April 1979 general elections were held for the 72 black seats in the 100-seat parliament. The United African National Council won 51 of the 72 seats and Bishop Abel Muzorewa became prime minister of Rhodesia-Zimbabwe on 1 June 1979.

At the Commonwealth Conference held in Lusaka in Aug. 1979 agreement was reached for a new constitutional conference to be held in London and this took place between 10 Sept. and 15 Dec. at Lancaster House. It was attended by the various factions in Zimbabwe-Rhodesia. It achieved three objectives: one, the terms of a constitution for an independent Zimbabwe; two, terms for a return to legality; and three, a ceasefire. Lord Soames became Governor-General of Southern Rhodesia in Dec. and elections took place in March 1980. ZANU (Zimbabwe African National Union) won 57 of the 80 black seats, ZAPU (Zimbabwe African People's Party) 20, and Muzorewa's UANCO (United National Council) 3. Southern Rhodesia became the Republic of Zimbabwe, with Canaan Banana as president, and Robert Mugabe as prime minister. Since then the country has moved towards a one-party state with Joshua Nkomo's party being increasingly opposed by the government. However, unity was stressed when, on 31 Dec. 1987, Robert Mugabe became the first executive president.

Further Reading

Verrier, A., *The Road to Zimbabwe, 1890–1980*. London, 1986
Wiseman, H. and Taylor, A. M., *From Rhodesia to Zimbabwe: The Politics of Transition*. Elmsford, N.Y., 1981

INDEX INCLUDING INDEX OF NAME CHANGES

The following index lists all the countries, and where appropriate their constituent states and dependencies, dealt with in *The Statesman's Year-Book Historical Companion*. It also includes popular variants of names (e.g. West Germany) and many of the name changes mentioned in the text. The formula for variants is: West Germany *see* Federal Republic of Germany; the formula for name changes is: Abomey *now* Benin.